The History of Legal Philosophy

Friedrich Julius Stahl

THE PHILOSOPHY OF LAW

VOLUME I: *The History of Legal Philosophy*

1A: *The Rise and Fall of Natural Law*

1B: *The Recovery of Historical Law*

VOLUME II: *The Doctrine of Law and State on the Basis of the Christian World-View*

PART I: *General Doctrines and Private Law*

BOOK I: *Philosophical Presuppositions*

BOOK II: *Principles of Law*

BOOK III: *Private Law*

PART II: *The Doctrine of State and the Principles of State Law*

BOOK IV

THE PHILOSOPHY OF LAW
Volume I

The History of Legal Philosophy

Friedrich Julius Stahl

Translated, edited, and prefaced by
Ruben Alvarado

WordBridge
PUBLISHING
εν αρχη ην ο λογος
AALTEN, THE NETHERLANDS

WORDBRIDGE PUBLISHING
Aalten, the Netherlands
www.wordbridge.net
info@wordbridge.net

German original: Friedrich Julius Stahl, *Die Philosophie des Rechts: Erster Band: Geschichte der Rechtsphilosophie.* Fifth unchanged edition. Tübingen and Leipzig: J. C. B. Mohr, 1878.

ISBN 978-90-76660-81-3

COVER ILLUSTRATION: "Samson Destroying the Philistine Temple," by an anonymous painter of the Bolognese School, early 18th century. This photographic reproduction used by permission, ©Kunsthaus Lempertz, Cologne, Germany.

NOTE ON THIS EDITION

Vols. IA and IB, previously published separately as paperback books, are here included one after the other in their original form. Page numbering, tables of contents, and indices are unchanged. The author's prefaces, which were not included in the paperback versions, are included here.

AUTHOR'S PREFACE TO THE THIRD EDITION

The third edition is merely a revised version of the history of legal philosophy contained in the first volume. The revisions will be noticeable in several places, most notably in the sections on Greek legal philosophy. On the whole and in essence, the edition is unchanged and does not require a new preface. Instead, I am including from the preface to the second edition what relates to the economy of this volume in its final form; and since the preface to the first edition explains the origin, motivation, and initial conception of the entire work, I felt it necessary to include it here in its entirety.

Berlin, November 20th, 1854

FROM THE AUTHOR'S PREFACE TO THE SECOND EDITION

For this first volume of *The Philosophy of Law*, the second edition has not undergone any significant changes from the earlier work, except for the omission of two chapters (on the relationship between expediency and ethics, and on Christian philosophy), the subjects of which have since been discussed in greater detail in the second volume. Nevertheless, this volume has been greatly expanded. First of all, further explanations have been added to several chapters—those on Kant, Fichte, Montesquieu, and especially Schelling and Hegel. In the case of Hegel, these additions were so extensive that a complete reworking of the entire section became necessary, and I believe that this edition provides a much better insight into the innermost core of his philosophical system. The counterrevolutionary doctrine and the doctrine of the historical school (previously in the second volume) have also been completely reworked and expanded. Yet the main expansion came from the addition of new chapters on subjects not covered there, such as the philosophy of law in the Middle Ages, the individual authors of natural law from Grotius to Rousseau and Locke, the French political writers, and Schleiermacher.

This may have led to differences in approach between the old and the new, and, despite my best efforts, perhaps even to inconsistencies in the details themselves, though hopefully not to such an extent that they would cause any confusion. In particular, the history of natural law is now presented in two parts (II and III of the third book), namely according to subject matter and according to authors; I did not think I could dispense with either, even if this meant that repetition could not be completely avoided.

***

The many valuable contributions that have been made since then to the history of legal philosophy and political science have served to encourage me and, even more often, to inspire me.

In this expanded edition of the book, I considered the title "History of Legal Philosophy" to be justified. However, even now, my task is not to write a literary history, but rather a history of legal philosophy. Therefore, I request the reader not to argue with me about the omission of this or that author or book. The aim is not to provide a complete account of legal-philosophical writings, but rather to provide at least an approximate completeness of legal-philosophical ideas and the process by which they developed and came to dominate public consciousness. From this point of view alone, I was unable to include the most recent legal-philosophical developments in my account. The course of this history of legal philosophy is simply as follows: The presentation of ancient and medieval legal philosophy (Books I and II) is followed by that of the legal-philosophical productions of modern times, namely from the Reformation to the Revolution, which are: natural law—the system of liberalism—constitutional theory—and finally, in embryonic form, communism and socialism (Books III and IV). The conclusion is formed by the legal-philosophical products of the most recent period since the Revolution: the counter-revolutionary doctrine, the doctrine of the Historical School of Law, and speculative legal philosophy (Books V and VI).

Berlin, April 27th, 1847

AUTHOR'S PREFACE TO THE FIRST EDITION

I hereby present to the educated world the treatment of a subject which, for many years, I did not believe could ever become the object of my investigation. For the lack of hope of ever gaining anything from philosophy, of ever arriving at a definite result, the discouraging example of the celebrated thinkers of modern times, who through philosophy have lost precisely what is most comforting and most sacred, had filled me, like so many others, with a complete weariness of all philosophical inquiry, and I withdrew exclusively to the study of positive law. It was my preoccupation with positive law that forced me to ask questions and conduct investigations for which I could no longer find the solution, or even the concept or designation, within positive law itself, and thus, without seeking or wanting to, I was pushed into a higher scientific field. Such studies and my love for them, as well as the encouragement of friends to replace the natural law I had abandoned with another appropriate field of study, persuaded me to begin my academic career in the winter with lectures on the philosophy of positive law. This compelled me to justify my approach ethically by means of a view of the nature of justice and to subject any opposing views to criticism. The various schools of legal philosophy fell into place for me in a step-by-step development. This laid the foundation for this book. —

At the same time, many favorable circumstances came together for me. The gloomy circumstances and mood in which I had been trapped began to lift. This included, in particular, my attitude toward Hegel's philosophy. Although I had been convinced of its falsity from the outset, I had been unable to identify the source of the error. Thus, it did not draw me to its beliefs, but it clouded and weakened my own, and as much as it repelled me, I was always compelled to return to it, if not in deliberate study, then in involuntary preoccupation, until I had acquired the means of overcoming it scientifically. At that point, I had at least come to a clear understanding of the situation. But in this one system, which had been taken to its extreme, I had also come to know the essence of all modern philosophy. This hostile power had ceased to seem terrible to me, and a new force of cheerfulness and confidence animated me and gave me the courage to try to find my own path. Finally, the decisive factor was the influence of

Schelling, who began lecturing at our university in the same semester. Through him, I gained many means for clearer analysis, expansion, and deeper justification of my thoughts; through him, I gained the courage to make positive and complete scientific use of convictions that one usually keeps locked away in one's innermost being as belonging to a separate realm and protects only against hostile attacks. I learned a great deal directly, and much was inspired in me. Above all, it is the fundamental idea of his current view that has guided me in all my scientific endeavors from that time on. With this fundamental idea, the concept of the historical view itself, which Schelling presented at the beginning of his lectures in a few strokes with a clarity and force that penetrated to the very core, a new era of philosophy begins. However, there can no longer be any talk of a school and followers, such as every philosopher has gathered around himself up to now. The system of freedom, as Schelling calls his, can by its very nature only find true love and veneration among independent individuals, and only among them can it find the care it demands and which alone it can tolerate.[1]

---

[1] Regarding my relationship to Schelling's newer system, I will quote here the relevant passage from my preface to Volume II, Part I of *The Doctrine of Law and State on the Basis of the Christian Worldview*, p. XII:

"In the second edition of this volume, which deals with these fundamental principles, I cannot avoid clearly stating my position on Schelling's new doctrine, which is the subject of widespread misunderstanding.

"I did not receive my convictions and direction in life and in science from Schelling. When I first set foot in his lecture hall seventeen years ago, my fundamental beliefs and my relationship to Hegel's philosophy were already the same as they are now; it was precisely because Schelling expressed himself in the same vein that I was won over to him. However, I do owe Schelling encouragement and very significant support in the scientific presentation of those fundamental convictions, as well as the general intellectual stimulation that one always derives from great, deeply thought-out treatises. However, what I accepted from Schelling, what I professed and still profess, is merely his polemic against the "rationalist" ("negative") principle and his juxtaposition of the "historical" ("positive") principle, and no one will consider this a philosophical system. On the other hand, I have never had any connection with Schelling's own special present system—his philosophical conception of the creation of the world, mythology, revelation, his doctrine of the three powers that form its center, etc. Nor does Herr von Schelling have any connection with any doctrine or exposition in my book, not even in the first volume, much less in the following ones, except for the basic idea in which I mentioned him and perhaps what is already directly and completely given in that idea.

"This is already evident from my statements at the time, although they were written without any calculation, out of enthusiastic gratitude. In the first volume of my *Philosophy of Law*, I have everywhere and expressly acknowledged only 'the one fundamental idea of Schelling's present view, the concept of the historical view itself' (VII) or 'the opposition of the logical as timeless and actless to the historical' (p. 55). I claimed only that this fundamental idea, the concept of 'historical philosophy,' was consistent with Christianity and prepared a place for it in philosophy (p. 56). Yes, as far as the delicacy of the relationship permitted, I expressly distanced myself from the obvious idea of 'a school and following, as every philosopher has gathered around himself up to now' (p. VII). On the other hand, it was obviously impracticable to describe my own teachings directly as not originating from Schelling. After taking perhaps excessive care not to appropriate anything that was not my own, quoting Schelling for even the slightest thought behind which I suspected a reminiscence (e.g., vol. I, p. 334), I was rather justified in expecting the reader, where I failed to do so, not to regard him as the author, and it was therefore neither my fault nor my intention that my teachings, e.g., the concept of freedom, the critique of Hegel's dialectic, etc., were frequently attributed to Schelling. Whether I did not already misunderstand Schelling's teaching in the basic concept to which I referred,—since it by no means rejects rationalism as unconditionally and without reservation as I do—only the famous originator of this doctrine has the authentic judgment, while I, however, also have the freedom of my own conviction and insight in relation to the genuine Schellingian understanding. I would be deeply sorry to have stated anything incorrect or inaccurate here, even though agreement with Schelling's views has never been and could never be a consideration for me.

"The erroneous opinion that I am a representative of Schelling's new philosophy, or that my philosophy of law is an outgrowth of it, has its origin merely in the fact that my whole point of view was not taken into account from the outset. I regarded Schelling's new principle of positivity as a great liberation from the philosophy up to that point, which had passed through the universe with some logical formula and thereby assumed

Thus, I formed a plan to thoroughly examine that hastily sketched history of legal-philosophical schools of thought, to trace their development in connection with philosophy as a whole, and to attempt, based on this historical foundation, to arrive at a new and more solid conclusion. —

I believe that I have undertaken a righteous task and in the right spirit. Legal philosophy is currently neglected and disparaged, especially by those of good will. But there are only a few men who, by a happy gift of insight, are spared the task of dissecting concepts. Such men deserve authority, but not imitation. Everyone should carefully consider where they stand in contrast to them; but their

---

to have grasped and understood things scientifically, according to which, then, my adherence refers only to this act of liberation, but immediately everyone, listener as well as teacher, approaches the matter (the positive object) independently of the other and seeks to investigate it. To attribute my philosophical theory of morality, of law, of the state, indeed even my concept of freedom from the point of view of its positive realization, to Schelling is then, under this presupposition, just as incongruous as, for example, to attribute my historical investigations into the Roman right of action to Hugo, because he broke the ground for historical investigations of this kind. Instead, however, a large part of the public did not allow themselves to be deprived of the customary idea that whoever refers to a philosopher necessarily assumes a ready-made system in which every matter is already accommodated. Thus, in spite of that resolute statement, my relation to Schelling used to be paralleled with the relation of Gans to Hegel, without considering that Gans had accepted from Hegel the all-determining method, the whole theory of natural law, the construction of world history, and thus the conception of every people and age, whereas I had nothing from Schelling but his characterization of rationalism. In the same way, Maurenbrecher even had the strange idea of describing my theory of the state as neo-Schellingianism, whereas it is now well known that Schelling, in the entire cycle of his lectures, barely mentions with one syllable the state and legal and political relations.

"Through this debate, as well as through the imminent publication of the Schelling doctrine, it is to be hoped that any such identification will be eliminated in the future. On the other hand, I am happy to leave it up to everyone to assess as highly as they wish the influence that Schelling's characterization of rationalism had on my philosophical formation. For the reader will gather from well-known events that it is not a craving for originality that compelled me to engage in this debate."

path is not one that everyone can safely follow. The rest of us have fallen prey to abstraction; even if we do not want to and do not admit it, we are drawn into it and will only free ourselves from it when we have followed it to its extreme. Savigny was entitled to venture into an investigation of the ultimate reasons for justice; his mind guides him safely, and through an artistic power he forms completely and perfectly what even the most strenuous philosophical investigation can only slowly and gradually bring about. He put forward a view of the origin of law—and from it, immediate practical requirements—which, as presented by him, provides a clear picture and is compelling in its inner truth. But when others, who lack this magic, try to understand and reproduce it in their own way, without really philosophizing, they will, as has happened, either resort to vague, ambiguous speech, or transform that living image into fixed statements and concepts, and what is attested there as rich truth will now become empty and meaningless or one-sided, even appear exaggerated to the point of being wrong and childish. The most intelligent people conceal from themselves where the historical view ultimately leads, and the disturbing questions are dismissed. That is why, since Savigny's writing, there has been no progress, no development in the historical view itself, however excellent the achievements of the school in history and positive law may have been. Within the school there is a lack of unity and clarity of consciousness, and it would be embarrassed to say what distinguishes it. From the outside, however, there is ignorance, misunderstanding, and unjust accusations.

This inhibition does not exist solely in the realm of legal philosophy, which is, after all, voluntarily abandoned; the treatment of positive law suffers just as much from it. For it is the destiny of the human spirit not to reject the highest questions, and nothing can flourish where it is opposed. If the historical view, in its vitality, reconciles science and practice, it is also the case that, when understood rigidly and abstractly, it widens the gap more than has ever existed before. Even where the new orientation has penetrated, only a faithful understanding of the past or of what still exists externally has been achieved, without recognizing the connection with present circumstances and their needs. This is the conclusion reached by the undeniable proposition that there is an indissoluble connection between different periods of time when applied in a scholarly manner. However, apart from civil law, where Savigny broke new ground, it has not yet been possible to introduce the historical approach. In constitutional law and criminal law, we see everywhere in the encyclopedia a futile struggle against inherited abstract concepts; they resist the new understanding, but no standpoint has been found through which they can be dispensed with, and precisely those that have the most scientific meaning are least able to resist them. Hence, a respected writer could claim that the historical view may well apply to civil law, but not to criminal law. Even in a complete presentation of civil law, who avoids speaking here about right and duty, perfect and imperfect, public and private law, etc.? And must not we here fill in the gaps in positive development with the dead concepts of a degenerate philosophy, instead of presenting a harmonious whole cast from a single mold?

No room should be given to the arrogant idea that man is capable of penetrating the eternal will and revealing the secret of all things. But it is permissible to hope that, through united efforts, we will once again achieve the community of knowledge that lesser times than ours have enjoyed. For the loss of this community is a depressing admixture in the depth and richness of scientific development that distinguishes our time. Everywhere there are divergent, opposing aspirations, countless parties, torn away from one another, each pursuing its own path, easily believed by its comrades, ignored by others, indeed not understood. A dying culture has woven the last threads of its existence into the new one that is dawning, and as the hostile forces interpenetrate, so arise the manifold confused views that criss-cross among us. We have fallen prey to the same spirit that we are fighting here. We use concepts and opinions without being aware of the total mode of representation to which they belong. If, in every field of knowledge, truth-loving inquiry pursued all questions to their end, if, with activity present everywhere, it linked the nearest and most external to the highest convictions, if it did not hide where it encountered new difficulties and where it had no more answers: then it should finally become clear what everyone believes and how this relates to the beliefs of others, where the point of divergence lies, what has been raised above doubt as a certain possession, and what remains as a common task. This would cause the centrist parties to disappear, all those who want to unite heterogeneous elements, or who, even in carrying out what they want to decide, are still unconsciously dominated by opposing forces. So let us attempt here to uncover the innermost core of the historical orientation. Its core, however, is not, as is commonly assumed, the view of the factual, of how law arises, but only the view of the ethical, of how it arises, what content it should have—the view of justice.

Here it must distinguish itself from the opposing orientation if it does not wish to be vain and futile in proclaiming itself new. Here its own essence must become clear, and only here can a decision be made as to whether, why, and to what extent legal philosophy as it has existed up to now is to be rejected. Only when it has demonstrated the untenability of the old philosophy, not merely in its results but at its very roots, will its own activity be secured against any admixture of the old error. Before this, it cannot be expected to gain general recognition. For ethical inquiry is indispensable to the human mind. As long as historical opinion does not show it a new way, the old way will not be abandoned; it will merely change its form, and even if its futility is recognized in one form, it will immediately gain new adherents in another. This is what the present moment teaches us. For if a system, hollow and untrue in its foundations, distasteful in its execution, and dismal in its results, could nevertheless become, if not the dominant one, at least the one that sets the tone, and that in an educated age accustomed to philosophy, then this is sufficient testimony to the deep and undeniable need for philosophical inquiry. —

In accordance with this insight, I have taken the greatest care in presenting and examining natural law, even though some may consider this superfluous in a matter that has long been settled. I have not shied away from discussing even familiar topics in detail, and have revisited certain considerations and questions that are usually regarded as insignificant. Above all, however, it was my intention to avoid terminology as much as possible, neither to create any myself nor to follow any of the existing ones, but rather to dissolve them into common language. For it is finally time that science, like its sister art, should come out into the open and be understood by all. Admittedly, new concepts require new words, and those who have never dealt with a subject before cannot expect to grasp the concepts that concern them immediately. But the inflexible use of words, which is not limited to individual new relationships but draws all existing ones under itself and thus transforms living language into a stereotypical mass—this characteristic of terminology is only the product of the one-sidedness and rigidity of philosophy itself. Any free inquiry that seeks the universal human cannot and must not resort to it. The word is not the container of meaning, but its living body. Free and mobile, similar to the spirit itself, it derives its meaning only from the ever-active connection and separation of thought, as it were through its momentary volition and action. Many philosophies might well find that when the garment of words is removed, lo and behold, there is no body to be found that it would have enveloped. Even if the following writing does not contribute anything new, it at least strives to dispel the fog of formulas in philosophical education and to compel the thing and the thought to come forward and stand up to observation. It is not at all the intention to find anything new; it is precisely the ancient, the belief of mankind from the beginning that is true. Only a few ever depart decisively and consciously from what the simple mind eternally recognizes as such, e.g., personality, the love of God. But the rest, although they generally admit it, become unfaithful to it in its application because they are overwhelmed by the richness of relationships and the ever-swelling mass of vague or erroneous concepts. To make such generally recognized truths universally valid and effective is the goal to which the path described above should lead.

According to the plan of this work, it will comprise two volumes; the second is to follow within a year at the latest. The first volume, which appears here, contains a genetic presentation of our knowledge of legal philosophy up to the emergence of the historical view. The reasons for this presentation and therefore for the division are explained partly here and partly in the introduction. And if views are included which are not usually regarded as philosophy, this will be justified in the presentation itself. — The philosophy of modern times shall appear here as a great intellectual development in which each step is motivated by the preceding ones, each thought penetrates all spheres at the center, and, as with organic products, only the fruit reveals where the seed was intended to grow. That is why I have usually indicated the course and the end in advance at the beginning of an orientation, and conversely illuminated the later epochs in the light of the endeavors of the beginning. The fact that the inner driving forces of progress thus become clear and the assumptions and systems naturally interlock is the guarantee I sought for the correctness of the presentation. That is why the only thing I ask of the reader is that they accept it in this form and not be discouraged from following it in its entirety and grasping the connections. The writer, who has strived with effort to connect scattered phenomena into a whole in a difficult subject, may well wish that his work not be read hastily and incompletely, and has a right not to be expected to be clear and instructive to such readers.

The second volume will contain a presentation of the historical view, divided into three sections. The first deals with law, its origins and development, and the last with justice as the central focus of this view. The middle section presents the historical view in its treatment of positive law, in its scientific conception, structure, application, and in the drafting of law books, and seeks to establish it in opposition to the rationalist view that has prevailed until now.

For it is not the slightest purpose of this writing to set up an eternal monument to rationalism. It must be fought in its own domain, with its own weapons, through the strictest and most precise sequence of thought, which is just as ready for the extreme abstraction that moves in empty conceptual definitions as it is for the contemplation of living activity in the world; but which strictly adheres to the path it has chosen and does not allow any wavering between the one and the other, or what has been gained on this side to be appropriated on the other. It remains to be seen whether rationalism can stand up to the test and pursuance it itself demands and calls for. Theology is still struggling with this adversary. Its victory will be made easier if such is also achieved in other areas. Schelling has now given the signal for this, which, in philosophy itself, has dispelled it for the discerning with a single breath, as it were. The task is therefore to uncover, with exhaustive completeness, all its expressions in legal philosophy and in the treatment of positive law in every respect. Where its falsity is not generally apparent in one field, it will be in another, and mutual confirmation will remove any doubt as to its nullity. It will become clear to jurisprudence that the countless evils felt and lamented by all in theory and practice, but sought in vain to be avoided, have their innermost seat only in it. It will thus reveal itself as an enormous error that permeates and consumes life and knowledge in all its ramifications. To achieve this alone seemed to me a worthy task. For once that hindering power is clearly recognized and thereby also repelled, the germ of life, which has been suppressed only by it, must burst forth of its own accord, creative and formative.

December 1829

The Rise and Fall of Natural Law

TABLE OF CONTENTS

Preface xi
Notes on the Translation xxiii
Introduction 1
Book I: Ideal and Empirical Legal Philosophy (the Greeks) 7
  Part I: Plato 9
    The Idea and Its Knowledge 9
    Influence on the Doctrine of State 10
    The Republic 12
    Assessment 15
  Part II: Aristotle 19
    Standpoint 19
    Principle and Course of His Politics 20
    Position vis-à-vis Plato 22
    Relation between Nature and the Ethic in General 25
    Value of the Ideal View and of the Empirical 26
    Explanation of the Conflict between Plato and Aristotle 28
  Part III: The Ethic of the Greeks 31
    Religious Standpoint of the Greeks – Unhistorical View of the World – Ethic Thereof 31
    Absence of Charity 34
  Appendix to Book I: The Romans 39
Book II: Theocratic Legal Philosophy (the Middle Ages) 41
  Part I: Augustine 43
    Speculative Conceptualization of World History 43
    View of the State 43
    Practical Political Tendency 45
    Verdict 45
  Part II: The Germanic Writers 47
    Thomas Aquinas' Outline of the Ethical Sphere 47
    The Political Doctrine of the Middle Ages: Aristotelian Element 51
    Christian Speculative Element 52

How the Two Cohere – The Theocratic Principle as Foundational Characteristic of the Medieval Conceptualization 55
Part III: The Reformation, and Preview of Subsequent Development 61
Anti-Theocratic Character of the Reformation 61
Lack of a Scientific Development of Its Principles 61
The Cartesian-Grotian Development and the Reformation 62
The Latest Approximation of Medieval Catholic Elements to the Protestant Standpoint 64
Part IV: The Start of the New Learning 69
Character of the Writers at the Start of the New Epoch 69
Thomas More 69
Francis Bacon 70
Jean Bodin 70
Book III: Abstract Legal Philosophy 73
Part I: Abstract Philosophy in General (Rationalism) 75
Essence of Rationalism 75
Motivation for Rationalism 76
Progression of Rationalism 78
Contrast with the Historical Viewpoint 80
Subjective and Objective Rationalism 82
Logical Pantheism – Spinoza and His View of Law 86
Standpoint of Natural Law 88
Part II: Genesis of Natural Law in General 91
Chapter 1: Ethics (Natural Law in the Earlier Sense) 93
The Conception of the Origin of the Ethic 94
History of the Conception of the Origin of the Ethic 94
Basic Concepts 98
History of the Basic Concept 99
Abstraction from Relations 100
Consequences of this Abstraction 101
Content of the Ethic 102
Chapter 2: Division into Moral and Natural Law 105
Factual Division of Duties 105
Scientific Division of Duties by the Greeks 105
… and by the Moderns; Thomasius, Kant, Feuerbach 105

The Problem of Deducing Law in the Subjective Sense 108
The Two Problems Facing Natural Law 109
Development until Fichte and Feuerbach 111
Chapter 3: Legal Doctrine (Natural Law in the Later Sense) 117
Equality [Concept of Man versus Ideal of Man] 117
The Deduction of Natural Law from the Concept of Freedom 117
The Concept of Primordial Rights and Its History 118
The Negative Character of Natural Law 120
Relation of Natural Law to Roman Law 120
Chapter 4: The Individual Institutions of Natural Law 125
The Two Conflicting Principles of Rational Philosophy and their Implementation in all Doctrines of Natural Law 125
Controversy over Innate Rights 125
Over Property 126
Over the Content of Contracts 127
Over the Binding Nature of Contracts 128
Over the Distinction between Alienable and Inalienable Rights 128
Over the State 131
Initial and Subsequent Position of Natural Law regarding Positive Rights 133
Unfaithfulness of Natural Law to Its Required Method 135
Part III: Development of Natural Law in Individual Systems 137
Chapter 1: Hugo Grotius 139
Principle of Law 139
Delimitation of the Legal Sphere 140
Contract as the Embodiment of Natural Law 141
General Ethical Significance of the State 142
Identification of Nation and State 143
Private-Legal Character of the State Contract 144
Evaluation 145
Chapter 2: The Natural Law Doctors from Grotius to Kant 149
Hobbes 149
Pufendorf 153
Thomasius (Gundling) 155
Wolff (Darjes, Höpfner) 157

Opponents of Natural Law (Selden, Coccejus, "Dubia Jura Naturae") 160
Chapter 3: Kant's System 163
Kant's Doctrine 163
Its Scientific Motivation 164
Kant's Relation to Spinoza 166
Contradiction in Kant's Demand on Reason 168
Usurpation on behalf of Practical Reason 169
Basis of the Deception 170
Three Resulting Inconsistencies in his Practical Philosophy 170
Impetus to Further Development: Transcendental Philosophy, Result of Fichte's and Kant's Standpoints 172
Chapter 4: Kant's Doctrine of Law 175
Fulfillment of the Rationalistic Character 175
Restriction of the Subjective Character 179
Necessary Progression to Fichte 180
Chapter 5: Fichte's System 183
Personality, not Law of Thought 183
Identity of Consciousness 183
Denial of Objects 183
Subjective Idealism 184
Task to Discover Everything a priori 184
Real Principle in Fichte's Doctrine and Its Consequences 186
Satisfaction of the Interests of Recent Philosophy by Fichte 187
Relation to Spinoza 187
Untenability of the Fichtean Standpoint 188
Chapter 6: Fichte's Doctrine of Law 191
Abstract Character of Ethics 191
Resultant Oppositions to Kant 191
Finalization of the Subjective Character 192
Deduction of Law 193
Separation of Law and Morality 195
Solution to the Earlier Contradictions 196
The Contradictions Return by the Back Door 196
Parallel of Natural Law and the French Revolution in Both Stages 201

Chapter 7: Summary of Results: Natural Law in Its Final Form 203
The Character of Natural Law as the Combination of Kant and Fichte, and Completed in the General State of Scholarship 203
Outline of the Textbook Doctrine of Natural Law 203
Part IV: Assessment of Abstract Legal Philosophy 209
Chapter 1: Logical Examination of Natural Law 211
Logical Contradiction in the Rationalistic Procedure 211
Application to Natural Law 213
Lack of Certainty for Pure Rational Proof 217
Contradiction of Content: The Basic Concept Required by Natural Law 218
The Institutions that Arise from this Contradiction 220
Chapter 2: Real Examination of Natural Law 221
Dissolution of Morality into Mere Correct Thought 221
Negativity of Ethics, Morality as well as Natural Law 222
Relation of Negative and Positive Freedom and Equality 222
Destruction of Public Law 228
The Truth in the Motive of Rationalism and the Law of Reason 231
Part V: The Revolution as the Finalization of Natural Law 235
Chapter 1: The Doctrine of Popular Sovereignty until Rousseau 237
The Relation of Liberalism and the Revolution to Natural Law 237
The Defense of Rebellion in Consequence of Church Movements (Buchanan, Milton, Languet) 238
Connection of Natural Law to the Doctrines of Revolt (Sidney, Locke) 241
The Jesuitical Doctrine 244
Chapter 2: Rousseau 247
Inclusion of Doctrines Developed to this Point 247
Rousseau's Doctrine 247
Doctrine regarding the Basic Relation of the State Association and its Correlates 248
Doctrine regarding the relation of government 250
Doctrine of the Purpose of State Association 252
Verdict 256
Appendix to Book III: Materialistic Legal Philosophy 259

Works Cited.....269
Index.....275

PREFACE

It is obvious to even the most casual observer that our age is in thrall to radical subjectivism. Which is to say: the individual and his or her[1] conviction is the driving force in the determination and assessment of social, cultural, political, and juridical mores, standards, values, and goals. There is no overarching standard that transcends individuals and what they, each in and for themselves, determine to be right and wrong, good and evil, worthy of praise or of opprobrium. As a result, there is no shared set of values by which individual self-determination can be guided or restrained; instead, what passes for a shared set of values is simply the aggregation of individual legislations pitted against similarly aggregated yet opposed legislations, whereby the winners impose their aggregated mass of particular interests on the entirety.

It used to be that such a result was accepted until the next election. But nowadays even that threadbare concession to objectivity has been jettisoned, at least by the subjectivist vanguard. If their approach ends up triumphing, the end result will be the termination of the experiment and the imposition of the permanent reign of whoever is able to secure and maintain power. Such does seem to be the next stage in our lengthy downward trajectory.

It is to such straits that we have been reduced; and it is rather a chore to have to trace out the origins, seeing as how there is so little prospect of redressing this catastrophic farce of a public order so as to restore it on sound foundations. But this is our calling, and we will not shirk it. Thankfully, there are not a few witnesses past and present, who have chronicled the career of the debacle the final stages of which we now are privileged (or condemned) to observe on a daily basis. One of them is presented in his own words, in the book you have before you.

Friedrich Julius Stahl (1802–1861) was a leading statesman and legal scholar in 19th century pre-Bismarck Germany. He was one of the century's great parliamentary orators, but because he labored in favor of a Christian-historical order of things, his work has fallen into oblivion. This is no fault of his, but of the

[1] That even these qualifiers have become problematic as being insufficiently inclusive, is symptomatic of the phenomenon.

turn toward the catastrophic we have noted; for his words are full of wisdom and caution, all which have gone unheeded. But regardless, they are well worth recovering and exploring, for they make clear the depth of depravity to which we have sunk, and how we have gotten there.

This book, which contains over half of Stahl's *History of Legal Philosophy,* traces out the history of one of the major contributing factors to our modern age. That would be natural law, something which hardly anyone talks about, or even knows about. This was not always the case; once upon a time, natural law was the vehicle of choice to propound all manner of systems of law and order. The leading idea in all of them being that in natural law we have a standard by which to judge all existing, "positive" (i.e., man-made) legal systems.

A fine aspiration, one would think. But the devil is in the details. And not even the details: it is in the starting point. For the methodology of natural law already contained in itself the seeds of natural law's destruction. And Stahl here traces out that course with masterly hand.

Before we proceed any further, we need to ask the question: whence cometh this thing we call natural law? How did it ever become such a central element in learned discourse in ethics, law, politics, and constitutionalism?

Stahl provides a clue when he remarks in passing that natural law is an "expression inherited from the Romans" (p. 179 below). Roman law is of course the primary constituent of the Western legal tradition, and its various rather cursory explorations of the concept mediated its reception in theology and philosophy. But the matter reaches farther back than that, and Stahl accordingly begins his exposition with the Greeks, Plato and Aristotle. Here he is concerned to describe their contribution to "the science of the just" (p. 1), which is his definition of legal philosophy. What he finds is that they contributed essential building blocks for the development of a doctrine of natural law, but without advancing it, without allowing it to run its course. The same is true for the Romans, who incorporate the idea of natural law into their legal philosophy, such as it was; but they, instead of developing it, focused on practice, in order to develop the real-world legal system they inherited.

Opposed to the natural-law philosophy introduced by the pagans was the conception of the will of the personal-infinite God being the source of the ethic and thus of law, characterized by Stahl variously as Jewish, Judeo-Christian, or Christian (pp. 31ff., 34ff., 80ff.). Working from Christian revelation, Augustine mediated the conflict between Plato and Aristotle by introducing the concept of the Fall of Man, "the middle term which alone can unite Plato and Aristotle." In this manner, "the contradiction between the absolute moral task of the human race, which imbues Plato, and the laws of nature and the natural constitution of man, which Aristotle makes into a standard, is solved" (p. 45). Hence, natural law as absolute unattainable standard (Plato) is reconciled with natural law as inherent life force (Aristotle); but the reconciliation comes at a price, recognition of the living God.

Thus from the start, Christianity had within it the resources to develop a higher law answering to the science of the just. But instead of developing this insight further, it took over the natural-law building blocks of antiquity and merely juxtaposed them with the Augustinian understanding of God and the world, thus without transforming them. This was the system of scholasticism, and its preeminent developer was Thomas Aquinas (pp. 47ff.). To accomplish this, Aquinas adopted the concepts of an eternal law (*lex aeterna*) and the natural law. Eternal law is "the world-ordering reason in the Divine Spirit" which in itself is of the nature of art, an example, an idea – *artis vel exemplaris vel ideae* – but which with regard to human action has the form of a law. Natural law is participation in eternal law without being equivalent to it, being limited especially by man's fallen state (p. 47).

The problem here lies precisely in the ambivalent concept of the *lex aeterna.* For Aquinas makes a far-reaching distinction with regard to how God Himself relates to it. In itself, the will of God is not subject to this *lex aeterna* – but with regard to the creature, the will of God *is* subject to it. "In and of itself, therefore, the divine will is one with reason, but in relation to the creation and rule of the world, it is subordinated to the standard of reason" (p. 47). The upshot of this arrangement is to divorce God's will from the reasonable eternal law, and thus from the reasonable natural law. God's will becomes a subordinate category; and *a fortiori,* His revealed will does as well. Therefore,

> regardless of how deeply and truly the source of all moral commandment is acknowledged to be in the divine reason and wisdom, as is likewise the unity of the divine will with the divine reason and wisdom, an unacceptable divide is introduced here between the divine will-substance and the divine counsels, which in its further development leads, and actually did lead, to the will-

substance or the eternal law in God manifesting itself as mere supreme rule, as something given, apart from any decision (pp. 47f.).

This was a fatal move, for it delivered the higher law over into the hands of autonomous reason. From this point, natural law could, and eventually would, take on a life of its own. Initially, the Christian scientific endeavor continued in the train of a juxtaposition of Greek, in particular Aristotelian, thought with Augustinian doctrine (pp. 51ff.). Then came the twin movements of Renaissance and Reformation, bringing a new element into play, the subjective: "The principle of subjectivity was first unleashed" (p. 62). For the first time, the thinking subject became the central factor in scientific analysis. And in its subsequent development, this principle of subjectivity came to express itself in terms of a new demand: the right, without acknowledging any authority or receiving any given content, to access and develop knowledge, hence, the right of autonomy. The science of natural law followed ineluctably in its wake. "The philosophy that only recognizes what follows from reason cannot very well look elsewhere for this source of the ethic than in reason. In this consists natural law" in its now-purified form (p. 93).

To be sure, scholasticism had already prepared the way for this development. In the *lex aeterna* it had devised a way to sidestep the personal-infinite God and His will; indeed, to do so was "the precondition, the first step that natural law had to take to clear space for itself" (p. 94). The *lex aeterna* "abolished freedom of decision and determination in God" (p. 95), making way for Grotius' – the father of modern natural law (p. 139) – famous adage that reasonable right and wrong would be what it is even if God did not exist. Grotius was not the first to enunciate this principle, for it was already expressed in medieval times – another indication of the preparation provided by scholasticism for modern natural law. At most, God could be considered the author of natural law in the sense that He caused it to reside in man's heart; but His will was relegated to the category of divine positive law, a subordinate and dependent category.

Grotius, the legal-philosophical counterpart to René Descartes, pioneered modern natural law. Natural law's first, Grotian, iteration was in the form of "sociabilism," with its starting point placed in the sociable nature of man. Hobbes turned this on its head, placing the starting point in fear and insecurity, but this was a side track. Thomasius took things a step further, introducing the pursuit of happiness (cf. pp. 139ff.).

But what lay at the heart of natural law was the centrality of autonomous reason. Wolff realized this and dropped the notion of a starting point in this or that drive of human nature altogether; rather, he zeroed in on the rationalist principle at the heart of natural law, making it itself the starting point. Taken on their own merits, his efforts were rather feeble, but they at least had this positive result: they constituted "an impetus for Kant to take the rationalist principle seriously" (p. 159). Following through on this principle, Immanuel Kant laid bare the basic conundrum faced by the doctrine of natural law: the conflict between two concepts, a timeless unchanging law of reason, on the one hand, and a world of concrete things, acting subjects, on the other. Try as he might, he could not reconcile the two, because "he contemplates reason as a static form, and consequently as a thing. A thing and another thing that is set over against it, will always remain apart." Fichte proffered the solution: "It was therefore necessary to regard reason as active; not as the determinations of thought and laws, but as the *activity of thought*. This was the precondition for explaining this connection" (p. 174).

In taking reason to be an active thing, as activity of thought, Fichte brought the natural-law tradition to its terminus, enthroning the subjective principle over the supposed objective, eternal, unchanging law of reason. Even more than this: he accorded exclusive existence to subjectivity, and denied the existence of an objective world outside of consciousness. Unpalatable though it might be, this was the inevitable conclusion to the subjective-rationalist train of thought. But the more practical issue of Fichte's philosophy has been the triumph of the principle of subjectivity in the area of law. With Fichte, the individual becomes the source of law and as such an absolute legislator. "Law has no power over people; its realization depends on their arbitrary will" (p. 198). How can such a sovereign individual coexist with others, you may ask? Fichte had no convincing answer. Without an overarching law to restrain individuals, what is left is power relations. "If you can, make yourself into the ruler of the world. Freedom of the individual as the principle of the doctrine of law necessarily leads to this end" (p. 201). The principle even extends to education, whereby Fichte purged education of received learning, "burdening the pupil with the production of the entire future fund of knowledge from out of his own pure thought-activity" (p. 193).

With Fichte we have arrived squarely in our own world. The radical subjective principle has taken over every area of thought and practice. Each individual has become a legislating god pronouncing his or her "LET THERE BE ..." and woe to whoever stands in the way of every particular "AND THERE WAS ...."

How do we escape this descent into the maelstrom? Although his major positive contributions are contained in Volume II,[2] Stahl already provides some answers here.

The core problem with natural law, having hitched its wagon to reason, converts reason from an instrument to discover truth into a, indeed the, source of truth. Thus, we look to reason, not to revelation or divine authority to discover the truth. But this is to put the cart before the horse. "The true, the just are therefore that at which reason in its activity arrives, not what it is; they are what is discovered *through it*, not *from it*. It sees the light and testifies of the light, but it is not the light and did not make the light. This is precisely what is wrong with rationalism: it turns the organ of truth into truth itself, and because of this, it thinks that by dismantling and examining this organ it has obtained the content of the true, which this organ was supposed to convey" (p. 216). To view reason as the source of knowledge and truth is akin to believing "that the corporeal instruments through which we receive and distribute food, actually *are* our food. Such a conception corresponds with rationalism's procedure" (p. 217).

This point of departure leads natural law, as we saw, to attempt to reconcile an eternal unchanging law of reason with human freedom. This supposed antinomy is a problem of its own making. For "the contradiction arises only from the fact that human freedom is founded on a concept. If it is deployed by the free will of God and as part of His specific moral order, then all difficulties are smoothed away: it reaches as far as it wishes to, it has its limits in how far it may alienate itself in the determination that He gave it; but within this boundary it has its truly free, change-effecting movement, because God, unlike reason, brings forth more than what is only logically necessary" (p. 130).

The missing link is the personal-infinite God of the Bible. Only He can unite law and personality, and only in His creative act can these both be brought

[2] The volume as a whole is entitled *The Doctrine of Law and State on the Basis of the Christian World-View*, comprising the subvolumes *Philosophical Presuppositions*, *Principles of Law*, *Private Law*, and *The Doctrine of State and the Principles of State Law*.

forth, into a world of manifold complexity which cannot be reduced to the forms of logic, to mere negative knowledge. Rationalism provides negative knowledge; God provides positive knowledge.

> What is found from reason (*a priori*) is, according to Schelling's deeply significant expression, not "being," but only "not-capable-of-not-being." Thus, for example, that a triangle has three angles that together add up to two right angles, or that, as Wolff deduces, "seeing is the property of an animal with eyes" (thus a seeing animal), is only a negative knowledge; on the other hand, that the earth is round and not triangular, that there are plants and animals, this is positive knowledge. Another would not be unthinkable. Positive, and the object of positive knowledge, is, if I may put it in an absolute and exhaustive manner, the person, what is specifically primordially determined for him (i.e., holiness, the love of God, etc.), his act, and the product of his act. Therefore, it is merely negative knowledge that there is a being, a power, a ground, by which the world exists, because the opposite would be contrary to logical concepts; on the other hand, it is positive knowledge that there is a God in the true sense, a personal, self-conscious creator; likewise, that this God is gracious and merciful. It is positive knowledge when we consider the world to be the act and creation of God, and only negative knowledge when we consider it to be the eternally necessary consequence of reason. Philosophy which derives all knowledge from reason, can have no other than negative knowledge (p. 81).

This personal-infinite, creating God produces positive knowledge and therefore also events, new occurrences, history; and His purpose in history is constitutive to law properly conceived, and thus legal philosophy. This understanding of history, Stahl avers, was lacking to the Reformation, as part of an overreaction to the Catholic emphasis on the authority of human tradition. We may dispute the details,[3] but we cannot argue with the fact that the emphasis on

---

[3] In particular with regard to the shortcomings in Stahl's treatment of Calvinism. His accusation that Calvinism completely ignored the historical dimension is overdrawn. His Lutheran predilections lurk behind the curt dismissal of Calvinist theology and ecclesiology as thoroughly ahistorical (p. 64). And his post-Revolution monarchist

history as a crucial determinant of a proper ethic and legal philosophy has arisen in the meantime, largely in response to the ostensible timelessness of the rationalist philosophy. As Stahl remarks, "These latest scientific endeavors should not merely scientifically give shape to the inherent drive, the principle of the Reformation according to its true, full, positive aspect, but at the same time revive an aspect which even the Reformation left to one side. That would be the ethical significance of world history as the work and manifestation of the World Power" (p. 64).

The Christian-*historical* approach, then, alone reconciles law and freedom:

> [T]he historical view is the one by which something has happened and is happening, according to which there is a free act. Schelling called the Christian view of the world the historical as opposed to the logical view of modern philosophy. For the latter would have it that the world and all particular things are necessarily contained in the essence of God, while the former says it only arose (came about) through His voluntary creation. I have referred to the Judeo-Christian view of ethics as historical for the reason that it views law as law because God willed it so. Thus, man had the ethic before any incident of his own; but he has it only by the act of God; it does not exist by itself, with the concept of its existence or of being in general. And the past is not the higher, the present is; and the highest is the future, because God leads the world and law to it (p. 80).

Likewise, it alone maintains a true ethic:

> According to the *Jewish* conception, it is the personal God, not limited by anything, who according to His free will rules the destinies of the world, and who prescribes to men their end. Ethical precepts have no foundation apart from His will. All establishments and regulations bear the imprint of His omnipotence:

---

sympathies cloud his judgment of the Calvinist Monarchomachs (pp. 238ff.). Stahl was not acquainted with the work of Althusius, which was rediscovered by Gierke only after Stahl's death. If he had been, he would have had to modify his conclusions, especially regarding the scientific nature of Calvinist political theology. Both of these issues – Calvinism's historical dimension and its political theology – are treated in Alvarado, *Calvin and the Whigs* and *The Debate that Changed the West.*

"Ye shall not deal falsely one to another, *I am the Lord your God*" [cf. Leviticus 19: 11.] Good and evil exist only because He willed it or forbade it, for His alone is the glory.... *History is only the work of an agent....* In Judaism, not only do human destinies have a history, but the disposing power over them does as well. In events, everything is foresight, preparation for a future destination, everything is the result of interaction of the free act of people vis-à-vis God and the no less free act of God vis-à-vis people. The Judeo-Christian narrative as a whole turns out to be a great stage play, the archetype of all tragedy, because it is the divine tragedy. The ethical commandments themselves are a history. There is no ideal closed off in itself as the norm for the manifold relationships that develop outside of it, but He who alone is the source of the ethic, for each event, when it happens, at the same time imparts the law, because nothing happens that was not present in His will (pp. 31f.).

And furthermore:

An ethic that creates the norm while simultaneously generating the conditions and circumstances, which itself moves in an uninterrupted ascent to its final form, and therefore may be something else for a different time and different incident, without contradiction – an *historical ethic* can have its basis only in the free and omnipresent will of a personal God. Thus in Greek philosophy, although it recognizes a positive and meaningful principle of things, yet already has the beginning of the unhistorical view, since the cause of the world and the ethic appears as unfree, *thallos*, something merely existing. This view reaches its extreme in modern, abstract philosophy and certifies here more clearly the untruth thereof, whence it is also necessary for philosophy to return to that ancient historical view, the *Judeo-Christian*, which has never ceased being valid in life (p. 34).

Given its abstract character, natural law lacks this historical dimension. Not only that, it also, its rationalist point of departure deprives it of concrete content. It cannot take life relations and elevate them; rather, it must eliminate them in order to create a new order of things. We are experiencing the inexorable logic of this rationalist subjectivism in our day, whereby every activist movement believes it can remake human nature after its own image.

Stahl laid bare natural law's ultimately anti-natural character, pointing out its inability to take created realities into account. Instead of accepting God-given verities, it determines to overthrow them and recreate reality in terms of its abstractions. This becomes evident in its treatment of social structures and the inherent purposes they contain.

> The innermost untruth of natural law, which must strike every unprejudiced observer as soon as it is stated, is that it completely disregards the *inherent purpose of life relations*. Every human life relation bears within it its own particular purpose and thereby lays upon people a vocation to fulfill it accordingly, to give shape to it. This is the basis for the moral requirements that pertain to it, and also the requirements of its legal arrangement. For instance, the inherent purpose of marriage (the union of spouses for full life community), and not the reciprocal relinquishment of freedom among spouses, is that from which the entire legal formation of marriage proceeds: the obligation of faithfulness and community for better or worse, the prohibition on polygamy, incest, arbitrary divorce; the purpose of parental relations from which proceeds on the one hand paternal power, on the other the sustentation of children. The same holds true for every other human relation: property transactions, occupational groups, political groups, local community, state, church. This purpose of life relations is the principle of both ethics and law. All actual law indeed aims for this, and law is rational to the degree that it is shaped in accordance with these relations.... This purpose of life relations is the ground on which true legal philosophy takes its stand in opposition to the false philosophy of natural law (pp. 229f.).

What impelled the career of natural law was the effort to discover a common ground for all right-thinking persons beyond the dividing lines of sectarian religion. If our times have taught us one thing, it is the absolute untenability of the notion of a such a natural law accessible to people of "good faith," regardless of conviction, on the basis of a common ground in shared nature, human or otherwise. The gradual elimination of all such shared bases, brought about by the inexorable march of logical consistency on the basis of contradictory presuppositions, regardless of how flawed they might be in themselves, should by now have disabused us of this fata morgana. Stahl had already anticipated such a turn of events nearly two centuries ago. As he wrote in the introduction to

Volume II of this work, "Every philosophical system of whatever name in the final analysis rests on a foundational presupposition that is nothing more than faith, no matter what claim it may make to so-called scientific certainty. Even unbelief is a faith – one cannot reason from naked doubt. We have no immediate or homogeneous view of the highest principles of things and thus no absolute certainty; therefore for philosophical systems a purely objective knowledge independent of all personal judgment, such as mathematics, the natural sciences, or even the positive sciences, is ruled out."[4] Modernism is not based on neutral science but on specific presuppositions enthroning autonomous reason, which, consistently applied, end up destroying life.

How do we avoid this fate? Generally speaking, we need to recover a Christian-historical understanding of life, the world, eternity. But in terms of systematics, Stahl proposes a novel solution. He notes that every system, however ultimately illogical, is based on some aspect of reality which serves as a presupposition from which all else is deduced. "All of these doctrinal systems in their ready-made manifestations are closed, self-sustaining worlds. But they are still created in the one real world, and if their movement of *thought* begins and ceases within themselves, they do have a *factual* ground, outside themselves" (p. 3). Intellectually, these systems are carried out in lopsided fashion because they focus on a specific human interest which in itself is legitimate and finds its basis in reality. "The various systems do not at all allow themselves to be united, because true and false cannot be united, and there is no community between opposing basic assumptions. But with regard to the interest that is specific to each philosophy, it is impossible to say in advance that one such would by nature exclude another. On the contrary, we might reason that each in itself, because it is human, is a true one, and that history desired its satisfaction, but is untrue in the product which it brought about in separation from the rest" (p. 4). Stahl's method is to deconstruct these philosophical systems in terms of the human interest which spawned each of them and which serves as its particular point of departure, and reintegrate them by joining these disparate interests into a comprehensive system embracing them all. Such is only possible through a comprehension of the whole man, of his true and original nature, because only his nature combines these interests. The knowledge of this, in turn, can only come

---

[4] *Principles of Law,* p. 4.

from his Creator.

And so, having passed through the subjectivist phase, finally turning away from his rationalist autonomy, there is only one alternative for modern man. "And when at last he sees himself compelled to turn back to the recognition of independent existence outside himself, he no longer can consider it in the Greek fashion, as held together by the idea or the laws of nature, but as the work of the freely acting God" (p. 38).

NOTES ON THE TRANSLATION

The usual translating conventions are followed. Square brackets [like this] are used either to show the original text in cases in which the translation is not straightforward or unambiguous, or to provide interpolations for better understanding, or to provide supplementary material.

A note about the notoriously difficult words "Recht" and "Gesetz": as is well known, English has no direct counterpart to them; they both refer to "law." Often they are used synonymously, but just as often they are not. This is similar to the Latin words "jus" and "lex," which confront the translator with the same ambiguity. Now then, there are three cases of contradiction referred to by these words. In one case, "Recht" refers to law in the more elevated, transcendent sense, while "Gesetz" refers to law in the positive, man-made sense. This is usually referred to as the contradistinction between natural law and positive law. But this is not the only kind of contradistinction they may denote. There is, in addition, the distinction between moral and juridical law, a distinction which plays a large role in the discussion of this book. In order to set juridical law apart from moral law, Stahl combines the words into one, using the term "Rechtsgesetz" for law which functions exclusively in the juridical sphere, and it is here translated that way. Yet another contradistinction is that between law and rights. Here, it is English which is unambiguous, German and Latin which are ambiguous. "Recht" in the singular I have almost always translated as "law" except where it was obvious from the context that "rights" were meant (e.g., p. 111); the plural, "Rechten," always refers to "rights," and it is here so translated.

Einleitung.

Rechtsphilosophie ist die Wissenschaft des Gerechten. Der Erwartungen sind nun verschiedene, welche man von einer Wissenschaft des Gerechten hegen kann. Man kann sich unter ihr ein System wirklicher Entscheidungen denken, ein höheres Gesetzbuch, oder nur eine Richtschnur des Urtheils über bestehende Gesetze. Das aber ist unbestreitbar: das Gerechte muß unabhängig von seiner Anerkennung unter den Menschen sein Daseyn und seine Tugend haben, und die Kenntniß desselben daher eine andere seyn als die des geltenden Rechts, eine solche, an welcher dieses selbst gerade allein zu messen und zu erproben ist. Manche sind wohl auch dahin gekommen, alle Einrichtungen für sittlich gleichgültig zu halten, oder zu läugnen, daß dem Menschen die Kunde des Wahren und Gerechten vergönnt sey. Es ist aber ein heiliger Glaube der Menschheit, daß eine Gerechtigkeit ist, und daß wir ein Wissen, sey es auch ein beschränktes, von ihr haben. Wo aber ein Wissen ist, da muß auch irgend eine Einheit, ein Zusammenhang in ihm seyn und ausfindig gemacht werden können, da muß es also auch eine Wissenschaft, in was immer für einer Art, geben.

INTRODUCTION

Legal philosophy is the science of the just. Expectations may differ regarding such a science. One can envision a system of legal decisions, a code of higher law, or merely a rule by which to judge existing laws. But one thing is undeniable: the just must have its being and its virtue independently of its recognition among men, which means that the knowledge of it must be something else than the standing law; in fact, standing law can only be measured and tested against it. Some have even come to hold all institutions to be morally indifferent or to deny that the knowledge of the true and just is vouchsafed to men. But it is a sacred belief of mankind that there is a justice, and that we have a knowledge of it, limited though it may be. But where there is a knowledge, there must also be some sort of unity and coherence to it, which can be identified, for which reason there must also be a science, of whatever sort it might be.

If one truly wishes to get on with such a science, the thought arises that the same thing has already been tried by others, in various ways, with various results. These previous attempts cannot be ignored, because it is human nature that we only be convinced and believe ourselves to be on the right track when we are aware of being in command of any conflicting belief. This puts us directly in the midst of the aspirations of our time. And even if the investigations into the just must have the same goal at all times, in each particular one a special way may be mapped depending on the state of the science which is found in it. But this means that our science will require quite a distinct approach. For not only is opinion divided and vacillating regarding individual institutions, it is so even regarding the standard by which their justice is to be assessed. Our legal philosophy cannot escape the total uncertainty of all knowledge and thought which is the fruit of the rapid succession of destructive systems of philosophy, while it also faces harrowing developments in its own field.

When at the end of the last century a long-held orientation broke into the open, it was the prideful freedom of human action and thought that led scientific efforts. Seeking sole dominion, like any new motive force, it expressed itself in the destruction of everything it encountered. The multiplicity of particular relations, the entire structure of the moral world would be torn down so that nothing would exist but what pure reason finds and brings forth out of itself. This orientation retained vitality until it used up its fuel and manifested its inability to provide a new world for the fallen one. At that point, the Higher Power once again was recognized and revered which, hidden to us, brings the human condition to shape and maturity. Once again the value of each individual life, each peculiarly formed institution, was asserted. And the law no longer appeared to be a product of the laws of thought, but a living member connected with all the relations of life of the peoples and the movement of history.

And so, this orientation was overturned, but mainly by virtue of a mere natural reaction. As in that case there was a hatred of all that exists, so in this case there was a hatred of all free reflection. Governments should maintain the existing condition; lawyers should know of the institutions of the present and their historical derivation, not judge them. In this manner, the fight against the philosophy of the times became a rejection of philosophy altogether. The power of life, the further development of relationships, which require examination and judgment, then also made this one-sidedness palpable; and in the Historical School[5] the need once again became manifest for a standard of the just, but without a specific view as to where it should betake itself.

Meanwhile, a new treatment of the philosophy of law arose in the philosophical system of Hegel. It not only opposes the other two orientations but generally demands a previously unheard-of way of thinking. We observe these three opposing scientific schools in the field of our legal philosophy. Next to them, partly based on them, partly independently, are writers who pursue practical interests without general scientific exhaustiveness. These are the representatives of countless political confessions.

So this is the ground on which the investigation of the just currently finds itself as it embarks on its course. It might take a course opposed to all of these viewpoints, or it might link up with one of them; whatever it does, it will encounter the opposition of the others. It therefore requires at the start a justification against them, namely one which they themselves must recognize. This would then constitute a grounded judgment over them. Without this scientific

---

[5] [The Historical School of jurisprudence as represented chiefly by Friedrich Karl von Savigny. It will be discussed in detail in Volume 1B of this work.]

justification, any investigation incurs the charge of arbitrariness. It cannot convict the opponent and therefore cannot consider itself to be secured. The same task also extends to the views of yesteryear, because our historical teaching transplants them to the present, and we cannot excuse ourselves from taking up a certain position vis-à-vis them.

But the difficulty of this task becomes evident already in advance. If a decision is to be made between opponents, it will not be possible otherwise than by they themselves recognizing common ground by which to measure themselves. Now then, every system which is to be secured contains in itself a supreme principle of law, in fact in part even a supreme law of thought and knowledge, thus the supreme thing against which everything else is measured; and it acknowledges this to be nowhere outside itself. Everything must be conceded to it, if one submits to its test of what is truthful. If, however, one denies this and chooses another, it can demand no further concessions. But this test of the truth, against what can it itself be tested? Whatever is established as a rule of justice, or as a logical law according to which things are decided and proven, is still only a new system placed alongside the previous one, equally isolated, rejecting and being rejected. It could not acquire authority over other ways of thinking, each of which is like a circular line moving around its own center, returned to its starting point, a self-sufficient closed world. But if one wishes to select what is true from among all of this, he must presuppose something that should be the result of his investigation – a standard. In so doing, he loses the recognition of all, and retains only a colorful composition, without unity and internal stability.

Hence, a community of the various views, each assured of its own rightness, seems impossible even before one begins.

All of these doctrinal systems in their ready-made manifestations are closed, self-sustaining worlds. But they are still created in the one real world, and if their movement of *thought* begins and ceases within themselves, they do have a *factual* ground, outside themselves. No system forms itself: it is formed by people. There must, therefore, be some drive, some interest in human nature, by which it is produced and gains its existence in an enduring manner. Its basic assumption cannot, by its very nature, be obtained by conclusions which it presupposes; rather, it is nothing else than precisely the interest that the thinker finds in his own innermost being, which he cannot give up. But the scientific method is always determined by the basic assumption – the manner of assuming, of deciding, of demonstrating, hence the entire system. The systems have therefore varied as the progress of history has brought forth a different character of the human mind and its various motives.

The interest that generates and maintains a philosophy is something higher than the philosophy itself, because the existence of the latter depends upon the existence of the former. The measure of philosophy is therefore likewise the measure that must be applicable to the interest that generated it. But its measure can only be a factual one. For example, that the good is good and evil is evil, cannot be demonstrated logically, but is true only while the primary source of good at the same time possesses omnipotence. Could humanity indeed break free from these ideas and the power that they contain, then the distinction between them would have to fall away in science as well. The historical progression, the real nature of man is the judgment over all motives of philosophy, and thus even over this. Science, as with the legends of the saints, must seek out the strongest lord.

The various systems do not at all allow themselves to be united, because true and false cannot be united, and there is no community between opposing basic assumptions. But with regard to the interest that is specific to each philosophy, it is impossible to say in advance that one such would by nature exclude another. On the contrary, we might reason that each in itself, because it is human, is a true one, and that history desired its satisfaction, but is untrue in the product which it brought about in separation from the rest. Now should it find a deeper, fuller interest that would contain all these interests in itself and alone generate them, then it would be satisfied through the satisfaction of all the others. The philosophy that exacted this would be the secure one. It would unite all the others; not their claims, but their true drives, by which alone both their false results and their true ones could become reality, the vital acting element in each one. This total interest with its rich content would be nothing other than the true and original nature of man, from which have emanated all conditions and motives, and to which they purpose to return. A view is certain not merely if it is grounded and agreed within itself, but if it satisfies the whole man, and also provides insight into how the others could arise; for no other position grants full overview of the others than the highest.

The task is therefore to present our philosophical knowledge genetically. The knowledge of the historical succession of philosophical views will not suffice here; instead, their own origin and inner gestation, the driving force in the human being that they produced, has to be revealed. Therefore, completeness of writers and their opinions cannot be the goal, but only the completeness of the scientific pathways; and with every system, the question is not so much which institutions it declares to be just, but what for it *is* the just, and whence it draws the knowledge thereof.

In this manner, the consideration of the past should lead to new results.

BOOK I: IDEAL AND EMPIRICAL LEGAL PHILOSOPHY (THE GREEKS)

PART I: PLATO

The Idea and Its Knowledge

Our eye receives the light and reflects the light, but it is not the light and did not make the light. Rather, Helios radiates the light; he gives things color and visibility, and our eyes the ability to see them. In the same way, the idea is the cause of good. She is the queen of the world of spirit, as the sun is of the world of sense. Indeed she even brought the latter forth, and set the light and the sun as her image in that world. Only through her is there a distinction of good and evil, of truth and falsehood, as the difference of color comes through light. Our spirit bears witness to the idea, but is not the idea; but by her it has received its ability to detect these differences. And were she to retire from the world, it also would no longer know good and evil, as when the sun goes down, the eye no longer distinguishes between colors and objects, although the power of distinguishing seemingly lies in itself.

This is Plato's parable.[6]

So the idea has an existence and therefore a quality, a determinateness other than the capacity in ourselves that, by its aid, sees its effects. And it must also be recognized as an independent entity in this way. Just as now no one investigates the eye in order to observe the sun and the light or to prove their existence, so Plato does not infer and find the essence of goodness from reason; but it itself is the first and original that there is, and of which the mind [Geist] has knowledge; not that it has to be there because some ground in ourselves made it necessary. The laws and the organization of the eye in themselves are nothing; the power and activity in it are stirred only by the light which ensures vision. Only through the idea is the power stirred that sees good and evil – the *vision of the spirit* [Anschauung des Geistes]. It is not placidly there, as sight is not placidly there in the eye, and does not have its possession in itself. Rather, it simply is, while it absorbs the object, like the rays of light, outside itself. If light and color are nothing other than what already lies in the organization of vision, from whence should it have its peculiar luster and the joy that it infuses in the

---

[6] *The Republic,* Book VI.

viewers? Now, if the idea is something outside of the laws and determinations of the mind, why should it be restricted to the paucity thereof, why should the good and righteous be merely formal, an epitome of general rules without special content? The idea in fact works according to its own nature, and nothing stands in the way of its having inward splendor and immense wealth, like the sun, with its rays breaking into manifold colors.

Influence on the Doctrine of State

With Plato, therefore, justice is no rule or system of rules, but a full display of manifold, quite determinate activity. Hence his republic is the pattern of concrete usage. He shows us his citizens in the full activity of their lives, how they meet their needs, what their employment is, what their spiritual aspirations are, how they are educated and informed, what they think to be good and estimable, bad and shameful. The constitution and form of the state appears in indissoluble unity with this particular life. These can as little be transferred to other citizens as its citizens could live under a different constitution. It is impossible to distinguish and delineate what in this state is the eternal, the ideal, and what is of accidental appearance. For if we were to abstract a principle from it and hold to it as the self-contained true and eternal, we would by no means hit Plato's meaning. It is not, e.g., the bare surrender of the individual to the whole that appears to him to be the true and magnificent; what matters is only the specific manner of surrender, the specific manner of activity, as it is conducted through all the diversity of human activity.

The ideal is so determinate and individual, determinate even for the moment in which it is presented, that it contains, as an essential element, even the mind and the worth of the ruling persons, who in fact change while the general principles of the constitution remain. Wise people are worth more than wise laws, this is what every simple man thinks: this judgment now makes its appearance in a scientific work, and it pertains to the idea of this state, that the wise (philosophers) govern it. In fact, for the mutual relations of its citizens there should be no rules at all. The sure judgment of well-bred men will decide in the particular case.

Hence, the notion that the general principles professed in its laws by the state, and presented in its constitution, contain the just, is quite far from the mark. The just does not aim for this stasis, the architecture of public life; rather, the just is a living condition, it consists in the particular action of the moment.

The scientific course followed by Plato, by which he discovers, tests, proves institutions, is nothing like *logical deduction*, by which, from given premises, others arise of necessity. He tests their *actual result* by assessing whether a situation arises that he desires for the whole. If the idea of the good and the just is something other than the organization of the mind, who then would require it always to desire a conclusion which of necessity follows from two premises, rather than from what the *whole* freely wills with a *single* will, regardless of how many components it might have? In a logical deduction, the connection is similar to a building, where the lower always carries the upper, without being carried by it; but contemplation [Anschauung] which is aroused by the idea is like a living body in which each member both holds and carries the other and is held and carried at the same time. The analogy that Plato uses between the unity of the people and the state makes it apparent that he does not seek the unity of the concept, but of the living. His picture of the state emerges in one step at the same time in all parts, complete, in the world, like wisdom from the head of Zeus.

Plato's facsimile from his archetype, or, in turn, others' facsimiles of his republic, is therefore completely different from those done according to abstract concepts and the more recent doctrines of state. The latter can be called the facsimile of stasis, the former the facsimile of the act. The facsimile of stasis is subsumption: juxtaposing rules having no intrinsic content and therefore lying ready at hand for any content – for example, equal freedom – with material otherwise indifferent, given apart from it – landholding, commerce, or whatever it might be. But Plato's facsimile does not impart a disconnected rule to the original which it only needs to take up; and no material is sufficient for it that was not already thoroughly shaped according to the idea. Any logical mind could therefore choose to introduce the justice of Kant or Hegel into a country, but whoever would undertake the formation of a state according to Plato, or a legal philosophy developed in the same sense, would have to be equipped with creative power.

Therefore, the facsimile of stasis must also mimic the image of stasis. To wit, actual institutions must mathematically satisfy the general principles of justice, and these must be amenable of realization. But the facsimile of act must mimic the original model of the act. The same spirit, the same effect must prevail in the facsimile as in the original. And so the painter's image of man cannot and ought not be equal in terms of ruler and compass, but should have the same effect as the original, i.e., the painting should bring forth the same perception in the viewer as the person painted. The question of feasibility is therefore the most incongruous measure one can apply to the republic of Plato. For the meaning is not that these laws are to be literally implemented in a state as he designed it, but that a real state bear the same spirit within itself, engender the same mind in its citizens, and through its institutions exercise the same impression on the beholders as upon him who designed it. It is this which is feasible, and if it cannot be achieved to that extent, at least nothing stands in the way of states making their institutions so as to approach it. And yet, in fact, this idea of the Platonic state is none other than what really moved the Greek states; in the period of their luster and their excellence, they together imitated it with greater or lesser success.

It has become prevalent in recent times to look at the real shape of things as the sole representation of the good and the just; and, while not admitting the existence of things apart from the idea, certainly not the idea apart from things. It has even been attempted to attach the Platonic ideas to this relation. But according to Plato, although the idea did bring about all things, its own existence is not conditioned by that which it produced; it is not just an aspect, foundation, form, or motive power of the product, but has a real independent existence, like the sun, which would still be the sun even if there were no objects for it to illuminate, no growth for it to unfold, and no eye to look upon it. To Plato the dissatisfaction of every great mind with earthly things is obvious. His ideal is nowhere in the world, as even his own visualizations could not show how things stood to his mind's eye. The reality that does not contain it, should first only strive to form itself in accordance with it. His knowledge is therefore not the same as that of a knowledge that is in the existing order, but of one that is currently outside of it, that only in the future perhaps will be in it – it is therefore a *preview.*

The Republic

This image of the state in Plato's mind's eye is the abundance of manifold forces corresponding to the human community, each fully unfolded in its own way, and all, in the entirety of all their activities, oriented to a goal, gained from an ordering sense in proper measure. "Justice" (we could more correct translate: perfection) for the state is precisely what it is for the individual. The first requirement is, that each develop his innate aptitude undisturbed, so that no force remains hidden, and all the wealth placed in the nature of man unfolds itself. The second is that each person be referred to his proper place and ambulate therein. The last, finally, is that these cheek-by-jowl, diverse aspirations and achievements all be mastered by a single will and interest – that the state also be *one* state.

Accordingly, citizens are divided into two main classes, one for the lower functions of material needs (the farmer, belt-cutter, potter, etc.), the other for the higher functions of military protection and spiritual leadership – the "Guardians." The separation occurs in an equitable manner if each is allocated the position to which he is called by his nature. Accordingly, even in the lower class, employment is not left to individual choice but according to aptitude and capacity, thus ensuring that each activity is brought to perfection. Equally, citizens are classified in the higher or lower class according to their higher or lower nature, their moral and intellectual gifts. For some souls by nature have gold mixed in them, others silver, others a baser metal. But the distribution in the two classes is hereditary because only a noble line yields noble offspring, and here still, precautions are taken against degeneration. However, this does not rule out members of the higher class becoming demoted if they degenerate, while members of the lower, if they ennoble themselves, become elevated to the higher. The lower class is further left out of consideration. It forms, according to the Greek manner, the base layer that is lowered into the enveloping earth in order for the splendor of the building to rise above it. The ruling class of Guardians alone is actually the state; in it alone is represented the perfection of human common life. Its members are relieved of any common concern and employment; the state meets the need. From childhood on they receive the most thought-out education; gymnastics and music bring all their physical and intellectual aptitudes to maturity, every great mind is nourished in them, every disturbing impression is kept away. Thus, imitative poetry itself is excluded because it endangers truthfulness and dignity.

The full development of the forces and the resulting proper distribution thereof has impressed upon it the seal of perfection by the *unity of the goal* that they serve. Everything is to be directed to the whole, to the state, not to any personal (private) interest. Citizens are not ends in themselves but merely a means for the state. In particular, the higher class of the Guardians, in which the perfect state is represented, imposing this utter self-renunciation and unconditional surrender on the whole – they are absolutely not allowed to have any particular interest. They are not allowed to travel on their own business, are not to make use of gold and silver, are to have no personal wealth. Even the bond of family is abolished among them. Marriages are holy, says Plato, but the most holy are those most beneficial to the state. Therefore the community of women and children should be introduced so that one should not have any greater concern and desire for those that concern him alone, rather than all others. No one is supposed to know who is his father, who is his son; one is to consider everyone to be father and son, so that a family love pervades the entire community. Only then will the state really be *one* state; all actual states did not deserve the name, because in each one there are several states, especially two, a state of the rich and of the poor, but actually there are countless, namely as many as there are individuals.

Therefore this state, preferably in its truest elements, the class of Guardians, is to contain all the noble powers, bravery, wisdom, gentleness, love of country, etc. But each of them has to attain the position which that they are appointed by nature to assume, and maintain it. Insight has to make the decisions, bravery has to execute them, strength that is determined by the idea of lordship must decree, those destined to serve must obey, and care is to be taken that none overstep one's own area into another's. Herein lies justice in the strict specific sense. But if this measure is kept, and if the scattered activities are to remain focused on a goal, it is necessary that the wise men stand at the head of the state – those who are not determined by the desire for money and delights, fear of death, but, equipped with strength of mind, with memory and mind are focused on the knowledge and execution of the good, who therefore do not look to appearance, but to the truth, above the changing and transient, and only strive after what is permanent and eternal. These, imbued with the greatness of the ideal and incapable of selfish volition, will share in the entire intricate motion of the animating rhythm. In them the summit of the Platonic state is reached, as it were in an unrelenting enthusiastic devotion, with which the people worship the idea of the good in the glory of the state which they form and which they present.

Assessment

What Plato calls the justice of the state is rather only the beauty thereof. Because what distinguishes the just from the beautiful is this: in the beautiful, the fullness of manifold existence is unconsciously united and without satisfying the parts; but the just grants every being its own existence, satisfaction and independent movement, so that it itself, as a whole, may freely engage the larger whole. But this is not found in the state of Plato. He sacrifices the human being, his happiness, his freedom, even his moral perfection. For this state exists only for the sake of itself, for the glory of its appearance; and the citizen is only destined as a ministering member to fit himself into the beauty of its structure. So it has a pictorial character. It is a work of art that seems to be there less for its own parts than for the spectator.

But an eternal law has it that even true aspiration, if pursued in isolation, when it injures another, at the same time destroys itself. Plato is prevented from attaining what for him is overriding – the inner harmony of the state – by the very fact that he disregards the interests of the individual.

Plato would even like his state to represent a higher harmony than nature, indeed the highest. But it can only do so by existing likewise as a realm of freedom, so that the beauty of its structure is not merely there, like nature, but is created in every moment anew by those who desire it and are enthusiastic about it. But this is made impossible by the institutions themselves. Nowhere is a right and a choice granted to the citizens; everyone has a position he must, rather than should, fill. There is no protection of the person but only of the abilities which he possesses, even against his will, so that here as well, it is not he who is protected but the archetype for which those abilities are used. In fact, it is not even intended, nor is any care taken, that he himself become a participant in the knowledge of the greatness which he represents. Everything that is an object of human control, possession, and desire is taken away from the class of rulers, so that even the possibility of devoting themselves to the state is taken from them. It makes of them a destitute rather than noble people. Harmony, as Aristotle interposes, does not refer to the same tone always being struck, but to many notes being struck in unison. Thus, the state must not merely be *one*, as Plato would like, but at the same time also *many*, in order to achieve beauty and harmony. It must consist of men who freely choose to act of their own will. Because Plato gives this up, he even pushes his state below the level of natural beauty.

When he does not take the happiness of its citizens into account, for example does not worry whether the class of Guardians will be satisfied with the position he allots them, indeed when he allows the infirm who are unable to serve the state to die, and banishes the doctors who would eke out a useless life for them – for he even believes a justification for life to be required – the intactness of the whole will of itself bring about the happiness of individuals, and it does not matter whether this or that class is taken care of, but only whether the state corresponds to its archetype. But the existence of the happiness of the people, and of a particular concern to that end as an end in itself and not a means to some other end, also pertains to the complete picture of the state. Such rigors as those do not adorn that picture. The forces of nature may go about destroying living existence and still remain sublime and beautiful, but human institution cannot imitate their relentless passage without violating their purport. Aristotle criticizes Plato for educating his warriors like dogs, to be mild to locals, rough and hostile to strangers, because an ungentle disposition is nowhere befitting. In itself, this institution holds no interest for us; but in it the great question comes to a head, whether the perfection of man or of the state takes precedence. Plato is not concerned with the human perfection of the warrior, but with the development of military power in the state. He promotes the inconsistency of a disposition of natural hatred against non-citizens because the human mind tends to gain greater strength in the direction that it unilaterally pursues. More disturbing than this is the education of women to male activity, to war and national defense. One is not permitted to become what he should be as human by nature, but only that by which the state has the greatest profit. Not only is the consummation of the individual sacrificed to the state; so also is the consummation of human relations and aspirations, for it holds true for these no less than for the state, that they fulfill that which nature has determined for them.

The bond of family is abolished so as to avoid any special interest. Poetry is banished, because, while it imitates the humble as well as the exalted, it does not promote the purity and lawfulness of the soul, which this state requires. The unity and cohesion of the state is no atonement for the fact that in itself high aspirations are lacking and sacred relations are desecrated. The Platonic state would have achieved a higher beauty if Plato had sought not merely beauty and enthusiasm, but also freedom and humanity. For the good, even according to Plato, must be of an even higher beauty than even the beautiful.

A sublime spirit runs through all these institutions of public life, the demand of unconditional boundless devotion without regard for self. However, with the state being made the object of this devotion, an unconscious structure is set over the people which cannot reciprocate, nor even feel, this devotion. How much truer and friendlier is the saying: "Man is not there for the sake of law, but law for the sake of men!"

Plato's doctrine is not free of the error that, while he pursues the *idea*, he insensibly imputes the *ideal* to it. Ideal, namely, is the perfection thought up by man by contrast with the perfection intended by God's command and purpose. The ideal therefore does have a trace of exaltation over reality, with all the bad and the common that adheres thereto; but it also has a trace of conflict with and violation of the natural order and thus true perfection, whereby it even falls short of reality. In this way, Plato fashions by human thoughts a perfection through devotion to and renunciation in favor of the state, which, while elevated over selfishness, nevertheless violates the right of personality and the vocation of sex and the bond of family as ordained by God's law.

Despite all this, Plato's doctrine of the state remains a model and an upbraiding teacher for subsequent times through its true goals, which are absent from subsequent science – the positive development of forces, the beauty of the design, and the inner spirit and enthusiasm which it recognizes as demands of public life.

PART II: ARISTOTLE

Standpoint

The Platonic idea of the good illuminates a future, and only a preview that it itself grants puts the mind in a position to recognize it. This preview, the special gift of Plato, is absent in Aristotle, who therefore must derive his knowledge of the just from what exists, what is observed with certainty, without enthusiastic intuition. His basis is the world as it is, and the laws that visibly receive and govern their existence. For him, the cause and measure of the just is not a freely designed shape that floats over reality futuristically, unattained and perhaps unattainable; but nature itself, the drive of which acts in unconscious things and the relations of men.

That institution which follows this drive is just. Aristotle's motto is "nothing can be good and noble that is against nature." So he derives the ethical law from the natural. The content is one and the same to him, only that with the former, freely-choosing beings *implement* it.

This assumption seems already to harbor a contradiction in itself. Nature, namely, acts with irresistible power, so that wherever it expresses its drive, no choice, therefore no ethical law is conceivable. Where, however, there is choice and resolution, hence room for ethical prescription, there also nature has retreated and accords no standard. Furthermore, nature arouses conflicting drives. Both selfishness and self-sacrificing love are its work, and it is certain that the ethic [ethos] usually enjoins precisely that a natural drive be overcome. If, therefore, a choice is made among these conflicting things, one would think that a different measure than the law [Gesetz] of nature would have to be found lurking in the background, a peculiar ethical law, from which the decision comes.

But Aristotle has no need of such. These contradictions have a basis only if one pays attention to individual effects. But for Aristotle the measure of the just is nature and its intention as a whole. An activity runs through the whole of creation which, while in appearance and in detail eliciting opposites, when taken as a whole acts in agreement. Unconscious nature everywhere manifests a creative drive, a drive seeking after preservation, propagation, increase of existence, through which creatures exist and multiply. It also displays the sphere of spiritual beings. It uses necessary wants to push people to combine, links them instinctively together, and so generates the various social relationships. Nature desires absolutely the richer, the manifold, the developed, even if, rebelling against its own goal, it here and there seems to wish to destroy existence and dissolve its creations into simple matter. It is therefore in accordance with nature that barriers of organic plant life restrain the raw elements; it is in accordance with nature that the reign of the drive to sociability and its constructions in the spiritual world be secured against outbreaks of selfishness. It is a natural drive by which man seeks the constant expansion of wealth, of luxury, since each activity is directed to its enlargement; but the general drive of nature sets a limit to him by showing that wealth is to be used only for one's own preservation, for the family and the state.[7]

So Aristotle requires no other measure beyond reality; instead, reality provides this measure to him, for he finds the universal in it and recognizes it for what it truly wishes, and should be. It does not necessitate irresistibly; rather, whether or not it will be obeyed in detail is an open question. It is not conflicting in itself; the conflicting drives are not the ones which run through it universally. And it is clear that its requirements are not to be overcome by the ethic, but rather correspond to what is recognized as ethical.

Aristotle's standard is thus the *purpose of nature* (τέλος). This is something quite different from what one usually understands by the concept of purpose (teleology). It is a purpose that lies in the thing itself (objectively), not arbitrarily set by man (subjectively), and it is ever already an effective and fulfilled purpose in natural or social formations, not one lying outside of them, by which therefore nothing is but a mere means, hence valueless in itself. Accordingly, Aristotle's method is *observation*. He traces the phenomena of nature in order to discover, through analysis and comparison, the intention and the inner aspirations of nature in those phenomena. By this course and in this manner he examines human life relations, beginning with the simplest and climbing to the richer, more developed; and this leads to his doctrine of the state.

Principle and Course of His Politics

The first human life relation effectuated by nature is the union of man and

---

[7] In *Politics,* Book I.

woman, the purpose of which is the propagation of the race. To this attaches the parental relation and the lordship relation (i.e., between masters and slaves); these differ essentially from each other in that the parental relation is for the benefit of both parts, the obeying as well as the ruling, while the lordship relation only serves to benefit the ruling part. Nature leads to other ties, to villages, hamlets, finally to the *state* (taking city and state in the Greek manner as equivalent).

The state is the supreme relation, it is the fulfillment of that which nature aimed at in those preceding relations, because it alone has self-sufficiency (αὐτάρχεια), while those others always require another and higher connection that receives or protects them. That is why the state is the final purpose of nature, and man is a creature destined for the state (πολιτικὸν ζῷον). He who wishes to live without the state, would have to be a being of a higher or lower nature than man. The state is therefore for the people, that is, the state is that which nature, already in the individual, aims at as its final purpose, as it everywhere refers the part to the whole, and in the part pursues the whole.

But the purpose of the state is first and foremost the *life* [Erhaltung] (ζῆν) of its citizens, thereafter the *good life* [Wohlerhaltung] (εὖ ζῆν). The latter requires many external circumstances (good soil, convenient location and the like), but above all it requires *virtue*, for it is in virtue, not in external goods, that satisfaction and well-being consist, and the education of the citizens to virtue therefore also manifests itself in Aristotle as the first task of the state.

Speaking of the constitution of the state, the first and general requirement, in accordance with this purpose, is that it, like the parental power, be oriented as much toward the benefit of the subjects as the rulers, and not like the lordly power, exclusively for the benefit of the rulers. Accordingly, in each of the three basic forms – monarchy, aristocracy, and democracy – we distinguish between a true representation and a degeneracy (παρέχβασις) of the same, depending on whether it meets that requirement or not. It is necessary to distinguish *kingship* (βασιλεία) from *tyranny*, depending on whether the monarch is restricted by laws to the welfare of his subjects or not; *aristocracy* from *oligarchy* depending on the whether the meritorious are appointed to positions of rule for the general benefit, or simply the rich for their own benefit; *polity* from *democracy*, depending on whether the rule, which belongs to the whole, is really for the benefit of all or merely for the benefit of the poor, who constitute the majority. The polity – which Aristotle considered to be the most perfect form of government – is to be achieved through a combination of oligarchic and democratic aspects, not simply through an organic expansion and arrangement of both classes, but rather by an intermediate path between the two principles, e.g., applying the oligarchic means of punishing the rich with fines for absenting themselves from the popular assembly, together with the democratic means of rewarding the appearance of the poor in the assembly with donations, with access to the popular assembly linked to a moderate income, and offices allocated not by lot or turn-taking (in the manner of Greek democracy), but by election with reference to competence.

Taking that general requirement – orientation toward the common utility – as given, the first standard of the constitution for each state is the *relative* one, i.e., the consideration as to which constitution is the most appropriate to its particular condition and the elements existing in it. Where by birth, wealth, education the citizens are equal to each other, the democratic form exists; where a smaller number predominate, the aristocratic form does; where one protrudes above all others, the monarchical form does. A constitution that would be generally and unconditionally commanded and just does not exist, because none of them can realize the purpose of nature in the state – the good life, education for virtue – in all circumstances, or at any rate in the best way.

Nevertheless, there is also an *absolute* standard of the constitution, namely that constitution – provided its appropriateness in terms of the given elements – that in itself approaches achieving that purpose most nearly, or one could also say, that constitution corresponding to the elements that are best for that purpose. This is precisely what the *polity* is, because in his *Ethics* Aristotle refers to the virtue which indeed is the purpose of the state as being a mean between two vices, e.g., between greed and waste, cowardice and foolhardiness. That is why the condition of achieving the purpose of the state is most favorable where the middle class predominates, because, without the temptations of wealth or poverty, it is most likely to go the middle way everywhere. Such a condition of hegemony on the part of the middle class corresponds to the polity.

Position vis-à-vis Plato

Accordingly, Aristotle shared with Plato the procedure of deriving knowledge from *objects* rather than from human *reason*. As the idea was for

Plato, purpose in nature is for Aristotle that which has content in itself that can be discovered, not by examining [logical] thought determinations, but only by an activity of mind directed to the object, i.e., observation, vision. Of course, Aristotle cannot find the purpose of nature by *direct vision,* as with Plato and the ethical ideal; he needs *abstraction.* For inwardly in the spirit Plato sees a future, and this vision is sufficient in itself to recognize what is just, because its content is precisely that which is contained in the idea, perfection; Aristotle, on the other hand, sees only what is real, which as such cannot be the measure of the just; he must therefore compare the manifold manifestations of what is real; he must discover the universal from the particulars. But this abstraction of Aristotle's has its proper use, which is the negative function of limiting, ordering, maintaining. It by no means itself provides him with the content; this he also derives from observation, which he engages in with every step. Currently, it is unjustly claimed of Aristotle that he understood pure thought free from sense-derived particularity, the logical law, to be the essence and the truth of things. But neither he nor Plato attempted to disregard actual things and infer the necessity of any existence from a thought. For him as well, justice is not a system of rules, but a condition of men. And legal institutions have their measure and their valuation not in consistency, but in the actual effects they exert on circumstances and the opinion of men.

The undertone is also the same for both: the state comes first, and people are subordinate to the purpose of its existence. On the face of it, Aristotle approaches to the modern point of view, especially in view of his objections to Plato. Since he blames Plato for rendering it impossible for his Guardians to exercise charity and moderation because of their enforced poverty, and for sacrificing the happiness and perfection of man to the state, he seems to desire personal freedom and satisfaction. But on closer inspection, Aristotle shows that at bottom he does not differ from Plato. He likewise, by virtue of that pronouncement that the state is prior to the people (i.e., that the state is the purpose of nature in man), considered man in all his existence to be a mere subordinate member and agent of the state without a higher relation independent of the state, because it is the absolute end. Similarly, the will of the people is not the purpose of the institutions, nor is it their cause. The noblest must rule whether the others like it or not, for otherwise, he says, they would only concede equal rights even to Zeus himself if he lived among them. In his constitutional doctrine as well, the idea of a personal claim to dominion or freedom, of an acquired right on the part of a prince or a state or nation, can nowhere be found; the crucial consideration is only ability, qualities [Eigenschaftung] to achieve success that will redound to the whole. Thus in terms of type, Aristotle shared with Plato this trait of the subsumption of men in the state, although in lesser degree and thus less conspicuously.

Aristotle is however opposed to Plato in this: Plato recognizes a purpose beyond all that the real world with its phenomena has to offer, even, it would seem, out of its reach. Aristotle recognizes no ought, no purpose (τέλος) of things other than what nature manifests to be its will, that it either already has attained or at least provides the means to attain. His opposition to Plato therefore does not carry the usual meaning: "these designs are certainly just and noble, but not capable of implementation," but "they contradict the preconditions of nature, wherefore they are not what the source of the ethic desires and pursues, they are untrue and unjust." Added to this is the uniform difference of character and treatment.

Aristotle requires the investigation of all that nature has hitherto formed, which is everywhere evident in changing and repeating forms. The diverse social conditions, the differences among people, their activities, earthly possessions, talents, their relations determined by preceding events, their desires and motives, the functions of state – judiciary, government, the armed forces, the possibility of their distribution, mixture, complementary position, whence the infinite variety of constitutions – all this, how it is produced, and what it in turn effects, Aristotle finds necessary to examine to find out what maintains itself, therefore what is in accordance with nature, what is just. He is therefore the creator of actual political science, i.e., the science of the natural action and reaction of the institutions that everywhere are found in the same or similar manner, and which relates to the living aspirations of every time and nation in the same manner as mechanical laws to individual organic beings. This knowledge, which is essential to the statesman for him to choose the means for his purpose, Aristotle requires, in accordance with his standpoint, in order to discover the ultimate goal.

So this is the basis and the path of his investigation. In this he limits himself to reality, and discovers the result from many isolated observations. But for all the acuteness of this investigation and the truth of individual observations, the final shape that ought to arise – the state, which fully conforms to the purpose of nature – is not at all clear. The investigation is like a stream which after a magnificent course loses itself in the sand. Plato, by contrast, does not require all of these investigations to discover the just. It is given to him directly, something more glorious than any comparisons of the real could grant. Filled by his archetype, he creates new forms, he aims only at the one single state, the perfect; he sees it all at once and outlines it with the clarity of real life. If in details, in which Aristotle is so trenchant, he often considers the unseemly, what is contrary to nature, nevertheless around the whole there hovers a halo of moral elevation that pertains to an entirely different world than the natural strength and safety of the Aristotelian institutions.

With such opposite starting points, these two also certainly must come to conflicting results. But it is one and the same power that effectuates the natural conditions and drives and also provides the purpose for which man and his chosen ties are to strive. This explains the relation between nature and ethic, which reality illustrates, and thus also the relation between Plato and Aristotle.

Relation between Nature and the Ethic in General

The conditions wrought by nature are the necessary *substratum* of the ethic. Marriage, parental authority are based on the natural drive of procreation, the helplessness of children, etc. But as such they not only receive a law from the ethic, they also lay down a law for it, only in a different way. The ethic prevails over nature through its act (actual [aktuell]), by what it positively wants, ordering nature in terms of its purposes, analogous to the master over the servant. In this manner it shapes natural copulation into the thoroughly ethical institution of marriage. But nature gives a law to the ethic by its character (substantial [substantiell]), by what it is, analogous to the servant vis-à-vis the master. Though something is demanded of him, nothing can be demanded that he is not able to accomplish. For example, a law could not effect the power of children over adults, even if it were absurd enough to wish it. Hence, true moral demands hereby run up against a barrier in the incapacity of earthly nature, and they become untrue, like nonsensical laws of that sort, if they do not take this restriction into consideration, but instead try to evade it.

But natural conditions are also the *prelude* to the ethical. They then form the first link in the great chain which forms the historical progress in the ethic itself. Already in the instinct of animals, in the insensate drive of the plant, there is that which, as morality, prompts men in ever more exalted form in the various epochs. This is Aristotle's justification. He can reason from the efforts of unconscious things to the ought of conscious beings, pursuing the uninterrupted climax.

Finally – besides the fact that nature is the substance of the ethic, and the less developed representation of the shapes thereof – nature has this in common with the ethic, that it leads to the same *outcome* in ethical relations, independently of the ethic. The natural drive is set up in such a manner that, purely in accordance with its own nature, it becomes a determinant in meeting requirements that do not share its same root. If people wished to isolate themselves, the natural need for aid would drive them to the state; and yet, the peculiar significance of the state is not this aid. The want of security calls for public punishment to deter crime; and yet, it is this public punishment as just retribution that is grounded in the higher order of the ethical world.

This is the basis of the community of Plato and Aristotle, through which they, pursuing opposites, on the whole not desiring similar results, still arrive at them. Plato requires a multiplicity of forces and their fulfilled formation for the rich harmony of his depiction; this leads him to the gradation of classes [Ständen]. Aristotle requires this gradation and shows the natural need of it, and this leads him to the fulfilled formation like Plato's. Plato has his state seek after the idea of the just, and as a result, happiness follows. Aristotle merely has it seek happiness, and this also results in virtue. It is a comparison of two architects, one of whom, by seeking merely to answer the purpose of the building, unintentionally makes a work of art, while the other wishes to answer all the demands of beauty, and so as a matter of course cannot leave unsatisfied any of the building's requirements.

Value of the Ideal View and of the Empirical

Both also recognize the *single spirit* that rules throughout all creation; but Plato believes he can see it immediately at a higher level than everything that exists, and can behold it without the aid of what exists; Aristotle wishes to recognize it in its expression in the lower levels, and thus be certain of the higher. This also portrays the only two true human ways of knowledge, ideal vision and empirical investigation.[8]

They also are inseparable. For Plato, the examination of reality always promotes elevation towards its primordial image [Urbilds], and if Aristotle were not already filled in advance with a harmonious vision, he would not have arrived at these results. Yet with each of them, the one or the other is repressed. Both approaches therefore are clearly presented right at the beginning of philosophy, thus guaranteeing the unity of its object – but no less its own inadequacy. The empirical way appears safe and all-attaining, mediating the law of its progress from the antecedent course to its climax and thereby determining its future stages. But progress in nature is not like a straight line in which two points determine a third, but is like the vibrant growth of a plant, whereby its flower and the fruit cannot simply be extrapolated from its seed and stem. So he who understands the significance of the beginning, would have to know the end. But just as true and apt is that which corresponds: we do not understand the importance of the beginning, because the end is hidden from us.

From this comes the continuous uncertainty and often the error of the Aristotelian analogy. "Every whole of nature is greater than the parts." From which he concludes: "The state is also higher than man." But with any natural whole, the invigorating drive proceeds from that whole and not from the parts; but in the state, it is people, not the state, that put people in motion. And who can guarantee that the highest vocation is not the perfection of man without the state, whereby, as Aristotle himself says, he becomes like the gods? While for every activity nature provides a tool which is not for itself, but for someone else, Aristotle deems slavery justified as a tool for the family and its care. But whether or not the higher sphere of free beings tolerates the existence of a mere tool like the lower sphere does, is something which that comparison cannot reveal.

Here, then, is the seat of the error which is the basis of the much-discussed defense of slavery. Although this institution is no longer recognized, the rationale from what nature enjoins is still held by many to be infallible. The higher level always has a law of an entirely new sort, if only because it is the higher. Wealth contains poverty, but poverty does not contain wealth. The observation of what precedes, and of the process itself, can only direct, determine the

---

[8] It hardly needs mentioning that empiricism here is not meant in the ordinary sense of a mere passive registration lacking the control and penetration of mind.

selection, confirm, but cannot of itself [für sich selbst] provide right knowledge. Therefore, in order to know what is known or ought to be known, an immediate perception is necessary, because this is what makes the preceding intelligible; it is not given in the preceding. This constitutes the ideal vision. But it is a special gift, and it promises, in accordance with its nature, only a limited knowledge. If the eye only sees by the sun, it will only see what Helios wills more or less to illuminate for it. So also, when the mind receives the power to recognize the good through the idea, which it itself is not, its knowledge is dependent on how far this Helios sends its rays into the world and to its eye. And so far it has not granted to mortals all the splendor of its light. Plato himself, who to this day is held to have the glory of the sublimest mind that has applied itself to philosophy, is likewise only struck by a ray of it. After him, history engendered higher thoughts, a life of nobler and deeper meaning than he imagined, and he could not even keep his likeness free of untrue, obfuscating features.

If empiricism and the vision of the ideal interpenetrate, knowledge will probably increase in degree, but deficient knowledge will not be made into perfect knowledge.

Explanation of the Conflict between Plato and Aristotle

Now the question arises: from whence does it come that these two paths here appear divided, indeed hostile to each other? Why does Plato not inquire into the real and concrete activities of nature; why even design the state partly contrary to its conditions; and even more so, why does Aristotle close his eyes to what is higher, and remain content with the imperfect world? The only explanation is the lack of *historical character* in Greek philosophy. They both assume the existence of a drive which is working towards a conclusion in simultaneous progressions from the lowest stages of unconscious nature to the highest stages of men and philosophers. But the same sequence of stages in time, the progress of generations and world epochs, and beyond that, the future transformation of conditions to which men are subjected on earth – these are things they do not take into account. So, the union of the given condition and its imperfection with the advanced condition and its perfection is wanting, and one-sidedness of one form or another is inevitable. Plato steadfastly maintains that the perfect ought to exist. But he finds no relation of it to reality, and this lack appears to him to be accidental, or at any rate unaccounted for: and yet he cannot learn anything from it, nor is there a reason to consider it. Aristotle on the other hand steadfastly maintains that the real does not allow for perfection. Therefore what seems to him to be the highest, in fact the final object, is precisely the imperfect. So he falls into the contradiction: nature strives after perfection, and yet it contains in itself the law that it cannot attain perfection.

PART III: THE ETHIC OF THE GREEKS

The common characters of the philosophy of Plato and of Aristotle have been revealed: the cause of the ethic, existing in itself and extrinsic to human reason – the lack of historical principle – the predominance of the state over man, whose happiness, freedom, moral perfection is sacrificed to it. Already what these two thinkers have in common, and the opposition they form, in part to older, in part to newer ideas, goes to prove that these characteristics of their doctrine are not the result of a particular line of reasoning, but a particular quality of their spirit – the culture [Bildung] of their nation.

Religious Standpoint of the Greeks – Unhistorical View of the World – Ethic Thereof

If the causes that are manifested in different ways in the various activities of a people are to be traced back to their common origin, one need look no farther than the highest conceptions of that people, in the consciousness of its relation to the deity. Now for the Greeks, the gods, endowed with personality as they are, are not in any manner the supreme rulers of things; blind fate dominates them and produces events. But the ethical world is under the sway of ideas, the highest thoughts or forms of the good, the beautiful, the sublime. Fate and the ideas, themselves without self-consciousness, determined neither by others nor by themselves, set everything in motion and wield the scepter over gods and men.

This manner of thinking is certainly not the oldest of all, nor humanity's original one. Allow us to compare it with another which has been preserved in the most ancient documents and handed down to the new world in a more elevated form, which is still the content of public faith among us, perhaps even among those who do not believe in its divine origin, and which can lay claim to consideration as the prototype of man.

According to the *Jewish* conception, it is the personal God, not limited by anything, who according to His free will rules the destinies of the world, and who prescribes to men their end. Ethical precepts have no foundation apart from His will. All establishments and regulations bear the imprint of His omnipotence: "Ye shall not deal falsely one to another, *I am the Lord your God*" [cf. Leviticus 19: 11.] Good and evil exist only because He willed it or forbade it, for His alone is the glory. Now among the Greeks this belief was converted absolutely into its opposite, as expressed decisively in Plato's *Euthyphro:* "The holy is not the holy because the gods love it, but the gods love it, because it is the holy" [cf. 10e]. This is to separate the divine essence in a different way than polytheism does. That is to say, not only is it divided into different gods, but personality itself, the willing and the contents of its will, the thing willed, are two powers entirely separated from each other, and these, the mere products, are set over their producers. For what appears to the Greeks to be fate, to be the idea over God, in reality is only that upon which they had decided upon, that which they put forward as task and goal.

The Supreme Being [das höchste Dasein] has thereby ceased to be a free and conscious entity; He has been diminished. But man, in the midst of these separated powers, has been elevated, made freer. He does not fear destiny, because it cannot do him any harm, as little as it can avert harm. It can as little pity the man as it can rage against him. But the gods are faced with the same necessity as man, and the hero is encouraged to undertake dangerous deeds of glory, because gods and heroes must fulfill their lot. Gods and men are subject to the same moral laws, and the extent to which the Greek recognizes them as his own, he also dares to apply to his gods. Thus, according to Herodotus,[9] a prominent Cymian overcomes a god who gave to his hometown the vile advice that it should hand guests over, by flushing the protégés of the gods, the birds nesting in the forest. This gives rise to the greatness of man, who with his free act overcomes unfree destiny, even the haughty greatness of Prometheus, who rebels against the immortal gods, a character in which the East sees only the abomination, and not the greatness.

Because an unconscious power is placed above the gods, the historical principle is automatically given up. *History is only the work of an agent.* Fate and the ideas merely *exist* from everlasting to everlasting, in them there is no decision, no act, no progress. In Judaism, not only do human destinies have a history, but the disposing power over them does as well. In events, everything is foresight, preparation for a future destination, everything is the result of interaction of

[9] *The Histories,* I.159.

the free act of people vis-à-vis God and the no less free act of God vis-à-vis people. The Judeo-Christian narrative as a whole turns out to be a great stage play, the archetype of all tragedy, because it is the divine tragedy. The ethical commandments themselves are a history. There is no ideal closed off in itself as the norm for the manifold relationships that develop outside of it, but He who alone is the source of the ethic, for each event, when it happens, at the same time imparts the law, because nothing happens that was not present in His will. Yahweh Himself ordains whereto destruction, whereto protection. The refusal of the incomprehensible – inhumane, as one would have it lately – commandment also meets with the divine wrath. And despite the existence of enduring institution and legislation, the Jewish ethic is still not exhausted; indeed, what is most essential in it would not be described if the individual commandments that run through all of history and form that history, were lacking in it. Therefore, like any history, it can only be depicted by narrative. Finally, in redemption all events attain their fulfillment, and law attains its transformation, its new, previously hidden shape. Free guidance and predestination rescind the contradiction of the inequality between beginning and end, and nevertheless the proclaimer of the truth, because He founded a new kingdom, said: "I am not come to destroy, but to fulfill."

The Greek view, however, sees their events go on without leading toward a goal; hence, an eternally recurring change of things. The archetypes, and with them the moral requirements, are the same at the start as they are further on. Always in the same way, man strives for them, and is unable to reach them. It is the contradiction that cannot be explained: the ideas had from the start to make the world in accordance with themselves, if they have power over it, and if the ideas are perfect, so would the world be. Therefore Aristotle diminishes their own content. He is perhaps the first philosopher gloomily to be resigned to the inevitable limitations of present nature as something eternal. A greater momentum elevates Plato over his nation; his lively aspiring mind could not do without the self-conscious creator and the final consummation of all things. So he closes the *Republic* with the prospect of an otherworldly future, which alone for him resolves the contradiction. But in terms of scientific application, he stands on the same line with Aristotle. Both ignore progress in history as a means to infer the content of the idea. In both cases the ethic is a form prepared from eternity to eternity; actions, which lie outside it, either comply with it or contradict it.

And God cannot be stirred by prayers, says Plato, because He cannot deviate from the idea of justice.

An ethic that creates the norm while simultaneously generating the conditions and circumstances, which itself moves in an uninterrupted ascent to its final form, and therefore may be something else for a different time and different incident, without contradiction – an *historical ethic* can have its basis only in the free and omnipresent will of a personal God. Thus in Greek philosophy, although it recognizes a positive and meaningful principle of things, yet already has the beginning of the unhistorical view, since the cause of the world and the ethic appears as unfree, *thallos*, something merely existing. This view reaches its extreme in modern, abstract philosophy and certifies here more clearly the untruth thereof, whence it is also necessary for philosophy to return to that ancient historical view, the *Judeo-Christian*, which has never ceased being valid in life.

Absence of Charity

Charity [Carität] is the peculiar characteristic of the Orient. It is the end of all the Jewish commandments, excluding those based on the historical relationship of the people to God, such as the exodus from Egypt, the promulgation of laws, etc. The divine love extends to all living things, from animals up to slaves, from strangers to the sons of the chosen people. But charity is only from person to person. Fate and the ideas are without sensation. Even the jealous God of the Old Covenant restricts the penalty to the fourth generation, while He blesses the thousandth. But the Greek avenger of morals [der Sitte] strides relentlessly across the earth. An intervening god may liberate after extended agony, but only rarely. The greatness of heroes is only elevated over the Nemesis through the atonement of a freely chosen downfall. Here then, charity ceases to be the driving force, the ideas cannot require it; they cannot reciprocate, because it is not their essence. They do not disappear; but they become something other than they originally and peculiarly were. Namely, not the person himself, whether God or man, is its innermost motive, but the beauty of their actions. This explains the hardness of Plato, the inhumanity of Spartan institutions, and generally the lack in Greece of laws with the welfare of the people as their final and energetic intention. This is perhaps the contrast generally between Oriental and Occidental virtue. The former has its ultimate source and its final goal only in a personality; the latter waxes enthusiastic about the highness of a thought, law, state, art, honor, so that even pride or stubborn assertion of one's own claims can be held to be duties.

The Greek life, one might say, is the initial astonishment of mankind when the Lord took from it the fear of His face, and it beholds, free and awakened, the immense splendor of the world. Mankind is set outside of himself and immersed in the world. To depict this beauty in the spiritual world, as it is expressed in the physical, is the task of people and of states. Here for the first time an occupation is bestowed on man, here first is there free state formation. He separates himself from the divinely given forms of life (the theocratic constitution) to create anew in accordance with divine models. In place of blind passive obedience comes man's own free reproduction. "Thou shalt not blur the boundaries of the things I drew, the sequence of stages in the whole of nature, but keep them holy!" is the idea manifested in a series of Jewish statutes: "Thou shalt not let thy cattle gender with a diverse kind: thou shalt not sow thy field with mingled seed: neither shall a garment mingled of linen and woollen come upon thee" [Leviticus 19: 19]. This order is not limited to unconscious nature, it also proceeds among the people, separates priest and Levite, and forms the structure of caste which is represented in the whole of the Orient. The same idea now is what causes Plato to consider the development of manifold forces, their measure and their delimitation, to be the justice of the state. But with the former, it is God's created beauty that is found and kept holy; with the latter, it is the creation of something new which is demanded by those models. Therefore, it is not regard in nature but in self-formed human relations, distribution according to ability, a separation and reconnection which man comprehends because he himself undertook it. With the former, the unity of the delimited elements is given by the divine purpose in all of creation; with the latter, man himself must first create them – *he finds them in the state.*

The state of Plato, in which this is the moral of the story, is proven here to be the same model pursued by all the Greek states. Thus, the Spartan state represents a vibrant body animated by a spirit, which as with a *single* will strains every sinew for the struggle. Athens developed a richer life. Art, philosophy, family connection, commerce, shipping, trade, all spheres of human activity are encountered here, and each is assured its own existence, as its nature requires. An abundance of magistrates and courts, each of which is assigned the care of a certain entity, spreads across the state. In the diversity of their education, their celebrations, the buildings for their assemblies, and finally, the leading interest of their object, they provide a rich picture, but they receive their proper boundaries from a shield under which they all repose, the supreme court of the Areopagus.

This rapture does not leave room to maintain a separate existence. Man only perceives himself as a part of the whole, from which he cannot separate himself, neither in fact, nor in thought. An irresistible urge propels him to intervene in its rhythm.

The ethic does not arise as a task of the individual but of the whole; it is something general (objective), directed to the world; man encounters it only as a member thereof. It therefore calls not for his actions (considered individually), but rather the existence of the moral order as a whole, the purity of the spiritual world. For this reason the Nemesis also pursues the involuntary act. And for those caught in the struggle of conflicting obligations, destruction is inevitable. However he chooses – Orestes may leave the father unavenged, or murder the mother – through him there arises either a gap or a discord in the moral world, and it must expel him. In this manner, in time out of mind the ancient royal houses fell, and in this manner within historical memory Timoleon falls into mental derangement, the punishment for murder despite its inevitability.

Even the state does not require the ethic from individuals, for them to give shape to it, but from the world, that it exist. It shall be, and shall represent a specific shape. Only from this do the duties of citizens issue, and not vice versa, the shape of the state from the duties of citizens. Therefore, there are ethical requirements that no human being, considered in himself, could recognize as his own, for example, the formation of classes [Ständen], and the perfection of the state is the first thing that is to be, and only then that of people. For it itself taken as a whole is the subject of the ethic. This explains the unnatural calling of women in Plato, the banishment of poetry, and the like.

Of law in our sense, according to which someone may do as he will within a certain sphere , there is here no conception. Nowhere does the Greek set his foot outside the world to which he belongs, his state. Greek liberty is not like Roman – protection of free disposition over a certain delimited object – but an ideal share in the actions of the state. It follows automatically that individual freedom is abolished in the Platonic state, in Sparta. Attic law could not leave off having standards appropriate to private pursuits, given its bustling trade and commerce. But nevertheless, it did not regulate them according to the principle of private law, that is, by the will of men, but sought to apply its own inherent ideas in an appropriate shape, as is readily demonstrated. The absolutely alien nature of the concept of personal entitlement to the Greeks is shown most clearly by a point in the first book of the *Republic* of Plato. Among all the possible determinations of the just which are to be assessed here, he comes also to the one in which "each is to be given his due." Here we think we have discovered the Roman *suum cuique tribue*, and thus law and entitlement in our sense. But he who studies this statement of Plato's accurately, finds in it that friends are to be treated well, but enemies badly. Under what is due (προσῆκον, *suum*) is not meant something that someone can dispose of at will, either to acquire or to leave aside, but something that applies to him with necessity according to a different standard than his will, even in opposition to his will. To suffer evil can be no enemies' *right;* nor can receiving good be understood to be a friend's *right.* This provision does not denote justice that protects individuals [schirmende], like the Roman legal principle does, but justice that visits retribution [vergeltende].

This is the objective character of the Greek constitution [des griechischen Wesens]: the ethic goes forth into the objective world and requires its perfection, not the individual human being's, and nowhere is action to be determined merely by one's own will, but everywhere by the order over him. The same character runs through science. Just as here the general question regarding the cause and the end of things urges itself, so does the investigator at no time look into himself, closed off to everything external, in order to find the answer. His thought always moves among the major objects of the world that surround him, which he in unprejudiced contemplation absorbs. The investigation pursues coherence in the things themselves, the sense [Verstand] that expresses itself in them. It does not have the obligation, nor even the permission, to seek a solution without taking into account what is to be solved. Therefore, Greek philosophy is [characterized by] free treatment, full of life. It draws on all the wealth of creation, it takes hold of development and growth, change and decay in all variety and tumultuousness, as life itself presents it. From this world, which it recognizes apart from the reason of the beholder, it had to arrive at a principle thereof which exists apart from his reason, an objective principle – water, fire, the natural purpose, the idea. To the degree that it considers this necessary to explain the world, it attributes to these a peculiar quality and effectiveness. Thought, on the other hand, only needs to refer to its own essence to do this, without taking the world into consideration.

In modern philosophy, the thinker withdraws into himself; he stands by the subjective principle, his reason. Hence the formalism. But he also finds freedom and personality in himself. And when at last he sees himself compelled to turn back to the recognition of independent existence outside himself, he no longer can consider it in the Greek fashion, as held together by the idea or the laws of nature, but as the work of the freely acting God.

APPENDIX TO BOOK I: THE ROMANS

The Roman world epoch embodies a major advance in legal and political consciousness: both the idea of the purely legal order which, while determined by ethical ideas, ought not be deflected by ethical motives in individual cases, and the idea of entitlement (law in the subjective sense) which here is not thought of in the way it is in our time, as a notion of human rights (either in the true or the false sense of the word), but manifests itself merely as a notion of the acquired right of the person, of a right warranted by the legal order.

And yet, the Roman world epoch embodies no advance in the awareness of the deeper reasons and ideas of law, no progress in the philosophy of law. In this, the Romans merely appropriated the products of Greek culture. Cicero, the main writer in this field, borrowed all his terms and principles from Plato and Aristotle, without any significant new thoughts. He does not even bring that which lived in the national consciousness – subjective entitlement – to scientific cognizance, and is not even aware of its opposition to the Greeks. The studies contained in his jurisprudential and political writings[10] revolve broadly around two issues: the existence of a natural moral law, and the best state constitution. He asserts the existence of a natural law (*lex aeterna*), as did the Greeks, especially with respect to the denial of Carneades; but he stops short at the general notion that morality [die Sitte] is true and independent, by no means a product of prudence; he does not concern himself any farther than this, in particular with the existence of a natural juridical law [natürlichen Rechtsgesetzes], which so recommended itself to the Romans. His investigations into the Roman constitution rest on the foundation of Greek political science, with the difference that, in accordance with patriotic sentiment, he comes to the conclusion that the mixed constitution, which he holds the Roman to be, is declared the most perfect. Even Stoic ethics retained with the Romans a peculiar strength of operation rather than a specifically scientific implementation, with more concern for the aspect of morality than the ordering of the social condition, than jurisprudential or political problems. Only the element in it of common humanity can be emphasized, which spread in the mind

---

[10] In particular, the *Republic* and *Laws*.

especially later (e.g., Seneca, Marcus Aurelius); but this did not give shape to legal and governmental institutions, neither in life, nor in their own teaching.

Much more important for the world-historical progress of legal ideas than the philosophical and political writers among the Romans, therefore, were the legal arrangements themselves, in part the conceptualization thereof by jurists of positive law. This has been dealt with in detail in other places of this work, particularly in the appendix to the volume on private law.[11] Therefore we may here proceed directly to the following period, which really does provide new scientific ideas, the legal philosophy of the Middle Ages.

[11] Stahl, *Private Law*, appendix: "Regarding the Value of Roman Private Law."

BOOK II: THEOCRATIC LEGAL PHILOSOPHY

(THE MIDDLE AGES)

PART I: AUGUSTINE

Among the Church Fathers, it is Augustine in particular who asserted Christianity in terms of a scientific philosophical presentation over against classical philosophy; he is the primary founder of Christian speculation, and he became decisive for the entire Middle Ages both in science and life [Lebensgestaltung].

Speculative Conceptualization of World History

The basic idea of his book *Of the City of God* (*De Civitate Dei*) is the antithesis between a heavenly state (*civitas Dei, civitas coelestis*) and an earthly state (*civitas terrena*), founded on the biblical contrast of God's children and the children of the world, albeit in a speculative formation. To wit, it conceives this opposition as a world-historical economy rather than as the mere nature of individual human beings, as the opposition of two coherent organized areas of sentiments, aspirations, tasks, but also institutions, destinies, world designs, running right through earthly life. It is, if one wishes to use a more modern term, a construction of world history. It begins the demonstration of this opposition at Cain and Abel, and conducts it on the one hand through secular history, the empires of the Assyrians, Persians, Greeks, Romans, and on the other hand through the sacred history of the Patriarchs, the Jewish judges, kings, prophets, up until the appearance of Christ and the Christian church. The end is the eternal glorification of the God-state and the downfall and the destruction of the earthly state.

The term *state* (*civitas*) is used symbolically in both relations, and therefore the question is, how does the real state on earth, the civic organization, relate to these two states? The expressions of Augustine on this score are not clear, in details perhaps even contradictory; nevertheless, the thoughts that form his total conception can be identified with certitude.

View of the State

The civil state is it not the same to him as the "earthly state" (*civitas terrena*), although he alternately uses the term *civitas terrena* for the realm of secular, and for the state. For he recognizes that the purpose of the state, earthly peace (as opposed to eternal peace), in itself is not blameworthy, and that Christians should wish for that peace and make use of it as long as mortality continues; precisely for this reason they also owe the state obedience, and to this end are to have community with the earthly-minded.[12] Accordingly, it cannot be something absolutely evil, as is worldly-mindedness; and that which is spoken of regarding the "earthly city" – that it will fall under eternal judgment with the devil – cannot refer to it.[13]

But yet he brings the state into the closest connection with the earthly kingdoms. For him the state, and not merely the current condition of the state, but the existence of a state generally, is simply the consequence of sin,[14] and therefore also a mere emergency institution, an arena of the passions and the oppression of the weak by the powerful. Accordingly, he considers interest in the state as something purely secular. Therefore the establishment of states everywhere proceeds from the earthly-minded; the heavenly-minded do not concern themselves with it. In this manner, the first state was founded by Cain, the original representative of the earthly kingdom – "he builded a city" [Genesis 4: 17] – while Abel was a stranger on earth and an exile.[15] Likewise, the Roman state was the state κατ' ἐξοχήν [par excellence], founded by Romulus, who, earthly-minded, also murdered his brother, and is a type of Cain. While the classical view considers the state to be the highest thing in human life, for Augustine it occupied the extreme opposite position, as something deeply subordinate for the true man. The degree to which the practice or allowance of pagan worship, which Augustine experienced in reality, influenced his judgment in this should not be left out of account.[16]

Nonetheless, he energetically asserts that only Divine Providence determines the formation of states and their destinies,[17] and he even takes it upon himself partly to show the moral motivations of this Providence in the governance of world destinies. In particular, he conducts a comprehensive discussion

---

[12] *City of God*, Bk. XV ch. 4, Bk. XIX chs. 14, 16, 17.

[13] "Aeternum supplicium subire cum diabolo" [eternal punishment with the devil], Bk. XV, chs. 1 and 4.

[14] Bk. XIX ch. 15.

[15] Bk. XV ch. 1.

[16] Cf. Bk. XI ch. 1 and Bk. XIX ch. 21.

[17] Bk. IV ch. 31.

of how the Romans were allotted the empire by God for the sake of their civic virtues.[18]

Practical Political Tendency

In accordance with such an assessment of the state, Augustine pays scant attention to its actual political tasks and allocates its main function only to the *protection of the church*. That and only that appears to him to be the truly ethical significance of the state, understandably so because in this way it enters into the service of the celestial empire (*civitas coelestis*). The practical goal in Augustine's doctrine of the state is therefore the maintenance of ecclesiastical prescriptions and the restriction and punishment of heretics by the external power of the authorities; that is the idea which most vividly fills Augustine and the one by which he became so decisive to the subsequent shape of Christianity.[19]

Verdict

Running through this whole conceptualization is the true insight, given with the Christian revelation, that the state, like the entire human condition, is estranged from its true eternal form, that an act changed the original condition of human existence, and that an act will one day again restore it. To the Greeks, this insight was absent; it is the middle term which alone can unite Plato and Aristotle. From it, the contradiction between the absolute moral task of the human race, which imbues Plato, and the laws of nature and the natural constitution of man, which Aristotle makes into a standard, is solved. On this basis, one neither needs, like Plato, to require an arrangement of human coexistence, of which man is incapable, for the sake of its ethical truth, nor, because of this human incapacity, does one, like Aristotle, need to tone down the moral requirement on the individual and the whole, and to hold the mere (negative) midpoint between two vices to be the nature of virtue, instead of recognizing the positive and infinite content thereof. As a result, the absolute devotion of the people, which Plato requires for the state, is referred to another realm than this ephemeral and tenuous one.

---

[18] Bk. V ch. 15.

[19] This notion is particularly implemented in a few of his letters: cf. epist. 93 ad Vincent., epist. 185 ad Bonifac.

Herein Augustine, by virtue of Christian enlightenment, extended moral- and legal-philosophical knowledge infinitely beyond classical wisdom. He gave it its true center. But he failed to recognize the independent and divine significance that earthly life relations, and thus, above all, the state, still have, even in their present turbid condition. Rather than penetrate the secular sphere with the recovered truth, he flees from it. The idea of the state as state, heroism, justice, wisdom, like the arrangements and tasks of well-ordered, properly structured public life, lie beyond his attention; they are not in themselves divine and worthy of Christian interest, and the significance which he concedes to one of the two great institutions of God, the state, is not that it solves its own problem, but only that it come to the aid of the other, the church, regarding the church's tasks. Basically then, for Christianity only the church can remain, and it makes use of the state to realize its rules externally – thus forcibly. Therein lies the origin of the hierarchical idea, according to which the church erects itself as a state, as a theocratic empire, and maintains the faith as a civil law, so that heresy, as the supreme civil crime, commands the death penalty. The state, as Augustine conceives it, is either completely unnecessary and worthless for Christianity, or the church must truly and fully use it. This is the result when the state is denied its own importance, and the protection of the church is acknowledged as its sole task. On the other hand, if one presupposes the independent importance of the state, then its connection with the church, which Augustine expressed, is an indestructible truth which has been tested from that hour to this among the Christian nations, and is being challenged at this time only because the peoples are no longer imbued with the same liveliness of the Christian faith. For the separation of church and state, today's solution, is only taught by those who either share this lack of faith, or cannot envision a different public condition than the one with which they are surrounded.

PART II: THE GERMANIC WRITERS[20]

Thomas Aquinas' Outline of the Ethical Sphere

The scientific ethics of the Middle Ages, if the *Summa* of Thomas Aquinas is representative, recognized, in accordance with its Christian basis, the living God as ultimate principle. For this purpose, it took over the traditional concept of a law of nature from antiquity, notably the Romans, and brought it into connection with that ultimate principle.

Accordingly, Thomas initially differentiated between the eternal law (*lex aeterna*) and the natural law (*lex naturalis*). The eternal law is the world-ordering reason in the Divine Spirit (*ratio gubernativa totius universi in mente divina existens*). This governing reason, in itself and with respect to the creation, has the nature of art, of an example, of an idea (*artis vel exemplaris vel ideae*), similarly to how an artist has an advance idea of his artwork (understood of the technical, not the aesthetic aspect); but respecting human action, which it impels to the same end, it has the nature of a law [eines Gesetzes]. The natural law then is nothing but the "participation" of people in this eternal law, as regards the distinction between good and evil, or the "impression" of the divine light in us. But it is not equivalent to that eternal law, because governing reason behaves differently in the regulator (God) than in the regulated (people); rather, it is imprinted in people only to a limited extent and scope, especially in man's fallen state. Yet everything that man, by nature, has of moral knowledge and requirement, is only the effect of that eternal law in God.

This now leads to the question: how does God relate to this eternal law in Him? Thomas answered with a distinction: the will of God in itself and in terms of its substance is not subject to the eternal law, but is one and the same with it. But the will of God in terms of what He wishes with regard to creatures (*circa creaturas*), is subject to the eternal law, insofar as the reason for what He wills lies in divine wisdom. In and of itself, therefore, the divine will is one with reason, but in relation to the creation and rule of the world, it is subordinated to the standard of reason (*rationabilis*). And yet, regardless of how deeply and truly

---

[20] [Subjects of the Holy Roman Empire of the German Nation, hence both Germany and Italy broadly speaking.]

the source of all moral commandment is acknowledged to be in the divine reason and wisdom, as is likewise the unity of the divine will with the divine reason and wisdom, an unacceptable divide is introduced here between the divine will-substance and the divine counsels, which in its further development leads, and actually did lead, to the will-substance or the eternal law in God manifesting itself as mere supreme rule, as something given, apart from any decision. Philosophically this is all the less well-founded because Thomas here did not even characterize this eternal law or divine will-substance as the eternal essence and holiness of God, but as His world plan.[21] In this manner we approach to a diminution of the inner freedom of the divine decree, binding it absolutely to reasons [Gründe] (*ratio*), while, as we shall see below, people are subjected to the will of God or His vicar [Statthalter], as the case may be, as to something apart from reason [grundlosen].

It is evident that, in this presentation, what is meant by natural law is not the legal sphere but, as with Cicero, the ethical sphere in general – in fact, only the moral sphere. But here the moral law, insofar as it inheres in human nature, is opposed to the law that is eternal in God and comes to man by way of revelation.[22] Therefore Thomas adds a third category: *human law* (*lex humana*). This now encompasses the legal sphere, but only in its character as *positive* law. Accordingly, with Thomas the legal sphere is only understood in terms of the aspect of its positivity, human sanction; and only this aspect, not the aspect of a particular content, a particular life-sphere [Lebenssphäre], sets it off against the moral sphere. A relation of positive law to natural law in our sense is not in question and, in accordance with this, cannot be; it is only the question of the relation of positive law to natural *ethical* commands [Sittengebote], and that is how it is construed: all positive law (*lex humana*) is only the outflow of the natural moral law (*secundum quam in particulari disponuntur, quae in lege naturae continentur*)[23] and only insofar as this is the case, is it justified. But on the other

[21] For a more detailed elucidation of the question itself, cf. vol. II, book I [*Philosophical Presuppositions*] of this work.

[22] In the book *De Regimine Principum* [On the Government of Princes] as well, book I, ch. 15, it can be seen that a distinction is not yet made between law and virtue.

[23] [See *Summa Theologica,* Benziger edition, II.I. 91, art. 3 conclusion: "It is from the

hand, the positive law (*lex humana*) cannot exhaust the full extent of the natural law (*non omnia vitia prohibere potest*),[24] because it pertains to the class of imperfect virtue. So there is no distinction between an idea of law and of morality; but positive law is nothing else than a partial sanction of moral law by means of human authority and penal administration.

Thus while the distinction between ethics and law [Recht] in relation to statute [Gesetz] and life-sphere (i.e., in terms of the objective side) entirely evades Thomas, he nevertheless has some, albeit very vague, notion of this distinction in relation to human virtue and the specifics of entitlement (i.e., in terms of the subjective side). He lists *justice* among the human virtues, and indeed a particularly excellent one, which for him consists in giving to each *his right* according to proportion (*aequalitas*). This virtue of justice is distinguished from the other virtues (*proprium inter alias virtutes*) in that it comprehends only action vis-à-vis other subjects (*ad alterum*), not action against itself; it therefore is not concerned with attitude (*non considerato, qualiter ab agente fiat*), and has only outward acts as its object, not inward, hence not the mastery of desires; all of this obviously has the character of the sphere of law [Rechtsgebietes]. Thus he takes law [Recht] into consideration merely as an object of virtue, that is, the moral character of the individual, not as a specific law [Gesetz] ruling human life, or as a sphere in its own right. He declares the just and the law (*justum* and *jus*) to be one and the same. It is in this sense that he conceives of the distinction between natural law and positive law, namely as that which is due to someone by the nature of the case versus that which is due according to the particular determination of the parties or of the people. This indicates that for him, the concept of natural right [Rechts] (*jus naturale*) does not even stand in the remotest connection to the concept of natural law [Gesetzes] (*lex naturalis*), which was discussed above. He does not even consider the judiciary (*judicium*) to be an element of a higher order, an institution, but rather a product of the virtue of justice.

But even in the sphere of (subjective) virtues, this virtue of justice, for

---

precepts of the natural law, as from general and indemonstrable principles, that the human reason needs to proceed to the more particular determination of certain matters."]

[24] [*Ibid.,* 96, art. 2, reply to objection 3: "Human law does not prohibit everything that is forbidden by the natural law."]

Thomas, does not always exactly correspond with the just in terms of object and character. Its more detailed description, namely, is this: as justice regulates man's actions with other men, it refers either to the whole of the human common condition, and orders actions for the common good (*bonum commune*), or it relates to other individual persons, and orders actions such that each is granted his right. The former is general (*universalis*) justice, the latter particular (*particularis*). General justice now is at the same time the general virtue for all earthly virtues, which does not mean that it contains all of them or is the same as them in terms of concept and essence (*essentia*), but that it determines all of them as cause (*causaliter*), namely, it orders them for the common good, which is the ultimate goal of all earthly virtue. It is therefore also to be named law-fulfilling justice (*justitia legalis*) since (earthly) law also seeks nothing else than the common good. Similarly, love is the universal virtue of the heavenly virtues, since their final goal is the heavenly good. Particular justice, which apportions to each individual his right, is again divided into *commutative* which, assuming the equality of persons, regards only things and processes respecting things as the measure of what is due to each, e.g., in purchase and exchange, and *distributive*, which regards the people themselves, their divergent worth and the merit of their personal actions, as the measure, e.g., the wise or the rich are entitled to a greater share in rule.

Accordingly, in this entire doctrine of justice, only commutative justice pertains by object and character to the sphere of law[Rechtsgebiet]. General justice includes all earthly virtue, and distributive justice, although it also intervenes in the sphere of law, is still not determined by a fixed external order, but by the reasonableness of contingent [jeweiligen], often merely internal relations. What imbues the basic conception of Thomas is the separation of heavenly and earthly virtue, while the separation of the moral and the legal order in earthly life itself escapes him; and it is the mingling of the (subjective) virtue of justice with the (objective) life-order of law which, since the characters of the latter make themselves felt in [outward] experience, brings him to consider the attitude of the actor to be a matter of indifference to the virtue of justice.

This is the outline of the system of ethics in the Middle Ages as portrayed by its most celebrated master.[25]

The Political Doctrine of the Middle Ages: Aristotelian Element

But with regard to the doctrine of state and (philosophical) state law in particular, the writers of the Germanic Middle Ages – Thomas, Dante, Occam, Marsilio, Andlo, etc.[26] – composed their teaching mainly of two elements, the philosophy of Aristotle and the Christian conception of the state, the latter especially after the example of Augustine, but each modified according to the standpoint and consciousness of time and nation. Essentially the same thoughts and the same manner of reasoning and presentation run equally through all of these writers. The legal-philosophical temper [Bildung] of the Middle Ages had more of a traditional than a successive and developing character. Now Dante, as far as philosophical deduction is concerned, was peculiar in the highest degree, emancipated even from Aristotle, just as he surpassed all other political writers in deep philosophical conception; [27] but precisely because of his

---

[25] With regard to all of this, cf. Thomas Aquinas, *Summa Theologia,* in particular *prima secundae quaest.* 91–96, *secunda secundae quaest.* 57–59.

[26] Thomas Aquinas (†1274), *Summa Theologia, loc. cit. Idem, De Regimine Principum* (the question regarding the partial or entire inauthenticity of this writing does not affect the argument here, in that it is in any case a document of the educated thinking [Bildung] of the Middle Ages – on the other hand, Thomas's commentary on Aristotle's *Politics* is of no significance to us, in that it only elucidates, and provides none of the commentator's own insights). – Dante Alighieri (†1321), *De Monarchia.* – William of Occam (†1347) *Dialogus.* – Marsilius of Padua (†1328), *Defensio Pacis* – (in Goldast, *Monarchia St. Rom. Imper.*), Petrus de Andlo (†1480), *De Imperio Romano* 1460.

[27] So, for example, Dante declares it to be the goal of the state (i.e., the Christian empire) that the human race as a whole engage the entire force of possible intelligence (*actuare semper totam potentiam intellectus possibilis*) initially for knowledge, and then for action, Book I, ch. 3. Like Kant, he distinguishes between freedom of the will and arbitrary will [Willkür], Book I, ch. 12. Sinning for him is nothing other than *progredi ab uno spreto ad multa* [to proceed from despised unity to multiplicity], Book I, ch. 15. Then: "Ex iis liquet, quod jus cum sit bonum, proprius in mente Dei est, et cum omne, quod in mente Dei est, sit Deus (juxta illud: quod factum est in ipso vita erat) et Deus maxime se ipsum

peculiarity, he had no effect on the further development of science.

Medieval political science took first and foremost from Aristotle the philosophical concepts and categories in general, e.g., the three categories of *ens, motus,* and *finis,* and the proposition that a mover must be above the moved, to prove that all rule is from God[28] – furthermore, those general propositions of natural observation applicable to politics, for example, that the whole is greater than the parts, that nature everywhere seeks for perfection – finally, however, in particular the lessons and propositions of politics itself, namely the derivation of the state from the social nature (πολιτικὸν ζῶον – *sociale animal*) of man, the doctrine that the purpose of the state is the good life (εὖ ζῆν, *bene vivere*), that this consists in virtue, that the distinction between true and false constitutions is drawn simply according to whether the rulers or the ruled are the goal, the classification of forms of state in *regnum, politia,* etc.[29] All this can be found equally in all writers.

Christian Speculative Element

In the same way, the Christian speculative conception of the state in the Middle Ages is based on the thought of Augustine, whereby the civil order is the result of sin, states are established by divine providence, two kingdoms run through earthly history, the Romans possess world rule because of their virtue

---

velit: sequitur, quod jus a Deo, prout in eo est, sit volitum. Et cum voluntas et volitum in Deo sit idem, sequitur ulterius, quod divina voluntas sit ipsum jus" [From these things it is clear that the right is a good, it is God's own, in the mind, and with all that in the mind of God, He is God (as it is said that what was in him was life;) and since God principally wills himself: it follows that the right from God, inasmuch as He is, belongs to the thing willed. And when he had the will and the thing willed in God is the same, it follows further that the divine will is the right itself]. These examples are sufficient to give an idea of Dante's speculative treatment. [Translations are from the Henry edition.]

[28] Thomas *De Regimine Principum,* Book III, chs. 1–3. Similarly Marsilius, Andlo.

[29] Thomas's investigations (*De Regimine Principum,* Book II) into the material conditions and material goals of the state (situation, climate, means of subsistence, highways) can also be viewed as a copy [Nachbild] of Aristotelian treatment, albeit a completely free facsimile [Nachbildung].

(also used as a justification of the Germanic empire, which indeed was viewed as one with the Roman), etc.[30] But there is nevertheless an essential, profound difference between the medieval conception, founded on the Germanic view of life, and that of Augustine. If with Augustine the state appears as a mere work and interest of the earthly kingdom (the worldly-minded), here it is the realization of God's kingdom in accordance with one of its aspects. Hence, in place of that contempt of the state, there emerges here an apotheosis of the state, i.e., of the Germanic-Christian imperial state which maintains justice and peace in the Christian world, by order of God. But nevertheless, here as well this recognition of the state is always due to its relationship with the church.

According to the famous doctrine of the Middle Ages which runs through all these writers, God set two swords over Christianity, the spiritual and the secular, the former in the hands of the pope, the latter in those of the emperor. They are directly ordained and vouchsafed by Him; He rules on earth through them, and every Christian – yea, because the true God also has power over those not yet recognizing Him, every person – is subject to both. Therefore, the legitimate supremacy of the pope and the emperor is asserted even over newly discovered and still unconverted princes and peoples, and in Christendom itself, division into several completely independent kingdoms instead of one empire is held to be as illicit as, in the church, its breakup into bishoprics rather than the papal primacy (Lampugnano). The dispute between the papal and the imperial party is only about the reciprocal relationship between these two swords. The teaching of the former, which was the first to be developed scientifically, is that the papal power is the higher,[31] because the spiritual and eternal stand above the worldly and earthly, just as, of the two lights, the sun stands over the moon; just as Levi and Aaron stand over Judah; even more, while the emperor receives his temporal power first through the pope, only the papal power comes directly from God, again by analogy with the election and dismissal of Saul by Samuel, and the offering of the three wise men (kings) before Christ. The pope was therefore the head of Christendom, the kings the arms, for which reason

---

[30] Thomas, *De Regimine Principum,* Book III, chs. 4–6.

[31] Thomas, *De Regimine Principum,* Book III, ch. 10. See also Dante's counterargument, *De Monarchia,* Book III, ch. 9.

only the pope is anointed on the head, the princes on the arms.[32] The further implementation is then: Christ conferred both swords on Peter and his successor, the spiritual for his own use, the worldly only as a sort of deposit until the future conversion of the Gentiles and of the state. For this reason Pope Sylvester reissued this sword to Constantine after he converted, on behalf of God. Under Charlemagne, however, the Pope as vicegerent of God transferred world empire from the Greeks to the German nation. This was the basis for its legitimacy.

The primacy of the spiritual over the secular seemed so evident that for a long time it captivated the mind of the Germanic peoples. Finally, though, the temporal power also acquired its scientific arsenal. It was countered that the spiritual and secular are two different spheres which are independent of one another without any relation of domination and subordination. This idea, so simple and so familiar to us now, was lacking then; and the imperial power had suffered from it. The shift took place in a decisive way with William of Occam. Dante separated church and state by the two purposes of human nature, corruptible and incorruptible, but he nevertheless acknowledged that the state receives the power of grace from the spiritual kingdom, which the papal blessing infuses in him,[33] and accordingly did not wish the independence of the secular power to be understood so strictly (*stricte*) that the emperor would not be subject to the pope (*in aliquo non subjaceat*); rather the emperor owes homage to the pope like the first-born son owes it to his father. Partly, public awareness was still too much in thrall to papal supremacy, and partly Dante was too profound to maintain a complete separation of the two spheres, like the defenders of Louis of Bavaria did. But the proper distinction, differentiating the spiritual

---

[32] *Decretales Gregorii IX,* I. 15, *de sacra unctione.*

[33] "Si ergo dico, quod regnum temporale non recipit ease a spirituali, nec virtutem (quae est ejus auctoritas) nec etiam operationem simpliciter; sed bene ab eo recipit ut virtuosius operetur per lucem gratiae, quam in coelo et in terra benedictio summi pontificis infundit illi" [In like manner, I say, the temporal power receives from the spiritual neither its existence, nor its strength, which is its authority, nor even its function taken absolutely. But well for her does she receive therefrom, through the light of grace which the benediction of the Chief Pontiff sheds upon it in heaven and on earth, strength to fulfill her function more perfectly]. *De Monarchia of Dante Alighieri,* Book III, ch. IV.11.

kingdom and the external church power, which already was intimated in the standpoint of Dante's, was, in terms of its fullest insight, only the work of the Reformation. Similarly, it was denied, albeit not entirely accurately in terms of history, that the papal coronation made Charles the Great into the emperor – rather, this supposedly took place by the will of the people (*acclamatio populi*). Finally, the independence of the secular authority, and its direct ordination by God, was set out in the great acts of state of the nations.

How the Two Cohere – The Theocratic Principle as Foundational Characteristic of the Medieval Conceptualization

Although the argument about the precedence of the two swords was conducted in this manner, still everyone was agreed on the idea that this dual sword, the papal-imperial empire, was based on immediate divine institution and had absolute prestige. It was thus a power erected for external earthly things as well as for faith and conscience, to which every Christian owed unlimited obedience. To this was attached Daniel's prophecy of the five world empires,[34] in that the last empire, which puts an end to every other one and endures into eternity, points not to the otherworldly kingdom of God (which, however, had already begun here on earth with Christ's appearance, but only as an inward, not yet revealed kingdom), but to the Holy Roman Empire of the German Nation, under pope and emperor. This was therefore regarded as identical with the kingdom of God, and usually thought to be an uninterrupted connection and future segue between the two.

This conception is found in the most exhaustive but also most glaring way with Petrus de Andlo. In his presentation, the Augustinian economy of the heavenly (heavenly-minded) empire is transformed into a formal dynastic succession. From the hand of God there first reigned Adam, Abel, the Patriarchs, judges, the kings and priests of Judah until Christ, and since then, again from God and in Christ's place, there reign Pope and Emperor, whom the Pope handed the secular power. The last emperor will lay down the trappings of his kingdom in the church, and there they will be taken up by Christ. Thus, from the creation until the resurrection not even the gap of an interregnum between

---

[34] Thomas, *De Regimine Principum*, Book III, chs. 12–16.

the divinely authorized rulers was left.[35]

Apart from this theocratic foundation of the state and its authority, the political theory of the Middle Ages also had another peculiar, although subordinate element, the analogy according to divine relations. Augustine, as did other Fathers, loved to conceive of the natural creation blatantly allegorically in order to explain ethical-religious relations. In similar manner, the scholastics and the political writers of the Middle Ages sought the solution of the question of state arrangement often in comparison with divine models. In this manner, the monarchical form of government was established by analogy with the unity of divine dominion;[36] similarly, the obligations of the sovereign and other things.

Both the theocratic element and this symbolizing one now everywhere appear much more emphatically among the representatives of the spiritual power. The supporters of the secular power are much more sober, and come closer to our present way of thinking [Bildung].

The writers of that time could not have been unaware that the doctrine of Aristotle, which they venerated, was not consistent with their Christian-ecclesiastical life valuation. They sometimes permitted themselves a different judgment than Aristotle's in specific cases, especially on the worth of the forms of government, where they almost unanimously declare not Aristotelian polity but, according to Christian-Germanic custom, monarchy,[37] usually elective

---

[35] Petrus de Andlo, *De Imperio Romano Regis et Augusti Creatione* [The Creation of the Imperial Roman Monarchy], Book I, ch. 1, ch. 13–15, and Book II, ch. 8 (pp. 11, 12, 45, 55, 65), finally in particular the conclusion: "de Romani imperii exitu et ejus finali consummatione" [Of the Issue and Final Consummation of the Roman Empire] (p. 140).

[36] Petrus de Andlo, p. 34. Thomas Aquinas, *De Regimine Principum,* I, 12. Dante (*De Monarchia,* Book I, ch. 15), according to whom it is not the rule of the state that approaches divine rule; the human race itself through unity (which yields it dominion) approaches God.

[37] Thomas nevertheless was able to reconcile this by characterizing the appropriate form as polity for the city (*civitas*) and monarchy for the territory [Land] (*provincia*). In the *Summa* he declares the mixed form generally to be the best. But it is traditionally the case in the medieval conceptualization that the concept of monarchy rules out

monarchy after the model of the German emperorship, to be the best form of government. On the whole, however, they seek to reconcile the contradiction of the two elements which they include in their teachings by distinguishing the spheres , attributing the secular to Aristotle, the spiritual to the Christian idea. The "Philosophus" (i.e., Aristotle) could have known nothing about the entire extent of revelation and grace, therefore also nothing of the priesthood, the spiritual regiment, hence the entire ecclesial side; but for matters for which no revelation exists, and which pertain to what man can attain with his natural capacity, the Philosophus is and remains the authority, and to this pertains in particular the arrangement of the secular regiment. The same distinction is applied to the purpose of the state, which is placed, in accordance with Aristotle's procedure, in the good, i.e., the virtuous life. Here also a distinction is made between, on the one hand, *earthly virtue*, recognized by reason and attainable by man in his own strength, as well as, in conjunction herewith, his earthly well-being – all of this forms the scope of the state (*regnum*) – and on the other hand, the virtue that can only be known through revelation and attained only by divine grace and the means of salvation, and corresponding to this, eternal well-being; this forms the sphere of the church (*sacerdotium*). This explanation is found in Thomas Aquinas[38] and others, but at its clearest and most complete in Dante,[39] although with him it does not serve to ground the relationship to Aristotle, but the relationship between emperor and pope. From this angle, inappropriate though it is to grace and revelation, is thus derived the task which was lacking

---

subordination to the laws [Gesetze]. Thus Thomas, *De Regimine Principum*, p. 300; Andlo, p. 32.

[38] Thomas, *De Regimine Principum*, I, ch. 15. Likewise Marsilius in Goldast, II, pp. 157–164.

[39] Dante, *op. cit.,* Book III, ch. 16.6, where among other things the following statement is found: "Propter quod opus fuit homini duplici directivo secundum duplicem finem: scilicet summo Pontifice, qui secundum revelata humanum genus produceret ad vitam aeternam, et Imperatore, qui secundum philosophica documenta genus humanum ad temporalem felicitatem derigeret" [Wherefore a twofold directive agent was necessary to man, in accordance with the twofold end; the Supreme Pontiff to lead the human race to life eternal by means of revelation, and the Emperor to guide it to temporal felicity by means of philosophic instruction (Henry translation)].

in Aristotle, that the state is to provide for worship.

Indeed, such a delimitation of the two spheres by no means eliminates the opposition between these two elements, in that the Christian idea also finds its application in the secular sphere ; and such is also found among these expositors. For this reason, throughout their entire presentation the contradiction remains unresolved. For instance, it is contradictory when in accordance with Aristotle they base the state on the socializing nature or the mutual need of man (*humana indigentia*),[40] but at the same time view it theocratically as God's representative; or when they in accordance with Aristotle's guidance investigate the worth of different forms of government, yet also teach that God has set monarchical power, and indeed a single one, over all of Christendom. For this lacks the coherence, for instance, of the application of Aristotelian notions to demonstrate the rationale of divine action, or that God established states because people need each other (which in fact was not entirely applicable), etc.; instead, these two run without connection alongside each other. Therefore, a dualism runs through the legal philosophy of the Middle Ages, there being two elements without penetration, without a unifying principle.

Similarly, they are also unaware of how the Aristotelian conception, which is derived from Greek life, is so dissimilar to the state of the Germanic Middle Ages, in which they lived and to which they were attached. Hence this intruding ancient mentality [Bildung] already contains the first seeds of the breakup of the medieval condition, and the furnishing of the European countries with a character approximating the ancients, such as they have at the present day. But even more than that: In their Germanic appropriation, the lessons drawn from Aristotle lack the Greeks' emphasis of the objective – the consideration of the state as a given, higher whole, in which the individual is subsumed. Therefore, where the Christian element, the positive divine sanction, recedes, the state will no longer manifest itself as a given power over the people, but rather, in the

---

[40] Thomas (*De Regimine Principum,* Book II, ch. 2) admittedly deduces the necessity of the state not merely on physical mutual need but also on the requirement of the community for intellectual need and the exercise of some virtues (particularly, justice and friendship). But entirely independently of this he teaches (Book III, ch. 9) a God-ordained hierarchy of authorities: men over animals and things, princes over men, the church over princes. Likewise Andlo, p. 12, cf. p. 11.

principle of subjectivity, as the work and the mere object of people.

In this manner the traces of today's doctrine of popular sovereignty are here and there already found in the medieval writers. This is very decided and well-developed in the case of Marsilius of Padua, who, of course, lived in the midst of alternative viewpoints. According to him, the people – i.e., the totality of the citizens or their *valentior pars* [stronger part] – is the legislator, or the first and actual efficient cause of the law. The same is likewise also the cause of the princely power (*principatus*) and also has the competence to punish the princes in cases of grosser violations of the law (*corrigendi*). The doctrine of Aristotle, whereby genuine state constitutions are those in which the government at the same time is directed to the goal of [serving] the subjects (the people), Marsilius conceives in this manner, that government must be conducted according to the will and the agreement of citizens (*voluntas et consensus civium*). He declares that for this reason elective monarchy is a more adequate form of government than hereditary monarchy.[41] All of this is indeed no longer specifically medieval, but already constitutes the transition to the modern political view.

But there emerges through these specifically medieval ideas a completely new principle in the philosophy of law: the *personal will of God*, which is nowhere to be found in ancient times, at least not as a scientific principle. Accordingly, the state not only has the ideal sanction of the good and the beautiful as with the Greeks, but also the reality of divine institution. Likewise, world history emerges under an ethical principle: the divine will. Among the Greeks, an ethical power is to determine the way in which states are to be constructed; but how they really are constructed is an affair of accidental human decisions and accidental events. Here, however, the real nature of states, the historical leading of their destinies, is determined by ethical power (the divine will). World empires and the contemporary construction of states manifest themselves as its work. The divine sway in history is here recognized, and also becomes one aspect, in fact the most important, of scientific conceptualization.

---

[41] Cf. Goldast, *Monarch.* II, pp. 169, 175, 185, 163, 165. When in opposition to this, Dante (*De Monarchia,* Book I, ch. 12) says of the king (emperor), "qui minister omnium procul dubio habendus est" [without doubt the Monarch must be held the chief servant of all] (with an expression similar to Frederick the Great later on), this has an entirely different, innocuous meaning [translation from the Henry edition].

This principle, which is true in itself, appears here in crude, external shape – as the *theocratic principle*. That is, it assumes everywhere a direct manifestation of God's will; accordingly, God ordained the authorities in church and state through a visible personal act (while Christ in person constituted the pope and through him the emperor), and their regard or majesty [Ansehen] is founded in this specific ordination, not simply in a general divine commandment.[42] Similarly, the events of world history are the direct expression of His will, and constitutional questions are decided according to His pronouncement. That God assigned world rule to the Romans because of their virtue, and the pope in the name of God conferred it on the Germans, is the ethical and legal basis on which science established the reputation of the supreme power of that time, and with regard to the former statement respecting the divine institution of the Roman Empire, the commandment of God that all nations must obey them and their successors was regarded as evidence of the virtues of the Romans, their victories as God's judgments, the oracle and finally the fact that Christ was born under Roman rule, that by which God recognized its legitimacy. This is the account even of the great and sober Dante.[43] The right of the Jewish people to destroy the Canaanites, which Michaelis inappropriately enough judges by today's principles of international law, had as its basis such directly expressed divine will and concrete command. The leading of the Jewish people was in truth theocratic by way of exception; for the Jewish people is the type of God's eternal kingdom. But the medieval writers treated the whole of world history in this manner.

---

[42] Cf. this work, Vol. II, Book IV [*The Doctrine of State and the Principles of State Law*], ch. 4: "The Divine Institution of the State."

[43] Dante Book II, pp. 120–128. Andlo, p. 100.

PART III: THE REFORMATION, AND PREVIEW OF SUBSEQUENT DEVELOPMENT

Anti-Theocratic Character of the Reformation

The work of the Reformation in relation to the social condition is simply the overthrow of the theocratic character.[44] The Christian element, the personal will of God, remains, albeit not in a theocratic way. The Reformers likewise base the ruling authority and the spiritual office on divine institution; but they base this on God's order and commandment, not on an immediate act of God, by which He introduced a particular constitution or ordained particular persons. Therefore, all of those investigations as to whether God set an emperor or many kings over Christendom, whether the Romans held world rule by right, whether the pope or the people transferred it to Charles the Great, all get dropped. In their place comes where and how ruling authority exists, it being from God and deserving of obedience. There is then no divinely prescribed form of the constitution of church and state, and the uninterrupted succession of the apostolate (*successio personae*) is no condition of the rightful church and its promises. In this manner the earthly world assigned to men is independent, and does not coincide with the eternal kingdom of God; the supernatural aura of express authority and its unlimited power over faith and action fades; the individual person receives a sphere in which he stands immediately under God and his conscience.

Lack of a Scientific Development of Its Principles

But this healthy evaluation of the ethical and political situation was still without scientific support, and initially even an attempt at any. Melanchthon's work on moral philosophy cannot be considered to be such. He deals with human duties, moral and legal, in pure positive fashion, under the direction and arrangement of the Decalogue, as those that just exist and are questioned by no

[44] Cf. my lecture, *Der Protestantismus als politisches Princip* [Protestantism as Political Principle], 1853, pp. 12–22.

one, without even examining the inner ground and the meaning thereof. For instance, he writes: sexual intercourse is necessary for the preservation of the human race, but God does not want stray copulation (*vagi concubitus*), so marriage is necessary. But why does God not want *vagi concubitus*? What is the meaning of this prohibition and its morally persuasive force, through which, even apart from revelation, it must be clear to us and so vouch for the authenticity of the revelation? Likewise: the human community must have a ruler, therefore mastery or subordination is necessary, as is obedience to superiors. The human race needs protection, so penalties are needed, war is needed, from which proceeds bravery, the champion of justice. The abundance of sound striking views and doctrines which this book contains in specifics does not make it into a book that builds on and executes a scientific principle, namely one that realizes the spirit of the Reformation. It is an expression of the life valuation of the Reformation, but not of the scientific system, for which it sowed the seed. Similarly, the natural law of Oldendorp treats legal commandments simply on the basis of the Ten Commandments, as a given, and the same is true of Winkler, namely giving a general introduction about ethics (natural law), which contains the Christian concepts of divine law, human nature before and after the fall, etc., without scientifically bringing them into contact with specific conditions, the legal system, the formation of the social condition.

The Cartesian-Grotian Development and the Reformation

It was therefore a necessity that, just as with the Middle Ages, the new world epoch founded by the Reformation should give shape to its life valuation in a scientific system. That was the impetus for the development that begins with Grotius and Descartes. But this only represents the life valuation of the new world epoch in its negative side: the overthrow of the theocratic character, the liberation of the earthly life-order from the ecclesiastical hierarchy, the liberation of science from any external authority. On the other hand, it also relinquished the bond to God Himself, which the Reformation held onto despite being liberated from mediating powers.

With the destruction of false authority, with the strengthening of the individual mind and its demand to exercise its own investigation and its own freedom, the principle of subjectivity was first unleashed, the power of free personality creating from itself and resting in itself, and it tore itself away from all authority and all content over itself. The complete self-sufficiency of human knowledge (of reason) by which it finds itself in its true condition, capable from itself of recognizing all truth, the complete self-sufficiency of human morality [Sitte], whereby man in his own thinking, separated from God and the moral order given by God (albeit formed in free economy), possesses the ground and content of all morality, and the ability to fulfill it – this is the fundamental character of rationalistic philosophy, indeed of the general scientific orientation from the Reformation to the Revolution. This cannot be held to be the science of the Reformation and of the world epoch founded by the Reformation, in the way that medieval philosophy is the science of Catholicism, since it only appropriated one aspect of the Reformation, and not even the decisive one – the negative polemic. Such is already confirmed beyond all doubt by its contradiction of the fundamental teachings and the life-principles of the Protestant church, while medieval science was in full compliance with the Catholic Church.

Nevertheless, rationalist philosophy in terms of its final destination, of which it was unaware, is the initial prod toward realizing the true and positive principle of the Reformation in science. Because even with all the error in standpoint and result, it is yet at the same time the innermost intellectual contemplation of man in himself. Making thought itself into an object of thought, seeking the connection to the eternal power in the withdrawal from the world into itself, only considering that which is clearly and distinctly acknowledged ("clare et distincte" in Descartes' expression), the systematic Only [Einige], to be truly known – this really is the precondition for Christian truth to penetrate completely into the sphere of science, similar to the way self-examination functions in the ethical sphere.[45] Nevertheless, the error lies in adhering to the sufficiency of human thought as a prerequisite, and thereby refusing the object offered to thought – experience and revelation. If this error is removed, then contemplation necessarily leads to an inwardness and self-awareness, notably also to a self-awareness in all knowledge about its relation to the Christian revealed truth, and thereby an assurance regarding it, hence a true intellectual enlightenment such as dominated the scientific insight of the past. To fulfill this and thus to bring the life valuation of the world epoch founded by the Reformation to scientific development in all its fullness according to its positive aspect as well,

[45] *Der Protestantismus als politisches Princip*, pp. 59–64.

from its center outward, is therefore the problem of the present time. The latest scientific endeavors in the aftermath of the Revolution wrestle to find the solution to this, more or less consciously, in greater or lesser approximation, and often partially in yet further aberration.

The Latest Approximation of Medieval Catholic Elements to the Protestant Standpoint

These latest scientific endeavors should not merely scientifically give shape to the inherent drive, the principle of the Reformation according to its true, full, positive aspect, but at the same time revive an aspect which even the Reformation left to one side. That would be the ethical significance of world history as the work and manifestation of the World Power. The Middle Ages comprehended this significance theocratically in the sense that the history of the world, as far as the possession of power is concerned, in church and state, was determined by the direct indication and formation of God. For its part, the Reformation completely prescinded from world history. It was only concerned with the ethical rule, the commandment; this alone is divine to it; by contrast, the whole of reality and history provided it no ethical defining moment. So, it measured the church purely in terms of doctrine which stands outside and above all history. By contrast, the historical realization of the church, the catholicity or the historical continuity (the unity and the connection of all those who confess Christ, and the uninterruptedness of the doctrine and constitutional development of the church throughout the ages) is not at all decisive to it.

For Luther this element is still active, but only as the residue of his Catholic education. It is not his own and therefore not his energetic principle. His preservation of the status quo is often only a concession. For Calvin, it is entirely absent, indeed it is fundamentally rejected. The standard of doctrine is applied at each moment anew, not only to rectify the church, but to decide whether the church is present, as if there had not been a church.[46] Similarly, science (ethics and politics) here simply has to do with the rule that stands outside and above all time in itself, and the world-historical progress of moral consciousness and the formation of states simply takes its place to be judged according to this rule, not to be considered a fellow determinant or manner of application of the rule

---

[46] *Der Protestantismus als politisches Princip*, pp. 71–88.

itself. The general ethical commandment and the action of individuals are the only factors, with the latter standing totally isolated over against the former, without any mediation by world-historical conditions. This trait characterizes not only rationalist but also Protestant education; it characterizes the scientific era from Melanchthon to Kant. This is the field of pure Protestant science.

It is unmistakably an enrichment of this purely Protestant conceptualization, indeed a resumption of an element pertaining to the medieval period, when in the wake of the Revolution scientific conceptions attribute an ethical significance to history itself in one way or another. Thus, speculative philosophy finds the highest ethical standards in the development of world history, the gradual progress of its ideas, and so constructs the history of the world in a manner similar to Augustine and his successors, and, in distinction to Melanchthon or Kant, as a divine work, although as the work of an entirely different God than the person in whom both Augustine and Melanchthon believed. This is the manner of the Historical School of jurisprudence, which attaches to everything that exists, everything that is traditional, a binding regard, an ethical necessity of recognition, a commitment to piety. Likewise the recent political school [i.e., legitimacy], which grounds the regard of historical dynasties not merely, as the Reformation did, in "where there is ruling authority, it is from God" – which *de facto* is true for every government – but is also suffused with the holiness of the divine dispensation in history.[47]

Nevertheless, the ethical significance which the true and evangelical principle must allow to world history is of a very different kind than that which the Catholic-medieval conceptualization ascribes to it: namely, it is always of only *secondary* ethical significance. The supremely ultimate must always be that which is above history: the Word of God and the ethical rule. If one does not wish to fall back to the theocratic viewpoint, there are only divine order and divine arrangements for the social condition (the state and the external church), not divine acts, not pure and direct divine sanction of specific circumstances and persons. The historical event is never the source of the ethic as it is in the Middle Ages, wherein ethics consisted in: thou shalt recognize the *event*, the *act*

---

[47] This thought also corresponds with the actual practice in all times by which, preferentially, only dynastic lineages come into consideration for a new occupancy of the throne.

of God, whereby He constituted the Pope and through him the Emperor, while all ethical rule (truths of faith, regulation of life, legal order) only indirectly issues therefrom (that is, as the current statutes of the pope and emperor). Rather, the source of the ethic remains the commandment (the rule) alone, and every event is ethically valued only by subsumption under the commandment. But this latter is recognized in its enriched content. While the older Protestant intellectual culture [Bildung] recognized the ethical commandment merely as a commandment for the *sporadic* actions of (individual) people, in this advanced insight it is recognized at the same time as a commandment for the actions of the human community in its *historically cohering unitary condition*, as a commandment: thou shalt not interrupt this coherence without reason, thou shalt have reverence [Pietät] for what has come about by God's *providence* or *allowance* in this condition, to the extent that it does not contradict the order of God (the God-given ethical rule) – the unified faith and the traditional consciousness of the church (which is not without the Holy Spirit) shall have an authority over you and yours, as long as it is not contrary to the clear Word of God – thou shalt not merely obey the ruling authority, where such exists, but thou shalt render piety and devotion to the dynasty rooted in history, as ordained by God.

This therefore distinguishes the *principle of legitimacy* from the *theocratic principle*. For the former, the chief ground of regard is always only the general rule that obedience is owed the ruling authority, although it not only is not conceived abstractly, but also in the deeper meaning that over a lengthy period of possession a divine arrangement is honored, and this deeper ethical valuation extends to long-existing, prescriptive power. By contrast, according to the theocratic principle the ground of regard is not the rule but simply the act of God, by which He ordained authority, and of course this must be a purely divine act without the human admixture which is in all mere historical dispensations of God. The theocratic principle therefore is not satisfied with the ever so lengthy duration of a dynasty, but it goes back to the divine source, to the appearing of Christ, in order to examine whether its absolute origin is really such a divine act. For this reason, the Protestant church does not consider the unbroken succession of bishops from the apostles onward to be a condition of the true church and its promises, but holds the ministry (even if, in an emergency situation, it were to have emerged anew out of the congregation, still directly) to be derived purely from itself, and thus manifests itself as something ordained and dispensed by God, not as prescribed by the congregation. Just as the ethical rule is supremely ultimate in the lives of individuals, while secondarily the divine guidance and the promptings they mediately contain, detectable by the foreboding mind, are likewise ethically determinative ("do nothing out of your own will")[48], so also secondarily there is an ethical guideline in the history of mankind.

Finally, that which according to the newer conception is considered binding, recognized as ethically significant in world history, extends not only to the mere acquisition of external power but also to the entire development of ethical consciousness and life-shaping ideas.

Herein, then, lies a resumption of, or at least a stronger emphasis on, an element left unheeded in the Reformation's manner of looking at things, albeit purified by this and therefore also homogeneous with it. What is manifested in the most recent trends in Protestant science, whether more manifest or more concealed, is a reconciliation of the Protestant and Catholic principle, as far as such is possible.

---

[48] [Perhaps a reference to Philippians 2: 3, "Do nothing out of selfish ambition or vain conceit" (New International Version).]

PART IV: THE START OF THE NEW LEARNING

Character of the Writers at the Start of the New Epoch

At the turning point of both ages, that is, at the beginning of modern history, there is a class of writers which does not, like Descartes, Grotius, Locke, bring to bear, in accordance with the framework of the modern world, a simple energetic principle, but instead makes the object of treatment an unprejudiced, often noncommittal conception of public life, without any clear-cut statement of the problem. Their writings are the product of education based in classical antiquity, which with its broad knowledge rather than a one-sided preoccupation with Aristotle had become widespread, together with the intellectual movement and sober assessment which was opened up by the Reformation. In the freshness of these newly acquired intellectual elements, they seek after the relations between civic order, which not long before had begun to consolidate, and scientific knowledge. Among these pertain especially Bacon and Bodin, and to some extent also Thomas More.[49]

Thomas More

In his *Utopia,* Thomas More provides a replica of the Platonic Republic, a description of an ideal state of human common life as it lies outside of reality and possibility. Even the form of government is platonic: an elected Senate of excellent families, with a lifelong magistrate from the ranks of scholars (Plato's philosophers) at its apex. Similarly, as with Plato, the main and fundamental idea of his ideal is the subordination of material interests and pursuits, their limitation to indispensable necessity, and the community of goods, or more precisely, a communal economy: fields distributed equally, the harvest brought to market and the requirement of every householder distributed to him without payment, legally determined daily working hours, and in small amounts at that, so that the remaining hours are free for intellectual pursuits.

---

[49] Thomas More(† 1535), *De optimo reipublicae statu deque nova insula Utopia,* 1517. Francis Bacon († 1626), *De augmentis scientiarum,* the chapter entitled "De fontibus juris." Jean Bodin († 1597), *De Republica.*

But in this picture More does not present the actual ideal of his nation, as Plato did; he provides, not a moral life assessment which is already active in the formation of states, but only the scientific expression. On the contrary, he completely abstracts from this, both from the conditions and the life assessment of his nation. His account is therefore nothing else than the enchanting game of a noble and educated mind, an attempt to prove itself in the newly acquired antique form, and from this it is understandable that it was and remains without effect. Incidentally, a complete sketch of the outlines of today's socialist economic system was given in More's book, only with the glorious difference that he did not make possession and consumption the final end, like the latter does.

Francis Bacon

Bacon is much more important. Compared to More, he once again represents the empirical standpoint, and does so with an independence gained from permeation in classical education, drawing from his own life experience and contemplation of national conditions, focusing on life, the national condition. With him there is no question of a peculiar scientific principle, of a system peculiar to himself. Rather, he enunciates profound insights which could have served to rectify subsequent systematic theory. Standing out among them are his conception of the state, by which public law ought not be restricted to being the guardian (*custos*) of private law, but also of religion, public mores, military power, public welfare; furthermore his theory of the origin (sources) of law, in particular the meaning and value of customary law and court practice. His teaching about the sources of law has only in recent times come to the fore again, through Savigny. As a philosopher, on the other hand, he planted the seed of a scientific development that immediately followed him, and in its later stages exerted the most important influence on the views of law and the state, although quite opposed to those that he himself held to; this will be discussed at the close of Book III [pp. 259ff. below].

Jean Bodin

Bodin's *Six Books on the Commonwealth* eminently manifests a new era of science [Bildung] arising in the sixteenth century. In terms of subject matter, it is similar to that of Thomas on the "government of rulers." In addition, in terms of structure one sees in it Aristotle's *Politics*. But the freedom of the modern era is already dominant here. Bodin joins Aristotle not only in concepts and doctrines but also in problems and the procedure of investigation. Likewise, the theatrical performances are eliminated. Hence, the legal-philosophical elements of the Middle Ages are all abandoned, and his book is therefore also completely or at least predominantly political theory (politics), not legal philosophy: herein it is the exact obverse of the subsequent work of Grotius. He seeks no principle, no basis and standard of all law; not even the legal basis of the state and the duty of the subject is a subject of his study. Although he presupposes the transfer from the people as the actual ground of state power, since everywhere the first and natural mode of conceiving the matter is the introduction of the existing constitution by conscious act, which can only be an act of the people, yet he admits that this in itself is not sufficient for the legal basis thereof. His aim everywhere is more oriented, on the one hand, toward laying out the extant, toward penetrating the richness of the existing political situation, and on the other hand toward recognizing the salutary, the wholesome, but not in order to establish some absolute legal necessity. He therefore begins by giving sharply delineated definitions of the state, of the family, of sovereignty ("majesty"), of the various forms of government, even the various types of monocracy (*dominatus – regia potestas – tyrannis*). He then seeks out the proper political maxims about conservation, change, the development of the state and its institutions. Finally, he compares the forms of government with each other in order to discover among them the more perfect, the more salutary. Especially prominent is his doctrine that the laws and forms of government necessarily must correspond to the conditions and manners of the people, together with the already extensive investigations he makes in that regard; for this reason he has rightly been characterized as Montesquieu's predecessor, while he himself had Aristotle as his predecessor.

But in terms of substantive content and intention, his book is mainly a scientific justification of monarchy. With the emancipation from Aristotle and the weakening of theocratic ideas, it was a requirement, indeed it first became a possibility, to comprehend the constitutional situation of the Germanic states, hence the monarchy and specifically the peculiar Germanic monarchy, in itself and independently, so that the nation, which emerged in terms of monarchy, also find its satisfaction in it, and especially that the true legal relationship between king and people (which theory and life might already have shaken) be recognized. Bodin meets this requirement. He teaches the advantage and higher perfection of the monarchical form of government, partly from earlier commonly-accepted reasons, partly from essentially new and often witty conceptions, but he only praises monarchy moderated by aristocratic and popular elements. He declares sovereignty ("majesty") to be a power [Gewalt] released from the laws, which, however, in his sense only means that the sovereign prince unites all regard [Ansehen] in himself and is subject to no judge on earth. Finally, in accordance with this he teaches the absolute illicitness of killing or dethroning the king when he really is king, i.e., sovereign.

It is with Bodin as it is with Bacon: there is no sharply delineated principle, or system based on that principle, but rather the considerations of a judicious man regarding political problems. There can be neither followers nor enemies of Bacon or Bodin; but anyone anytime can learn a great deal of truth from them, and base much that is truthful on their authority. The writings of both contain richness and solidity of ideas. But this entirely unprejudiced conception, which however does not penetrate to the ultimate grounds and is not systematically rounded off, had no lasting effect on the age. It pursued thoroughly conscious and self-contained knowledge, and the intellects which extracted a single aspect from the wealth of the subject, but situated it in all its sharpness and carried it through to the final consequence, were therefore, despite their one-sided fallacy, the ones which initially achieved scientific predominance.

The beginning of the world era which followed the Reformation is also characterized by the higher esteem in which the ethical element is everywhere held. That element is nurtured more carefully in science even than the material and mechanical, and ethical significance is recognized as supreme, especially with the state. Thus, Melanchthon declared the respectability of outward behavior to be a goal of the state (*honesti mores in externa vitae consuetudine*), Bacon likewise with regard to the common good (*bene vivere* in the sense of Aristotle), namely religion, discipline, etc. Bodin discusses in detail the notion that the outward comforts of life form a very subordinate purpose of the state vis-à-vis its moral purposes, and among these sets the "contemplative" purpose (the worship of God) as the supreme one. More, finally, starts from the complete suppression of material interests. It was the subsequent period that came to the profane conception that the protection of life and property is the actual, indeed sole task of human community.

BOOK III: ABSTRACT LEGAL PHILOSOPHY

PART I: ABSTRACT PHILOSOPHY IN GENERAL (RATIONALISM)

In the free treatment of the Greeks, every philosophical doctrine, indeed every conception, had its own independent life, and the ethics of Plato or Aristotle can be understood and appreciated without taking into consideration how, in their view, the existence of the world and the coherence of it is to be explained. This is not the case with modern philosophy. Logical consistency, through which alone it aims to attain all its knowledge, establishes the particular in its entire existence on initial assumptions. Each branch of philosophy stands and falls with the supreme philosophical viewpoint [Ansicht]. Therefore, for insight into the newer philosophy of law it is absolutely necessary to take the entire system of philosophy into consideration, and the former only as a consequence of the latter. This is true not only of the particular form of natural law as given by the founders of the particular systems, but quite as much of its general development. Because its entire existence is a result of the viewpoint of abstract philosophy in general.

Essence of Rationalism

The essence of abstract philosophy is: only accept what follows from reason, what is logically necessary. That something exists, is not sufficient; the opposite must be impossible. Every particular content with which reason is filled, is initially manifested as something random which could just as well be something else. What cannot be thought otherwise if it is to remain reason, is reason alone, what it is, its own laws, forms, and determinations: for example, the rule that something cannot be its opposite at the same time, the idea of the one and the many, the finite and the infinite, the relation of cause and effect, etc. Only that which already contains these has the character of logical necessity. That something follows from reason is the same thing as saying that anything else would cancel the determinations of thought. Hence, pure reason – thought prior to all content outside itself – is the principle of abstract philosophy. What it contains, is also to be recognized from itself, prior to all experience (*a priori*). And on the other hand, that which is known through experience can never have the character of logical necessity. For experience shows only that something is, never that the opposite would be unthinkable.[50]

Everything that is to be proven, must therefore be found purely *a priori*. This is true of the things of everyday perception no less than the invisible objects of faith. The proof of the existence of God, for example can only be conducted when it is shown that the non-existence of its concept, which one has to construct apart from any experience, is a contradiction (the ontological proof); the proof of the immortality of the soul, when the characteristics of which the concept of the soul consists, logically exclude mortality.

Common to all investigation and knowledge is reason in a *negative* sense, i.e., the elimination of everything that contradicts the laws of thought, as the standard. The peculiarity of the rationalist orientation is reason as a *positive* standard: only to recognize what these laws already contain in themselves, and to exclude anything that in terms of them might be this way, might be that. Insights should be discovered not merely *by* reason, but *from* reason. Reason is not to be the means and organ, but the source of knowledge; it is not through its activity to find a content lying outside of itself, but to find the entire content solely from its own nature and its laws. That is why this orientation is appropriately referred to as *rationalism*. It is like holding the eye to be the source of light, and wishing to see things not by looking at objects, but from the internal structure of the eye and its analysis.

Motivation for Rationalism

The motivation for this is not skepticism, because the philosopher who destroys the world by means of abstraction, has in advance the hope of rebuilding it out of himself. Nor only admiration of the intellect, because this for its own sake, as experience shows regarding the Greeks, leads to the quest for meaning in things, not to prescinding from them; rather, it joins to itself the *interest of freedom*.

The independence and inwardness of man (the principle of subjectivity) is what propels the entire history of the modern age and the European-Germanic populace – an insight that has been widespread among us for a long time. It has

---

[50] "Experience teaches us that something is constituted in this or that manner, but not that it could not be something else." Kant, *Critik der reinen Vernunft* [Critique of Pure Reason], p. 3.

become the basis of the current aesthetic view. Regarding the legal institutions and the formation of states of the Germanic tribes, it is also recognized that their origin consisted in free self-determination and personal ties. In like manner, scientific investigation resists the constraint which the objects outside it exercise upon it. One comprehends when one allows something to impact him, when one allows himself to be determined by it. Cognition [Erkennen] presupposes recognition [Anerkennen]. The Germanic spirit – liberated by the Reformation from the church's authority and energized in its innermost depth – does not wish to be determined by anything but what it itself determines. A world pre-existing outside it acts oppressively upon it; it is a foreign power, to which it is to submit against its will. It frees itself from that world by abstraction, and refuses to submit as long as it finds no compulsion to do so within itself. Only when the thought determinations themselves demand it, is room made for that existence; for then, the recognition is based on its own existence, not on this other's.

Such disdain to accept the real as real because it is not derivative of self would have to be reckoned the height of arrogance, if it were certain that it occurred arbitrarily. But this process is reflected in the entire development, without any awareness of choice and intention. It permeates all branches of knowledge and constitutes at least the scientific form even for the positive content. It is as if scientific treatment could not otherwise go about its business. Therefore, reason is also defended in general; but the attempt to justify its *particular* use, which is the important thing, is not even made, because one believes it not to be something particular, but the general and solely possible. And indeed, the possibility of abstraction leads of itself and almost inevitably to this conclusion, until the complete trial first makes clear the enterprise and its necessary end, in doing so safeguarding against it.

All philosophy, in fact, is only intended either to obtain a guarantee for specific results (God, immortality, etc.), or to recognize the unity in the mass of diverse things. The former can be called its practical, the latter its theoretical interest. Both are universally human and eternal. It must look for something unconditioned for both ends, which imparts the guarantee and unity to all others. If it is possible for human consciousness, through reflection, to break away from all existence outside of it, to feign even for a moment that it is alone, that everything else apart from it either does not exist at all or does so in a very different character than it really is: what is more natural than to seek that supreme guarantee in what one can no longer think away – one's own existence, and thought itself? The desire to gain certainty about God and immortality, to rescue these from the destruction of that flood of thought washing everything away, must lead to the attempt to see whether they were not already given in those first assumptions. The same free activity of thought that is cognizant of the ability to accept or not to accept any existence or the validity of any commandment, also removes the correspondence between man and the world. It has found what the Greeks stipulated in vain, a position outside of the world and thus a capacity to act against it. It is itself its own world. It stipulates recognition by necessity, it feels everything to be dependent solely on its choice. It is no longer incorporated into the world, and when it wishes to eliminate the contradiction and restore unity, no attempt lies closer to hand than to incorporate the world into itself, to find the world's coherence with it in its thought determinations, just as it finds coherence in itself. If all of this is achieved, then it appears to it, and to the thought pertaining to it, to be the harmony in all things, the only cause from which it imagines something existing to be such; and it possesses for its desired results the confirmation that it alone can be sufficient, its own existence. It has achieved what all philosophy desires, and has achieved this in the manner that its motive force and sense of independence wished for.

In the early period, the practical interest is still predominant. It proves the immortality of the soul – the reality of which is, that we can only be certain of it through faith in the revelations and promises of God – from the characteristics of the soul (its intangibility, its non-compositeness), thus in a way that God Himself could not annihilate or make mortal if He wanted to, any more than He could make a round triangle. Later, from the time of Fichte this interest recedes completely, leaving only the scientific [i.e., theoretical] interest: to derive the world from one's own reason.

Progression of Rationalism

This explains the entire process. Philosophy must find everything *from* reason, *in accordance with* reason. The motive of abstraction – to have the absolute in itself – likewise sets the restriction on its own thinking and existence. Besides, one might just think away even this, and how then could anything be found? That is what is meant when philosophy supposedly emanates from nothing.

Abstraction is immediately carried out until it arrives at some very simple idea, of which one cannot divest himself if he exists and thinks, which underlies all thinking, e.g., substance, the concept of being, the absolute, and the like. All determinate existence must proceed from these remains of abstraction – the simplest that reason contains – and it must do so according to reason, the merely logical. It must contain things such that their opposite is unthinkable. This applies just as much to the systems of necessary opposition, which have to form one thing in opposition to another (Fichte, Hegel), as to those which merely follow from the principle of contradiction. In both, science can accept no object, no concept as something that is there; it must itself build everything in its own way, by showing that with the preceding – beginning with the first assumption – this likewise is posited according to the laws of thought, and their not-being or being-something-else is a logical impossibility. It must then in the same way be possible for it and incumbent on it, conversely, to resolve objects apprehended by it in some manner into the simplicity from which it made them. This is the meaning and the high importance of *definitions*. The characteristics of the definition should be entirely adequate to the defined, should exhaust the matter; these features, even themselves in turn defined in the same way, should be able to be converted into already given general conceptions. In such a way one is to arrive at that which is simple, the general substance. It is, when one completes it, the transition backward, which the philosophical system aims to take forward.

Thus, all living coherence in the world is now repealed, freedom is impossible, the relationship of cause and effect is only appearance, in truth everything is as it is in logic and geometry: mere ground and consequent. Every cause, namely, can be distinguished in its effects not only in thought but also in reality. It is possible for the former to be extant and the latter not to occur, for example, when the sprouting of a seed is suppressed. Besides a positive cause, then, one can accept a negative one, the non-existence of possible prevention, if it should manifest itself. Yes, it is at least conceivable that the cause itself is free either to produce the effect or not, for example, a man and an action. Time – it might now be a true or a false idea in itself – at least refers correctly and clearly to the relationship of cause and effect, separating them both. By contrast, in the logical context the generating and the generated – ground and consequent – can be kept apart in thought but not in reality, as for example with the nature of the triangle and its consequence that its three angles together are equal to two right angles. We cannot put the notion of time between them, nor a prevention of the ground by the will or any other way. We know, as soon as the ground is there prior to all investigation, that the consequence is likewise inevitable, because it is not separate from it; it is the thing itself. Therefore, if all existence is inferred from the initial assumption according to reason, then that existence must already be given in it, apart from any process, and it is inconceivable that anything could have been done differently than it is, or rather that it should be different than it is. And rationalism must stand fast on this conceptualization. For if any free production were to exist in the world, i.e., something else likewise feasible and conceivable, then it could not know from mere thought determinations that precisely this is real. And what follows from reason, cannot be the result of a process, an act, or otherwise it would not have existed before these events, and it would really have been a logical contradiction. Just as little can things be exhaustively defined when they are effects and not mere consequences. The radius being logically *contained* in a circle, is absolutely nothing other than everything else that is already given for all circles. By contrast, the son as *engendered* by the father is by no means denoted even by that descent and by all that is posited in the concept of the father.

Reason as the principle of philosophy, therefore, does not tolerate any occurrence, any creation; it endures nothing new, nothing only adventitious. It is nothing more than what follows from it, and what follows from it could never be lacking, because it is it itself. *The entire development of abstract philosophy is actually continually driven forward by one single postulate: There is no change!* This postulate necessarily led – as will be shown below – from the early stage to Kant's, and thus connects the new systems with the ones preceding his.

Contrast with the Historical Viewpoint

The historical view, which, as was maintained above, the Greeks lacked, here is thus virtually denied. Now this emphasizes all the more that the historical view is not to be understood as if there were eternal change without unity of purpose and control, or as if the past had a higher value than the present, or as if one wouldn't know anything if it hadn't been for events from which one could learn. Quite the opposite! In fact, the historical view is the one by which something has happened and is happening, according to which there is a free act. Schelling called the Christian view of the world the historical as opposed to the logical view of modern philosophy. For the latter would have it that the world and all particular things are necessarily contained in the essence of God, while the former says it only arose (came about) through His voluntary creation. I have referred to the Judeo-Christian view of ethics as historical for the reason that it views law as law because God willed it so. Thus, man had the ethic before any incident of his own; but he has it only by the act of God; it does not exist by itself, with the concept of its existence or of being in general. And the past is not the higher, the present is; and the highest is the future, because God leads the world and law to it – just as the uniqueness of the Historical School of jurisprudence consists in nothing other than having this as its ultimate foundation, as will be shown below.[51]

Herein likewise lies the difference between negative and positive knowledge. What is found from reason (*a priori*) is, according to Schelling's deeply significant expression, not "being" [Seiende], but only "not-capable-of-not-being" [Nicht-nicht-sein-könnende]. Thus, for example, that a triangle has three angles that together add up to two right angles, or that, as Wolff deduces, "seeing is the property of an animal with eyes" (thus a seeing animal), is only a negative knowledge; on the other hand, that the earth is round and not triangular, that there are plants and animals, this is positive knowledge. Another would not be unthinkable. Positive, and the object of positive knowledge, is, if I may put it in an absolute and exhaustive manner, the person, what is specifically primordially determined for him (i.e., holiness, the love of God, etc.), his act, and the product of his act. Therefore, it is merely negative knowledge that there is a being, a power, a ground, by which the world exists, because the opposite would be contrary to logical concepts; on the other hand, it is positive knowledge that there is a God in the true sense, a personal, self-conscious creator; likewise, that this God is gracious and merciful. It is positive knowledge when we consider the world to be the act and creation of God, and only negative knowledge when we consider it to be the eternally necessary consequence of reason. Philosophy which derives all knowledge from reason, can have no other than negative knowledge.

According to that view, then, the entirely consummated All is merely an

---

[51] [Book VI, Part II; included in vol. 1B of this translation.]

emanation of empty determinations of thought. God, as was referred to above, is what remains of abstraction. The latter, and thus God Himself, is likewise the world – logically, it is contained in Him. This is logical pantheism, which rationalism necessarily must confess or else give up its peculiar method, that is, itself. Different things were adopted in the different systems as what is most simple, which is where the abstraction has to halt – thus, as the god of the world of reason. For Spinoza and Hegel, it is general being (for the former as real, for the latter as thought); for Kant, the notion of the categorical, necessity itself; for Fichte, the I (the concept of self-consciousness). But all assumptions can be traced back to a dual basis, the real existence of the thinker (the I) and the pure determinations of thought. Both principles, as we have shown, are given necessarily with the abstract method; they alone are what remains. Therefore, they confront us immediately in the motto of the first founder of this orientation: *cogito, ergo sum*. But they are *in conflict with each other*. In terms of its essence, the real existence of that which thinks [das Denkenden] is living, acting, generating something outside itself as effect. Reason, however, is static, ready-made, including in itself everything it has produced as a result. The former is free, self-determining and freedom-demanding; the latter is merely determined, necessary, and necessity-imposing. Therefore, what is built on the one is destroyed by the other; thought-necessity abolishes the freedom of the I, and the free activity of the I does not allow for everything to be thought-necessity. They thereby attest to the falsehood of the motive, which encouraged both in a form such that they could not be carried out at the same time.

Subjective and Objective Rationalism

These principles, depending on whether the one or the other is used as a basis, divide the systems in two main directions. The one may be called subjective rationalism, the other objective rationalism. For the latter, impersonal reason is God, while for the former – if it were capable of accomplishment – thinking man himself is God. The representative of the first is Spinoza, the last is Fichte.

These principles come into conflict in the individual systems themselves and in the various branches of science, above all in the philosophy of law. The law of reason continually receives the impetus for its development only from the vain attempt to unite these foundations, and only from them is it possible to look into its innermost working. However, since the living cause of the entire orientation, against the power of which no logical consistency makes headway, is only independent personal existence, then of course subjective rationalism must predominate. It attains predominance right after Spinoza, and maintains it up until Fichte.

Only in the modern period has it been ousted, and all power again turned to the objective, namely by Hegel's system. For there arose a certain awareness that severance from the world does not lead to what is true, and it was believed that objective rationalism avoided this. But this is deception. Pure thought, which it makes into a principle, may not be the person of the thinker; but nevertheless, it has no existence elsewhere than in the abstracting individual. Hereby was the person connected to his own forms of thought, but not to the creation. And if one absolutely refuses to refer all particular existence to a cause that is outside us, recognizing it only insofar as the determinations of thought that are inseparable from our consciousness contain it, then nothing else could have prompted this than the subjective motive whereby man in his isolation wishes to be the center of creation.

Objective rationalism, where it is sincere, is also well aware that it denies a personal God and the historical creation. This is not always so with subjective rationalism, which is wont to invoke the scholastic distinction between the principle of being and the principle of knowledge.[52] Reason is not supposed to be what causes things, but only what causes our knowledge of them. Such an appeal might be less deceptive with general systems of philosophy, in which things can be traced all the way back, than with individual doctrines, for example in theology and natural law. Because reason is to be the *principium*, the originating thing, what is intended here is not a merely negative standard added as a second one to the positive standard, in order to test its conceivability. The distinction would yet have weight if reason were taken merely as the beginning and starting point of the *investigation*, as a fact which is itself to be explained — but not as the ground which alone grants the explanation. For then it would immediately have to go beyond itself. One would have to call for help from laws outside of it to attain to the principle of things. If, for example, I explain the

[52] [Apparently a reference to Kant's appeal to the distinction between *ratio essendi* and *ratio cognoscendi* in the Preface to the *Critique der praktischen Vernunft* (Critique of Practical Reason).]

existence of a Creator by the fact of my existence and the forms of my reason, then this happened according to a rule learned from experience. For according to which logical laws is a Creator given in the concept of my existence? How does it follow from the forms of pure reason that it is not me that is the Eternal One?[53] Supposing we had now arrived at the true principle, then the procedure would take on its enduring shape in terms of the nature of this principle, which does not already contain reason. If, for example, this principle were a personal almighty Creator of the sort that rationalistic theologians have found it to be, then it is clear that He could not prescribe to Himself things to do or have done beyond those from which He could not refrain; for example, there could be no miracles, simply because *reason* can produce nothing other than what it must produce.[54] With such a method (which is no longer mere rational inference, but empirical-historical) there would then be no reason as to why *pure thought* is made the starting point, and not rather our whole manifoldly filled nature, thought and desire, volition and conscience, and the endless supply accumulated in it through experience and history. This totality as undeniable fact is the agency from which one would have to proceed in order to discover, likewise with the help of our whole faculty of knowledge, the cause of the forms of thought, observation, intellectual vision, even intuition. For only if we seek the logical unity of the world in ourselves do we have to conceive of ourselves as simple.

The difference of the scientific course as here described, appears to me to have been meant by Plato in the sixth book of his *Republic*, and he would have delineated it more clearly if he had been acquainted with rational philosophy in its modern iteration. There he esteems the mathematical and similar sciences to be lower and insufficient, because they abstract general forms from visible things, and from these abstractions as assumptions move *forward* to results, which then, in order to have some meaning, need the sensible things through which (not from which) they were obtained. True science, on the other hand, must first explicate *backwards*. It must start from the objects, certainly, but

---

[53] Similar reasoning by Kant also refutes this kind of demonstration (*Critik der Urtheilskraft* [Critique of Judgment], pp. 331ff.).

[54] See for this generally, Kant's *Religion innerhalb der Gränzen der bloßen Vernunft* [Religion within the Bounds of Bare Reason], Book Four, Part One.

considers them to be conditioned [bedingte] and therefore seeks not that which is in them (the general form), but an independent cause outside them, as the absolute [das Unbedingte]. If it goes to work like this, then, when it has ascended to this absolute, it will no longer need the sensible things from which it proceeded, but will move among the pure forms. Among these forms (εἶδος) Plato certainly understands not that which is without specific content, the abstract, but rather the opposite of the sensible (αἰσθητόν), the intellectual, in constant freedom, not inhibited by any immovable substance, acting – the creative archetypes and counsels of God.

But all of this is precisely opposed to rational philosophy, including the subjective kind. Here, pure thought is the beginning. With this, we directly relinquish the creaturely character. According to the pure consciousness of existence and the pure forms of thought, we would have to consider it eternal if it only were possible to abstract from the particular sensations which we have at every moment and the changing conceptions with which we must fill those forms. Further, with this thinking as starting point, explication can only occur in the forward direction, according to its own laws. What then results cannot be a cause outside of it, but only a consequence in it. If with the existence of reason everything that truly should be is already logically necessarily posited – and this is the requirement – then there is no need for a Creator outside of it, and according to the same laws of logical necessity, there cannot even be one. If one were to postulate Him, thereby making the concept of Him real – erroneously, because what it requires of existence must also be there even without a Creator, as necessary as logic itself – then the Creator Himself could only be a creature of reason, which is the higher Creator, as can be seen from the Kantian proofs of God.

It therefore comes as no surprise that the logical systems lead to atheism. Rationalism does not first end there, it has already begun there. It immediately *denies* by its own method, *prior to any investigation*, the question the *affirmation* of which it is in the practical interest of all philosophy, even rationalism, to *attain certainty about.*

Admittedly the abstract method largely lingers midway, unconscious of its basic requirement and its inevitable outcome, contenting itself with eliminating details the logical needlessness of which is evident.

Logical Pantheism – Spinoza and His View of Law

Spinoza is the example to which all later efforts of this sort refer as the most solid model, even when they are battling amongst themselves. That does not come because of his exceptional intelligence alone, but also from the special nature of his scientific work. All the later philosophers implement specifically rationalistic systems, but *Spinoza did nothing less than set up the canon of rationalism itself.* Thus, with him it is the magnificence of the enterprise, without the pettiness and inconvenience which in the execution (for example, by Fichte and Hegel) it inevitably gets caught up in. And he, like everyone devoted to him, can find no doubts and no difficulty against his view, because he does not try to put it to the test. He assumes that the only thing in the world is rational coherence. And he does not show how specific objects really follow from reason, but only what kind of coherence with it and with each other they must have according to that assumption. What he says about this cannot be refuted, because, as people are wont to repeat after him, it is true. One simply has to deny the assumption itself, the rational coherence of the world.

The essential content of his teaching therefore consists merely in the character traits of rationalism, which we give here as the generalities of every logical system:

The absolute (*causa sui*) can only be something the existence of which follows from its concept (i.e., the non-existence of which would be logically contradictory), and this is Being itself (substance): this is God. There can only be one, which is simple (because the original idea of thought is necessarily empty, undifferentiated, therefore simple and indivisible). Every cause must lead inevitably to its effect, which is to say, there is no cause and effect, but everything stands in the correlation of ground and consequent. All specific things are only necessary consequences (modalities [Affektionen]) of pure Being (God). He is in them like the essence of the stone (*lapideitas*) is in individual stones. He has no mind and will; He had no freedom to create the world or not to create it; rather, He contains the world, according to necessary laws. There is no freedom at all, as little for God as for men. We consider our actions to be free because we do not know their causes. For what exists, and therefore every individual action, is only a consequence of general necessity, is already given with the substance itself, therefore inevitable, etc.

Ethics in the true sense cannot be expected of Spinoza, for the essence of objective rationalism excludes the freedom of the actor. The universal law [Weltgesetz] is everything; no action takes place that did not follow logically from it (from God). Anything which happens there, therefore cannot help but be lawful, good, and right. Injustice would only be that which did not follow from this necessity, but precisely for this reason is also not possible – "what no one wants and no one is capable of." Human beings can act against religion (the revealed), but not against the eternal law of God. There is therefore no injustice, no sin. What we call such refers only to the consequence that an action has for us, for the well-being of people, not to its intrinsic character.

The objection that there is evil in the world is thereby obviated, in that it is denied and the notion of it is declared to be a sham. Spinoza's entire view of law is only the implementation of this idea. People need to enter into the state, bear its dominion, in order to gain security; because nature drives them to choose the lesser of two evils. If they did not enter into the state, then nature has effected this as well and they do no injustice thereby. By unifying, the government gains power, and therefore right, over all. It may order what it wishes, because it can do so; citizens must obey because they are unable to resist. The government must ensure the public good, because this consideration is a lesser evil than imminent rebellion and thereby doom. But if it does not wish to, it does so at its peril, it does no injustice because nature has given it the power not to. Citizens may not transfer their rights fully and unconditionally to the government; that is, it is physically impossible to give up their (natural) power completely and forever. If they could, the government would no longer be obliged to govern well, namely, it would no longer have the mechanical drive to that end.[55]

Seemingly, and in terms of a literal reading, Spinoza's view of law has the same basis as Aristotle's – nature – the power of generating everything by necessity. But a closer examination shows most clearly the difference between the empirical and the abstract method. Aristotle recognizes a nature with characteristic laws and purposes which his thought does not possess, but which he learns from observation. Spinoza's nature at bottom is nothing other than the abstraction of a logical necessity. Aristotle always derives new data for his knowledge from the world around him; he finds an existence of an entirely

[55] See the entirety of Spinoza's *Ethics* and *Theological-Political Treatise.*

different sort in conscious than in unconscious nature, and accommodates his knowledge to this, here establishing freedom and a true ethic. Spinoza, closed to any experience, to everything newly adventitious, holds firmly to his initial assumption, and conversely forms the objects according to the shape of his knowledge, and denies freedom and ethics. For Aristotle the equitable is what free being does, in correspondence with nature. For Spinoza it is what nature itself does, and that's it.

Standpoint of Natural Law

So the peculiarity of objective rationalism is that, carried out logically, it allows for no ethics. All actions that can occur are given with the initial adoption of general substance by ineluctable necessity. Even the question regarding justice must cease, because it would foresee an independence and a condition of being severed from this general necessity. But the logical interest which is satisfied thereby is only derivative. What is original desires causality, not on the part of the laws of thought, but of the living person, which calls for a doctrine of obligation that recognizes his power and freedom, which makes his personality the center while allowing the realization of logical deduction to depend in the first place upon him.

Such is the natural law as it has progressed from Grotius up to most recent times. Natural law thus owes its existence and formation to subjective rational philosophy. Because it emanates not only from reason but also from the existence of the thinker, this philosophy is at once aware of the freedom to exercise in action what is demanded or not by thought; it therefore derives from reason only the prescriptions, while leaving actions to be effected by the free person. So the prerequisite of ethics is not lacking. For this it eschews the postulate that everything is just reason, since free actions, which it admits, may just as well be *counter* to reason.

This is what distinguishes natural law from the legal view of Spinoza; it is the difference between subjective and objective rationalism in general. The basis and the characteristics of natural law are already given with the generic characterization of abstract philosophy, and only need to be substantiated in the particular subject matter. For in no other scientific orientation can the treatment proceed so evenly as in this one, the essence of which is precisely to regard what is newly created not as something newly generated from the appertaining life principle, but as given with the universal, in terms of its concept. Natural law takes on a different shape when it manifests itself as an integral part of a universal (subjective-rationalist) system, with Kant and Fichte, or when it is formed from a doctrine as independent as it is isolated, such as from Grotius up until recent times, whether because its cultivator did not practice philosophy as a whole, or because his philosophy consisted of individual fields without connection. In the latter it is more dominated by the characteristic of the object, in the former more by the specific, often random results of theoretical philosophy regarding this object. It will thus be altogether appropriate to illustrate the development of natural law first according to its general motives in the thread of the subject matter, and then according to its peculiar shape in the individual systems in the thread of the preeminent practitioners.

PART II: GENESIS OF NATURAL LAW IN GENERAL

Chapter 1: Ethics (Natural Law in the Earlier Sense)

The question: How can I tell what is just and what is unjust? presupposes the higher question: how is it that there is just and unjust, what causes these differences, what is the source of all ought? The answer to the latter question is therefore the decisive one for any sort of ethics. The philosophy that only recognizes what follows from reason cannot very well look elsewhere for this source of the ethic than in reason. In this consists natural law.[56]

---

[56] For the development of abstract philosophy in general, and therefore for this entire approach, it is of the utmost importance that reason be held in the truly intended sense of pure thought, rather than to presume any specific content (e.g., a design [Absicht] or attribute of God supplied up-front), which of course solves many problems, but also abandons the basic requirement, which is to accept nothing without logical necessity. Now the threat of such tacit assumption is greatest in ethics. For a long-standing custom that is hardly ever doubted, by which existing mores [Moral] are derived from reason, has lent to this term the signification of morality itself, a word which everyone understands immediately; this might lead one to wonder whether our derivation of obligation from reason is well-founded, since reason is understood to be equivalent to morality. This is further supported by the current confusion of language in philosophy and the usage adopted by many since Jacobi, whereby reason is understood to be the immediate perception of everything divine, holy, good, just, thus precisely the opposite of discursive reasoning [vermittelnden Denken].

The principle upon which natural law and the entirety of rational philosophy is based, is pure thought. It does not wish to proceed from mores and justice, but rather to derive them from itself. Further, it is static, merely existing thought: the epitome of the pure determinations and laws is what it *is,* not what it by its activity produces.

What is proper to the rationalistic treatment can be explained from this, and apart from it, could not arise. Reason in those other meanings would lead to a legal philosophy of an entirely different character. Even the teachers of early natural law stated that by reason they understand thinking, e.g. Pufendorf, *De Jure Naturæ et Gentium,* Book 1, ch. 1, §. 2 [English translation: *Of the Law of Nature and Nations*]; Thomasius, *Institutiones Iurisprudentiae Divinae* [English translation: *Institutes of Divine Jurisprudence*], Book I, ch. 1, §. 38, who refers to a statement of Descartes: *homo dum intelligit, cogitat,*

The Conception of the Origin of the Ethic

The Platonic idea of the good, by which what corresponds with it is good and what conflicts with it is evil, is a source of the ethic outside of reason. It has an original independent existence. And Plato could not even raise the question, why exactly is it that the good is good, and that it should exist? The newer ethic, on the other hand, is based on this question. What does "ought" mean; is it something good or bad? I can deny all of that, even abolish these conceptions, and still exist and think without contradiction. I will only consider the "ought," the "good and evil," to be something if, apart from them, my thinking itself would cease to exist. The good must therefore be logically deduced and must be defined, that is, it must be composed from pure thought-determinations, able to be decomposed into them again. With Kant, for example, it is only the form of all thought itself (necessity and universality); with Hegel likewise, a product which the empty *thought-determination* of being brings about with the *law of thought* (dialectic), *apart from any other component.*

History of the Conception of the Origin of the Ethic

Prior to philosophizing, the Christian world recognized a cause of the ethic independent of reason in the will of God and in the content thereof, divine holiness, which is of specific determinacy, positive, not susceptible to and without need of any further (logical) deduction. To remove this cause was therefore the precondition, the first step that natural law had to take to clear space for itself. The beginnings of this were already given in the philosophy of the Middle Ages: in the *lex aeterna*, which the scholastics set in holy nature over God, which was

---

dum vult cogitat, dum sentit cogitate [Man thinks while understanding, while willing, while feeling]. And though subsequently even important men, such as Leibniz, quite often attribute moral laws which are independent of thought, to thought, as contained in the *ratio;* though they occasionally understand active examination and not logical elaboration as *ratio;* this is merely a lack of consistently clear awareness in their work. Since Kant, who emphasized precisely this clear awareness, there is no longer any such wavering among rigorous philosophers; but non-philosophical writers are now taking all the meanings of reason and combining them into *one* meaning, to turn that into a principle, namely reasoning from reasons [Raisonnement aus Gründen], as did the late lamented Wolffian school.

in Him prior to any resolutions, from which they believed they needed to derive the ethic (*convenientia cum sanctitate divina antecedenter ad voluntatem divinam*). This abolished freedom of decision and determination in God, and it was now requisite to explain reason as that which by necessity is determinative of Him and the world. This took place by asserting that the differences of right and wrong would stand according to reason, even if there were no God. Because in that case God could not possibly be the cause of them, neither His *sanctitas* nor His *voluntas* – otherwise without Him the consequences would lapse as well – this cause could only be reason. Leibniz took this assertion, which was adopted by the founder of natural law, Grotius,[57] (although he by no means was its author), under his wing against adversaries, and emphatically asserted: as the laws of geometry would have to be found necessary even if one denied God, so also the laws of justice. And the differing requirements which, according to the Bible (which Leibniz acknowledged), God issued at various times, form no hindrance to this, because these exemptions are no less necessary consequences of reason than the rule;[58] God Himself is praised because He is righteous, and acts *ut omni satisfaciat sapienti* [to satisfy every wise person].[59]

Wolff[60] posits the law the source of which is the will of God, as positive, over against the *lex naturalis,* which has a *ratio sufficiens* in the nature of man, a classification that can still be found in most textbooks of standing law. As can be seen, it is not the intention here that, as was indicated, good and evil exist by themselves (*perseitas honestatis et turpitudinis*); but that good and evil are such by the laws of thought. This view was indeed contradicted by prominent natural law teachers. Following Pufendorf, there is no good and evil without the *impositio* of a suzerain, and this is God; man did not even have the *socialis* and *rationalis natura* in a manner *ex immutabili quadam necessitate* but rather *ex beneplacito Divino.*[61] Thomasius protested against the distinctions of the

---

[57] Prolegomena, *De Jure Belli et Pacis*, §. 11.

[58] *Observationes de Principio Juris,* c. 13.

[59] *Monita quaedam ad Samuelis Pufendorfi principia*, in Dutens, *Opera Omnia,* vol. IV, part III, p. 275ff.

[60] *Institutiones Iuris Naturae et Gentium*, Part I, ch. 2, §. 39.

[61] *De Jure Naturae et Gentium,* Book I, ch. 2, §. 6; *De Officio Hominis & Civis Juxta*

scholastics[62] – comparing their *lex aeterna* to the matter of pagan philosophers – and also against this assertion of Grotius,[63] and declared that while his principle of reason should be the standard (*principium* ***cognoscendi***), it should by no means be the cause of the ethic (*principium* ***obligationis***).[64]

But all of this was only words, without application and consequence. The treatment proceeds in such a manner as if everywhere the opposite view were accepted. And this could not be otherwise, if reason is to be the standard of the just, regarding which no doubt prevails amongst the collective caretakers of this doctrine. Because now, what is just is what reason itself contains, not what a cause external to reason requires, a cause the effect of which reason views as if such were independent of it. Reason, then, is not merely the eye, but itself light and color. What reason is, could not suffice to find the differences between right and wrong if there were anything else outside it which caused the differences. The assertion, then, that God is the cause of the ethic is therefore annulled by the other assertion, that reason is the (positive) standard thereof. Certainly an association could lie in God having given us reason, and that therefore He wills what follows from it.[65] But in that case, did God only create the pure determinations of thought and the concept of our nature, stripped of any specific life, and not our specific ethical determination? Should what unfolds in history, which He in fact likewise directs, not similarly be acknowledged? And how can we arbitrarily attribute to Him the wish to have the drive for morality produce its requirements in the same way that logic produces its results, given that the former is given to produce deeds, the latter simply to take up and grasp objects of thought [Gegenstände]?

Legem Naturalem Libri Duo [English translation: *Of the Whole Duty of Many and Citizen*], Book 1, ch. 2, §. 2.

[62] *Institutiones Iurisprudentiae Divinae,* book I, ch. 1, §. 31; "Dissertatio Prooemialis" [Introductory Dissertation] in *ibid.*, §. 39.

[63] *Programma* [apparently the "Collegium Privatum über seines Institutiones Iurisprudentiae Divinae," in "Die Grund-Lehren des Natur- und Völker-rechts, nach dem sinnlichen Begriff aller Menschen vorgestellet...," pp. 57ff].

[64] *Fundamenta juris naturae et gentium ex sensu communi deducta* [English translation: *Foundations of the Law of Nature and Nations*], Book I, ch. 6.

[65] E.g., Wolff, *Institutiones Iuris Naturae et Gentium,* Part I, ch. 2. §. 43.

Hence, it is not merely individual statements by which Pufendorf, Thomasius, and those professing to follow them, come into conflict with themselves. Just so does Pufendorf require that every suzerain, from whom all obligations proceed, not only have the power but also *justus causas et rationes.*[66] The *impositio* as the final cause of obligation thus itself has a higher cause of obligation over it, rational laws, a contradiction already criticized by Leibniz. So Thomasius praises the benefits of natural law in order to have a law common with pagans and atheists.[67] Therefore, for him, *ratio* also has force *etsi daretur Deum non esse* [even if it is given that God does not exist].

But this is not all; their systems in their entirety are driven by the rationalist principle. In practice they everywhere bind the will of God, which they make into the cause of the ethic, by reason. He shall not be subject to the *lex aeterna* and His own *sanctitas;* but it is prescribed to Him that what follows from the drive to sociability etc., and that alone, is what He shall will, while He shall not will other things outside this. Therefore, with them as well as with their opponents, He plays no other role than a *Deus ex machina.* To wit, He has to undertake everything that reason can no longer achieve. He must invest moral duty with its real power over people,[68] secure entitlement,[69] and be the cause of such obligations for which one can provide no *ratio,* for example, the prohibition of incest. With such an approach, controversy is entirely in vain; though initially the subject of the most careful debate, during the course of that debate it also became increasingly lackluster, since God increasingly disappeared,[70] until finally Kant expressly declared reason to be the *cause* of the ethic. Since Kant, the relation of God to duty is no longer discussed, and it may well be surprising to see this controversy once again stirred up here as something of importance.

Thus, from the start of abstract philosophy, the opposite mode of conception is everywhere connected with it. But already here, the effectuating element in scientific treatment is reason alone. It only need be expressed unequivocally

---

[66] *De Officio Hominis et Civis* [English translation: *The Whole Duty of Man according to the Law of Nature*], Book I, ch. 2, §. 5.

[67] "Dissertatio Prooemialis," at the end.

[68] Wolff, *op. cit.,* Part I, ch. 2. §. 41.

[69] Thomasius, *Institutiones Iurisprudentiae Divinae,* Book I, ch. 1, §. 84.

[70] Compare Gundling, Darjes, Nettelbladt, Höpfner, with earlier generations.

to banish entirely even the appearance of that conflicting element.

Basic Concepts

Reason, from which the ethic is to follow, now requires a basic concept from which it is inferred, which, as goes without saying, must still remain after all abstraction is accomplished. According to the subjective-rationalistic standpoint of natural law, this concept is the existence of the thinker, human nature. In reality, this nature is always something specific, determined by individuality, environment, fate, time, matter, in short, by history. But in such determinacy, it possesses no logical necessity. The only characteristics which are inseparable from the concept of man are sensibility and thought. A man without moral feeling, even if he has never yet existed, is at least still conceivable; but a man without physical existence or without the capacity for thinking would be a logical contradiction.

The *sensorial-rational* (i.e., thinking) nature of man is therefore the basic concept of abstract ethics. It is actually premised by all natural law doctors. But initially one did not know how to make any direct use of it, and was forced to found the system on some drive of the human being, for example, the drive to sociability, which one hoped would suffice for the inference. The premised concept of thinking nature was only used to justify the rational *inference* from the drive as law. What is of note here is that every system of natural law is built exclusively on such a drive, and no attempt is made to derive such a system from *all* of the drives of human nature. This has to do with the abstract treatment. In our nature, the manifold instincts and feelings are actually connected; but they have no logical unity, no concept that is common to all and yet individual to each. But rationalism urges just such a simple principle. It contradicts living fullness as principle, but no less what is merely aggregated. Syncretistic treatment does not show up as long as there is vitality; such comes along only at the time of exhaustion, when the original confidence to achieve simplicity has abated. To take an isolated drive as ground, therefore, lay of necessity in the character of the natural law; what was arbitrary was the choice of one or the other.

Therefore all possible exchanges were made between sociability, fear, happiness, perfection, etc.; the whole gamut of human drives was run through, and the natural law schools succeeded each other following this thread. The development knew no rest until at length Kant secured that basic concept and summed it up in its complete abstraction: thinking nature as mere consistency; the sensorial as the restriction of that pure consistency contained in any of its expressions. From this point, the concept of a being that thinks, but is limited by sensoriness (finite) remains as principle. Only this has a logical necessitation, it is the last remnant that is left standing after abstracting from the existence of man.[71] And from the concept of thinking nature, it is also only by pure reason– as required – that it is possible to deduce. Any other drive than that of logical consistency itself, for example happiness, acts externally and is energized externally. In order to say what it requires, both the consequence of action in the world and the repercussions of the external object on one's own condition must be observed.

This provides the concept from which nothing more can be abstracted (the necessary beginning) and from which now the entirety of ethics must ensue, merely from logical reasoning; as Wolff previously expressed it: *Principium ex quo continuo ratiocinationis filo deducuntur omnia* [The principle from which, by the continuous thread of reasoning, everything is deduced].

History of the Basic Concept

In the series of ethical systems, Hobbes is customarily highlighted as opposing rather than promoting the development of natural law. But this is certainly unjust. He is in no way any different from the others, since he simply elevates one drive from human nature, just as they do; only he elevates the drive of fear rather than some other drive, and from this he deduces his results, to which he certainly has the same right. It follows from the conception of a fearing being that protection is sought for life and limbs – *pax quaerenda* [peace-seeking]. It does not follow from it that agreements are kept outside of the state; for when

---

[71] Hoffbauer (*Untersuchungen über die wichtigsten Gegenstände des Naturrechts* [Studies regarding the main objects of natural law]), prompted by Kant, thought that he had to go farther. The *abstractum* of man is still too concrete for him, and so he arrives at the concept of a rational being, which is not like this, and therefore is not exactly human. The original and acquired rights that are derived from this concept of the rational being thus form the pure natural law, those derived from the concept of man, the applied natural law.

such agreements are kept, they provide security which at the same time harms someone else. Therefore, for Hobbes the state of nature is without rights, and one takes offense at this. But it follows from the drive of fear that a civil condition be established in which the supreme rule must be *pacta servanda* [agreements are kept].

For this reason Gros unjustly accuses Hobbes of confusing what people do with what they ought to do. This is because to Hobbes, this utter arbitrariness [of what they do] is really nothing more than the minor premise; prior to this he has the major premise, what they *ought* to do: "protect themselves" – as elsewhere: "please themselves" – from which the state follows as conclusion. Equally unfounded is Thomasius' objection that the *pacta* presuppose a law. This law is just dictated by human nature as fear. Even Hobbes is not empirical. If he was, he would have made the multiplicity of drives in human nature, which experience demonstrates, into the principle. Because he is not empirical but abstract, and only for that reason chooses the one of fear only, and has everything proceed from it as reason would have it, *necessitate quadam non minore, quam qua fertur lapis deorsum* [a kind of necessity, not less than what is said of a stone falling]. So in every respect he belongs to the development of natural law. He stands or falls on its foundations and is far from opposing it; his approach is only a variation on the theme, consistent with the others in principles, requirements, and procedures, and is only distinguished from them by an entirely incidental assumption.

Abstraction from Relations

Turning now to individual ethical requirements as conscience makes them known to everyone: the diversity thereof is linked to the diversity of circumstances in which we function. In industry, we feel obligated to be diligent, in trade to be honest, in social interaction to be benevolent; one particular course of action is required for the family, another one for the state. So it would be natural to seek the reason for the difference in these circumstances. To this end, it would not suffice for these to be regarded merely as different material, but as a different source. Each must be conceded a peculiar moral objective that has its origin in itself; but then the unity of these various objectives would have to be sought outside man.

And so rational philosophy immediately annihilates these relationships, in order to recognize them again only if they contain its fundamental concept of ethics. This abstraction stands in relation to the condition of the *state of nature*. Such has been constructed in different ways, as a historical fact, as a presumption, a fiction, finally, arriving at self-understanding, as a scientifically necessary abstraction. In all these ways, the drive to its adoption is the same: since I can imagine myself without the state, such is therefore not *a priori* required by reason; I must now assume that the state was not in existence, in order to see whether my concept as a thinking being leads me to it. In the same way, one can oppose the state of nature to the condition of the family or of social interaction (mutual contact), and this has been done, even if not expressly. If, for example, with regard to the question of breaking up landed estates, the necessity and the objective of agriculture is not the deciding factor, since the freedom of the individual should decide everything, this presupposes that it is not the actual relations of agriculture but the prescinding thereof, the state of nature, that is taken as starting point.

Consequences of this Abstraction

Since the actual existence of these conditions is abandoned, their actual requirements are as well, and they can only apply, and apply to that degree, if this deduction yields them. Thus, the configurations of the ethical world no longer impose laws on persons; instead, they receive these first from the concept of persons' existence, and therefore *of necessity are entirely different* than what the nature of these configurations requires.

To wit, when man conceives himself to be released from any connection and still recognizes a rule over himself, this rule can only be enacted for him as an isolated case – he is its exclusive subject. Only what he is capable of, only what still makes sense when one looks at his action and fulfillment in isolation, is his goal. And it is satisfied when he fulfills it, when he attaches no blame for it to himself. A general condition the achievement of which also depends on the participation of others, cannot be demanded of him, and thus cannot be the object of the rule. Thus, for example it can only command: "Thou shalt be prepared for the state!" not: "The state shall exist!" Otherwise he would not be summoned as an individual but as part of a totality. So while the Greek ethic is directed to ordering the world, and is to be established to satisfy this without considering how people's actions are constituted, here the quality of these actions is what is requisite. The result, and what is constructed by the same in the world, is only adventitious, and is not the originally willed.

Nearly all of the earlier systems of natural law begin with the concepts of action, its kinds, its attribution, etc. Hence with the Greeks, the duty of the citizen is discovered from the ethic of the state; but with the modern versions, the duty of the state is imagined from the duty of man apart from the state. This has supreme influence on the content of the ethic. Because with the former, requirements must arise for man which could never be made for him if one thinks of him individually. With the latter, however, the state itself is robbed of its peculiar duties because the individual cannot or may not meet them. The meaning of punishment, for example, cannot be retribution; because which persons are entitled to administer justice? That it therefore likewise does not accrue to the state, is then self-evident.[72] The existence of social ranks [Ständen] must be abandoned as an ethical requirement ahead of any investigation, because it is not a matter of my action. If every rank, exclusively pursuing its orientation, excels in doing so, but only while accompanied by extreme one-sidedness – brave but brutish warriors, pious but shiftless priests, highly educated but effeminate scholars – then this view would rightly deprecate the imperfection of the individuals, but it would not notice the admirability of what they provide in the way of wealth and power to the entirety. This is because *the content of this entire ethic consists merely in commands over the isolated actions of individuals.*

Content of the Ethic

What actions these might be, should indeed, according to the requirement, arise from the basic concepts. But since, as will be demonstrated in the issue, such abstraction never leads to positive results, the interest of the school as a whole gets immediately involved. Accordingly, the goal of bidden actions is simply man. Either rationally to pursue one's own satisfaction – as Hobbes, Thomasius – or, since virtue does entail a certain sacrifice [Hingeben], to pursue the satisfaction of others, their welfare, their freedom, etc. Apart from the beings who resemble him, his abstracting reason and its interest offer him no object. Unity, the development of the strength of the state, the symmetry and

[72] E.g., Fichte, *Grundlage des Naturrechts nach Prinzipien der Wissenschaftslehre* [translation: *Foundations of Natural Right*], Part II, p. 129.

beauty of life, faith, devotion, honor recede into the background or disappear entirely. They do not provide well-being to the individual. Kant consequently removed the duties towards God from ethics, which the ancients and many of the moderns held to. Hence, the duties towards Him (who, in terms of His concept, is the absolute cause of all being and duty) obtain their sanction through a second absolute, the nature of man, and take their place alongside other duties, even though the duties to God – assuming they exist – are the only thing which make these other into duties. This is tantamount to a Kantian wishing to range duties to the moral imperative alongside the duties to neighbor, parents, children, and spouse.

Now after abstracting or prescinding, reason finds a goal outside human existence, which is itself, the form of thinking. To satisfy this in action is its own fulfillment. Such is conceived partly as a second task in addition to the satisfaction of others, partly as the epitome and ground of all other tasks. But its concept is none other than the uniformity of action according to principles, regularity, immutability, unaffectedness by changing emotions.

This negative virtue of never contradicting itself is found in Spinoza's view of the rule of the soul over the emotions, in the *pax interna* of Thomasius, which consists in discouraging the passions, and at its most conscious, finally, with Kant in the supreme rule of ethics: act according to a law which is a universal law, one through which a contradiction with itself can never arise.

Chapter 2: Division into Moral and Natural Law

Factual Division of Duties

Now reality shows two kinds of ethical [sittlicher] prescriptions, their obvious difference being that, with the one, compliance is compelled by the state, while with the other, compliance is left to the individual; and in accord with this, the latter focuses on disposition, the former on the act. Science has to demonstrate the basis for this difference.

Scientific Division of Duties by the Greeks...

The Greeks found this difference in the subject of the ethic, whether it is directed to people individually or to the state as a whole. It aims for the same everywhere and in the same way. But the requirements it puts on the state, when the state fulfills them, are thereby in themselves automatically compulsory for the individual. The state, which has the obligation, is therefore not compelled, and the individual who is compelled, does not automatically and directly have the obligation, and his disposition is irrelevant.

To the Greeks it is not at all strange that man is limited in his actions so that the world can reach its perfect form. There is thus no necessity here for a distinction in the ethic itself. Plato distinguishes between the just man and the just state. Aristotle distinguishes between ethics and politics; apart from the state (πολιτικὸν δίκαιον) there is only *one* justice (ἁπλῶς δίκαιον). In general, the Greeks do not seem to consider the question as to how the ethic relates to the individual, whether in compulsory fashion or not, to be of great significance.

... and by the Moderns; Thomasius, Kant, Feuerbach

In modern philosophy, however, precisely this must be the cardinal question: how does the law affect me, does it merely exact, or does it compel me? Now then, the newer philosophy does not even recognize duties originally placed on the state; how much less, then, a restriction on the individual stemming from the state? A sufficient ground to coerce the individual must be given with man himself, even apart from the state (in the state of nature). By one basic rule, therefore, and for one and the same subject, the necessity of the variety of commands, enforceable and unenforceable, external and internal, must be demonstrated. This can only be done if an original division of the same is identified, two different objectives of the ethic, each of which by its concept demands compulsion for the one, excludes it for the other – juridical law and morality.

The subjective principle of the new philosophy was constrained to find this difference. Although the task remains to purify this discovery from the dross of abstract treatment, still it is a great step forward. For the Greek conception can explain neither the dependence of compulsion on the will of individuals (law in the subjective sense), nor the dissimilarity of law to other public objectives.

To Leibniz is owed the honor of having predicted the shape of the newer ethics – its division into morality and law. The execution, however, was carried out by Thomasius. The sociabilistic[73] system, even in its development by Pufendorf, knows only these two ethical sciences without subdivision: the positive, i.e., theology, and the philosophical, i.e., natural law. Pufendorf also has them correspond to the distinction between the *forum internum* and *externum*, so that all inward, or as we now say, moral, obligations are referred to theology, while the outward are left to philosophy, i.e., natural law. But this does not keep him, in the title *de promiscuis officiis humanitatis* [of the common duties of humanity] from treating alongside each other the rules of international law, *de accessu ad litus alienum* [of access to foreign shores], *de foro praebendo* [of granting a market], and the duties of charity and gratitude.

By contrast, Leibniz, in his letters discussing Pufendorfian natural law, claims the internal forum also for philosophy. He concedes that the inward duties are not appropriate to natural law proper; but neither may they be left to theology; they have to be discovered from the *ratio*. Therefore he sets up, separate from natural law and (positive) theology, a rational doctrine of inward duties, i.e., a *moral philosophy*.

It was left to Thomasius, this man who, even though devoid of ideas (as is the entire orientation), nevertheless through the freshness and bluntness of his mind, contrasting as much with the earlier scholastically crimped treatment, which he combatted from the outset, as with the dullness of Wolff and his successors, put into effect what Leibniz surmised. His first writings were indeed

---

[73] [German *sozialistische,* i.e., the system, initiated by Grotius, that derived law and society from man as a creature of a sociable nature, seeking social life.]

occupied with implementing the sociabilistic system in the received manner, nor is the title *de promiscuis officiis humanitatis* absent there. But the arbitrariness with which the *forum externum* and *internum* are intermingled with the sociabilistic thinkers, caused him to seek a principle of ethics enabling him to give a peculiar basis to each of the two classes of obligations, so that their different characters could be derived from reason, with evidence, as he says, that must be clear even to the most narrow-minded (*stulto*).

For this reason he jettisons the sociabilistic system, the principle of which, the drive for sociability, could not accommodate such a separation, and substitutes for it the drive for happiness. From this follows that double law: to seek outward and inward peace. This distinction corresponds to law and morality – the negative duty not to violate the other, and the positive one, to do to him what he himself wishes for – *forum externum* and *forum internum* – enforceability and unenforceability of duty. Thomasius is therefore the first to provide a foundation for the classification of perfect and imperfect duties, which was already found in Grotius; he first truly distinguishes the obligations according to the criterion of enforceability, in the *regulas justi* and the *regulas honesti, decori, officia humanitatis*.[74] The first book of his later work, *Fundamenta Juris Naturae*, is occupied with the discussion of his new principle; the subsequent ones, which maintain the arrangement of his first work, the *Institutiones Jurisprudentiae Divinae*, are merely intended to specify the later deviations from it. These deviations consist nearly entirely in separating out all the obligations which exist for the sake of inward rather than outward peace – which he earlier, following the sociabilists, had treated together with those and largely characterized them as enforceable – and characterizing them as unenforceable, for example, the paternal power.

The Wolffian school did not progress any farther in this.

The system of Thomasius achieved the mutual correspondence between the material character of inward and outward peace, positive and negative duty, and the formal one of compulsion and non-compulsion, albeit not in such a way that the formal manifests itself as a necessary consequence of the material, which is what is demanded. Namely, no ground is given as to why the

---

[74] *Fundamenta Juris Naturae,* Book II, ch. 6, §. 4 [p. 217]. This was attributed to his students, unjustly so.

commandments which have inward peace as their object rule out enforceability, while those with the object of outward peace demand it. Whether they should be fulfilled or not could be left to free will either for both types or for neither.

In order to be able to provide this ground, and thus to be able to deduce the different effects of morality and law as necessary from their different natures, inward and outward *freedom* had to be substituted for inward and outward peace. This was Kant's accomplishment. In terms of its content, inward freedom excludes constraint. The laws which merely have this as their purpose – which do not directly resolve upon specific acts – contradict themselves when they compel. The laws that have outward freedom as their objective, however, must compel, because outward freedom cannot result from accidental fulfillment and non-infringement, as can, for example, well-being, because freedom ceases where the result depends upon others, even if this result actually comes about. For example, if someone gives me my thing, but he was not compelled to give it to me, then even though I did receive the thing, my freedom over the thing did not and does not exist.

In this manner, morality contains the laws for the purpose of inward freedom, while natural law contains those for the purpose of outward freedom. Although the difference existing in life between enforceable and non-enforceable obligations only prompts the quest for a principle by which this difference can be justified logically, and only guides that quest, so conversely, what exists now gets assessed by this principle. The separation in life must now be just such a one as can be deduced from life. Therefore, from this point on it is held to be decided, as a requirement of reason, that *only those laws which have outward freedom as their purpose, shall be enforceable.*

The Problem of Deducing Law in the Subjective Sense

This development could have concluded here if not for the fact that the characteristic concept of the legal sphere, to which outward freedom likewise automatically leads, remained unaffected – *law in the subjective sense.* Just as the compulsion which juridical law of necessity requires must accord with the peculiarity of its object – freedom – so also does this compulsion depend on the discretion of that freedom, the freedom for which the law exists. Because even if I securely obtain the object of my freedom, if my obtaining it or not does not depend on me, then I am not free. The compulsion by which I obtain what is mine, must absolutely be the result of my will, if my freedom is to be attained. The ethic wills this freedom. And the decisive thing here is: not only does it have this freedom as its objective, in favor of which it requires others to act, but it imparts it directly. He for whom it is established has the awareness that freedom does not first have to be produced for him, but that he already has it and may make use of it. It is not like, say, the good, something which, although required by the ethic, yet only arises in fact and exists in fact, but it is an effect of the ethic and is itself ethical.

Since the Romans, this immediate sanction of freedom can be found decisively in human life and consciousness, especially in the Germanic. It is a fact; science could not remove it and not deny it, it had to assimilate it. But it also generated a new distinction between morality and law. What is moral merely effects a requirement and only has a consequence for those subject to this requirement. The person for whom something results from the fulfillment of its command, e.g., whose good is to be effected, has no connection to *the command itself*. His relation, which Grotius calls *aptitudo*, is therefore without any ethical significance, and the concept of *aptitudo* was also soon lost to ethics. But juridical law not only imposes a requirement, it also imparts freedom; it has a double relation not only when it is fulfilled but by the very fact that it exists, the one to whom it is given, the other for whom it is given, to the obligated and to the entitled. Even coercion itself, because the duties of law are different from those of morality, materializes only as a result of that freedom, and as evidence of this, it is not directly applied by law, but only by the person entitled, if he so desires. In this manner, requirement, which law imposes just as morality does, recedes as secondary, while freedom, which law constitutes, emerges as primary – [subjective] right [das Recht]. For this reason, Feuerbach ended up expressing the difference between morality and natural law like this: *morality is the science of duties, natural law the science of rights.*[75]

The Two Problems Facing Natural Law

But this separation embroiled ethics in two contradictions, the solution of which is its problem. The first is that between the moral and juridical law, on the one hand, and what those laws entail by way of requirement, and on the

[75] *Kritik des natürlichen Rechts* [Critique of natural law].

other. The second is between the laws and competence.

Firstly: since reason posits outward freedom as its goal, it will inevitably come to the point that the same actions that it secures as law, it forbids as morality. According to juridical law, no one may stop someone who wishes to kill himself or to waste his substance, from doing so, even though the moral law demands that such acts not happen. For this reason, the Wolffian school restricts competence to morally licit actions. But morality permeates all action, and since idleness is against morality, we would lose the competence to be idle; by the same principle, given the existence of needy people, we would lose the competence to use property. Kant seeks to resolve the contradiction by having reason impart outward freedom as a means for its own ends, as a way for its commands to be freely met inwardly. A person would not contradict himself in such a case. Reason might lead one into temptation, to make the victory all the more glorious; it might not at first will what it actually ends up willing, out of consideration for the final end. But this relinquishing and restriction of self for future purposes, this free choice of tactic, is not the essence of a rational law. Outward freedom is by no means rationally necessary for inward freedom. Experience shows how much they interact, but in terms of their concept, they are independent of each other. When people are prevented from suicide, dissipation, idleness, by outward force, still their inward disposition can also be that they not waste, not commit suicide, not be idle. If this were not the case, reason would have to ensure not only against restriction by other people but also against restriction by nature. For example, it should make all people rich so that they can be frugal voluntarily, and also make them all poor so that not abundance but honesty deters them from stealing.

Indeed, the contradiction goes even further. As morality, reason demands that force be withheld; as law, the contrary, that force be applied. But because reason as morality extends itself to all actions, it comes about that reason needs to prescribe the same act in two ways, on the one hand having to do something (force), commit something, that on the other hand it cannot permit. The law obliges me to pay my creditors, so according to reason I must be compelled to do so. But now morality commands the same thing of me; it is then contrary to reason that I be compelled. Therefore, Kant made this distinction: morality also imparts to legal obligations their sanctions, although the content of those sanctions is given not by it, but by the law.[76] But that does not resolve the contradiction, for as morality also makes legal obligations its own, it is compelled to require the uncoerced decision for these as well.

That is why, in the later period of natural law, the ambition is everywhere expressed to provide an independent principle to rights [dem Rechte] completely divorced from morality. This, it was believed, would remedy the contradiction. But it is not sufficient to separate law and compulsion from morality; rather, they must be separated from ethics altogether. This was accomplished by Fichte, and he was aware of finally having satisfied a long-recognized requirement.

Secondly: rights [Recht] and juridical law are contradictory in terms of their concept. The question here is not why a juridical law exists, a law that forces me to protect another's freedom, even when opposed to moral purposes; rather, given its existence, how a competence can be derived from it. Because right, the freedom to do or not to do, cannot possibly follow from a law that only contains what is necessary. Trying to combine these two concepts is the locomotive engine in the history of the fundamental concepts of natural law.

Development until Fichte and Feuerbach

The earliest practitioners did not yet feel the need for such a combination. With them there is a sudden break from the deduction of law [des Gesetzes] and obligation, in order to treat of rights [Recht] as a *facultas moralis*, as a *potentia activa*, the cause of which is then only perfunctorily attributed to *natura, lex, consensus,* or *Deus*.

A serious endeavor to find a systematic relationship here soon emerged. Because it was conducted in terms of the abstract character, the viewpoint which held competence to be a new concept was resisted as long as possible. The next attempt therefore was to consider it as being another side of obligation, positing it immediately with obligation. "What I ought to do, that I also may do;" therefore in terms of its concept, every command already contains entitlement [Berechtigung]. Thus Wolff, Nettelbladt, et al. But that is not entitlement: for entitlement may be refrained from; furthermore, there are rights to things that

---

[76] *Metaphysische Anfangsgründe der Rechtslehre*, pp. xv–xvi [p. 21 in *The Metaphysics of Morals*].

one ought not to do.

Entitlement was now sought in the obligation of others rather than one's own: "if I am obligated to you, then you are enabled; my limitation is in itself an enlargement for you." Thus Heydenreich, Hoffbauer, et al. But it does not follow from the fact that I should allow myself to be compelled, that others may compel me. If I act unreasonably by not allowing myself to be compelled, it does not follow that others act reasonably by compelling me. The freedom of the entitled would thus factually exist if the obliged party actually fulfilled the command; but it would not have the ethical content which is intended by the concept of law, and its actual usage would even be irrational, because one may not at all limit the freedom of another.

Likewise the other characteristic of legal obligation, e.g., that its fulfillment is to be preferred before moral obligation, can be explained only if its essence is that an antecedent right requires it. But then one cannot turn around and derive a right [das Recht] from it. The deduction of a right from a duty, be it one's own, be it another's, had then to be abandoned. Now there remained no choice but to derive obligation directly from law. The concept of law, as it was posited, contains that of entitlement as well. But here one ran into the contradiction of the *lex permissiva*. A law [Gesetz] can only command and not permit, and so the specific content of the juridical law would cancel the general nature of the law [Gesetzes], which is absurd. Now of course, a law imparting freedom is indeed not at all contradictory if we are speaking of actual, functioning laws. Because it can never be said of any living cause, prior to experience, what it is capable of and what it is not; and experience shows that freedom arises according to laws. Thus, the natural law of procreation makes the son independent of the father, the law of the state sanctions the freedom of the citizen, and the command of the lord frees the slaves. But the law of reason cannot grant freedom; because the actions for which it should provide, it must contain, as consequence, in order to prescribe them. The generally perceived contradiction in the *lex permissiva* therefore by no means concerned this truth: no freedom can arise from a law, but rather this one: what should arise logically cannot arise as something possible, but only as something necessary.

Still, there was no turning back, and entitlement had to be found entirely in the concept of juridical law. Kant then resorted to the expedient that the law does not contain competence immediately but mediately: the law which commands or forbids some things but not all, thereby establishes an empty sphere, out of which action can be taken arbitrarily – this is competence. But this is only negative, not positive allowance; a non-prohibition is not yet a right. Freedom here, notwithstanding the obligation of compulsion of others, would follow only as something *de facto*, and the peculiarity of legal obligation would be left unexplained, just as it was with the attempt to derive a right from the duty of another. Thus the law must contain competence immediately as positive permission – lately even Feuerbach insisted on this – which on the other hand is not possible, since a positive permissive rational law is a contradiction.

Hence the final step of natural law had to be taken: the right of man [das Recht des Menschen] had to embody the condition of something original, from which even the juridical law arises. The progression, then, runs like this: first, it appeared to be the result of obligation – for it is in the nature of the ethic to will obligation originally; then as ground of obligation, but still a result of the law; and finally as ground of the law itself. But thereby it ceased to follow from reason, for it is itself the initial assumption; and it also no longer need acquiesce to the empire of law; natural law drops from ethics. This step was taken in this respect, as in the aforementioned, by Fichte, and is only an integrating member in the formation which all of philosophy gained through him. For this reason, both it and its consequences are to be considered there.

But we must now answer the question: why does natural law strive in vain to derive right from obligation or obligation from right; why can it not have both, at one stroke, follow from the juridical law? Then the character of perfect obligation would be explained from rights posited at the same time with obligation, and vice versa, positive entitlement explained from the simultaneously posited obligation of others. The only thing standing in the way of that conclusion is that such production is no longer logical. In a living body, certainly, something is at the same time cause and effect of another. But rational deduction can only find the one in the other; or both, not mutually conditioned, in higher concepts. The attempt to have right and obligation emerge at the same time, which by no means was lacking towards the end of this school of thought's career, is therefore merely syncretistic; they emerge alongside each other rather than becoming a whole by means of a living drive; and therefore, as Feuerbach already demonstrated,[77] this attempt cannot attain what was intended. Abstract ethics, as stated above, does not exact conditions, but only actions on the part of individuals. The law cannot speak into the world: let there be the state! because only isolated persons hear it. Nor can it say: thou shalt be secured in your freedom! because this is not an affair of its power. It can only say to the one: I do not forbid it! and to the other: you are to acquiesce in this! But what is said for the one has no existence for the other. Each must declare what refers to him, as a right or an obligation, to be his "own reason," which speaks to him but not to the other.[78] The non-prohibition of the one and the restriction of the other come as little into connection as do two people dreaming of each other. It is not a real power over them and not a real condition around them, which associates them. The law would only appear as a natural result of the law of reason if the latter read: thou shalt secure thy freedom, claim ownership! With this it really would impose a necessity. But the law does not read like that, and if it did, only obligations would exist, not rights.

Natural law, due to the character of its principle, necessarily encountered all of this difficulty. Reason cannot give rise to heterogenous things which freely restrict each other. Reason cannot generate a product independent of itself. Man, thinking in isolation, is encouraged only to isolated actions; no condition to which he pertains with others can make known to him regulation or sanction.

Therefore one cannot consider the difficulties and contradictions laid bare here to be superfluous subtlety. What is subtlety is above all the effort to get results through such reasoning, which adheres strictly to the characteristics of the *concept* alone, and does not acquiesce in, or take up, the living reality constituted from the *matter*. And in what consists abstract philosophy other than this endeavor? Its essence is subtlety, and to investigate what can be attained hereby is the only way it can be understood and appreciated. It would have won the day if the requirements that it generally lays down and busies itself to accomplish were not linked to its works, to which it was strictly referred. It would not have it any other way. Because everything that this subtlety necessitates, as we have shown, is actually recognized by the outstanding intellects of this school of

[77] *Op. cit.*, pp. 209ff.

[78] So declares Feuerbach most decisively, *ibid.*, pp. 147–148.

thought, and scientific progress has been arranged in terms of it. That which was claimed above, is here demonstrated: the historical progression itself forms the tribunal.

Chapter 3: Legal Doctrine (Natural Law in the Later Sense)

Logic can be called the heart of the newer philosophy, which emits its pulses and receives them back in itself; natural law is its countenance, in which its soul is reflected. For the freedom of man, the secret driving force in all its efforts, is here manifest as express principle.

Equality [Concept of Man versus Ideal of Man]

If freedom is inferred from the *concept* of man, then it must arise for everyone in equal measure. And if this freedom is the exclusive objective of all coercive laws, then there is nothing that could abolish that equality. Now then, an ethic that derives from the objective of relations leads to inequality of the law. If a rank [Stand] of honor, a representative of the divine majesty is to exist, then the latter must be permitted sanctity and inviolability, the former advantage of birth. The purpose of the family assigns a different legal position to the man than to the woman. The *ideal* of man, the highest quality of being for which he is intended, would *mandate* inequality of the law. The closer the approximation to it, the greater freedom and entitlement it would generate. The *concept* of man, however, is present in all men and in all circumstances. Therefore, complete equality before the law is the requirement of the law of reason; it is made by all the doctors of natural law, from the earliest to the latest. Consistently implemented, it prohibits advantages of birth, rights of majesty (at least those that are irrevocable), the taking of individuality into account, whether in terms of wardship [Bevormundung] or in recognition of the ideal [of man]. It leads to women being granted an equal share in the affairs of state along with men; even children who have attained the age of rational thought, in which, therefore, is the concept of man, should have the right not to be put under wardship, and to be granted the same position as the rest. The Platonic principle: "to each the position appointed to him by nature!" and the principle: "to each the same!" are complete opposites.

The Deduction of Natural Law from the Concept of Freedom

Freedom as a principle of natural law is initially without content, that is, without a particular object and without restriction. The natural thing would be for every right first to be determined by its object, and its restriction to follow from that. But here, the determination must proceed in the opposite direction. For the object cannot be found from that empty freedom, but the restriction can: in such freedom on the part of others. From this restriction, then, the specific objects of rights are to be derived, if they are to be derived merely by reason. The various objects of experience are posited as minor premises under the concept of the equal freedom of all as major premise, and the conclusion must yield the specific rights and institutions. It is precisely the business of natural law to carry this out.

The Concept of Primordial Rights and Its History

Among the objects subsumed [as minor premises], two classes immediately can be distinguished according to their generic difference. To wit, there are objects regarding which man is already in possession by virtue of his existence, for example, one's own life, own thoughts, the use of limbs, etc.; and there are those with which he comes into contact only in different ways, combines with them and again separates from them, or which do not need to be conceived in connection with every human being. This is the distinction between *innate* and *acquired* rights (*jura connata* and *acquisita*). The diversity of relations already leads to this in the process of deduction. One only needs to analyze the existence of man to get the *jura connata*, and he gets specific ones. I have a right to these, i.e., my limbs, etc. For the *jura acquisita*, on the other hand, objects external to people must be subsumed, events must be subsumed, in which case we only get them as abstract rights, such as rights over things in general; the factual first decides to which things we have a right.

The relevance of the distinction manifests itself directly in the consequences. According to the postulated equality, innate rights must accrue in the same way to the one as to the other, while with regard to acquired rights the question is first, to what degree was that original equality effaced by the occurrence which led to them, and to what degree is it effaced in specific cases. This yields the consequence for alienability and burden of proof. For this reason the earliest writers already had the distinction between innate and acquired rights. Pufendorf's distinction between *obligatio connata* and *adventitia* is entirely of a piece with this; because to the former he reckons the "obligatio omnium hominum adversus quoslibet homines qua tales, per quam invicem jus naturae usurpare socialemque vitam agere debent."[79] But with Thomasius the definition is still imprecise. For him, *jura connata* are those which one has apart from the consent of the obligated party, which means that *patria potestas* also pertains to them. Wolff comes closer: *jus connatum homini ita cohaeret, ut ipsi auferri non possit* [the innate right of man cleaves to him, so that it cannot be removed]. Hoffbauer summarizes the difference in all its sharpness.[80] He separates innate rights not merely from those that presuppose any occurrence of contract, but all that presuppose any particular occurrence at all.

This is the generally leading concept, even though it is not everywhere clearly recognized. But Kant seemed to have abrogated it. The earlier proponents, namely, treated the natural equality of human beings and the *jura connata* quite separately from each other. Kant, systematically penetrating, sought their connection; he found it in the fact that they both explain one and the same concept. He denied the majority of innate rights and derived them all from what is none other than primordial, content-free freedom itself, according to Kant's definition: the right not to be a mere means for another. From this point, the *concept of primordial right* [Urrechts] took the place of the *jura connata*.

But Kant had to concede that innate rights when taken individually, for example, the right to a good name, not being directly expressed, first have to be deduced logically, and that this deduction is of a different sort than the one involved with property, contracts, etc., a difference which shows itself to be operant in the burden of proof. Hence, although he banished the words *jura connata*, he did not banish the fact. Rather the empty concept of freedom, the primordial right, is now the midpoint of natural law, from which first arises that which is immediately contained in it, and then that which requires other occurrences.[81] The analysis of the existence of man yields the rights to one's own life,

---

[79] Pufendorf, *Elementa jurisprudentiae universalis libri duo*, Book I, defin. 12. §. 1. [English translation: *Two Books of the Elements of Universal Jurisprudence* (Indianapolis: Liberty Fund,), p. 109: "the obligation of all men towards all men whatsoever as such, by virtue of which they ought to employ the law of nature in their relations with one another, and to live a social life."]

[80] Hoffbauer, *op. cit.*, pp. 122ff.

[81] Kant, *Metaphysische Anfangsgründe der Rechtslehre*, p. xlv [p. 30 in *The Metaphysics of Morals*].

limbs, reputation, the possibility of acquisition. When the objects outside of him are subsumed, then there result the rights to things and to the actions of others, either temporarily or in permanent relations. This is the system of natural law.

The Negative Character of Natural Law

The abstract character in natural law lines up in just the same way as in philosophy generally. In both, everything is only the logically necessary consequence of a basic concept. In philosophy, this basic concept, from which no further abstraction can take place – substance – is empty being, while in ethics it is the concept of the thinking being. This in turn becomes the basic concept of the philosophical doctrine of law, so that all individual rights and institutions only manifest themselves as its modalities. Therefore, natural law bears a negative character like abstract philosophy does generally. Just as the substance of Spinoza or Hegel is that which cannot be thought away, pure being without content, mere not-not-being, so also here, what is taken as the basis of freedom is not positive power (like the freedom of God to create the world, the freedom of the Platonic wise men to govern the state), but something without content, only that for which, if absent, the concept of freedom no longer exists – the *not-being-a-means, not-non-person, not-being-a-slave*. In the same way, the development of this concept is a negative, i.e., a merely logical one. Namely, no right, no institution, may emerge that first arises and then is joined to that empty concept of freedom as something new, but only those of which it can be shown that when they are expressed, their non-existence is likewise impossible.

Relation of Natural Law to Roman Law

The affinity of natural law with Roman law is generally recognized. This already indicates that Roman institutions could be received into the natural law textbooks, and this in fact took place. To elucidate natural law, therefore, nothing would be more conducive than clearly to delineate its agreement and divergence with Roman law, and to demonstrate the basis of each.

Roman law, like natural law, recognizes a right of the individual independent of any divine requirement over him. But where a person, in whatever relation, ever breaks from the connections in which he was created, there arises a paucity of cultural drive and force, and thus the abstract character. With the ancient Germans – although they towered above the Romans in independence and the love thereof – yet every right was also permeated by obligation; honor – perhaps only another expression for freedom – inspired their lives; it was not merely an inviolable good but also a sacred power that required as much of every act as it authorized that act. That is why the Germanic legal viewpoint is always situated within the totality of life; every entitlement is created, develops, varies, with the manifold relationships that, all around it, passively and actively affect it; and it is constantly assessed together with them. By mutual permeation with them, there arose ever new kinds of applications that had not been originally delineated by their mere existence; Roman law, on the other hand, in that it conceives of every entitlement in isolation, precisely thereby prescinds from all living relations, and could only receive that which is given invariably with its concept. Herein consists the Romans' abstract procedure of reasoning from existing rights and the laws which indicate their content. Emptied of life, the logical character everywhere emerges automatically; for there is nothing [new] to be expected, but only what must always remain. When the force that forms anew recedes, then everything remains as it is and is fixed spellbound in an immovable concept.

To this degree, Roman law and natural law agree. But Roman law only conceives the already existing entitlement in isolation. Its abstract procedure of reasoning thus begins first from given rights and laws. These themselves, however – the starting point of the rationale – have come to it from out of the totality of the consciousness and the relations of the nation; religion, patriotism, family, forms of diet; these living causes have determined it, which by their nature effect something positive, having to produce something which they were not already. For this reason, it embodies a variety of rights and laws, each of which has its own existence, which are not included in any concept – one may presume whichever one he likes. It is positive law. By contrast, natural law isolates people right from the start. What emerges here has already arisen in the abstract. The origin of rights and legal provisions is the empty concept of freedom, and nothing new must be added to this basic concept. Not only the application, but the production itself is stamped by the absence of life.

Alongside personal entitlement and in agreement with it, there could also exist in Rome an independent law of the state, a recognition of the public condition not dependent upon men. For the legal condition had a living source there. Natural law seeks logical unity; it can only have one concept as basis. In that it emanates from the rights of the individual, this rules out its deduction from the state, and it tolerates no obligation of compulsion which does not proceed from the freedom of individuals. Ultimately, as explained above,[82] all logical connection is timeless. What reason demands is contained in it before any occurrence, and what is based on an occurrence does not follow from reason.

By contrast, rights which have arisen through history and presuppose it are not logically necessary. Roman law recognizes the real manner of the functioning of action and incident; it does not abstract from time and history. On the contrary: what it grants to every man according to specific statutes at a specific time, is precisely his inviolable right (*jus quaesitum*) and this is held to be sacred to him. This explains why the nation, with the same virtues and defects, nevertheless manifests such opposite action in its two classes [Ständen]: in the patricians, the recklessly passionate pursuit of their prerogative, in the plebeians, unprecedented moderation while enduring outrageous hardship. It is the sanctity, in the eyes of the nation, of every acquired right, i.e., rights arisen in history. In the entire struggle, the upper class manifests itself as that which protects its own, for which reason the use of any means is not viewed as a bad thing; the lower, by contrast, as the one that offends without justification. And it is certainly not prejudice or ignorance on Livy's part when he conceives the struggle in this character, leans as a Roman to the patrician side, and even in the speeches of leading plebeians, characterizes the undertakings of this class as riots and illegality. The characteristic Roman sentiment holds everything which is acquired to be inviolable, regardless of the results to which it leads, how its use is related to humanity, and finally, without any regard to what would exist if we think away the occurrences by which it was acquired, it being conceivable that they had not happened.

Now the logical derivation of rights leads to quite the opposite: the disregard and annihilation of all acquired rights. In every moment reason requires anew – for it requires it incessantly – that incidents be ignored, that the truth be discovered from it alone, and therefore that anything formed outside of it be destroyed.

This is the train of reasoning that abolished all prerogative of rank and guild,

---

[82] Book III, Part I.

in order to restore the eternal condition of reason, that is, a condition outside of time and action. Certainly the disregard of the condition then existing contained in itself an emphatic requirement; but it was not taken into account that this desire to allow only the logically necessary to exist would lead to continuous acts of destruction for the goal to be achieved, precisely because life, it being life, is not without history and change. So then, the principle of freedom developed purely logically does not in any way secure the rights of living people; on the contrary, it abolishes them, so that only consistency can exist.

The description of the peculiarity of Roman law, by which each entitlement is more isolated than even the natural-law deduction, is reserved for another place.[83]

---

[83] See Stahl, *Private Law*, appendix: "Regarding the Value of Roman Private Law."

Chapter 4: The Individual Institutions of Natural Law

The Two Conflicting Principles of Rational Philosophy and their Implementation in all Doctrines of Natural Law

The real existence of the thinker, and the law of thought, were referred to above as the two necessary principles of rational philosophy, and the conflict in their modes of production was also highlighted.[84] The general development of natural law contains just these principles, and therefore also their conflict. Because of this, rights [Recht] and juridical law could not be brought into connection – natural law makes human freedom into its foundation, and yet does not recognize acquired rights.

The genesis of the individual institutions is now also nothing more than a repetition of the same difficulty, the same mutual fuss, when one tracks any one of them. The exclusive principle of law must be freedom. If one comprehends this as real freedom, then right is what it *does*; if one comprehends it as the concept of freedom, then right is what it *is* (in both cases, excluding curtailment by others). In terms of the manner of operation of real freedom, there results from it a change in the initial condition which can progress to its complete opposite, in which it cancels itself and tolerates no restriction. But in terms of the concept of freedom, no change is possible. The condition is given by necessity, and freedom does not have freedom if somewhere it is restricted from effectuating anything in opposition to the logical conclusion. For the mode of action of freedom and of the logical conclusion are precisely opposed, in that the latter ever only posits what it already is, while the former can indeed bring about something else. This is the reason that in natural law one finds two opposite opinions regarding each and every institution, one of which is unconsciously based on the former principle, the other on the latter, and which are never able to arrive at a final settlement.

Controversy over Innate Rights

With respect to innate rights – rights to life, body, honor, opportunity to acquire property – logical deduction demands that their being flow directly

[84] See above, Book III, Part I [e.g., p. 88].

from the concept of man. Therefore they are always necessary, and it is contrary to reason if for one moment they do not exist. As such, giving them up cannot depend on discretion. But if life or reputation really are my rights, objects [Sache] of my freedom, then I should be able to keep them or not keep them, and even to renounce them if I so desire. Hence, Fichte[85] admits that one legally could sell his freedom of thought, if factually this were possible. According to the latter line of thought, the murder of a man who himself demands it, is no violation of the law, *non fit injuria volenti* [injury is not done to a willing person]. According to the former, it is such; because although it is not against that which this free person wished, it is to act against what follows from the concept of his freedom. Therefore, one and the same writer, and no second-rate one at that, can profess first the one, then the other opinion.[86]

Over Property

Consistency stemming from equal freedom would correspond to the arithmetically equal allocation of objects, community of goods, alternating use. But this contradicts living freedom, which cannot allow objects to be allocated without its will; it itself must be the cause of possession; but if it desired and took them, it wishes to lord over them exclusively, because by its very nature it must be able to effect something, and it cannot do so in a community of goods. To it corresponds property and the original acquisition thereof by seizure, the derivative acquisition thereof by transfer. But now it happens that the legal condition is determined by events which might or might not have occurred. One person is deprived of objects by the act of another, which he could not prevent, and an inequality arises in actuality, in the particular case, even with initial and, in terms of the idea, equal opportunity for control of the external world. In Roman law this is completely consistent, because Roman law recognizes the deeds of the free man as the determining factor of the legal condition; but natural law recognizes only the logical consequences from the concept of his freedom, and

---

[85] Fichte in the anonymous publication, *Beitrag zur Berichtigung der Urtheile des Publikums über die französische Revolution* [Contribution to Correcting the Verdict of the Public regarding the French Revolution], Part I, p. 228.

[86] Feuerbach, *Revision,* 2nd ed., Part II, p. XXIX, and *Lehrbuch* [Manual], 1st ed., §. 40, note.

a condition is not logically necessary which did not have to be effectuated.

Over the Content of Contracts

The history of the philosophical doctrine of property therefore manifests the eternal vacillation between the horns of this dilemma. According to Grotius, there follows from reason a community in all things, as now exists in public places, such as the theater. No one can acquire a lasting privilege vis-à-vis another for one particular object; he only has a right not to be disturbed in the factual possession thereof, not by virtue of a right to the thing but by virtue of his personhood, and only as long and as far as this factual relation extends.[87] Pufendorf, following the moderns in this, misunderstands Grotius when he attributes to him the idea of a positive-law community of goods. Pufendorf's own opinion only differs from Grotius' in that he denies this claim to non-disturbance of the factual condition: if someone collects fruit, another may snatch it from him again.[88] Although Thomasius rejects the latter as a *jus Hobbesianum,* which Pufendorf had actually already refuted, he returned to the view of Grotius.[89] Later, however, he seems to consider a positive-law community of goods to be the rational one.[90] This is decisively the case with Nettelbladt,[91] although all practitioners of natural law before Kant agreed that the community of all goods (*communio primaeva*), of whatever sort, flows immediately from reason, and the possibility that several property arises through occupation could only have its legal basis in an express or implied contractual establishment. Even according to Thomasius, reason advises occupation; but not so *praecise* and *distincte*, that a *pactum* would not be necessary for this.

Kant is the first to go the opposite direction and allow things to be linked permanently to one's legal sphere [Rechtssphäre] through his voluntary action. In this he is followed by the later Fichte and by Fries, although they again, like the earlier proponents, justify the institution of property solely from the

---

[87] Grotius, *De Jure Belli ac Pacis,* Book II, ch. 2, §. 2.

[88] Pufendorf, *De Jure Naturæ et Gentium,* Book IV, ch. IV, §. 3.

[89] Thomasius, *Institutiones Iurisprudentiae Divinae,* Book II, ch. 10.

[90] Thomasius, *Fundamenta Juris Naturae et Gentium,* Book II, ch. 10 [pp. 232ff.].

[91] Nettelbladt, *Systema Elementare Universae Jurisprudentiae Naturalis* [Elementary System of the Universal Law of Nature], §. 255ff.

agreement of the people; but they arrive there from a completely different position. Whether and why contracts are sufficient to transfer property, or to make the institution itself rational, does not pertain to the doctrine of property. The concern here is only whether the free act of an individual who has been granted the capacity to appropriate, can abolish equality, which lies immediately in the concept of freedom.

Over the Binding Nature of Contracts

The controversy which can be called perhaps the most important one of natural law, namely the *binding nature of contracts* (although only becoming the general subject of treatment in the later period) revolves around this same pivot. Any objections to this are based on the fact that one does not adopt a historical, act-generated relation between the moments of consent and of performance, but rather, in accordance with the abstract character, measures each against the concept of freedom. But this cannot explain how I must do something now simply because I once wanted to. Suppose I once made a lawful promise, but on false pretenses; now, i.e., without reference to time [zeitlos], my freedom entails that I am *not* obligated to keep that promise. Enforcing the contractual obligation is therefore contrary to reason. The binding nature of contracts is to individuals what legal inequality is to the whole. The deeds of the nation yesterday, even the deliberate ones, could not bring about the existence of a situation today that did not already have to exist apart from any deeds. And as with the people regarding its history, so can and must I abstract from my history, namely from what I did and wanted yesterday.

In opposition to this, the defenders of contractual obligation reason from consideration of the living person. He must act, connect the different times of his actions, and thereby make something happen for the legal condition. This, however, creates something contrary to his present freedom and hence likewise against the concept of his freedom. This dispute about the binding nature of contracts is made clearer in its essence when it is extended to the possibility of its contents.

Over the Distinction between Alienable and Inalienable Rights

Contract is the predominant institution not only for the emergence of legal claims, but for natural law as a whole. In it, everything is effectuated by the will of man: the right, the obligation, *that* they are, *what* they are. A system that is driven by the interest of human freedom can use no other lever than contract. With it, one seeks to actuate the most heterogeneous, the most peculiar, in the same manner. From it, one tends to derive even the validity of testaments, and thereby indirectly, intestate succession as presumptive testament.

He who is permeated by this spirit even for a short period – and who has not been! – must remember how this solution everywhere initially presents itself. But if contract itself is an act of freedom, then its opposite comes to pass simultaneously with its completion: he who has acted freely, is now bound. So with contract, it is only for a moment that freedom exercises its full existence. Like a flash, it dies with its birth. And with contract, natural law has called upon a dangerous assistant. One uses it to justify what one wishes, but does not consider that he also justifies that which he does not wish, and that, if it should have the power to build, it must also have the power to destroy. The rights of subpoena [Strafandrohung], of property, of paternal authority, the rule "sale breaks rent," if they cannot be derived directly from the principle, become established by contract. By contrast, compulsory morality, prerogative of nobility, tax exemption, trade restrictions, which their defenders must have the right to ground on tacit agreement, are unconditionally rejected. And where will the limits be set on what can be agreed upon? Will one, like the old Germanic tribes and the earlier natural law, allow contractual slavery? Will one limit the duration of a function, like the French Code prohibits the permanent hire of services, or the scope, and to what extent?

Therefore, it was in the latter period of natural law, when everything in rapid development hurried to its end, that one became preoccupied with the separation of alienable from inalienable rights. No tolerance could be found for acquired rights which, in view of the fact that they only could arise because of a fact, could only lapse because of a fact. The difficulty first became apparent with innate rights. It was already demonstrated above that those two principles require on the one hand their alienability, on the other their inalienability, and therefore neither of these opposing conceptions has lacked defenders. Nevertheless, both led to results that could not be accepted.

Alienability could not be accepted, as it made even full slavery possible. Nor yet inalienability, because innate and acquired rights are in such indissoluble relation that, with the rigidity of the former, the latter would also lose their flexibility. The possibility, for example, for someone to acquire things by his actions, to move about at his own pleasure, as contained in primordial right, must at least be relatively abandoned in order to engage any run of the mill contract. To find the boundary here, one would have to separate, in abstraction, the innate right, without any specific content, from this content, declare the latter of any sort to be alienable, the former alone to be inalienable. So to be consistent, we arrive at this: the original right itself, that is, the not-being-a-slave, cannot be abandoned, but every specific use of it can be, as long as only it itself remains. Hoffbauer, one of the clearest and sharpest proponents of this orientation, distinguishes: "I can abandon individual rights which I have as component parts of my innate right; but I cannot deliberately give up one of my original rights such that nothing more of them remains to me."[92] Fichte, who in his anonymous work on the French Revolution[93] conducted a sprawling investigation into the alienability of rights, and whose interest is precisely their inalienability, nevertheless comes to no other result than what has just been delineated: pure personality is inalienable, while everything specific, in which it expresses itself, is alienable. Thus he admits that someone can entirely divest himself of his right to engage contracts, and even can enter into slavery; only in the latter case, the right of the slave to be nourished by the master remains as a right, so that the concept of a person, the primordial right to life, is thereby preserved.

Natural law itself thus accomplished the reduction of inalienability to this mathematical point, so to speak, and thereby believed it had brought those contradictory principles into harmony. But it did not achieve this, because it is entirely impossible to achieve. Either there is a historical connection between the act and its consequences – in which case, slavery is not against freedom, when it is only willed; because it happens to him who is now a slave only by his will, and therefore he is not treated as a means. Or there is no such connection, and it cannot by any means justify being bound by a contract; because he who is compelled does not now wish to be so, and thereby is treated as a means.

The solution of this dialectic is this: the contradiction arises only from the

---

[92] *Op. cit.*, p. 254.

[93] *Beitrag zur Berichtigung der Urteile des Publikums über die französische Revolution* [Contribution to the Correction of Judgments by the Public regarding the French Revolution].

fact that human freedom is founded on a concept. If it is deployed by the free will of God and as part of His specific moral order, then all difficulties are smoothed away: it reaches as far as it wishes to, it has its limits in how far it may alienate itself in the determination that He gave it; but within this boundary it has its truly free, change-effecting movement, because God, unlike reason, brings forth more than what is only logically necessary.

Over the State

Among contracts, the *social contract* plays the leading role. Through it, even lasting relationships of mutual dependence (marriage, parental relationship, the state) which are removed from freedom, can be derived from freedom. *Nullum imperium sine pacto.* These relations, which by their very nature dominate mankind by their inherent idea, are thereby brought under the social contract. For any society [Gesellschaft] only has a passive object and does not entail any submission other than that which reciprocally exists and is mutually adopted. In this way, the existence and the arrangement of the family, the state, continually depend only upon the arbitrary will of the parties to the contract. Its shape is only governed by the restrictions of private contracts – where such is recognized. Hence the state is, e.g., denied the right of capital punishment because private individuals cannot dispose of their lives – as if they had a greater right arbitrarily to dispose of their health, their freedom.

Thomasius distinguishes himself in this, that when he was still a sociabilist, he derived the law of society and the power thereof from the goals of these relations themselves, rejected the *consensus tacitus* and *praesumtus* of the other natural law doctors, and grounded paternal authority directly on divine institution. Consistent with this, he declared in his later works that the relationship between parents and children involves no compulsory obligation.[94]

In terms of this school's interest, the essence of the state must likewise consist solely in the satisfaction of the individual: It is an institution for either the good, or the moral perfection, or the freedom of individuals. But the task also was to derive this logically from the basic concepts: "Without the state, power or difference of opinion would topple the results which follow from the equal

---

[94] Thomasius, *Institutiones iurisprudentiae divinae,* Book I, ch. 1 §. 86; Book III, ch. 4. *Fundamenta juris naturae et gentium,* Book III, ch. 4.

freedom of all. But freedom calls for the protection of its results; this protection is the state; therefore, the state is included in the concept of the equal freedom of all." This is the final result of natural law from first to last. It was only in the later period that the attempt was also made to insinuate morality or happiness as an end for the state, in contradiction to the innermost motive of orientation and in contradiction with consistency. Because to be justified as a legal institution, it may only follow from freedom. Hence the will of the individual to be protected is the exclusive goal of the state.

But this still does not satisfy the leading interest. Because the state puts limits on this goal as well, and even protection should not be imposed. The will of the individual, therefore, must not merely be the exclusive goal, it must also be the only cause of the state. The state is founded on *contract*, express or implied, real or supposed. This reduces the institution [Anstalt] the power of which is obvious to the people, and which cannot be avoided like, e.g., the church can, but factually cannot be done without, to the individual will, at least in theory. And here the character of the whole orientation speaks most directly: outright rebellion against every given regime; subjugation only to a chosen one. From start to finish, all significant natural law doctors are therefore agreed on the creation of the state through contract. Even with Spinoza this is at least the form with which he cannot break, regardless of how much the thing itself contradicts his system's character of necessity. The bottom line for him is not consent but the real alienation of power; yet he characterized this everywhere as a contract.

That this ongoing contradiction must also prevail in the deduction of the state, is obvious. It follows from the *concept* of freedom that freedom *must* be protected – hence compulsion by the state and a certain unalterable form thereof. *Living* freedom, on the other hand, requires free choice in its establishment (state contract) and discretionary arrangement. Now this contradiction was not so evident to the older writers, but ever since Kant it has set everything in motion; hence the manifold opinions as to whether the state contract is voluntary or necessary, whether it is morally or legally necessary, whether it grounds duty to the state generally, or only to a specific one. This controversy as well can as little be brought to an end as can the one set forth above; and it is merely coincidence, or rather the interest of the antagonists, which has proven to be the decisive factor every time. Therefore, in different relations the most contradictory principles prevailed. Namely, with regard to establishment, the view generally was adopted which follows from act-oriented freedom: the state arises and exists legally by contract, so that if people did not want it, it would not arise or exist. By contrast, in the doctrine of the arrangement and formation of the state, almost all profess the result of the opposite principle: only those arrangements are permitted in the state which include the concept of freedom, and public legal institutions that do not follow from this concept are unjust, even if the people willed it that way.

Initial and Subsequent Position of Natural Law regarding Positive Rights

This, then, is the course of development of natural law taken uniformly as a whole, albeit with individual differences and disputes. For a time it both mingled with religious and devout notions[95] and tolerated positive legal institutions within itself, e.g., the feudal law, until finally it stripped itself of all foreign elements to present itself purely in its peculiar character. Initially, it was nothing like at odds with existing institutions, the intent of the deduction being to demonstrate the rational necessity of these as they really are, in order to sanction them. But it increasingly pushed against them until it finally forcefully tackled and upended the entire existing state.

A principle, and probably the most important one, which was followed above in its development, shows this clearly. This would be the principle separating out compulsory obligations. This was initially sought in order to justify the status quo; in the end, it was used to demolish it. Even the actual content, the primordial right of man – that he may not be a slave – which is what the entire development seeks, was obtained only at the end of that development. Oldendorp even venerated slavery and deduced it from the commandment, Honor thy father and mother, while also appealing to the authority of Aristotle.[96] Thomasius called for a less restrictive relationship in accordance with natural rights, e.g., *non invitus alteri vendi poterit servus perpetuus* [one cannot be

---

[95] To this pertain as well the investigations regarding morals and law prior to the Fall, regarding the Kingdom of Christ and the Devil, etc. Hobbes and Thomasius in particular busied themselves with this.

[96] Oldendorp, *Iuris Naturalis Civilis et Gentium Isagoge* [Introduction to the Law of Nature, Civil Law, and the Law of Nations], IIII Praeceptum [Fourth Commandment].

sold into perpetual slavery to another], but nevertheless calmly listed alongside it what positive law has enacted differently.[97] Wolff deems it justified by contract and insolvency; by birth, only until such time as the master recoups the costs of education;[98] Hopfner merely by contract. Only the subsequent period (Montesquieu, Rousseau, Kant) rejected this absolutely.

If one now looks back to the first requirement – to derive everything simply by logically subsuming passive objects under the ethical rule – in order to see whether it has been met, then we have to conclude that it by no means has been satisfied. Admittedly, property and obligation [Forderung] could be regarded as the object of such subsumption: things brought under the concept of freedom are property, etc. But with regard to the legal necessity of the state, the deduction is by no means only logical, but also derived from effects. Here not only is the object of freedom taken from experience, the rule that the state should exist is as well, and is founded on those premises, on the observation that people apart from higher authority do not respect rights, but that such an entity secures them. Already the concept of the end of the state, which underlies the deduction, entails this. For now the question is no longer: what lies in the concept of freedom? But rather, by what is that which lies in the concept of freedom achieved according to the laws of empirical nature? But what is found by this approach lacks the character of logical necessity. One can be persuaded that things subsumed under freedom yield property in the way that two times two equals four; it is not contradicted in terms of form. But that human drives make the state necessary already lacks this necessary form. For reason assures me neither that the state will really be capable of protecting me in my rights, nor vice versa, that they will be violated without it, even though to this point all experience, which in reality always has exceptions, speaks for both. For this reason the great divergence between Hobbes and the others had its foundation not in ethical but in experiential propositions.

The same is true for the various institutions of the state. For this reason, the objection has been lodged against the theory by which punishment, like the state, is considered to be a means (namely a means of protection): it needs to be seen whether punishment *always* achieves this; apart from this, it would be

---

[97] Thomasius, *Institutiones Iurisprudentiae Divinae,* Book III, ch. 5.

[98] Wolff, *Institutiones Iuris Naturae et Gentium*, §. 959.

lacking a rational test. This objection is entirely justified in terms of the requirements of abstract procedure, but it is valid with the same justification against the deduction of the state for the purpose of securing law as it is against punishment. Namely, in both the *continuo ratiocinationis filo deducere* [continuous deduction of the thread of reasoning] is given up, in order to turn the workings of experience, which are not without exception, and are not logically necessary, into the thread of reasoning.

Unfaithfulness of Natural Law to Its Required Method

But natural law is compelled to this infidelity to its method, because while it derives ethical rules from reason, it borrows the material thereof from experience. Now the outside world stands everywhere not only in logical, but in real connections, and the ethical construction itself must be affected by this. For this reason natural rights, as abstract philosophy generally, always had the urge not to borrow relations from experience, but to find them *a priori* as well as in their ethical arrangement. This took place with Fichte and Hegel. With them therefore, and preeminently with the latter, the uninterrupted thread of logical reasoning is implemented. For them, the state and its institutions do not result because they are needed for a goal, but because they are included in the basic concept of natural law by a rule of pure thought, without anything needing to be added from outside, as will be shown in greater detail below.

We have hereby characterized natural law in its general outlines. The final evaluation of it will be suspended until its various iterations with individual compilers have been pursued. Our purpose here has been to emphasize the internal contradictions which impelled its development.

PART III: DEVELOPMENT OF NATURAL LAW IN INDIVIDUAL SYSTEMS

Chapter 1: Hugo Grotius

Hugo Grotius is the originator of the system of philosophy of law which goes by the name of "natural law" and which for more than a century was the only one applied and cultivated; indeed, it was the only one held to be possible, because the various systems which were customarily distinguished during this period (sociabilistic system, system of fear, external peace, etc.), were merely particular implementations of one and the same system.

Principle of Law

His work *On the Law of War and Peace,*[99] in which this is laid down, had the law of nations as its intended and actual task. The old foundations – feudal law, knightly battle customs, ecclesiastical orders and temperaments – gave way for this, and new ones needed to be laid; indeed the evidence had to be provided that in relationships among sovereign states and especially in war, not merely advantage and violence applied, but justice. But standards to legislate and enforce among sovereign states over which no supreme authority exists, presuppose the idea of a law which is valid not by positive sanctions, but by its own intrinsic regard. It was therefore a necessary preparation for Grotius' task to show the law to be given by nature (*jus naturale*) and valid apart from any positive legislation, and indeed such a one that is invented and introduced by man not for the sake of utility and selfishness, and which therefore can be bypassed for the sake of utility, but which rests on an ethical reason, which binds man absolutely. To refute that doctrine of utility and prudence such as represented in particular in antiquity by Carneades, and to establish an ethical principle of law, is the endeavor of the Prolegomena of Grotius' work, with which the new era of legal philosophy mainly begins.

He constructs this law, in itself ethically binding, upon the gregarious nature of, or the drive of sociability in, man (*socialis natura, appetitus socialis*). Man has a drive for community with others, indeed a drive for a "peaceful and rationally ordered community." Grotius did not conceive this urge to community as mere reciprocity of physical needs, but much more broadly, as good will towards

---

[99] Grotius, *De Jure Belli et Pacis*. [On Grotius, see also Alvarado, *Calvin and the Whigs; The Debate that Changed the West.*]

others, especially in opposition to mere utility. It is to him the love of a condition in which common satisfaction is achieved for self and others. The gregarious nature in this sense now becomes the principle of law. What follows from it is the law of nature (*jus naturae*), is just, is commanded, while the opposite is unjust and illegal; and it is immutable (*mutari non potest*), and is the supreme law for all times and for all peoples. Thus did Grotius establish a principle for a system of natural law, a *purely ethical* one disregarding utility (*jus non solius utilitas causa comparatum*), and a purely *rational* one disregarding positive regulation. (It is not rationalistic because of its independence from positive law, but because of the source from which it is drawn, namely, human reason abstracted from God and the God-given world order, in which it, as shown above [p. 95], goes so far as to claim a validity for the same even on the assumption that there is no God.)

Delimitation of the Legal Sphere

The sphere that stands under this principle and is to be regulated by it is, according to Grotius' specific declaration, simply law in the actual or strict sense (*ejus juris quod proprie tali nomine appellatur*). He therefore firstly rules out law in the "broader" sense, which we call morality [Moral], namely the control of desires (fear and lust), as those regulated not by the drive of sociability, but by a different drive of human nature, namely, value judgments regarding the true lasting value or lack thereof of things, and secondly, as part of this broader law, the wise arrangement (*prudens dispensatio*) of the particular conditions of every man or every state, thus politics.[100] Therefore there remains to the sphere of law

[100] This is the undoubted sense of §§. 8 and 10 of the Prologue. Many places indicate that Grotius understood law in the broader sense to be morality, preeminently Prolegomena §§. 41 and 44, where it reads: "cum injustitia non aliam naturam habeat, quam alieni usurpationem, nec referat, ex avaritia illa, an ex libidine, an ex ira, an ex imprudente misericordia proveniat" [Whereas the very Nature of Injustice consists in nothing, else, but in the Violation of another's Rights; nor does it signify, whether it proceeds from Avarice, or Lust, or Anger, or imprudent Pity, or Ambition, which are usually the Sources of the greatest Injuries – Barbeyrac/Tuck, I, p. 121]. Likewise Book II, ch. 22, §. 16: "Illud quoque sciendum est, si quis quid debet non ex justitia propria, sed ex

[Rechtsgebiet] (the sphere that stands under the principle of the drive to sociability) nothing but *respect for mine and thine*, namely property recognition, fulfillment of contracts, damages, and upon transgression, the punishment that pertains to this (*alieni abstinentia – promissorum implendorum obligatio – damni culpa dati reparatio et poenae inter homines meritum*). The deduction of these legal propositions is simple and obvious, they being undeniable conditions of peaceful coexistence, and is exhaustive in terms of that principle; because for the mere purpose of peaceful coexistence, nothing more is required.

Contract as the Embodiment of Natural Law

As a result, only the sphere of private law as such is derived from the principle of natural law. From this Grotius arrives at the state only indirectly, namely, through the medium of *contract*. It is a command of natural law that contracts must be kept, because (for the peaceful community) there must be some sort of mutual obligation among men and none other than contract is conceivable (*fingi potest*). But then it must be assumed on the part of those who form a state (who have joined with a *coetus*), that they have promised by express or implied

---

virtute alia, puta liberalitate, gratia, misericordia, dilectione, id sicut in foro exigi non potest, ita nec armis deposci" [This we are also to understand, that if a Man owes another any Thing, not in Strictness of Justice but by some other Virtue, suppose Liberality, Gratitude, Compassion, or Charity, he cannot be sued for it in any Court of Judicature, neither can War be made upon him on that Account – Barbeyrac/Tuck, II, p. 1112]. In this sense, therefore, Grotius also judges the duty of parents to nourish their children to be such a one that pertains not to law in the strict but in the broad sense (hence, morality): Book II, ch. 7, §. 4. This entire construction of the ethical sphere of Grotius' can only be explained on the basis of then-extant scholastic teaching [Bildung]. That which there was divided subjectively into various virtues, Grotius established objectively as separation into life-spheres [Lebensgebieten]. The sphere of *justitia commutativa* is what he construes as law in the strict sense; as law in the broad sense he allocates control of appetites, which according to Thomas was the object of other virtues but not justice, and the wise distribution of goods and positions according to the inner worth and calling of persons, which according to Thomas was the object of *justitia distributiva*. But when he transfers the separation to objective life-spheres, it automatically becomes a compartmentalization of the legal sphere over against morality and politics.

contract, to obey either the majority or those to whom authority has been transferred. For this reason, even according to Grotius' expression, obligation from agreement (*obligatio ex consensu*) is the "mother of all civil law." Upon it, in fact, is based the power that gives rise to civil law.[101] Indeed, even in the sphere of mine and thine he also derives the validity of several property from contractual introduction.[102] So it is only contract that directly binds according to the law of nature, everything else is derived from it, and one might say that the entire essence of Grotius' doctrine of natural law, without him being aware of it, is nothing else than merely *the binding nature of contracts.*

General Ethical Significance of the State

As Grotius proceeds from a general ethical basis for law, he also, in the same way and in accordance with this basis, attributes general ethical significance to the state. The state is the perfect union of free men, through which that law [Gesetz] of nature, a peaceful and orderly community, is to be realized.[103] In accordance with this general ethical significance, the state, as differentiated from the person of the prince, as a human community, is the subject of public legal relations and public authority. There remains, therefore, the state itself, and its rights and obligations continue through all change of rulers, dynasties, and even forms of government – the immortality of the states (*civitas immortalis*),[104] and the actions of the regent are binding on any successor, even those who are not his heirs, so that they are acts of state (*actus regii* as opposed to *privati*).[105] Similarly, the purpose of the state according to that general ethical significance is the common enjoyment (mutual recognition) of rights and the common utility. The public good is thus the supreme standard for decision (*salus publica suprema lex esto*), to which all individual rights must yield. From this in particular he derived the right of eminent domain (*dominium*

---

[101] Prolegomena, §§. 15, 16. Cf. also Book II, ch. 5, §. 17 and 23.

[102] Book II, ch. 2, §. 2. no. 5.

[103] "Est autem civitas coetus perfectus liberorum hominum, juris fruendi et communis utilitatis causa societas." Book I, ch. 1, §. 14.

[104] Book II, ch. 9, §. 8, nos. 1–3 and §. 3.

[105] Book II, ch. 14, §. 1, nos. 1 and 2; §. 11, no. 2; §. 12, no. 2.

supereminens).[106]

Identification of Nation and State

With this entire conception, the state is for Grotius entirely the same as the nation or people [Volk], the people [Menschen] united, and the public signifies only what is of common utility to all, not what is a higher necessity over them all. Certainly he considers the people to be the state only insofar as it is imbued with a spirit, namely, just that full civil life community (*vitae civilis consociatio plena*) the first product of which is the supreme authority.[107] But the state never manifests itself to him as a unity or institute [Anstalt] to be distinguished from the people; this is also expressed in the fact that he everywhere uses the concepts *civitas* [city], *communitas* [community], *coetus* [gathering], *populus* [people] as synonymous terms. In consequence, he grounds that identity of the state and perpetuity of its rights and obligations not on the unitary institute but rather on the fact that the rights and liabilities are *that same people's*,[108] and mediates the binding nature of the acts of state on the successor not through the state but through the people, because of its being obligated by the actions of earlier rulers acting as its representatives, and tacitly transferring this obligation to the later rulers, who derive their power from it. In consequence of this, and this is the main point, for him the people are the subject of supreme authority (*summa potestas*). In free countries, it remains so completely, while in monarchical states it is not the exercise but the right (*imperium in se retinet, quanquam non exercendum a corpore sed a capite*). Therefore, here the people remains the general subject of authority, while the prince, to whom it transfers that authority, becomes the special subject (*subjectum commune* and *proprium*), similar to the whole body being the subject of sight even though only the eye is first and foremost. Therefore the authority also reverts back (*redit*) to the people when the

---

[106] Book II, ch. 14, §. 7.

[107] Book II, ch. 9, §. 3.

[108] "Non desinit debere pecuniam populus rege sibi imposito, quam liber debebat, est enim *idem populus*" [A Debt contracted by a free People, ceases not to be a Debt, because they are at present under a King; for the People are the same – Barbeyrac/Tuck, p. 673], Book II, ch. 9, §.3.

dynasty dies out, as having proceeded from it.[109]

Grotius nevertheless does not arrive at any practical inferences against monarchy from this implemented theoretical popular sovereignty; on the contrary, he emphatically combats the then revolutionary doctrine of a supremacy and especially penal authority of peoples over their kings. This is because, according to his doctrine, the king, although only gaining authority by transfer from the people, nevertheless thereby receives it truly and irrevocably; the people forever remain subjected to his own will and act. Grotius teaches a sovereignty of the people and a sovereignty of the king, but the former is only potential, and therefore can never do harm to the latter.[110] Nevertheless, this conception, by which Grotius disposes of the natural consequences of his basic assumption, again is only possible through an inconsistency, a lack of awareness regarding his position, of the kind he is afflicted with generally.

Private-Legal Character of the State Contract

That is to say: in contradiction to the general ethical and thus necessary significance that Grotius ascribes to the state, he conceives the contract founding the state in strictly private manner, as of arbitrary content, and since, as the state in general derives from contract, so necessarily do the specific form of government; all forms of government are declared legitimate by the backing of such a contract or similar title, such as, in particular, conquest, which according to Grotius' position can be considered a (compulsory) contract. In this sense, he recognizes in particular the legality of a class of states which he already distinguished using private-legal characterizations such as patrimonial states or usufruct states, in which, namely, the ruler has full ownership of state authority, either because he has subjugated the people through war or contractually it has passed so completely into his hand that nothing is excluded.[111]

---

[109] "Nam imperium, quod in rege est ut in capite, in populo manet ut in toto, cujus pars est caput: atque ... adeo regis familia extincta jus imperandi ad populum redit" [For that sovereign Power which is in the King as Head, rests still in the People as in the Whole, whereof the Head is a Part: So that ... if the Royal Family be extinct, the Sovereignty reverts to the People – Barbeyrac/Tuck, p. 672], Book II, ch. 9, §. 8; Book I, ch. 3, §. 7.

[110] Book I, ch. 3, §. 8.

[111] Book I, ch. 3, §. 11.

Certainly this term patrimonial state initially signifies only the irrevocable and unconditional jurisdiction of power (including the power of alienation [Veräußerungsbefugniß]),[112] not absolutism. But in other places Grotius also allows the content, purpose, and scope of state power to depend on any contract whatsoever. In the way that a man of his own free will can give himself over to slavery, so also can the people bestow the sovereign power over itself in whatever way it wishes, because it is not utility but only will that is decisive according to the legal point of view, and therefore states are also justified in which the state power is intended solely for the benefit of the prince and not the people, thus entirely equal to the power over slaves, in accordance with the then prevailing Aristotelian characterization.[113]

There is obviously an inconsistency with regard to the concept of the general necessary essence of the state. If the legal basis for all relations only lies in the satisfaction of human desire for a peaceful and rationally ordered community, then a contract cannot be legally valid that allows the public authority to be used not for this purpose, but for the benefit of the ruler. This inconsistency had to be removed, and this led, from the other premises of Grotius, to the doctrine of Rousseau.

Now the same thing that holds for the state and the people within the state must also apply to the nations mutually. For these as well, there exist standards by agreement (among which, undoubtedly, not only express but also tacit agreement is to be understood) which have as goal not the benefit of an individual state but the benefit of that great unity of states (*magnae illius universitatis*). Accordingly, war in particular is also based on fixed laws. There are only certain cases in which it can lawfully be conducted, mere advantage is no authorization, there are rules and restrictions according to which it must be conducted, and there are even temperaments of humanity by which not everything allowed by principles of law should actually be implemented.

Evaluation

With this program of ideas [Ideenkonception], Grotius opened a new path for various scientific fields. Already for ethics generally, he laid the foundation

---

[112] *Ibid.* and Book II, ch. 6, §. 3.

[113] Book I, ch. 3, §. 8, nos. 1, 2, 14.

for scientific treatment by laying claim to an independent field separate from religion, and an independent body of knowledge separate from revelation; because if he also fell into error in this, by entirely separating God Himself from this purpose, he yet extracted the problem of recognizing the moral commandments not in terms of arbitrary divine commission, but their inner reason and essence.[114] Still more decisively, he is the founder of "natural law" as an entirely new science which did not exist before him. Not only did he establish a new principle for the philosophy of law, the socializing nature in his sense, but he provided a new boundary for its subject matter. He was the first to separate out the actual sphere of law, which until then was mingled with others. He established a natural law (*jus naturae*) as distinguished from morality and politics, while also distinguished from positive law. Legal principles shall exist which are not based on positive law and yet are not merely desirable principles worthy of pursuing, but which already are actually valid, legally binding principles that have nothing to do with the question of the appropriateness of the state constitution and state institutions, but are valid across all state constitutions and state institutions plain and simple, as unconditional legal standards. Such a science of general law, which is not morality, not politics, not the epitome of mere law-ideas, and not positive law, is precisely the specific nature of the discipline of "natural law" that Grotius founded and the entire construction of which, at least in its outlines, he already prefigured with a steady hand; and here again the mighty progress he achieved in distinguishing the legal idea from the political idea needs to be recognized, regardless of the untenability of his notion of such a law.[115] For regarding the doctrine and law of the state, Grotius mainly asserted the viewpoint of the public commonwealth as opposed to mere private entitlement to rule, as has already been pointed out in other places of this work.[116]

Above everyone else, however, Grotius accomplished a service for the law of nations, which was his intended task. Since it was no longer the church that maintained a joint order among the mighty of the earth, and no longer the emperor who was recognized as the supreme arbiter of their disputes, in international relations it was only the absolute will of the individual sovereigns which

---

[114] See Stahl, *Philosophical Presuppositions* (Vol. II, Book I), §§. 24 and 28.

[115] See Stahl, *Principles of Law* (Vol. II, Book II), §. 17.

[116] See Stahl, *The Doctrine of State and Principles of State Law* (Vol. II, Book IV), §. 37.

was valid, and there already had appeared the theory of mere utility which handed the European condition over to the thirst for unlimited aggrandizement on the part of courts. It was therefore a great thing to bring about the validity not only of utility but of law in the relations of nations, such that even in war laws are not silenced, and that even what the law allows, humanity does not permit. Grotius stands above all the subsequent practitioners of natural law up until Kant, not only by being the initial originator, but also in the execution, richness of thought, and the perception and living conception of conditions, as a result of which (which is also noteworthy) with him falsehood does not emerge as determinedly as with others; in part (in particular the severance from Christianity) it even remained hidden from him.

But as undeniable as these lasting merits of the Grotian doctrine are, he also, with this same doctrine, was also the first and already full-blown founder of that one-sided and therefore false orientation which in its consistency ends with the destruction of morality and justice. He sketched out the enterprise of implementing a legal construction by abstracting out not only the Author of the moral order but also the content of the actually given (objective) moral order, abstracting simply from the nature of man. He gave the initial expression to the manner of presentation in which the state has no authority over men in itself, but only gets it through their contract, and has no purpose in itself, but derives such from the purposes of (individual) men. This point of view is the decisive factor. The fact that Grotius personally and incidentally endorses the Christian revelation could not prevent the consequences of this from manifesting themselves.

This also clarifies his relationship to Aristotle. The tradition in which the social nature of man contains the basis of law and the state began with Aristotle and proceeded to Grotius; to this degree, the sociabilist system has been regarded as nothing new, and not as the Grotius' work. But the same expression has a completely different meaning in Grotius than in Aristotle. The same expression with Aristotle means nature as the power in the universe which appoints people to social life, while with Grotius it means nature as the character or desire of men. According to Aristotle, nature in the state seeks *its* completion for that which it establishes in smaller circles, and this is the reason that man is by nature gregarious. According to Grotius, by contrast, man has a social need, which is why the state is an end of nature. Therefore Aristotle comes to an (objective) doctrine as to how the state must be arranged according to *its* very nature, while Grotius comes to a (subjective) doctrine, how it must be designed to suit the nature of *(individual) men*.

Hence with Grotius a principle came to life which in its further development necessarily led to the doctrine of Kant and Rousseau, and eventually to the French Revolution. The doctrine of Grotius, that the duty of subjects has its basis in their tacit contract, is in itself quite insignificant and innocuous. But it only needed to be developed in all its content and its consequences to become what a century later would overturn the order of Europe. Likewise, one snowflake which dissolves on the mountain peaks is inconspicuous; but [when combined with others] it rolls along and falls as a crashing avalanche into the depths.

Chapter 2: The Natural Law Doctors from Grotius to Kant

Hobbes

Thomas Hobbes[117] countered the doctrine of Grotius with another, taking the same point of view but from an opposite presupposition. Human nature is not the desire for community (shared satisfaction), but selfishness. Man seeks community not for the sake of comrades but merely for his own sake. The origin of great and lasting societies is therefore not mutual benevolence but mutual fear. The detailed implementation is as follows.

The state in which people by nature, i.e., prior to their mutual commitment by contract – the "state of nature" – is one in which all have the same rights to all things, but also the same inclination to hurt each other, particularly because of the desire for things. The state of nature therefore is a perpetual war and perpetual reciprocal threat and fear. But now the law of nature (*lex naturae*) or – a term Grotius used as meaning the same thing – right reason (*recta ratio*) is self-preservation (the protection of life and limb); what happens in accordance with this is justified and responsible, having taken place *juste* [justly] and *jure* [lawfully].

The fundamental precept of nature, therefore, is to seek peace. From this flows two corollaries: the first, that you cannot retain the unlimited right of the state of nature, but must partially transfer it in order to possess what you retain in peace; and the second, that you must keep contracts, because only in this way can peace be attained. From this source equally arise the duties of compassion, gratitude, etc. (in short, all moral obligations), since their reciprocal practice serves self-preservation. So Hobbes reduces everything having to do with law and ethics to selfishness.

Yet all of these commandments which follow from the law of nature are not binding as long as the state of nature endures, precisely in terms of their own principles; because as long as one is not sure of fulfillment by others, one's own fulfillment does not serve self-preservation. That is not only why the civil laws are silent in the state of nature, but the laws of nature as well; in it, there is no

---

[117] Hobbes, *Elementa Philosophica de Cive* [Philosophical Elements, the Citizen] 1642 (*Leviathan* 1651).

other legal standard (*mensura juris*) than actual benefit. But for this reason it is the law of nature to abandon the state of nature (*status naturalis*) and to establish the civil condition (*status civilis*), that is to say, to bind each other in overwhelming numbers to reciprocal assistance against disturbances of the peace. This combination is the state, and only from it proceeds the mine and thine, the obligation to respect other people's property, because only through it does the assurance exist that others will do the same.

Yet this security coming from this connection should not be a mere agreement (*consentire*) but a union (*unio*); that is, participants must cease to be separate independent entities, but instead need to become one will, so that individuals retain no will and no right of themselves, but rather transfer all their rights and all their power (*jus virium et facultatum suarum*) to a person or a consilium, waiving resistance and reversal of the transfer. That is the supreme power (*summa potestatis, summum imperium*) or, as we would say, sovereignty. In this manner the state is itself a person (*persona civilis*), distinguished from all individuals that make it up, so that all these taken together are not to be regarded as a state, excepting he who represents them (*repraesentant*). A dual contract is therefore necessary for the establishment of the state: the one through which anyone contracts with anyone, and the other through which they all contract with the future holder of the supreme power, to submit, and indeed to submit unconditionally.

This complete transfer of all right and all force to the supreme state power necessarily makes it absolute (*imperium absolutum*). In terms of its concept, there can exist neither a higher power over it nor a restriction on it, for the latter assumes a higher power. It cannot be bound by laws. There can be no right of subjects against it that it must take into account, no property, indeed no conscience, no judgment over good and evil, but in this as well, subjection to the judgment of the supreme state power (the sovereign) is unconditional, and therefore, whoever acts in obedience to state power does not sin. The opinion that the subject might have an independent judgment regarding good and evil, and that a sinful act that he commits by command of the sovereign is a sin for him, is a false and a revolutionary doctrine (*seditiosa opinio*).

Finally church teaching, i.e., the interpretation of the Holy Scriptures, must take place by state authority (albeit by means of the bishops of apostolic succession) because the individual, if he had the competence to such interpretation, would attribute to himself the highest standard of conduct, which would cause all civil obedience and indeed all of society to cease. Therefore, for Hobbes the church also coincides completely with the (Christian) state, which is to say, by the church he understands Christians united under an external authority. Here below, the inner invisible church is merely a church in *potentia* [potentially], not *actu* [actually]. Given the reasons already brought forward, such power may be no other than precisely the supreme state power. Only such a unified will, against which wills that are competing with and combatting each other cannot stand, is able to ensure the security of peace, which is the supreme law of nature. Selfishness, which is the core of human nature, can only be tamed by such unlimited irresistible power.

Accordingly, Hobbes stands unmistakably on the same presuppositions that are peculiar to his time, and which were first expressed by Grotius. Like Grotius, Hobbes does not recognize a given order standing over men with inherent ethical laws, but wishes to derive such only from the nature of the individual. He too, therefore, established the civil condition on an arbitrary contract of subjects, so that even the validity of majority vote, this "beginning of the civil condition," can only be decided by unanimity, and he knows no other concept of injustice (*injuria*) than that of contract infringement, so that no injustice can be committed against those with whom one has not contracted.[118] What is unique to him, though, is that he de-ethicized [entsittlicht] law and the state, indeed morality itself. The natural law (*lex naturae*), on which alone he erects law and ethics, is not ethical at all but the mere physical drive of self-preservation; his right reason (*recta ratio*) is a mere law of prudence. No less peculiar to him is his political result: the absolutism of the state, which before him had never been taught, nor after him, at least not to that degree, such that he even excludes the moral accountability of subjects, namely in the way that citizens are subjected, not as in Plato to a higher harmony, but to an arbitrary will. Hobbes arrives at this result by being consistent: The vacuity of social relations which is here assumed, the divestment thereof of ethical ideas in order to base them purely on human will, must lead to the absolute power of the united human will. Rousseau later attained similar results, in other ways. Grotius would have had to arrive at them, if he had exhaustively drawn the consequences from

---

[118] Book I, ch. 1, §. 3.

his principle *salus publica suprema lex esto.*

But Hobbes was also led to his absolutist doctrine from a practical motive. The religious and political divisions, the [English] civil war, the readiness of religious conscience to revolt that surrounded him in his own country, filled him with longing above all for peace and unity, and the idea that such cannot exist where any power of resistance, especially for the reason of conscience and religion, could burden it. In both respects, both in his materialistic conception of life and in the practical power of his political result, Hobbes is an excellent representative and cultivator of the orientation that found its development in the West, in opposition to the more ethical and inwardly contemplative manner of vision suggested by Grotius and cultivated particularly in Germany, even though the outcome of that orientation was quite different, indeed the opposite of the one Hobbes strove after. But Hobbes' deep insight into the foundations of the state had true scientific merit, namely, the notion of the unity of the state in contrast to a mere society; and connected to this, he first expressed the idea of sovereignty in all its profundity; in this he stands above Grotius. For Grotius distinguishes the state merely from the prince, while Hobbes also distinguishes it from the people.[119] In particular, Hobbes substantially developed the system of legal philosophy begun by Grotius; he brought many and significant doctrines to clear discussion which, although already available, were only veiled in the system of Grotius. In particular, these would be the doctrine of a state of nature, the deduction that the supreme principle of law cannot be fulfilled in the state of nature and therefore postulates the state, the description of the course of events (or the legal relation) by which the state is established by contract. These doctrines, if not true in themselves, are necessary for the position, and therefore built the construction of "natural law" up until the last moment.[120]

---

[119] With Bodin, the concept of sovereignty is certainly more concrete, is determined more vividly than with Hobbes, but merely as something given; it is not deduced from the essence of the state.

[120] Hobbes and Spinoza have often been set in parallel. This has been prompted by both the mightiness of the two intellects, and by the impression that with both, actual ethics disappears and is replaced by a natural power; and indeed, with both of them the nearest

Pufendorf

Pufendorf[121] is considered to be the one who implemented the principles laid down by Grotius, and in so doing to have perfected the sociabilist system. If one understands by this that he applied those principles consciously and logically to the subject matter, then that would be inaccurate. Such inner systematic development cannot be found in him, not even to the degree of Grotius

---

expression thereof is the natural law of self-preservation. Yet they differ from the ground up. Certainly, Hobbes founds law and custom on the natural instinct of self-preservation; but what he derives from this natural drive is for him nevertheless a demand such that man should freely fulfill or violate; his law, therefore, is truly ethical (at least regarding the form, i.e., the manner of accomplishment) even though in terms of content it is only physical. By contrast, Spinoza founds law and custom on the power of nature, i.e., the metaphysical necessity of the universe. His law of nature is not to be met by man, but by nature itself and inevitably, and man does not have the freedom to violate it. There is no demand, no ought in the actual sense. The form of ethics is also absent, the working of the law is not ethical but merely natural. The pantheistic position allows ethical content to the law, as for example self-sacrifice (Hegel's doctrine would later demonstrate this), even though there is not much of this to see in Spinoza himself; but it does not allow an ethical mode of action to the law. On the other hand, Spinoza did not share the absolutist result, and indeed he was concerned that he would be categorized together with Hobbes, who was hostilely regarded on this score. A sentence in his *Tractatus* refers to this: "People may not transfer all power to the authorities, because they cannot," and in his letters (*epistola* 50) he himself points up the difference between his doctrine and that of Hobbes: "quod ego naturale jus semper sartum tectum conservo, quodque Supremo Magistratui..., non plus in subditos juris, quam juxta mensuram potestatis, qua subditum superat, competere statuo, quod in statu naturali semper locum habet" [I will always firmly maintain natural right, and that the supreme magistrate ... does not have more of a right over his subjects than according to the degree by which his power exceeds that of a subject, which is always the case in the state of nature]. The position of Spinoza has no other refutation against this absolutism than that such is not possible according to natural law, and where the power of nature is everywhere acknowledged, the difference between the state of nature and the post-contract condition cannot be established.

121 Pufendorf, *De Jure Naturæ et Gentium*, *De Officio Hominis & Civis.*

himself. But Pufendorf did implement the material of the ethical and jurisprudential discipline in a completeness and external order that hitherto did not exist, and thus gave to the Grotian doctrine an outward systematic form. Moreover, he brought the philosophy of law into connection with the overall philosophy of his time, as it in the meantime had been founded by Descartes, albeit only superficially, in that his system of natural law presupposes the philosophical results thereof. It must also be recognized as an achievement, that he investigated the anthropological foundations of law – intellect, will, action – precisely in consequence of the general philosophical point of view and thus provided the instigation to cultivate significant legal doctrines, in particular, imputation [Zurechnung]. All this taken together assures him a place in the history of natural law. But that he furthered natural law in terms of content as well, must be denied. He rather renders the notions of Grotius superficial than develops them; he summarizes the drive to sociability not as Grotius does, as mutual benevolence, but merely as mutual need; he decisively renounces the bond with God and the Christian revelation, which Grotius (albeit inconsistently) still maintained, and declared (despite the opposition of theologians) natural human reason to be the sufficient source of moral knowledge; he binds God to the natural law not as Grotius does, by virtue of moral necessity, but because God mechanically cannot maintain people otherwise than via the drive to sociability; he thoroughly confuses the spheres of law and morality, which Grotius separated. In fact, he transforms the pure discipline of law founded by Grotius into a discipline of moral philosophy, a doctrine of duties. Nor did he contribute any new aspects for the systematic expansion of the natural law system. In the final completed form of natural law with Kant, therefore, one is reminded of Grotius, Hobbes, and Thomasius, as those who provided the elements, but not Pufendorf. Rather, his main significance is only the external dissemination of doctrine via his catchy exposition.[122]

---

[122] Pufendorf is best evaluated in Warnkönig, *Rechtsphilosophie* [Legal philosophy], pp. 50ff.

Thomasius (Gundling)

By contrast, Thomasius[123] established inner and indeed essential progress in the discipline of natural law through his separation of morality and law, as was treated in a previous chapter [pp. 106ff.], by which the provisions for inner peace are moral and cannot be compelled, while those for external peace are legal and can be compelled. But this is not a completely new element, because even Grotius himself, as is evident from the above presentation, separated the legal sphere [Rechtsgebiet] from the moral under the names law in the stricter and the broader sense, and ranged them under different principles, the former under the drive to sociability, the latter under the proper valuation of things. Indeed, the innermost character of the doctrine founded by him is precisely that it strives to highlight pure legal principles. But the distinction is not presented by Grotius in clear concepts and is not energetically executed. Hence it was that Grotius' successors blurred, indeed completely lost this distinction: Hobbes derived the duties of compassion, gratitude and the duty to fulfill contracts equally from self-preservation; and in the same manner Pufendorf summarized the right use of language (not to lie) and the right use of things (property) in the same chapter, and the like. With Thomasius, the separation of the two spheres is secured for good, in that he emphasized a different motive or goal (inner and outer peace), a different ethical character (*justum* and *honestum* – *decorum*)[124] and a different effect (enforceability and unenforceability), hence delimited it in terms of all relations, and set for himself the specific task of implementing the distinction through the entirety of ethics.

Moreover, Thomasius was governed here by a practical motive, which pertained to the innermost driving force of the entire development, by which his distinction procured a very different result than it did with Grotius. For him, namely, the important thing was to keep external force far from the inner moral, especially the religious sphere . It is mainly the interest of freedom of religion that drove him to make the distinction between the two spheres , and

---

[123] Thomasius, *Institutions Jurisprudentiae Divinae; Fundamenta Juris Naturae et Gentium.*

[124] With Thomasius, *decorum* comprehends duties towards others, *honestum* duties to oneself, and therefore they are based on the Pufendorfian system; but both together are opposed to *justum* as a completely separate sphere of coercible duties.

therefore he first formulated it, prior to the publication of his *Fundamente des natürlichen Rechts* [Foundations of Natural Law], for a practical reason, namely to defend the Pietists against religious oppression by the orthodox, which he did in the publication *Das Recht der evangelischen Fürsten in theologischen Streitigkeiten* [The Right of Protestant Princes in Theological Disputes]. This led him to the result that, for the purpose of salvation and thus of piety and faith, no provision of a legal nature, hence coercible, can exist and be maintained,[125] and therefore he emphasized not only, as Grotius did, the different origin and purpose of moral and legal precepts, but also and especially the different effect, the coercibility and uncoercibility thereof. In this regard he brought in one mighty stride not only the scientific system of natural law but also the lively intention that underlies it, closer to the goal, so that Kant only had to apply the finishing touches. This is reflected also in Thomasius' practical achievements, his struggle against torture and the witch trials.

Since then, the formal criterion of the legal sphere [Rechtsgebietes], coercibility, which would not again be forfeited, was especially emphasized and developed by Thomasius' successors, Gundling, Gerhard, Fleischer, *et al.* The distinction between the two spheres, a vital question for Thomasius, became an academic subject and remained so up until Kant. The scientific result of that distinction manifested itself in full evidentness with Gundling, Thomasius' most significant successor. His natural law (*jus naturae et gentium*) is a pure doctrine of law to the exclusion of morality, which he treats in another work under the name of ethics. Gundling is to be regarded as a pure follower of Thomasius, even if he did not admit to it. Certainly, he often goes back to Hobbes and establishes his proper position against widespread misinterpretation. He also seeks to rectify various and sundry controversies according to his own manner, selecting the proper viewpoints from among all previous authors. But his basic concepts

---

[125] In my book *Die Kirchenverfassung nach Lehre und Recht der Protestanten* [The Church Constitution according to the Doctrine and Law of the Protestants], I referred to the erroneous nature of this Thomasian doctrine in relation to the church, by which he confuses coercion regarding individual salvation and individual faith with coercion for the maintenance of ecclesiastical order, hence public doctrine, preaching in the name of the church. See the more detailed treatment of the territorial system founded upon this, in the same place.

and teachings are from Thomasius: happiness as the principle of ethics, its division in terms of outward and inward peace, the restriction of the legal sphere, and the perfect or enforceable obligation, to the former: this is how he constructs natural law. If he sought to found that principle of happiness more deeply, by attributing to the laws given to mortals the object of the conservation and perfection of their nature, while this conservation and perfection consists precisely in happiness – well then, this is hardly worth mentioning.

Wolff (Darjes, Höpfner)

A different method for dealing with natural law came on the scene with Wolff.[126] Wolff deals with natural law entirely as a moral philosopher. The principle he newly issued for morality, the perfection of man, is for him the law or right of nature *tout court*, and he implements it throughout the entire sociable condition. He does not entertain a separation of law and morality like that of Thomasius. While he retains the distinction between perfect or coercible and imperfect or non-coercible obligation, this distinction is incidental, marginal, and does not determine the shape of his system; he did not have a standard, like Thomasius, for determining which duty is coercible and which is not.

For this reason he again divides the entire ethical sphere merely in terms of the moral system, as sketched by Pufendorf: duties towards himself, towards others, toward God; and competence is only the result of (private) obligation, and actually is nothing other than permission: what I am obligated to, I also need to be free to do. Wolff's moral principle is certainly more correct than the earlier one of happiness.[127] But for natural law he accomplished nothing as far as content is concerned, for nowhere did he either enrich or more narrowly specify it. At the most, one can thank him for the development of various concepts: the *status moralis*, which consists in being the subject of law and obligation, the distinction between absolute and hypothetical rights and such like, as a promotion of clarity in the ethical sphere. If anything, he lost the measure and delimitation of the ethical sphere gained by Thomasius and furthered by

---

[126] Wolff, *Jus Naturae Methoda Scientifica Pertractatum* and his *Institutiones Juris Naturae et Gentium*.

[127] Nevertheless, on this point cf. *Philosophical Presuppositions* [Volume II, Book I of this work], §. 29.

Gundling. He took a wrong turn that quickly had to be retraced. On the other hand, he gained significance for the formal or general scientific character of natural law by applying the demonstrative method.

In general, Wolff's philosophy is of a character whereby demonstration is its innermost essence. Other philosophers are led by some material foundational view, which to them is the supreme truth, or at least the supreme problem. For example, Spinoza by the oneness of God, therefore His impersonality and the absorption of the creatures in Him; Leibniz, by contrast, by the formation and existence of independent individual creatures (*principium individuationis*). On the other hand, for Wolff there is no such supreme material truth; rather, for him the syllogism as such is the supreme, only truth. He takes from Leibniz the two principles of demonstration, the principle of non-contradiction (*principium contradictionis*) and the principle of sufficient reason (*principium rationis sufficientis*), and implements them through the entire sphere of knowledge. That which he and every other person knows, he presents in the form that it does not contradict itself (because "the essence of a thing is its possibility," that is, precisely conceivability, non-contradiction) in that everywhere he takes the features from the definition which he himself put in it (according to experience), which then for him is valid as having been demonstrated. For example, "seeing is founded in the essence of an animal that has eyes," thus it is a characteristic thereof, which obviously is to say nothing other than that seeing is the characteristic of a sighted animal.[128]

The most characteristic aspect of this method and of Wolff's intellectual organization is that he thinks that we have no immediate certainty even of our own being, but gain it (even if, for most, this occurs without realizing it) only by means of a deduction: "If we wish clearly to realize how we are convinced by these reasons, that we are, then we will find that the following conclusion is contained in this thought: Whoever is aware of the being of himself and of other things, is. We are aware of our being and that of other things. Therefore

---

[128] When Wolff allows himself to act beyond this purely analytical manner, it goes badly for him. Thus, for example, he proves: because God had to create that which is most perfect, the planets must have inhabitants. He could just as well have proven from the perfection of the divine creation that people do not have to have only legs, but also wings.

we are."[129] Hence not even Wolff believes that he is, if he is not convinced by reasons for it. Wolff also applies this syllogistic method to the ethical sphere, and if in itself this is nothing more than an absurdity, nevertheless the requirement which underlies the rationalist philosophy, to find results purely from reason, is thereby first actuated, and the inevitable alternative is therewith posed for a subsequent, more rigorous scientific conception, of either abandoning this requirement, or making an attempt really to use bare concepts of reason. Wolff's demonstrative treatment of the entirety of philosophy and hence the philosophy of law has no other value than that of being an impetus for Kant to take the rationalist principle seriously.

Subsequent legal-philosophical treatment closely adhered to Wolff. Yet there was still the need, even without full awareness of it, to return to the more correct position of Thomasius that had been lost. Wolff's most significant and most successful student, Darjes, indeed retained the entire structure of the Wolffian ethical system, but he used the second part, obligations towards others, to derive the Thomasian segment, the field of compulsory duties, or, as he calls it, to gain "jurisprudence" as opposed to "ethics." But with Höpfner the diminution of the Wolffian system and the return of the Thomasian one is on full display. Höpfner unites the perfectibility- and happiness-principle and treats them synonymously; he departs from the Pufendorfian-Wolffian division of natural law into three classes of obligations, and instead delimits his discipline according to Thomasius' and Gundling's method as the doctrine of "natural compulsory duties." Nor does he treat primarily of obligations in order to derive rights from them, but rather everywhere originally treats of rights. At the same time, the way in which the general texture of ideas leads to Kant is already reflected in him, in that the will is already roundly asserted to be the ultimate principle of rights, thus especially in the deduction of property as well as contract. Wolff's doctrine in relation to legal philosophy is only a provocative episode between Thomasius and Kant.

---

[129] Wolff, *Vernünfftige Gedancken von Gott, der Welt und der Seele des Menschen, auch allen Dingen überhaupt* [Rational Notions of God, the World, and the Soul of Man, likewise All Things in General], §. 6.

Opponents of Natural Law (Selden, Coccejus, "Dubia Jura Naturae")

Resistance to the natural law system was by no means lacking during this period of its development and rule. Such resistance stemmed from the accurate realization that the natural law system completely dissolves the bond between the human world and God. Selden and Coccejus take this position,[130] as does Crusius later on, in relation to moral philosophy. But these opponents were not able to indicate either the innermost seat of error and separation from God, nor were they able to provide any doctrine maintaining the bond with God which scientifically sufficed.

Selden objected to the grounding of natural law on mere human reason by referring to the absence of a binding power in human reason, and the conflict of reason among a number of people and doctors, which all point to a higher author of, and a higher sanction for, natural law. But his own reasoning contains nothing further than this: the natural law that comes from God has an obligative and a permissive component; the obligative is that we must remain faithful to the contracts and state constitutions that we, again by contract, have entered into (*pactis ac regiminum formulis civiliter initis standum*); the permissive is that the sphere left free [frei gelassene Sphäre] can be precisely determined by the people through their agreement in a binding manner,[131] however, the binding force does not arise from the contract as such (*ex simplici hominum ratione et consensu*) but from God's permission that they by mutual agreement prohibit or enjoin what is free in itself (*ex consensu mutuo inhibere*). Finally, however,

---

[130] Selden, *De Jure Naturali et Gentium*, in particular Book I, chs. 7 and 8. Henricus Coccejus, *Disputatio Juridica Inauguralis de Principio Juris Naturalis Unico, Vero, et Adaequato* [Inaugural Juridical Disputation regarding the Only True and Adequate Starting Point of Natural Law], and in particular in the *Positiones pauculae & generalissimae loco quasi postulatorum explicationi juris gentium & praelectionibus Grotianis praemissae.*

[131] "Simulatque ex ejusmodi permissione quid ab hominibus sociatis coercitum, vetitum seu constitutum est, ad illud in quod sic consenserant ipsi (sive pacto sive deditione sive aliter) .... observandum obligatos esse" [Similarly from such permission by which human society coerces, prohibits, or appoints, regarding that to which they consented (whether agreement or capitulation or whatever) ... they are obliged to observe it]. Book I, ch. 8, p. 106).

God's laws are promulgated by the revelation in Scripture, which are mandatory everywhere and of necessity.

Hence Selden fought a side of the natural law system that was the least relevant, because the natural law doctors themselves often and gladly admitted that obligation has its final (remote) ground in God, and his own result coincides with natural law's in the essential thing, that at the origin contracts are the source of all law. The only thing in which he has the advantage is that, clinging to the divine origin of all moral precepts, he can vindicate the supreme position for the immediately revealed commandments, which the exclusively rational moralists left completely sidelined.

Coccejus essentially agrees with Selden in his polemic: he does not see a binding power in human reason and (admittedly less decisively expressed) a content for commandments necessarily arising from the principle of social and peaceful life. His own doctrine, however, which he sets in opposition, is more thoughtful and decisive than that of Selden. The divine will, which he makes into the principle, is to be recognized from His deeds and works and the perfection of the divine essence (without any mention of revelation). From this will proceeds the entirety of the commandments of natural law – freedom of action, the prohibition of harm to another, the necessity of the common life among men (*societas communis*) and the rights which arise therefrom, the legal effects of declarations of intent, disposition over one's own, the right of inheritance of children, domestic authority, the necessity of the state, the regard for and power of the magistracy – rather than by means of contract or deduction from one simple principle, which supposedly includes everything.

To this degree Coccejus truly opposed the error in that system, the ratiocination and foundation of the legal system on the human will and contract; and the accusation lodged against him at the time, that he did not teach anything different than Pufendorf, because the latter also recognized reason to be a work of God, was unfounded. But there is lacking, firstly, any mediation between the divine will (His deeds, His perfection) and the results that Coccejus teaches to be the content thereof; we do not see how the inheritance of children, regard for government, and so on, follow from divine perfection; secondly, the ethical and legal order in itself is not at all comprehended by him, indeed he contributed little to their deeper understanding; it is all set down as positive [as opposed to natural], and indeed the basic concepts thereof (the concept of law, competence, and the like) are much less sufficiently and correctly comprehended than with Grotius and his more significant successors.

And so, such opposition to natural law achieved nothing.

Other objections to the same thing, especially as recited by the author of the then highly celebrated writing *Dubia juris naturae*, were based on mere skepticism and therefore even less likely to affect its reign.

Chapter 3: Kant's System

Kant's Doctrine

As is well known, the train of Kant's system is this: we form all our knowledge by means of certain forms and concepts which we do not draw from experience, but which we must already have within us before we are capable of experiencing, as for example the relationship between cause and effect. We would never consider the real causes and effects in these conditions to be anything but isolated phenomena if this relationship were not already implanted before all perception. The embodiment of these forms of thought and law is reason.

The question is now whether reason, without which we cannot experience, is also able to furnish us with perceptions apart from experience (*a priori*). Here we are not speaking of such perceptions which contains nothing but what reason itself is, a mere extension of what lies in the essence of those forms (analytic knowledge), for example, that the cause precedes the effect, which indeed the concept of cause declares. Rather, this has to do with the perception of objects outside of those forms (synthetic knowledge), for example, God, immortality. The question is, "are *a priori* synthetic judgments possible?"

This is the question that rational philosophy of necessity must raise when it has arrived at consciousness of itself; in fact, it is that in which its consciousness consists. The result of Kant's investigation is this: we have no pure rational knowledge (no *a priori* synthetic judgment). For reason only vouchsafes the form of knowledge, while the material comes to us through experience, i.e., by means of the impressions of external objects upon our senses. Only both factors together provide knowledge. For example, the statement of pure reason: "everything that occurs has a cause," is not yet knowledge; a specific occurrence and a specific something that is its cause are obligatory for it to become knowledge. All our knowledge, then, is experience-knowledge, and beyond possible experience, hence of extrasensory [übersinnlichen] things that do not affect our senses (God, freedom), we can have no knowledge at all.

But more than this: Even our actual knowledge, thus experience-knowledge, is untrue, for we only attain it through the medium of our two sensory perceptions, *space* and *time*, and these are merely our (subjective) inherent forms without truthful (objective) existence. It is not the existence of things that is subject to doubt, but the opposite: without them, we would have no sensory impressions and thus no conceptualizations at all. Only its true quality (*"the thing in itself"*) is not perceived, because things (objectively) do not exist in space and time, even though we can only observe them as they are in space and time. Our perceptions therefore obtain only phenomena, not the things in themselves. And the objects of our knowledge (not, of course, the objects in themselves) comply with our manner of perception, and not the other way around.

The sum is this: we have absolutely no perception of transcendental things, and our perception of sensory things is mistaken, it yields us only the phenomenon, not the thing in itself.

This, then, would be a renunciation of all knowledge. But now comes help: all of this is only true of theoretical reason, that is, thought directed to perceiving objects that exist outside of itself. By contrast, practical reason, that is, thought directed to the generation of objects (actions) that are not already in existence, thus where it manifests itself as Ought, discovers these objects as goal without external impressions on the senses and therefore apart from the medium of space and time, purely from its own laws. To wit, there is a commandment of the good within us, which we do not derive from experience and which commands us to do the good without taking experience into consideration, i.e., without taking a consequence, a utility, a convenience to us, into account, but only for the sake of the good – a "categorical imperative." This then is pure rational knowledge. From this unconditional commandment of the good follow, purely *a priori,* freedom, immortality, God: freedom, because without it a commandment would be preposterous; *immortality* or a world beyond this world, because reward and punishment do not follow upon fulfillment or violation of that which reason consistently must require; *God*, because without Him reward and punishment could not be realized. Practical reason, accordingly, is the area in which truly pure rational knowledge (*a priori* synthetic judgment) exists; through it alone, therefore, we gain knowledge of transcendental things, and only its perceptions are true and reliable, while theoretical perceptions, because they borrow from experience, are fictitious.

Its Scientific Motivation

Obviously this fictitious nature of all experience which Kant takes as the basis, is not mere doubt but a positive confident assertion, and at once presents itself as the actual character of his system. How Kant was forced into this conception must be demonstrated in order to clarify the essence of the critical philosophy.

The basis upon which it rests is the assumption that space and time, chiefly time, is merely a notion pertaining to our own sensorial nature, corresponding to nothing in the object. Certainly, from the fictitiousness of the notion of time, Kant inferred that time has no subsisting and inherent existence in things, and therefore is not a derived concept. But such reasoning about an individual element of knowledge cannot possibly be the deepest mainspring of a system upon which a philosophical epoch is grounded. With the same reasoning, Kant could have denied the truthfulness and objectivity of all logical forms (ground and consequent – unconditional). Rather, a much deeper mainspring underlies it which itself determines this line of thought.

Every glimpse of the world shows change, act. But rational coherence is timeless – "universal and necessary." Should Kant wish to recognize this changing world, he would have to recognize a cause and a coherence of the same, which is not reason, and therefore cannot be discovered by reason. That would be impossible for it, because it would contradict the basic conception of rational philosophy. If he should wish to deny the existence of changing things, then he would also find this to be impossible, in that he very well saw and declared that without the existence of these things it would be absolutely impossible to comprehend why we imagine this or that and not always the same thing,[132] and that the thought forms are not yet knowledge unto themselves [für sich], but require an object and content to arrive at knowledge.[133]

There remained only one escape for him: maintain both: there is rational coherence, *and* things really exist, and only deny the rock of offense, the mutable character of the latter. He builds his system upon this foundation. Space and time are only fictitious because they are the forms of mutability. In Kant's view, if we weren't bound to these forms, "the same determinations which we now perceive as change, would yield a perception in which the conceptualization of time and *thereby that of change* would not even arise,"[134] and in that case we

[132] *Critik der reinen Vernunft*, pp. 274, 275.

[133] *Ibid.*, p. 146.

[134] *Ibid.*, p. 54.

would recognize the true nature of things. But now, space and time are the medium for all knowledge of extant objects; this can, then, only yield phenomena. In this way he solves the difficulty in which he denies mutability, causality, act, along with time, indeed denies reality itself as nothing other than "time-filler," so that only mere logical relations remain; everything shrinks to mere determinations of thought as in a mathematical point.[135] This is the basic viewpoint that rationalistic philosophy by no means derives from investigation, but rather unconsciously smuggles into the investigation. Kant believes he can flee from such a result's absence of result, to the area of practice. That is to say, thought as ethical demand requires objects that are timeless, eternal, immutable. For it was the undoubted presumed conception of his time, that the ethic be a system of bare logically connected rules, and this conceptualization cannot be refuted as mere logical coherence in physical things could, by any and every glance at the world. But the ethic could only therefore be assumed to be such a system if it were based upon bare rational coherence. Here or nowhere could pure *a priori* be recognized, and the results thereby attain the certainty of logical laws. God, immortality, and freedom had to be demonstrated on these grounds in order to be elevated beyond any doubt.

Kant's Relation to Spinoza

Thus, this entire system develops from the basic assumption of rationalism: there is no change. Spinoza asserts the rational coherence of the actual world. Kant, by contrast – both the later Kant, and the Kant prompted to investigate

---

[135] For Kant, even our *a priori* function is contaminated by the mixture of a false perception of time. That is to say, even the *a priori* judgment, in that it applies the categories to an object (if not to a specific one, then to any conceivable object) which comes to our observation from the sensory world, contain a time relation, e.g., "that which occurs has a cause" is constructed upon the unity of time, denying thereby that anything can begin anew, or can drop out of the unity of time. For this reason our judgments *a priori* are by no means valid for the objective relation, but only for our experience. They are the foundational principles according to which alone we can have an experience, but they are not the laws of the objective world. Accordingly, Kant even establishes contradictions ("antinomies") in reason itself, in connection with its supreme conclusions or ideas, which have their origin in the fact that they everywhere are based on the view of time.

by the Wolffian school's endeavor – gained the insight that the world of experience does not allow the problem to be solved, because we here find undeniable change, freedom, act. He therefore abandons this world as fictitious, and flees from it with his rule of reason into another, which he first fabricates by his thought, in which he is capable of completing the task because he first arranges it in terms of the task.

He seeks something unconditional, a *causa sui* in Spinoza's sense, i.e., such a one that is not, like God, the first that *is,* but is the first in terms of what we *think of.* For him, this is the notion of unconditionality itself, with the character of universality and necessity that necessarily adheres to it. From this, likewise according to logical laws, all actions must flow; in this consists the ethic. It may produce nothing else, or else the absolute would no longer be what its concept testifies, the foundation of the conditioned.

For this reason it postulates freedom of the will. That is to say, it denies that it is determined by covetousness (thus by objects outside of thought), but it likewise rejects every motive outside of rational thought itself – love, enthusiasm, as well as self-interest – as being contrary to morality. Hence, reason requires actions categorically, unconditionally, only as consequences of itself. Good and evil are not characteristics that precede our thought, and condition it; rather, they first arise through the form of universality and necessity that underlie our thought.[136] But the ought itself is yet a real power and contains in itself the notion of change, since an action is to be generated which does not yet exist. It therefore had to be referred to the world of phenomena. Thought manifests itself to us as ought, the imperative, as commandment and prohibition, only because we belong to the fictitious world of change. Apart from this, there would be no question of ought; rather, reason itself would faultlessly accomplish the actions that flow from it;[137] considered more precisely: there would be no ought and no act; rather, reason would exist simultaneously with its consequences. Not only the condition of action but also the condition of the intelligible world would be deduced from that absolute. As a statement of universality (non-contradiction) it contains the agreement of the act corresponding to it and its consequences for happiness, thus a condition of allocation according to

---

[136] *Critik der reinen Vernunft,* p. 102.

[137] *Ibid.,* p. 36.

desert ("the highest good") and a world disposer that makes this happen – God. The latter, as product of that absolute, is therefore bound to the law thereof, and cannot exercise pardon and grace. The actual God is therefore also in this intelligible world the abstract thought of logical universality and necessity, a God without understanding and will, as with Spinoza.

Contradiction in Kant's Demand on Reason

This makes clear that Kant completely grasped and followed the canon of Spinoza. The construction of his intelligible ordering is arranged entirely in accordance with it, even though for the things of observation he surrenders it. For this reason, a double world runs through the Kantian system: that of the phenomenon, i.e., the real coherence of act and event, and that of the essence, i.e., logical coherence. Spinoza, for his part, solely recognized the latter, and believed he had resolved the former only because he insufficiently took it into account. For Spinoza, the world as we observe it is merely the unconditional in terms of its concept, with its necessary consequences. Kant identifies these observations as something wholly other, and therefore also as fictitious; but for him as well, the ethical actions, the intelligible ordering, i.e., the true existence of things, is only the substance which underlies all thought (universality and necessity) and its modalities. Spinoza denies freedom (the choice to do this or that) in the real world. Kant accepts it and names it freedom of choice [Willkür]; but at the same time he denies it in the true world, where everything is necessity: reason contains the actions appropriate to it, the last judgment [das Weltgericht], etc., without choice [Wahl]. This unavoidable determination by reason Kant calls freedom of the will [des Willens] in contrast to freedom of choice [Willkür]. With Spinoza nothing can occur in the real world which is not necessary and thus just. The distinction between good and evil drops out; but with Kant such can occur, and it is only in the kingdom that we ourselves have to construct, or that lies beyond our experience, that this infallibility lies. He therefore does not need to justify the evil shown by experience; in the realm of phenomena he can praise and reject, and is empowered to establish tasks which are not already fulfilled, and for which – as we see ourselves – we are given the choice, and so can contrive a real ethics.

It turns out, then, that both of these apparently scarcely related systems, which above all construct the shrillest contradictions in ethics, nevertheless in turn are based on one and the same basic requirement.

Usurpation on behalf of Practical Reason

Kant is generally accused of a string of inconsistencies, but these have their deep-seated origin in the task that he gives to all philosophy, which he must of necessity give to it, holding fast as he did to rational philosophy while nevertheless not being blinded by it. For this task is in itself contradictory. He requires synthetic perceptions from pure reason, i.e., perceptions in which predicates are not derived from a concept, are not already given with that concept, but to which others are added, which are not contained in it. "Which are not contained in it" – what is that, other than: those which, according to reason, are not inseparable from the existence of reason, thus are not bound to reason through a cause outside of reason. If Kant thereby only wanted rational coherence and knowledge from reason, he would have required no synthetic judgment, he would simply have had to deny the possibility of such. Or, there is synthesis. There are effects, predicates, which are not contained in their causes, but could be produced or omitted by them. In that case, however, there is, truthfully, act and change, even if the form of time and space would be the prejudice of the senses. In that case, it is not possible to consider the relation of things as truthfully immutable, because it is change; nor to recognize it through the power of necessity (reason), because it is something free; nor as *a priori*, because it is directed not in terms of the laws of thought but in terms of causes which precipitate change.

We might attempt to consider this dilemma even to be a product of our prejudice, the truth being that the unchangeable is in fact a connection of new, and thus an object of synthetic, knowledge; but that would be inconceivable to us. That would have pushed us beyond all ground of human thought and imagination, where no further examination could follow; but such an appeal would by no means be in Kant's spirit. For he only rejects the forms of sensory observation, not the logical law of contradiction. But now it is demonstrated that without reference to time and space, simply in terms of thought, synthetic knowledge and change are inseparable concepts, while synthetic knowledge and mere rational coherence (thus discovery from reason) contradict each other.

Basis of the Deception

Therefore, it is quite natural that this greatest of all investigators, who by virtue of the strict account he everywhere renders, undoubtedly lays claim to the rank of the most thoroughgoing and venerable of all rational philosophers, was led by his investigations to this place: reason vouchsafes no synthetic knowledge in the theoretical sphere. But when in the practical sphere he nevertheless commits the contradiction, he is deceived by the following mistake: our sense of ought, the drive, the longing within us, really precedes all sensory impressions, and to that degree is *a priori,* and certainly also has a synthetic force; it impels us to certain actions, requires conditions, and points with certainty to a relation with God, the future, and blessedness. *But this drive is not reason,* it is a real power, and in terms of its innermost essence continues to have an effect as act and change, by no means in a logical manner, by no means according to the nature of reason. It is also, even though free of visible influences and elevated above them, still not an initiating cause but rather effected by a higher cause preceding it and distinguished from it. Precisely the character in it by which it is what it is, and by which it alone can have the synthetic power to generate something from itself, namely what is real, what is capable of action – it is precisely this character that Kant denies to it and declares to be a delusion. What he allows to remain to it as truthful, the emptied thought of the *a priori,* is what the synthetic power does not have. He thus makes use of the actual drive (which he denied) in order to attribute its force to thought, which in terms of its nature it cannot have.

Three Resulting Inconsistencies in his Practical Philosophy

From this stem the inconsistencies in Kant's practical reason, among which these three can be distinguished: that a real moral law follows from pure reason; that on the basis of this moral law, not only actions but general conditions can be commanded; and finally, that not merely practical but also theoretical knowledge can be derived from it.

The world of action, in which, because knowledge is directed toward what exists, thought is transcended, is precisely what Kant needs for the knowledge of what is to be produced. Like every idea, every commandment must also have an object, and this – the act, the human relation – pertains to the world which he regards as mere appearance, and which thoroughly bears that character. He cannot escape the fact that the essence of practical reason itself does not otherwise appear to us, for it is affected by this world, as an ought, as a free production of something new. The rational law of universality and necessity can as little be a practical commandment as can the categories, or the unity of apperception, be knowledge. If in accordance with this law of reason Kant assumes the content, "act in such a way that all rational creatures can exist in accordance therewith," then he has thus drawn upon the entire world of appearance, and that which he denied in theoretical philosophy, he acknowledges as true. Because living things, and the fact that they may exist or be annihilated – pure thought knows nothing of them. That a wound yields death, that deprivation of food causes hunger, which one does not have from eternity, in short, continued existence and destruction, all of these are change, already in terms of thought. The highest truth and the summit of the system, the last judgment [das Weltgericht], presupposes that there has been action, and arbitrary action; that there has been alteration, and thus analytically contains that which is categorically denied. How can practical reason, since it must draw upon experience, extend beyond the limits of possible experience, and how can truth arise? But if it does not draw on experience, the law of universality and necessity requires nothing other than that something not cancel itself, and this something is again nothing other than the form of conceptual unity itself, as it also underlies theoretical reason. The only content that the imperative can have is that thought be thought.

If reason is the cause of the practical commandments and therefore determines their content, then they, as shown above, can only make demands on the actions of the individual. Yet in Kant, their object is also the existence of general conditions, for example the state, directly and in its entirety, or punishment as retributive justice. Kant confesses that this contradicts the original essence of reason, but that it is capable of "expanding itself *a priori* by such postulates." But reason is not capable of such an expansion, such a pursuit of the world outside us; only the real drive of the ought within us is capable of this.

Through such expansion, Kant finally also succeeds in deriving theoretical results from practical thought. Namely, God, immortality, the last judgment, regarding which practical reason does not vouchsafe the insight that we effectuate them, or that they *should* exist, but that they really *do* exist, where, therefore, practical reason, contrary to its own concepts, is directed not to the production of objects but to the knowledge of existing ones. In this, Kant is supported by his denial of time and change; for with this the difference between theoretical and practical knowledge is really abolished; future and present, will and being become the same. The act, the choice, which, already in terms of words separates the practical from the theoretical, is precisely what is abandoned as untrue.

Now here as well, the inner contradiction of the system should be most striking. Because reason calls for conditions of a certain sort, Kant recognizes the truth of its requirement (the future, which depends upon choice), but not the fulfillment thereof, for example, that a state should actually exist. But in invoking conditions of another sort, he recognizes not only the requirement but also the fulfillment as being inevitable, e.g., God, immortality, the last judgment. He should have said: Reason demands the state, criminal justice, God, the last judgment; and its requirement, its ought-to-exist is true, and it is so because reason commands it, which can have no other standard of truth; but whether they really exist is a question with which practical reason has nothing to do. Or, he had to say: that which practical reason demands, also exists necessarily – but in that case, not only God and immortality, but also the universal reasonableness of our actions; and this obviously contradicts the facts.

This is Kant's attitude toward rational dogmatism, both the consistent version of Spinoza and the vague arbitrary one of the Wolffian school. The latter deduce the existing world of change from its unchanging laws of thought. Kant shows this to be contradictory, but then he himself makes the same contradiction, by deducing from just such premises a moral world which also includes action and change.

Impetus to Further Development: Transcendental Philosophy, Result of Fichte's and Kant's Standpoints

The essence of Kant's criticism contained the impulse toward a completely new development. The contradiction between pure thought and the real world produced his system, and his activity, therefore, had to be directed toward sharply separating these opposites. Hence, rational philosophy was not merely brought to the consciousness of its enterprise, but also brought to inward awareness, since the separation makes reason an object of its own reflection. Those who preceded him contemplated the world, into which they tacitly transported thought. Kant contemplated thought itself. In technical terms: this is the emergence of transcendental philosophy, the philosophy which observes its own consciousness, while it takes up its objects, looks upon the activity, the means of which it makes use.

This measured separation of the faculty of knowledge from its objects, however, necessarily provokes a new philosophical question, namely, how is not merely the perception of the truth possible, but perceptibility at all? How do the two divorced worlds, reason and the objects outside of reason, unite into one idea, even though it be erroneous? This question is deeply rooted in the essence of abstract philosophy and the subjective principle. The man who breaks away from the world must wonder: how can this world still excite conceptions in me? The investigations of Descartes, Spinoza, and Leibniz on the connection between the body and the soul are already echoes of it. Now, however, the entire fate of philosophy is laid upon its shoulders, and at present it is crowding out everything else which ultimately must be dealt with, which Kant himself pronounced to be the actual tasks, those regarding God, immortality, freedom. The development of philosophy is now continuing on this path, and it is as if humanity will have attained its goal if it could explain how it came to conceptualize anything.

The explanation which first presents itself, of which Kant therefore, as the starting point, avails himself, is this: things make sensory impressions upon us, we lend to these impressions the form of reason, and both together make up conceptualization. But a close inspection reveals the inadequacy of this explanation, and this led to the system of Fichte. The impression on the senses, namely, is quite without reason, it being purely physical; it cannot, therefore, become something intelligible, no matter the elevation; otherwise, one would be able to construct thinking just as well by using physical ingredients. A thing is not a thought and can never become a thought, and the thought form can only be affected by a thought, not by a body and a physical effect. Hence, the connection between the two would be impossible. Kant did not here, in theoretical reason, usurp the *truth* of imagination, as he did in his practical deductions, but rather the *existence* thereof.

But why is it that he cannot establish a connection between reason and things, since, as experience shows, such really exists? The reason for this, as

Fichte demonstrates,[138] is that he contemplates reason as a static form, and consequently as a thing. A thing and another thing that is set over against it, will always remain apart. It was therefore necessary to regard reason as active; not as the determinations of thought and laws, but as the *activity of thought*. This was the precondition for explaining this connection.

In what manner it was to be explained, however, was in turn motivated for Fichte by the stage of the Kantian system. The previous philosophy generally had the conviction that only reason is true. Kant shared this conviction, but at the same time expressed what it entails, namely, that things are untrue. Nevertheless he asserted their truth, but only as a veiled one. But this cannot mean anything other than: if things had been properly recognized, it would have to be understood that they too are nothing but reason, but that means that they are *not* – the *only* thing that is, is *reason*. Kant thus unconsciously asserted it, and Fichte had only to explain it.

But in doing so he completed his explanation of conceptualization. In other words, reason is both the forms of thought and the things, but it is both only by producing them in their activity. If, for example, the relation of cause and effect, which is of reason and not of experience, is analyzed, then there is already in it this, that a thing produces another thing. Hence, pure reason contains objects, and the Kantian distinction cannot be preserved at all; rather, the inevitable spillover from the form of reason to the object outside of it proves that they are not separate things – indeed, they are not things at all – but only products of an undivided activity. Thus one can no longer ask how, by means of matter and the capacity to conceptualize, conceptualization and knowing are possible, for it is not matter, nor the capacity to conceptualize, but merely conceptualization and knowing.

This step was thus inevitable for rationalism, since it insisted that there was no truth outside of reason, and yet had to make comprehensible the possibility of a conceptualization.

---

[138] This transition from Kant to Fichte is manifested most vividly in the essays of the latter in his and Niethammer's *Philosophischen Journal* [Philosophical Journal].

Chapter 4: Kant's Doctrine of Law

Fulfillment of the Rationalistic Character

Kant resolutely extended the rationalistic character of ethics and natural law to its farthest limit, and executed it with deliberation. In the practical field, too, he excluded all that is empirical, all that comes from objects other than the laws of thought, and sought the sum of the ethical only in the latter. This is the position he occupies in the development of moral and legal philosophy.

He confessed without hesitation the assertion of Grotius, and the so-called *perseitas* [perseity] of the good, without making a distinction between *principium cognoscendi* and *principium obligationis*: God can be imagined to be the author of obligation vis-à-vis the law, and furthermore to be the one to whom everyone owes obedience *according to* a law, but not to be the author of the law itself – this is, and can only be, reason; otherwise the law would be contingent.[139] God is so little the author of the law that He himself stands under it. Even God can act in no other way than under a maxim or such-like, may only treat other rational beings as ends, not as means, must conceive of Himself as a participant in the kingdom of ends, even though the chief one, cannot add anything to the content and motive of the moral law,[140] and thus is the constitutional monarch of the kingdom of reason.

Kant also expressly states something that his predecessors only groped after: there is no ethic in the relations and dealings of life (as something made by God and not reason), but only in what remains in our thinking after all abstraction. From here it enters first into actions and then into relations. Hence for Kant it is not a question of the nature of the individual act which interferes with the real world, which either fulfills or abandons its purpose, but only of the general rules which have been formulated without regard for the present, principles for which the goal of all action is not to contradict them. This shows what Grotius

---

[139] Kant, *Metaphysische Anfangsgründe der Rechtslehre,* p. xxviii [p. 19 of *The Metaphysics of Morals*].

[140] Kant, *Grundlegung zur Metaphysik der Sitten* [Foundation of the Metaphysics of Morals], pp. 74, 75, 85.

and Pufendorf were after when the former[141] asserted that the moral laws do not have the certainty of geometry because they cannot be separated from matter, while the latter asserted the mathematical certainty thereof, and writes of the necessary instability of relations in such a way that the moral law is by no means affected by them.[142] He was impelled, although less clearly, by the idea that the ethic exists only as a rule, and not as an act.

In the same sense Kant separates the motives of the will. Nothing in which the will is determined by an object outside of thought – pleasure, desire, affection, love – is an ethical motive. The only ethical motive is respect for the law, and indeed, the law of reason. Laudable acts out of the love of God or man are as little moral as are laudable acts out of ambition and selfishness. Inclination and love, far from increasing the ethical quality of the act, rather detract from it, as Schiller's epigram justly brings out:

> Willingly serve I my friends;
> but, alas, I do it with pleasure;
> Therefore I often am vex'd
> that no true virtue I have.[143]

Finally, for Kant the content of all ethics is solely the law of thought, consistency. His predecessors, even philosophers like Leibniz, had everything that should exist be a requirement of reason, and suddenly the content of the good for them is again love, humanity, equal rewards and punishments, without their being aware of and explaining how these are required by the laws of thought, or even connected with them. But Kant accepts nothing as ethical of which he is not at least convinced that thought itself contains it inevitably, and therefore ruthlessly eliminates everything regarding which he is consciously aware that such a proof is impossible. For Kant, the moral law must be *categorical*, not hypothetical (valid only under certain conditions of experience). It must therefore be *merely formal*, that is, have no object, no content, no material. As such, the moral law is nothing other than the law of thought: universality and non-

---

[141] Grotius, *De Jure Belli ac Pacis*, Book II, ch. 23, §. 1.

[142] Pufendorf, *De Jure Naturæ et Gentium*, Book I, ch. 2, §. 9.

[143] *The Poems of Schiller*, trans. E.A. Bowring (New York: John B. Alden, 1883), p. 268.

contradiction. It reads: act according to a maxim which, made into a universal law, does not contradict itself (actually, which made into a universal law does not destroy the social state of the world of experience). Or, according to a different expression: act according to a categorical purpose, that is, not according to something that you posit arbitrarily, but something that every rational being must posit. Nevertheless, there is only one such purpose: reason or the rational being itself, and therefore: you must have the rational being, both yourself and other rational beings besides you, as an end (here Kant unknowingly confuses reason/the law of thought/consistency and the rational being/personality/the real subject).

From here he constructs the moral world; for him, it is a kingdom of ends, inasmuch as all the rational beings set themselves the purpose of treating themselves and one another simply as ends. According to all of this, the good, as Kant himself emphatically emphasizes, is not an original concept which thought discovers; rather, it follows from the law of thought, as derivative.

In the same manner, in the theory of law, external freedom is first shown to be contained in the essence of reason, in the notion of the absolute, of universality and necessity. It goes like this: the nature of reason is that it itself, i.e., its law of necessity, is the original and solely effectuating factor in action. For this it is necessary that the will *really* not be determined by impressions of the outer world (which implies as a postulate that it must have the *possibility* of not being determined thereby – freedom of the will). Such impressions of the world are twofold: desires aroused from within, and force from without. Thought must surmount both in order to be the absolute. By requiring the first, it is the moral, by the second, it is the juridical law. Morality is therefore internal legislation, self-compulsion; juridical law is outward legislation, removal of outward force, coercion of others.[144]

But because the concept of external freedom has been gained from reason,

---

[144] Hence, it is not the subject aiming at this rational, that is, aprioristic action, who is coerced by juridical law, as with morality; rather, it is others who are so coerced. In this manner reason, because it dictates moral and juridical law, secretly switches the subjects to whom it speaks. This follows from the inconsistency criticized above, that Kant allows reason to dictate objective conditions. Its command here is really this: on the one hand, *you shall* overcome your desire, on the other, *it shall not be* that you be coerced!

it everywhere becomes a subject of investigation as to whether the opposite of a given institution [Anstalt] would contradict this concept – for only then is it recognized. For example: "It is possible to have each external object of my will as my own. Suppose there to be a maxim entailing that such an object of the will must remain ownerless. If this were made into a law, it would be *repugnant* to law."[145] In this manner, Kant stands on the same level as his time, which tore apart everything that was not necessary in this manner. Institutions [Institute] of feudal law, the church, which claimed their place in the natural law of the older protagonists, are expelled from it. The national economy collapses, and taxation falls only under the purview of the protection of rights. Kant was the first theoretically to derive institutions which do not follow from freedom but which nevertheless cannot be done away with in any actual state, as means for those that do – such as maintenance of the poor, education, the prohibition of public immorality, public health, contributions to the church. He has been followed in this expedient of his by the entire mass of modern proponents of constitutional law, as well as the natural-law textbooks.

Recognizing the world of phenomena alongside reason, Kant found the laws by subsuming the various materials under the general rule of reason. He thus fell into the same necessity as the others, not merely of subsuming objects of experience, but taking the ordinary effects of them as [if they were] premises of the rule itself. Yet Kant was the first to realize that this does not accord with the philosophy of reason; he knew what *continuo ratiocinationis filo deducere* [continuous deduction of the thread of reasoning] means. He tried to prove that he did not discover the state through this observation, but without much success.[146]

This finalization of the abstract character therefore corresponds to the fact that, since Kant, the philosophy of law changed its name. The earlier prac-

---

[145] *Ibid.*, p. 56, §2.

[146] *Metaphysische Anfangsgründe der Rechtslehre*, §. 35, p. 192. [*The Metaphysics of Morals*, pp. 89–90.] Kant here demonstrates *a priori* that people are not simply [the embodiment of] reason, but also at times unjust to each other, as well as aberrant in their judgments. This is something that Pufendorf demonstrates more appropriately from experience: *quis est, qui ignoret?* in *De Jure Naturæ et Gentium*, Book VII, ch. 1, §. 10. Cf. pp. 134ff. above.

titioners, as shown above, had some empirical drive as principle, and only the inference from this was purely rational. For them, therefore, the expression inherited from the Romans, *natural law*, was still appropriate. But the principle of Kant being consistency, thought-necessity itself, the only characteristic name now is the *law of reason*.

Restriction of the Subjective Character

But if Kant in one fell swoop finalized the rationalism of ethical laws, by comparison he comported himself toward the subjective principle in such a way as partly not to favor it, and partly even to prevent its development. For the acting man and his freedom belong to the world, a world which Kant maintains is untrue, and although Kant necessarily tolerates him, like he does this world generally, he subordinates him to his higher world, the law of reason. This manifests itself both in the scientific deduction of the basic concepts and in the results of his legal doctrine.

Legal freedom is not given for man's sake and does not follow from his living existence, but follows from the existence of the forms of reason, and exists so that one may act *a priori*, that is, so that thereby the logical law is the first cause of an intelligible world. It is not so much the freedom of the individual, as the thought of freedom which is the same to everyone (the maxim of coexistence). Therefore, it is already primordially restricted for each; there is a juridical law (the consequence of that thought) before all agreement (the consequence of individual active freedom). From that idea, the state follows of necessity. It is therefore an imperative, required directly and unconditionally by reason. The civil authority stems from this concept of reason, its sanctity and its power can therefore not be doubted; the people of the world of phenomena cannot decide on it; hence Kant's disgust regarding the judgment of the French people over their king.[147] The freedom (law) of the living man only follows from the idea of the equal freedom of all, which does not consist in the permission [Erlauben], but only in the uniform restriction of each; it follows indirectly, as an emptied sphere ; it is a non-prohibition. Reason here makes the right of man [das Recht des Menschen] into its right, which then follows from it and exists for it, and

---

[147] *Metaphysische Anfangsgründe der Rechtslehre*, pp. 207ff. [pp. 97–98 in *The Metaphysics of Morals*].

therefore for the most part is withdrawn from man's power of disposal, which after all is the only way that it could express itself.

Moreover, reason also directly manifests itself as being invested with rights and prescribes to man enforceable duties which are no longer due to the idea of universal freedom. The subject of these rights Kant calls humanity or man in himself, in opposition to the man of phenomena, thus not the man of action but the one inexorably determined by reason, by the logical law itself. The duties of the family, between the spouses, between parents and children are derived from this right of reason (even though they do not follow from it), and evidently do not stem from the freedom of the individuals, which is why, likewise according to Kant, they cannot be waived by mutual consent. This right of reason demands punishment as retribution. Punishment, then, is not a means of preventing people from being injured in the future, but a necessary consequence of reason, which would be violated immediately by its omission. The law of non-contradiction, of uniformity, has a right to exist, and its existence is just the *talio*. Non-punishment of crime does precisely the same thing against the law of reason that violence does against the living man.[148] Furthermore, the law of reason makes acts into violations of rights which do not infringe the right of any living human being (unnatural sins.) So it is only man as such (reason) who, as a member of the popular assembly, helps to form the court of law and, for example, issues the sentence.

Necessary Progression to Fichte

The existence of two principles of law – reason and the I – appears in Kant's system as perfectly consistent, in that they correspond to its two opposing worlds. His system as a whole justifies the inclusion of the contradictions that

[148] This was the least comprehensible thing of all; it made Feuerbach believe that, given this theory of retribution, Kant must have been decrepit when he wrote his doctrine of law. It is natural that the results from Kant's purely objective rational principle would not be understood, given that the whole development could not stand still with him, but aspired to the pure subjectivity of Fichte, to which Feuerbach already most certainly adhered in his view of punishment. Cf. von Linck, *Über das Naturrecht unserer Zeit als Grundlage der Strafrechtstheorien* [Regarding the Natural Law of our Time as the Foundation of Theories of Penal Law], Part II.

permeate the law of nature, and to that extent he can also be called the true representative of it. This explains the general following that he gained at the time, and the authority which he still possesses among all abstract legal philosophers. His doctrine of law resembles the momentary balance of a tipping body that delays its fall, and so seems to be true bearing and consistency. The real change took place only with Fichte, who for that reason also encountered less of a reception.

But being justified in terms of his system is not yet being justified in the thing itself. The right of real people has no association with that of people as such, as little as, in the system as a whole, the world of appearance has with that of reason. Here is no explanation as to why phenomena are there and why everything is not reason, which is why, in our conceptualizations, we cannot determine where the truth ends, and where the deception begins. Thus in ethics it is not evident why freedom of choice [Willkür] (i.e., of people) exists and not merely freedom of the will [Willens] (i.e., of reason), why compulsion, if reason demands it, depends on the pleasure of the claimant, why there is a right of unreasonable people alongside the right of people as such. So then, here too it is not possible to determine with necessity what belongs to one person and what to another, to what degree reason should limit individual freedom or leave it untouched. For there is nothing higher over both, which sets for each its limits; but the right of man in itself, in terms of its concept, excludes all freedom of real human beings, and vice versa.

And so Kant cannot do anything else than attribute, entirely arbitrarily, something to reason here, something to man there. For example, he allows wealth to depend upon the regulation of human beings, while he allows family relations to be governed by reason. He wants the state to be necessary, and yet he cannot give up its contractual formation. In order for the sovereign to have an unlimited right, it is necessary at the same time that everyone who obeys be himself (in his reality) and be a member of the sovereign, and yet it is not the real man at all, but his reasonableness, which votes in the assembly and passes judgment in the court; the one who obeys is something else altogether.[149]

This dualism, this inner, all-pervading contradiction, makes it necessary to

---

[149] Cf. *Metaphysische Anfangsgründe der Rechtslehre,* p. 195 along with p. 320 [pp. 91, 102 in *The Metaphysics of Morals*].

progress towards an undivided principle. But the restriction of personal freedom also pressed in this direction. This alone, as the living mainspring of the development, could not receive more than an initial impulse from Kant's reaction, who with scientific circumspection submitted it to the law of reason; but with this impulse it was enabled with equal resolution to rise above that law.

Kant revealed the insoluble difficulties of deriving the juridical law from reason: the impossibility of deriving from it the right and entitlement of the individual; the question as to why reason, if it must compel freedom, cannot compel other purposes; and why it protects the same actions in one case which it forbids in another.

It was imperative to give up the law of reason as a basis for legal freedom, and to locate that basis in the real man in his free activity.

In this specific doctrine as well, the phase of Kant leads to that of Fichte.

Chapter 5: Fichte's System

Personality, not Law of Thought

Reason became something different with Fichte than it was in its earlier development. No longer was it the epitome of thought determinations; instead, it was the thinking being, the person himself, inasmuch as he acts according to those determinations. I myself, self-consciousness, am reason. The highest conviction of rationalism – only reason is true – hereby received a new meaning, one completely different from the old one: only self-consciousness, only the thinking, the personal, is and has reality. That which has no consciousness of itself, a thing (the forms of thought itself as such), is not there at all, "and he who thinks differently does not understand himself" – this is the thesis that Fichte carried through with all his resolve, as the first and last result.

Identity of Consciousness

Right now, our consciousness seems to bear witness to the existence of these unconscious things. But that is deception. Those things are not truly there; they cannot, therefore, be the cause of our conceptions of them; only our consciousness is, and those things are only there because it conceptualizes them to itself, and therefore are there only as conceptualized (for us), not as being (for themselves).

But if you ask: why do we conceptualize things if they do not exist apart from ourselves, and why do we have the consciousness that we of necessity conceptualize them? The answer is: the law of consciousness (or more significantly: the concept thereof) says that objects must be conceptualized. Such is discovered by self-observation, which is the outcome and the precondition of all philosophy. I am not conscious in any other way of myself – hence, I am not there at all – without also setting some object, even if only my own self, over against myself as something distinguished from me. This act is not an affair of pre-existing consciousness; consciousness only arises with it.

Denial of Objects

But I see this act by which I set the object, and distinguish myself, the active (subject), from what I set over against myself (object); even if this opposite is itself nothing else than myself; because it is just my activity. So, the subject and the object are both only the one and the same I in its actions; this is the identity of self-consciousness, which exists only by being active in this opposite way, as a subject-object [Subjektobjekt]. The double series, the activity which posits objects (the real I), and the activity which looks at and differentiates them from itself (the ideal I) in its inseparability (identity), is reason. The objects cannot therefore be anything separated from it, outside of it, because its own concept is just the positing of these objects. I have to posit objects before all experience, because before I posit them, I do not even exist. But this means as much as: there is no experience, that is, no conceptualizing, which is effected by a cause outside conceptualizing. Rather, the activity which, in accordance with its nature, posits and looks at objects – reason – is the only being. It is only to the unphilosophical consciousness that the effects of the law of this activity seem to be experience.

Subjective Idealism

The way in which the I opposes itself to itself and distinguishes itself from itself is manifold, and from this arises the diversity of conceptualizations. Two main types of activity are above all distinguished: in one, the act which posits objects (the not-I) precedes, and the view [Beschauung] is determined by it — *perception* [Erkennen]. In the other, the view, the concept (the original I) precedes, and the positing of the object depends on it — *action*. In the first case, everything is necessary; for the law of the I acts without me knowing how I must set these objects; the real activity is a necessary one. In the second case, the ideal begins in me, pure activity, which, since it has no object, can choose this one or that; hence I am free. The concept of action therefore demands that the pure, free I actually not be determined by an object in any manner, but instead that it determine the object out of itself — this is *the ought*.

Task to Discover Everything a priori

Fichte demonstrated, as was shown, that the positing of objects is contained in the notion of self-consciousness. However, if the viewpoint that there is no object and no experience is to be demonstrated, it must be shown how self-consciousness is compelled by the law of its activity to conceptualize precisely such and such objects, indeed all those which everyone feels bound to conceptualize to himself, which, according to an unphilosophical way of thinking, exist outside of him. The whole world of experience must be discovered from the laws of self-consciousness (*a priori*). This then is the task of the Fichtean system.

Hence, it is not merely the form of perception, but also its substance, the things themselves, which are to be derived from reason; not merely the ethical rules, but also the relationships which they determine. That plants, animals, other people are there outside of myself, that the race is maintained through reproduction, my body by food which the earth vouchsafes me, must as necessarily reside in the concept of self-consciousness as do reciprocal legal restriction, marriage, property; for how else would I know all this, since I do not get any conception of it from the outside, and with the non-existence of things, cannot do so?[150] This task, which cannot be ignored in the Fichtean system, has aroused the greatest astonishment and, through its clash with all ordinary thinking, and certainly with the actual existence of things, has hindered its spread. But as ridiculous as the enterprise seems and as unfeasible for the unbedazzled, it contains the truth that the substance of things and their restriction, the ethical rules and the relations for which they exist, cannot be separated from one another; the one has no existence apart from the other; they are the product of *one* act. The fallacy is only to consider this act to be one of human consciousness. But Fichte not only *a priori* derives external objects, but also the forms of thought themselves. While Kant only comes across the categories and tabulates

[150] This alone can be the criterion of reality even according to those presuppositions. If we distinguish the conceptions of real objects (horses, lions) from fantastic (dragons, gnomes) by the fact that the former exist in the outside world, the latter only in our conceptualizations, then with Fichte the difference cannot lie here, because for him *everything* exists only in conceptualization, with the difference being that the former are conceptualized according to the law of self-consciousness, thus in a necessary manner, while the latter are conceptualized apart from this law, in arbitrary acts of conceptualization. The further question of how it comes about that, among these objects which of necessity form the perimeter of our entire conceptualizing, I also at any moment in time necessarily conceptualize just those of which the empirical consciousness says that they surround me right at this moment (e.g., the house, the street in which I live, the people who just then walk across the street), this question, to which his system peremptorily leads, Fichte does not even raise.

them and arranges them schematically, Fichte undertakes to demonstrate their necessity, to have them emerge from the one supreme assumption of his system, that of the actuality of self-consciousness according to the law of I-not-I. In this as well, he is the forerunner of Hegel, who likewise does not submit to the categories as given, but undertakes to generate them by the dialectical movement.

Real Principle in Fichte's Doctrine and Its Consequences

Fichte incorporated the real, which remains after all abstraction has been accomplished, the self-conscious acting I, into his system, which from this receives a livelier character.

The previous method was subsumption, which was used by the Wolffian school, the natural-law doctors, and Kant. It is based on there being, apart from the rational rule, which is the major premise, also matter separate from it, as the minor premise. Scientific activity brings both together and draws a conclusion. Fichte does not have two such halves and can spare them, because his living principle produces something besides himself. His scientific activity does not bring together what is separated, but pursues that indivisible production. For him, the essential organ of philosophical perception is the vision [die Anschauung]: it envisions the activity of the I in itself; only then does the abstracting mind derive characteristics from it, and retain its contents as something static, no longer alive – as a concept. It is demonstrated here that wherever there is only a spark of life and action, the forms of reason no longer attain to perception, but rather a capacity is required which does not separate relations, but is all-encompassing, which we call vision.

Furthermore, with Kant the content of the ethic is the law of reason; the freedom of man to be determined by this law is just the precondition of fulfilling it. With Fichte, this freedom of the I to be determined by reason – i.e., in this case the concept of its own existence – is itself the content: "the ought is the *drive* of absolute self-*activity*." Thus, legal freedom is not a consequence of the commands of reason, but a direct act through which the I posits itself as free. Accordingly, with Kant the band that holds together the different spheres is a logical one: the law of reason contains the forms of perception, the prescriptions of action, and the imperative of legal freedom. In Fichte, it is a real one: the active I perceives, is driven by itself to the ethic, posits itself as free.

Satisfaction of the Interests of Recent Philosophy by Fichte

This system corresponds to the innermost interest of the new philosophy. The world no longer lays down a necessity for man to conceive specific objects and recognize laws; necessity lies only within him and the nature of his consciousness. He does this all for no other reason than because that is what he is; it obligates him to nothing than his own existence (equal to God). On the other hand, the logical interest of rationalism is also satisfied by the fact that everything that exists is already posited with the concept of self-consciousness, in such a way that it cannot be thought away. But that is why, in principle, the first satisfaction is undone; for man, although free from all the outside world, has an inexorable ruler in the laws of logic of his consciousness. In terms of the same *a priori*, he can be told which objects he should conceptualize, which requirements he should set for himself. And yet he is not himself this law; for although it may be his nature, it is not his will. He gains nothing in the exchange. Nevertheless, this is the most that could be done for human freedom; for man to make all objects and moral laws at will, so that his free will is the cause of conceptions and ethics, cannot be asserted because it contradicts the undeniable facts. The best that could be done was to posit the necessary law of his consciousness as the cause, and this is only an apparent satisfaction, an unproductive gain.

That is why in this system, the life spark that wishes to flare up is repeatedly suppressed, like the Greek god who devours his children at birth. The universal act of consciousness is observed through vision and is a matter of empirics, so that only its *existence* is *exhibited*, not its *necessity demonstrated*. But this act is at once comprehended in a concept, and now, as in the other systems, deduction from the impossibility of the opposite takes its place.

Relation to Spinoza

Hence, Spinoza's rules are paid full homage. The I is the substance, the world its necessary consequences. With Fichte, it is not that the world is *produced* by the *activity* of the I – as appears to be the case – but rather, that the world is *contained* in the *concept* of self-consciousness, and it is given as something that is.

Yet as far as the *content* of Spinoza's doctrine is concerned, Fichte is precisely opposed to him. He makes the inconceivability of objective rationalism clear. There is no impersonal world-law or universal existence such as Spinoza would have it, since there is only what is self-conscious. The career of the entirety of abstract philosophy can be summarized as follows: Spinoza's assertion of logical pantheism, and the procedure of the Wolffian school to demonstrate everything from the laws of thought, challenged Kant to investigate whether the coherence of things corresponded to the coherence of reason, thus to a separation of thought and its objects, leading straight to the question of knowability. And with Fichte this led to the insight that there is only actual thought, only personality, and thereby to the rejection of logical pantheism of the Spinozan sort. So it strode in the opposite direction, with Fichte bringing subjective rationalism to completion in the place of objective rationalism. As did the Wolffian school before him, Kant proceeded from himself, the thinker, and to this degree, the unity of apperception is for him the focus of reason; but he then detached reason from himself and treated it as an independent objective power. But with Fichte, reason exists only as the I; this is therefore actually and generally the principle, it is God and the world, as substance is with Spinoza, and it cannot really be distinguished as the one or the other; for it is first itself when it imagines the world to itself (in both meanings of the word[151]), and the world is only there while imagined by it.

Untenability of the Fichtean Standpoint

Yet this, when it becomes clear, entails the fearful thought: only I, the individual, the I known as so and so, am; and I am the entire world, and if I cease acting, I die, there is nothing more. Fichte could not bring himself to admit that other self-conscious beings could exist, for how should these various I's come to each other, affect each other, and impart the consciousness of their existences? Every not-I is only my I. My conception of other people, like anything else, cannot be brought about by their existence, for it is the product of my own thought activity, which is sufficient to engender it, and nothing outside of it is capable of this. These other people with whom I interact, strangers, friends, relations, are not truly self-conscious acting beings, but are only conceptualized as such by me in a necessary manner, like the beings of dreams. The same is true of God, should a follower of Fichte's believe in Him. He could only be the creation of his intelligence, his I, which he sets over against himself, not something else;

[151] ["imagines" – *sich einbilden* – can also have the meaning of a false impression.]

only for him, not for Himself, only something conceptualized, not something existing.

To think in this manner is insanity, and Fichte does not admit that his system promotes such thinking. He deceives himself by conceiving the I not as the existing, but as one of the existing, or as rational being in general. But such an I fills the entire world, and it is not evident how another such I can exist alongside him. So then, if Fichte wished to make a universal I into God, which only individualizes Himself into many people and separates them from Himself, then this was the step which Schelling took immediately after him, but which also abolishes Fichte's system. For according to Fichte, the I is not there at all prior to its positing itself over against itself, in so doing coming to awareness,[152] but this is to consider an individual I, Fichte or any one of his readers, as the only one; the universal I would not be conscious of one of himself. This individual I runs through the entire system. Should the universal I be the principle of law [Recht], positing itself as free, then there would be posited as free a necessary law [Gesetz] like the Kantian man as such, or even Spinoza's nature; that you or I are free is not thereby stated, but denied. And upon this latter is what Fichte's natural law is based. When furthermore it is demonstrated with natural law that the I must see other I's opposite him, then this only makes sense with the individual.

Nevertheless, in his later writings (which certainly were not true to his earlier ones) Fichte did involve the universal I, although he did not make proper use of it. But only the system of "My I" influenced the progress of philosophy and his own doctrine of law.[153] Fichte thus conducted the isolation of persons

---

[152] *Grundlage des Naturrechts nach Principien der Wissenschaftslehre*, p. 11.

[153] Fichte's I is, however, equal to Kant's unity of apperception (of which it is merely the more vivid expression), pure I, not the empirical I; in itself it is abstracted from every material determination that I perceive in myself, and the mere pure thought-activity conceived with it. But just because it is *pure* I, it is by no means yet *objective* I. Just as is that unity of apperception, it ever remains subjective thought-activity, positing objects for a (subjective) consciousness, just as the characterization "I" indicates. For this reason it is necessarily individual, albeit not individual A or individual B, but individual as such. Fichte speaks precisely in this manner in his *Das System der Sittenlehre* [Science

to the extreme. He who philosophizes, views himself as the midpoint and, as follows of necessity, as the cause of the world. But this position also makes clear that he cannot get back to those from whom he has freed himself, given that every bond with a real world and with real people has been severed. Man and his thought cannot be the midpoint of things or the knowledge of them.

---

of Ethics]: "Now it is certainly, as we have seen, involved in Egohood [i.e., I-ness], that each Ego [I] should be an individual, but only an individual in general, and not this particular individual A, B, C, &c.... Hence since it is accidental to the Egohood in general, that I, the individual A, am precisely this A, and since the drive of self-sufficiency is to be a drive of the Egohood in general, as such, this drive certainly does not crave the self-sufficiency of the particular individual A, but of reason in general. The self-sufficiency of reason as such, is our ultimate purpose; and hence not the self-sufficiency of our reason, in so far as it is an individual reason" [*The Science of Ethics as based on the Science of Knowledge,* p. 243]. Fichte's I can therefore be conceptualized at most as the general law of subjective consciousness, not however as something objective, separated from this consciousness (similar to Schelling's absolute I). But then it is something abstract like Kant's reason; if it is to be real, then it is just the thinking of the individual. Even when Fichte later (not perhaps without being instigated by Schelling) progresses to the fact that one must conclude from the I (actually real subjective thinking) to a basis thereof, and the basis of that existence is God, this god may not be so construed as a reality but merely as a picture, a silhouette, from which the activity of the I, which consists precisely in depiction, image-making, proceeds. That archetype, the god, is not on behalf of itself and in itself, but merely the source or the law of the conceptualizing and acting activity of the I, and accordingly the world is not immediately produced by this god but rather is conceived by the subjective I (consciousness) in accordance with that image or law. Among all the shapes it takes, Fichte's doctrine therefore remains pure idealism, pure subjectivism and pure movement without contentual being. It is nothing other than Kant's system of categories set in motion.

Chapter 6: Fichte's Doctrine of Law

Abstract Character of Ethics

In the practical field as in the theoretical, Fichte only furnishes a modification to Kant's system, whereby what with Kant is a static thought-form, with Fichte becomes the activity of the I. The entire outline of the system remains the same; only the lines shift in terms of this differing viewpoint. In this manner, Kant's doctrine of the ethic, which consists in nothing else than *a priori* action, is maintained. But with Kant, *a priori* action is that in which action is undertaken in accordance with the logical law of universality and non-contradiction, thus according to a maxim which does not contradict itself when executed; with Fichte, on the other hand, *a priori* action takes place when the I acts out of itself, thus in terms of its conviction, which it recognizes as duty. Here and there, action is considered in terms of the effect of external objects and the pleasure and pain they excite – empirical action – as something opposed to the ethical, and the ethical is nothing else than being free from this; or, as Fichte expresses it: thou shalt use nature as the means for reason (i.e., the law of the actively thinking I), not vice versa. But for Kant, action coming from inside is conformity with the laws of logic, hence the universally possible maxim, while with Fichte it is the actuality of the I as such. Action from enthusiasm [Begeisterung] is therefore the final solution of Fichte's ethics.

Resultant Oppositions to Kant

And so, Fichte's principle of enthusiasm has as little content as does Kant's law of universality and non-contradiction. For Kant, the ethic is a formal (abstract, contentless) law; for Fichte, it is formal (abstract, contentless) enthusiasm. The charge that he puts to the ethical world (the community of rational being), to encourage one another to act from *conviction*, obviously provides no content to the conviction. According to that modification of Kant's point of view, Kant's two postulates – recompense in accordance with desert, and God as Judge – take on a different shape with Fichte; or rather, after having become shadowy figures with Kant, they drop off entirely (as do all parts of the object). Recompense, or salvation, as the case may be, is not to be sought in an enjoyment of a sort of "liberation from all dependence" but only in a complete such liberation, i.e., it is not to be sought in a good apart from extrasensory (rational) action, but only in such action, and it is the moral world order, although incomprehensible (actually quite easily comprehensible), that such action in accordance with reason (i.e., in accordance with freedom from the senses) also leads to this liberation. Nor is there any external (in the objective world) consequence attached to the action, as Kant postulates beyond temporality. For this reason there is no need of judges and executioners who distribute these consequences, no God, for God is nothing other than the epitome of the relations of this extrasensory order on my moral action.[154] For this reason, religion itself is nothing else with Fichte than this purely formal, non-empirical action being willed and believed as religion; salvation, i.e., freedom from all dependence is tied to this, whatever its consequences may be in the empirical world. This faith is religion.

Finalization of the Subjective Character

Accordingly, religion has absolutely no object, no God outside of us, no world beyond this life, no special commandment; it is nothing else than the consciousness of the moral, i.e., unempirical action of its unempirical nature. Moral community and the church therefore entirely coincide. They are just the endeavor of mutual encouragement to such aprioristic action.[155]

This abstract enthusiasm, enormously stimulated and exalted above external goods but completely devoid of content, runs through Fichte's *Reden an die Deutsche Nation* [Speeches to the German Nation]. Among all the German philosophers, it is precisely Fichte who is celebrated as the philosopher of practical

---

[154] "Man summarizes and establishes the relations of that order on himself and his action, when he discusses them with others, in the concept of an existing being *which he perhaps calls God.* This is the consequence of the finitude of his spirit, but it is benign if he does not use that concept any further for anything." *J. G. Fichte's ... Appellation an das Publikum über die durch ein Kurf. Sächs. Confiscationsrescript ihm beigemessenen atheistischen Aeusserungen* [Fichte's Appeal to the public regarding the Elector of Saxony's decree to confiscate alleged atheistic statements made by him], p. 38. Indeed, it is quite naïve to offer such a confession as a *justification* against the charge of atheism, and yet it is even more an imposition on the part of philosophers that we are supposed to accept this confession as such.

[155] Cf. regarding all of this *Das System der Sittenlehre*, pp. 304ff.

morality. He merits this because he animated the nation to elevate itself above material conditions and interests and its selfishness (over possession and enjoyment), to pure enthusiasm and self-sacrifice for an idea. Certainly this forms part of true ethics (formal); but that merit was likewise due to the contribution of a fortuitous provision of life – the liberation of the Fatherland. At the time, it was a call to powerful spiritual elevation in the face of external force and internal weakening. But Fichte's doctrine can never serve as an enduring example, as a proclaimer of true and complete ethics, either from the practical or the scientific side. In the latter character, it would signify the ruin of true ethics. That nation which had the mere act of enthusiasm, the surrender to any idea regardless of moral content or commandment for human life-relations, as the sole bond of its moral community would wear down or disintegrate. Any goal undertaken with enthusiasm and with elevation above the material condition [die Sinnlichkeit] would then be considered moral, even if the most sacred commandments of the objective moral order were left unpursued or even violated. Where only the grandeur and self-satisfaction of the subject has validity, rather than the ethical order grounded in itself, there the extreme of the subjective orientation is the basis. The untruth of this doctrine later manifested itself in the most tangible aberrations both in literature and in life. Fichte introduced the same notion of content-less I-activity into pedagogy, whereby the main content of his speeches to the German nation was geared to eliminating all positive knowledge and learning from education and nurture – burdening the pupil with the production of the entire future fund of knowledge from out of his own pure thought-activity.

Deduction of Law

With regard to the doctrine of law, the first thing to consider is that Fichte not only finds the ethical rules *a priori* but also the relations and objects thereof, the existence of desire, the earth, other people, my own body, etc. I must ascribe to myself a body, accept the existence of other beings, etc., not because I find them outside of myself but because of reason in me, and indeed these external objects are deduced in a peculiar way, not from ideas of nature but from the ethical ideas. As such, natural philosophy drops out entirely; everything is ethics. In fact, in terms of Fichte's standpoint nature has no significance of its own as an expression of thought, but is only there for reasonable beings to have as the object of their reasonable actions, namely their mutual self-restriction. The world is only "the sensory material of our duty; duty is what is actually real in things, it is the true ground of all appearance."[156] Its meaning is therefore that it be something shared, regardless of what it actually is. All of this only follows from his view of perception and concerns his method in general, without having a particular significant influence on the content of the doctrine of law. What is essential to his doctrine of law is that it finalized the subjective character of natural law, as Kant finalized its rationalistic character.

For Fichte, legal freedom does not follow from the ethic (practical reason) but from the real existence of the I. From the start, then, legal freedom is the freedom of the individual, not the notion of general freedom and equality. It does not have the ethic as its goal; it is its own goal. It is not something that has to be realized, an object of the ought; it is something already existing. Through its real power, the I posits itself as free, and when it observes itself, it can only find itself to be free. "Freedom is philosophically, not ethically necessary." Coercion is already given in its concept, and thus does not follow from the ethic. With Kant, the freedom of individual persons is already originally restricted because it first proceeds from general freedom, which itself furnishes measure and boundaries when it distributes freedom to them. With Fichte, it has no measure or restriction because the I itself posits it immediately. It consists "in the right of reasonable beings to be the sole cause in the world of sense." The power of coercion contained in it must of course be as free of restriction as it itself is. This, *my* immediately existing and therefore initially unrestricted freedom and possibility to exercise coercion, is the principle of the doctrine of law.

The law of self-consciousness requires that the I accept other thinking beings; this must be demonstrated in theoretical philosophy; individuality, self-consciousness only arises through this opposition. If other thinking beings place themselves in opposition, one must ascribe to them the same unrestricted power as one does to oneself. But furthermore, he cannot give up his own initially-posited freedom as the only reasonable being, and must also require the recognition of this from those posited over against him. To this end it is necessary, first, that he restrict himself freely; otherwise, he would not be a reasonable being standing in opposition to them, because the criterion of a reasonable

---

[156] *Appellation an das Publikum,* pp. 46–47.

being is its own restraint. Secondly, others must restrict themselves in the same act of mutual conditionality. In order to maintain everything as initially posited – my rationality and freedom, and the freedom of others which is deduced from it, including their action – and not to annul one of them and thereby to commit a contradiction — the *community of law* is necessary. Its content is the juridical law, which thus follows consequentially from the concept of the free individual.

Separation of Law and Morality

In this manner, Fichte attained what natural law was after: he provided to law a unique principle separate from morality, without forfeiting the scientific connection; and this was possible only through the standpoint of his system. It would appear that this was already discovered by the earlier theorists, above all Kant: morality is the inner legislation (self-coercion), law the outward (coercion of others); hence, entirely different legislations (!), with the unity of these two being practical reason, the law of universality and necessity. Yet precisely because the unity of both lies in a law or concept, the separation is entirely useless; it does not accomplish what is sought from it. Both legislations, namely, need to function in concordant manner in terms of that concept, and when they take on an opposite character, as is actually the case, this manifests itself as a contradiction of practical reason in itself.

Fichte, on the other hand, secured for his separation the achievement of a living unity of self-conscious being, rather than a logical one. Every living creature can be active in various ways in terms of its nature; the concept, the law cannot. The I contains on the one hand a drive to a certain activity – this is how morality is generated; on the other hand, it is already an existence, a power, something freely willing, acting – this is how the law arises. In terms of their essence, drive and power have an opposite effect, and the I, which they both are, nevertheless remains one and the same. In this way, Fichte could say "as the moral frame of mind is love of duty for the sake of duty, so on the contrary the political frame of mind is love of self for the sake of self... love yourself above all things, and your fellow citizen for your sake!"[157] Kant's law of reason, by contrast, can only have as goal the rational necessity of all action everywhere.

---

[157] *Grundlage des Naturrechts nach Principien der Wissenschaftslehre*, Vol. II, p. 114.

Solution to the Earlier Contradictions

By means of this separation, consisting not merely in words and appearances [Dekorum] but in result, Fichte is able to solve the problem that prior to him was vainly grappled with. It is no contradiction of reason that coercion take place in the sphere of law [Rechtsgebiete] even though legal obligations are also required by morality. For it is not the I as my drive (as ethic) that coerces here, but the I as existence and power, mine that coerces others, and others' that coerce mine. It is no contradiction that the same actions that are forbidden here are protected there. Law could only consistently command and prohibit them in one and the same way: "it is impossible to understand how it is that a law of permission can be derived from an unconditionally commanding moral law which thereby extends over all things."[158] Namely, that it uses something as means (permission) which initially and immediately annuls its goal, in order perhaps to get to it indirectly, contradicts the nature of a law. But the I, which here protects free action, is no law, it is immediate existence itself. It is quite removed from the contradiction involved in competence following from the law. For it does not follow from the law, but is already there before the law, from the I, and the law itself is first derived from it and only contains restriction, not freedom – as must be the case for law.

The Contradictions Return by the Back Door

Fichte's predecessors had already sought to remove these contradictions; but the point of view by which Fichte alone was able to remove them leads at the same time to other consequences which at the least were not cultivated in natural law. In terms of its nature, my drive (morality) is binding, unconditionally commanding. But this is by no means the case with my unbounded power (basis of juridical law); on the contrary, in terms of its nature this excludes every law [Gesetz]. Putting into action that which rationally follows from it cannot be unconditionally commanded, precisely because it is freedom. Whether it will submit to this depends on itself: "because they (people) are set free, such a boundary cannot lie outside freedom, as something by which freedom is annulled; but this is by no means the case if freedom is restricted; rather, through

---

[158] *Grundlage des Naturrechts nach Principien der Wissenschaftslehre*, Vol. I, Introduction, III.

freedom everyone should set these boundaries themselves, i.e., everyone should *make* themselves into law, in order not to disturb the freedom of those with whom they stand in mutual interaction."[159] The consequence from the concept of my freedom, the legal community, is therefore by no means practically necessary but only advisory, as to how to establish it in case I wish to correspond with the consequences of that concept, "in case I *wish* to be consistent." "Law is not practical, but technical-practical."

The necessary following step is: rights to specific objects, in the manner of property or family rights, are not immediately given, in the way Kant derived them from the law of reason. For anyone, when he does not freely restrict himself, is entitled to everything unlimitedly, so that restrictions arise first through arbitrary agreement. "All rights to something are based in a contract."[160] The primordial right [Urrecht] of man, which he had prior to civil society, is not, as in the past, freedom restricted in accordance with the maxim of coexistence, which in this restriction is also ethically secured. Rather, it is the unlimited power with which one threateningly opposes another, and there is no other safeguard than the possibility of uniting and establishing a state. The state here truly arises from a contract, because its construction is arbitrary, and so is its design. Now the law prescribes both tentatively, in the event that one wishes to be consistent. It may be repealed and rebuilt at any moment; this explains Fichte's decisive approval of the French Revolution. It is true that Fichte, like Kant, also allows the compulsion that forces the rebel to enter into the state.[161] With Kant, this compulsion is the consequence of rational necessity, which commands the state unconditionally; with Fichte, however, it is only the consequence of the unrestricted arbitrary will of those already united. With equal justification they could have coerced the recalcitrant to dance a minuet; and he has the same freedom to reciprocate their coercion, should he be the stronger, for what requires him to be consistent? In any case, it is not a rational necessary coercion, for his freedom is not restricted by itself, nor is it annulled. What is

---

[159] *Grundlage des Naturrechts nach Principien der Wissenschaftslehre*, Vol. I, Introduction, II.

[160] *Grundlage des Naturrechts nach Principien der Wissenschaftslehre*, Vol. II, p. 266.

[161] *Grundlage des Naturrechts nach Principien der Wissenschaftslehre*, Vol. I, Introduction, II.

here proven, as has been said above, is that subjective rationalism makes the thinking individual into God, just as objective rationalism does with impersonal reason. The free I as the absolute beginning of jurisprudence can as little be bound as can Spinoza's world law. With the latter, all actions are lawful because nature effects them; with the former, they are lawful because the I effects them.

The first character trait of Fichte's doctrine of law is therefore: Law has no power over people; its realization depends on their arbitrary will. The question then becomes, what is its content in case someone actually wishes to comply with it? For this also characterizes the system. The law [Recht] of the law of reason [Vernunftgesetzes], of the Kantian man as such, must succumb: *only the personal is entitled.* The freedom of living people is the exclusive cause of coercion. In this manner, the law of marriage is removed while adultery is freed: "the state can neither issue laws nor establish punishments against it, nor against whatever sort of extramarital satisfaction of the sex drive. Whose rights would be violated by this offense?"[162] In this manner, punishment cannot be retribution, for the notion of correspondence has no rights, and whose (which person's) right would be satisfied by retribution? The law of uniformity, which with Kant is reason, is with Fichte a mere thing without self. Fichte has to ask: what is this marriage, or this retributive justice, that it should exercise compulsion over me? Can it conceptualize, distinguish objects from itself, set goals for itself? Is it an active self-conscious being like me? And if not, then it does not exist at all; it is merely my production. How could I as a free and entitled person think of this as capable, as cause in the world of sense, which is not even capable of positing a world of sense?

Just as with the first relation, in which we say freedom may only be restricted *by freedom*, so with the second, we say freedom should only be restricted *for the sake of freedom*. Hereby in the first place, man in his personality is the exclusive principle of law. I may be subjected to coercion only when I will it, and when I subject myself to it; I only do so for my own security in accordance with reason. "Love yourself, and your neighbor for your self's sake!"

On this point, natural law is necessarily pushed into a corner, and on this highest point its untenability once again manifests itself. To wit:

---

[162] *Grundlage des Naturrechts nach Principien der Wissenschaftslehre*, Vol. II, p. 201.

Only the separation of the self into drive and freedom makes it possible to alleviate the earlier contradictions. But with that, the mutual penetration of both is also abandoned. Freedom *can* and *should* be subject to drive, but that is the manner of the ethic generally; the peculiar thing about the sphere of law, that freedom must be subjected to it, is no longer attainable. The living self, which recognizes an ideal ought, but really is independent of it, can only be bound if the cause of the ought also has a real power. With each of the problems that Fichte solves, a new difficulty arises precisely opposed to the previous one. It used to be impossible for natural law to gain freedom from the binding force of reason, from which it proceeded; now Fichte cannot go from freedom, which he makes into a principle, to a binding force. The law of *reason* indeed ceases, leaving a completely lawless arbitrariness behind.

While Fichte justifies the coercion of law by deriving it from the original freedom of the I rather than the ethic, in exchange he forfeited the ethical significance of coercion. What remains is merely factual power, and he can only incite the feeling of an accidental defeat on the part of the coerced. It is similar to the so-called law of necessity of the earlier doctors and Kant. He who is pushed off of the plank because someone else has the power and there is no law above them, will not consider this to be what was owed to him, as for example a debtor would consider being forced to pay what he owes. Even in the state, law has no ethical guarantee. The state is based on contract, but on what is contract itself based? In terms of the legal concept of the state, I need to keep the contract only if I wish to, including the contract which contains the community of law, the state itself. Only the strength of the united persons binds me, as with Spinoza, and could just as well force me to do something else than this consequence of my freedom. The coercion exerted by the entirety of the citizens against an offender is thus no different than the violence unleashed by the offender in the transgression.

If it is consistent that the law permits what morality prohibits, because permission and law are based on freedom, then everything becomes permission and nothing remains of law. To the degree that the concept of law as inner drive truly obligates, there is nothing else than morality, as Fichte himself claims; as such, its separation from morality and its actual treatment by Fichte is far less grounded than it is with the other writers. To the degree, however, that it does not inwardly demand, and thus is something else than morality, to that degree there is *no demand at all;* it is a game, instructions on how to rigorously set up something of complete indifference, for which you happen to be in the mood.

All of this was no secret to Fichte, but he nevertheless considered his doctrine of law to be well-founded. Yet the nerve itself, apart from which no law of reason and indeed no law at all can exist, is diseased. This is the restriction on behalf of others, even if merely uncertain. Here Fichte obscured the consequences of his principle, because if he acknowledged them, he would have to give up the principle, which he cannot do if he does not wish to fall back into the old contradictions. To wit, Fichte gained the concept of competence, of positive entitlement, not by deriving it from the restricted law of reason but by positing it as the originating thing. But it is simply impossible in terms of consistency to get from it to restriction, leaving entirely to one side whether it must subject itself to this consistency, or only should do so, or merely do so as a matter of entire indifference. By contrast, consistency requires that I not restrict myself but that I subject others to myself. "Love yourself above everything" follows from my unrestricted freedom, but "and your neighbor for your own sake" does not. Fichte arrives at restriction and legal community only through a twofold deception. The reason by which he expressed it positively is this: "As I, the reasonable being, have established myself as free and others as free, I must also wish for them to recognize me as a reasonable (free) being; I can only achieve this if I restrain myself." The actual restriction (indeed its possibility) does not, however, lie in the essence of freedom but in the essence of the ethical drive, and it is as free that I have made myself the basis of law, not as impelled by reason. If the latter were the case, my freedom could not even emerge alongside it, it would already be determined through and through; I must act perfectly to be recognized by others as reasonable, and we find ourselves precisely in the same place as those who discover law from the ethic.

But Fichte seeks to distance himself from the obvious inconsistency that I commit here when I first posit myself as infinitely free and then restrict myself, by claiming that the restriction exists only for the sake of freedom. But that is only the confusion of *my* freedom with *universal* freedom or the freedom of others, the distinction of which is the basis of the system. As the first principle was: my freedom can only be restricted by *my* freedom (not by others or the notion of freedom), or else it is not restricted but abolished as freedom, so must the second be: in accordance with consistency, my freedom should be restricted only for *my* freedom (not for others' or universal freedom), otherwise....

The one position requires the other. If Fichte withdraws the first statement, then he has a different principle than the free I, which exercises coercion, and has returned to the Kantian standpoint. If he insists on it, then he must also stand on the second, in which consistency requires first from my freedom: maintain yourself, do not enter into slavery, be prudent and restrict yourself where you might otherwise lose, dissemble, keep your word when necessary! in the way that Machiavelli implemented this system. And then, secondly, positive: make your freedom, which you first posit as limitless, against which you have placed others only in order to gain consciousness through the opposition – now make your freedom really limitless, by subjugating those who are endowed with freedom and capable of resistance, and by receiving them in submission. If you can, make yourself into the ruler of the world. Freedom of the individual as the principle of the doctrine of law necessarily leads to this end.

Parallel of Natural Law and the French Revolution in Both Stages

Life is everywhere more consistent than science. While the rationalist orientation in German science does not consistently keep both principles – thought-necessity [Denknotwendigkeit] and the real I – separate, but, as was shown, trembles for the latter largely for its consequences and festoons it with the results of the former, the history of France placed each alongside each other in their total finality. It is the parallel between natural law and the French Revolution, which immediately meets the eye and has long been recognized. Nevertheless, the parallel exists not only in general, but even in the gradations. The Republic (of course, not in its origin by executing the king, but in the principles of its existence) accords with the Kantian standpoint. Here everything which did not follow from the concept of freedom was destroyed; but the notion of freedom and equality is still a necessity which stands over every individual, from which each first receives his right. Reason, the impersonal, holds the scepter, but as with the Kantian version, it has no real power to maintain itself. Living persons do not follow its mathematical lines; it wishes to rule over the personal, but the personal is stronger.

There then arises the system of the real personal I, of Napoleon, who has no other notion over him than his *own* freedom, which he restricts when he wants to, and only for *his power*. He is bound by the rational consequence from his own will, and this distinguishes him from other conquerors. For this reason he does not digress in random ventures, in useless inclinations. It is as if the calculated execution of power delights him more than its actual arbitrary use. But *only this* consequence binds him.

> Ideas live easily alongside each other,
> But things in space bump up against each other.

Fichte could deceive himself and deduce a restriction for his original freed I. But the living I, which does not owe its freedom to the laws of the republic and its equality, but to its own real power, could not commit the inconsistency and impose a restriction on itself for others. And when it is consistent, the world only has room for one such I.

Chapter 7: Summary of Results: Natural Law in Its Final Form

The Character of Natural Law as the Combination of Kant and Fichte, and Completed in the General State of Scholarship

Natural law as founded by Grotius was brought to its scientific conclusion with Kant. The subsequent treatment by Fichte by no means superseded and displaced Kant's standpoint; he only exercised criticism of it which Kant could turn around and exercise against him. For their oppositional relation is only this: of the two poles between which natural law swings, the free self and the logically necessary law, of which it is not possible to stand on both at the same time, Fichte takes his position on the former, Kant on the latter.

Taken in its entirety, Fichte's doctrine hereby appears to be extreme by contrast with Kant's moderation. The shape in which natural law lately has come to be completed in German science is therefore predominantly Kantian. The entire edifice of natural law is taken from him; tendencies toward Fichte only crop up in details, in those instances in which the general superficial conception of man's arbitrary will (the empirical I) is more satisfactory than Kant's categorically necessary commandment (*homo noumenon*).

Here is how the relationship is presented in the most popular and most often consulted textbook of the time, that of Gros.

Outline of the Textbook Doctrine of Natural Law

The content of natural law, loosed from a connection with any particular system of philosophy as the general scientific manner of understanding, can be summarized as follows:

The doctrine of "natural law" or "the law of reason" must proceed from the *state of nature* by contrast with the civil condition, i.e., a condition of natural arbitrary will, without law and the state. Not that such a condition need have existed; but it must be assumed in thought, it must be abstracted in thought from the existing law and state, in order to derive the necessity of law and the state, the rule by which they are to exist and the degree to which they are obligatory, purely from the nature or the reason of man (the individual).

It now arises from the nature or reason of man that man as a sensory-reasonable being must have *freedom*, both internal freedom, i.e. to be determined only by reason (the logical law) independently of outward impressions, and external freedom, in accordance with which he can be active in the world of sense as a rational being (i.e., in accordance with that logical law). The laws that follow from internal freedom and on behalf of it, form the sphere of morality, while the laws that follow from external freedom and on behalf of it, form the sphere of law.

The external freedom accruing to man as reasonable being is in itself unrestricted. But because such unrestricted freedom is due to every person, and the freedom of everyone is oriented toward one and the same object, the world of sense, the freedom of all would mutually nullify itself. Hence there follows from reason, as the law of non-contradiction, the basic principle: each must restrict his freedom to the degree necessary to allow others to exist alongside him. This is the *maxim of coexistence.* It is the supreme, indeed the only principle of natural law. All others (regarding property, marriage, the state) are not self-existing legal principles, but only applications of this one principle to various factual relations, and what does not follow from this maxim, hence what does not have as goal the mutual recognition and self-restriction of freedom, could possibly pertain to the moral sphere but not to the legal sphere, and therefore cannot be prescribed coercively. It is precisely this infinite freedom with the restriction by the equal freedom of the others that is the *primordial right of man.* (The primordial right is only the subjective expression of that which is expressed objectively by the maxim of coexistence). The primordial right therefore characterizes the right of man not to be obligated to others for anything other than that for which they can be obligated to him.[163] It also entails that man not become a mere means for others, and so cease to be an end.

This is the deduction of the legal principle, the first and chief work of natural law; there now follows the second, the subsumption of relations under this principle.

First, the coexistence of freedom implies the mutual non-injury of the person – bodily existence, free spatial movement, honor – these being *innate rights* (not to be confused with the primordial right). Directly following from this is *property*: for external freedom and absolute efficacy ("causality") of people in

[163] In this concept of primordial right as given by Kant, the influence of Rousseau's notion that freedom is based on mutual reciprocity is nowhere to be seen.

the world of sense requires that any particular thing be able to be subjected to his will, and the coexistence of freedom requires that one person not disturb another's such relation to a thing. The act of such subjection is occupation. Finally, there follows from this the *binding nature of contracts;* for by virtue of that absolute efficacy in the world of sense, one must also be able to subject the actions of others to his will, since they also belong to the world of sense (his "arbitrary will as the determining basis of actions in taking possession"); nevertheless, by virtue of the concurrently existing freedom of others, it extends only as far as others agree to. But the latter have the possibility of agreeing to this because the capacity freely to restrict oneself also pertains to the essence of external freedom. The act of such permission, thus the expansion of freedom on the one side and self-restriction on the other, is contract. (If this agreement alone is the basis for the binding nature of contracts, it follows that the content of the contract is legally indifferent, and that any contract, whatever its nature, is equally binding; nevertheless, natural law doctors list only those species of contracts which they find in common law.)

Anything beyond this can hardly be directly inferred from the maxim of coexistence. Whatever is held to be a legal institution therefore has validity only by means of contract. Marriage is a contract for the mutual use of the sexual functions. A different goal, namely life community, does not lie in the legal nature of the marriage contract, unless through an accessory agreement, and all content of the marriage contract (temporary marriage, polygamy, incest) is legally admissible and valid by virtue of the both parties' agreement. This according to, e.g., Gros, following Fichte. For his part, Kant sought to demonstrate exclusive sexual community as the necessary content of the marriage contract and indeed directly from the maxim of coexistence and the primordial right of man, by reasoning that the opposite turns the other party into a mere means. With regard to the education of children, there is no legal obligation upon parents (not merely according to the original practitioners, such as Grotius and Thomasius, but also Gros and others), although Gros gave everyone (not only the parents) the right to educate minors, they being legally incapable. But Kant here asserted a natural-law obligation on parents to educate their children on the basis that whoever brings a person into the world "*without his consent*" (in a sense violating the person's will) is bound to reconcile him to his condition. The law of inheritance is likewise a contract, but with the modification that a moment of limbo enters between the tender (which only upon death is an irrevocable and thus actual tender) and acceptance, during which time the community [die Gesammtheit] safeguards the matter for the heir (Kant). Intestate succession of course is held to be presumptively testamentary. In this manner, family relations rest entirely on arbitrary contract or, in the view of most doctors of natural law, drop entirely out of the legal sphere.

One species of contract is the *social contract*, i.e., the voluntary association of several persons for a common purpose, for which rights and obligations of the participants are established. Such societies include the business corporation, marriage, the church, and preeminently the state. Every other association is legally indifferent, i.e., in terms of legal principle it is a matter of indifference whether they are entered into or not. This is the case with the trading company, marriage, the church. Only one association is legally necessary, the state. To wit, the supreme principle of the law of reason commands the mutual recognition of freedom (inviolability of the person, of property, of contract); but people individually do not fulfill it, by virtue of their sensory composition; its fulfillment can only be attained when people join forces to establish a power which coerces every individual should he refuse it. The association to this end is the state. For this reason, it and it alone is the postulate of the legal principle.

Accordingly, the state is the association for the coercive realization of the maxim of coexistence. Its purpose is the protection of individuals' rights as they follow from this maxim. What therefore does not follow from this maxim and serve it cannot rationally be an object of the state association, state laws, in short, state coercion, e.g., public education, public mores, public welfare. The exercise of coercion in these matters violates the legal principle. (The many institutions in actual states for which such coercion exists are by some rejected in terms of rigid consistency, by others rescued by detours: they either indirectly serve the protection of rights, by reducing the risk to life and property of the well-bred, well-educated, and well-to-do, or, in addition to the actual state contract, the members of the state also established an implied contract for these other purposes.)

Now then, if the state in general is a postulate of the legal principle, then it can only come into existence among a specific set of people, by virtue of the freedom of rational beings, though their own agreement, thus *by means of contract*. Whether states actually arose through contract is a matter of indifference;

but legally the power of states and the duty of obedience on the part of subjects is based on an implicit contract and can only be assessed in terms of the consequences of such.

This is the entire content of the doctrine that goes under the names "natural law" or "law of reason," after the material drawn from elsewhere has been eliminated and its own structure is showcased in its purity. Its particular treatment is the derivation of law and the state from the nature or reason of (individual) persons. Its characteristic doctrine is firstly the restriction of coercible commands and state purposes to the protection of the rights of individual persons, secondly the denial of all self-existing power and the exclusive justification of power in the consent and mandate of the underlings. Law and the state accordingly exist only via individual freedom and only for its purpose.

PART IV: ASSESSMENT OF ABSTRACT LEGAL PHILOSOPHY

Abstract legal philosophy must be regarded as culminating with Fichte, even though rationalism still rules in later systems and in a certain sense first received its completion through Hegel. For the latter system merely complied with procedural requirements, while the orientation's interest, to the degree capable of attainment, was satisfied by Fichte. At this juncture, at least initially, it stepped away from the events of the world and from the aspirations of science to make way for a new one, which initially even contradicted it. Hence it is that in the later systems, in which the abstract character – and thus indisputably the mainspring of human isolation – prevails, there is no desire to admit it; furthermore, the results of legal philosophy, which to this point pursued individual freedom, from this time forward took the opposite tack and therefore, although established by abstraction, nevertheless violated the interest which leads only to abstraction, as is decisively the case with Hegel. From Fichte onward, the desire completely to accommodate rationalism is accompanied, even unawares, by the opposite, to be freed from it.

As long as the principle of rationalism was still the principle of life, it was allowed to show itself as such, and could find general recognition. Now it has become a mere principle of a school; it is opposed to the times, to which it must accommodate itself, not entirely successfully.

For this reason Hegel's system was not allotted the same glorious lot as previous systems. For these had gripped the entire age as if with a giddiness, whereby the luminaries of each discipline willingly gave themselves over to carry them out and seek their glory in them, while even the lesser circles of the educated world were soon filled with the new conception or mindset. This latest system, on the other hand, is both limited to the narrow circle of the school, and finds no support, and even the most determined reluctance, among the leading men.

With Schelling it was precisely the antirationalistic characteristic that initially and especially took hold of the most quick-witted, which with the sense that this had not yet penetrated [the broader culture], subsequently inhibited its spread. The further presentation will confirm all of this. Here this provisional remark was necessary in order to justify the assessment that natural law maintained its place even with Fichte, and the later systems were sometimes affected by it as well, as far as the general traits recurring in them are concerned.

Chapter 1: Logical Examination of Natural Law

Logical Contradiction in the Rationalistic Procedure

It is easy to claim *in abstracto:* "Everything is the production of a necessarily working law. This (God) contains the world by its very nature, and it could become nothing but what is; but what is, had to be." This idea appears to be the simplest, the one most in agreement with itself, the only one capable of fully satisfying the thinker by the unity which it extends across all of existence. But whether this law truly expresses and makes comprehensible how all things derive from it, is something that can be put to the test. The bulk of those who seek salvation in such philosophy neglect to penetrate that far. They content themselves with that assumption, believing it *without* thinking, as such demonstrating most precisely the eternal saying: half a philosophy distances one from God, true philosophy returns to Him.

Indeed, whoever would discover that law and the way in which it produces things, would have to be capable of discovering, from out of himself, the whole existing world without having experienced anything of it, since only such things exist which, according to that law, could not be omitted. Such a person would have to know the future; he would have to be a prophet in much greater degree than those of the primordial world. He would be illuminated not merely by individual rays of light communicated by another being: the entire future until the end of the world must be revealed to him. And he could not generate such knowledge otherwise than from his own thinking, which must know best of all, it being the god that brought forth the present, and will complete the future. After centuries of trying to get to know the simple law and the way of its production, after having had such a large quantity of its products made available, it should finally have succeeded!

But no system can yet boast of this discovery. Spinoza stopped at the assurance that things are only the necessary forms of expression of a substance: he did not demonstrate why the substance had to take on precisely these forms, or even could do so. Fichte in his earlier period, Schelling, Hegel sought to provide this demonstration, and it is not difficult to show that they did not succeed. In principle, Kant positively gave up on this. Nevertheless, there is no need here to turn to the invariable experience of failed systems; the demonstration failed because the proceedings it presupposes are contradictory in themselves and therefore in any case impossible – this being a bare negative assertion, it can be proved from the selfsame concept of these required proceedings.

As little as unity can be abandoned by science, so little can multiplicity, which is a circumstance requiring irrefutable explanation. The question is, how can this multiplicity exist along with that rational unity? There are two paths here: either it emerges from simplicity itself – this is decisive, self-evident rationalism. Exemplars are Spinoza, Fichte, and Hegel. Or it assumes a manifold matter outside of reason, through which reason expresses itself multifariously in addition to simply. This is the case with Kant and the school preceding him.

The first path immediately reveals its contradiction. The simple, the undifferentiated, which works only according to a necessary law which is always the same, cannot bring forth a variety. Why do I derive from the absolute (whether the general substance as per Spinoza, or the concept of self-consciousness as with Fichte) a plant here, an animal there, and not always one and the same thing? When I proceed from *as-yet indeterminate* substance or intelligence, it is impossible for me to do so. I must therefore assume to this end a multiplicity of various determinations in the absolute, prior to my deduction. But then unity itself is given up, which consists precisely in there not being anything differentiated prior to the deduction, and the differentiated emerging only through this movement, despite its being uniform.

The other path, which allows multiplicity to exist in matter, which itself gains unity only through reason, is incapable of establishing a connection between the two. The simple law of thought and manifold matter are entirely heterogenous and cannot bring about anything in common. To become connected to variety in a necessary manner, there must already be various relations corresponding to matter in thought itself, hence a multiplicity must be given. Nevertheless, various conclusions thought to be necessary were derived from simple, pure laws of reason and from this matter. Such was the procedure of dogmatic philosophy prior to Kant, and Kant as well in the practical portions of his work.

Here, however, the conclusion is usurped, just as in the first path the minor premise was. Both are attained by assuming various differentiations as an undifferentiated postulated principle prior to all deduction, while thinking them to have been gained by deduction. If one is consistent in the second path, then the multiplicity of things and rules is not derived from reason but is ready-made and given prior to reason and has no portion with reason. But then the unity that is predicated is only a unity of thought itself; matter, from which reason stands apart without any necessary connection, cannot thereby attain unity.

Hence, here as well either the unity that is the scientific requirement must be given up, or a midpoint outside of thought must be sought from which actual multiplicity could emerge, i.e., rationalist philosophy must be abandoned. Kant recognized this inadequacy of reason most deeply. If we do not assume any matter (things outside of our reason), then we cannot give a reason for the various conceptualizations we have; but if we assume this manifold matter, then reason, which allows of no multiplicity in the true sense, is not the principle or origin of things and cannot find anything outside of itself. This is the narrowness of Kant's system. He therefore had to give up the derivation of the world from pure thought and *a priori* knowledge not merely in theoretical but also in practical philosophy, and not only provisionally and relatively, because of the way we conceive change, but definitively and absolutely. Instead, he sought to satisfy the contradictory requirements by postulating a contradictory condition: synthetic knowledge without change, i.e., a multiplicity which is not manifold.

Application to Natural Law

Natural law therefore exhibits both of these attempts, and the impossibility of implementing them. From their simple premise, Fichte and Hegel wished to derive by this same logical process not only legal rules but the various human relations themselves. This is especially the case with Hegel. As simple premise, Fichte had the concept of self-consciousness without any other content as the characteristic of the opposition of a not-I to the I. This opposition is the concept of self-consciousness, and it is such even without any particular thing having to be the object of opposition. Why should the ever-uniform concept of self-consciousness demand the opposition of an organized body, or of other people, or the need for food, housing, education, etc., from which the majority of legal institutes arise, in terms of a necessary conclusion, and not arbitrarily but just exactly as the particular manifestations that crop up? The answer Fichte had prepared for this is the additional ground of determination for the second, by which the one had to turn out differently than the other; for example, if I first recognized reasonable people besides myself directly from the law of self-consciousness as necessary, then I now, but even only just now, must conclude that it is possible for me to have an effect on them, and so I must have a body. The untruth is firstly, that the abstract influence – the specific body had to be; but then it is already entailed that the first conclusion gave a certain result. The concept of consciousness, when it truly clothes itself with the opposition of the not-I, when something truly is, can by no law of thought produce a *specific* not-I, whether it be a body, other people, or whatever. There is an unbridgeable gap between the abstract and the concrete of any sort.

The natural law doctors as a whole and Kant, on the other hand, presupposed the manifold relations outside of reason; but what is just in them would always be the simple law of reason. Only insofar as a proposition necessarily has arisen by subsuming the ethically indifferent relationship under this rule, is it just. The only hindrance standing in the way of this is that such necessary propositions do not arise. The law of reason ever remains what it is, the immaterial, while the relations ever remain what they are, ethically indifferent. The rule takes up the material that is subordinated to it, but it might just as well take up another; the two do not combine to form an indivisible product. In the logical law of non-contradiction, which Kant, under the names universality and necessity, made into the principle of morality as pure law of reason, the consistent morality of a Franz Moor[164] would be just as appropriate as the Kantian, should one not assume a purpose for humanity [menschlichen Wesens] and relations in the world lying outside that law, which indeed contradicts such a morality. In that case, though, this purpose, not that law of reason, is the positive principle of morality which generates the multiplicity and specific nature of the laws.

Just as little does the abstract concept of freedom, and the uniform restriction thereof for others, generate a specific legal institution. In this freedom, a right over one's own life or over things, etc., cannot be accepted prior to subsumption. The mere restriction to equal protection for others has first to produce the *specific objects* of freedom from out of the infinite freedom comprising all objects. Therefore, in the same way that we deduce from this a right to things that excludes the right of someone else, we could deduce a right to conduct vendettas [Fehderecht] in terms of specific equal norms. For in what closer relationship does the empty concept of infinite freedom stand to someone else's

164 [A character in Friedrich Schiller's play *Die Räuber* [The Robbers], cold, calculating, and without conscience.]

members than it does to things, all of which, in terms of this same concept, pertain to it in the same way that those members do? Contracts are by no means necessary, even if we assume a historical connection between the moment of promise and the subsequent ones: is freedom not violated if I lie assertorically? Why then if I do so promissorily? Why does Kant consider it a violation of the freedom of the intelligible man, which lowers him to a means, if his spouse does not have him exclusively as her spouse; why is this not also the case in other relationships, e.g., in which more than one person are employed at the same time, as with domestics?

If one sets human relations under the concept of equal freedom for all, then one set of relations could just as well flow from it as another, and either without contradiction. What impels the right choice is only the divine vocation, to which freedom is given in actuality, the content of which *is* given, instead of which *must be* given according to the laws of thought. It is the vocation of man to maintain himself through commerce, to be bound by contracts, to live in exclusive marriage. Only the purpose of things, the way in which and the purpose for which they are used, decides whether they should be *res communes*, communal property or private.

Relations have thus already produced a multiplicity of ethical determinations prior to the deduction of reason. Reason only recognizes these, it does not produce them; and if these relations had not produced them, reason would not be able to. Thought is not the effectuator of the ethic, and science must seek a different principle than reason in order both to recognize specific ethical requirements and to maintain unity in them. Certainly, the true cannot anywhere contradict thought, and those logical rules or the concepts abstracted from the given institutes must be found in all ethics. A provision that contradicts itself would not be a just one, because it never existed. Freedom and restriction are the ineradicable features of all law, and the eternal just law is therefore inconceivable without them; but they are not yet themselves a law, and they cannot produce one, regardless of what material is provided to them, not only a just one, but none at all. They are merely the restrictions of the same, which can tolerate the most opposed content. *From Spinoza to Hegel, this is the untruth which always recurs in changing forms, the eternal self-deception of the rationalist way of thinking: it borrows from reality things, ethical requirements, and assumes their development; and anything which does not* contradict *a form of thought is then passed off as* required *by it.*

Everything that is necessary is of an analytical character. With all deduction and movement, it can only posit that which was there prior to the deduction, and what necessarily pertains to the concept prior to the deduction. If Spinoza's statement, the nerve of rationalism, is adhered to: "the effect is given inexorably with the cause," then everything is analysis, there is only monism [Eines]. This is either simple, undistinguished – for in that case, with all conceivable lawful development, nothing can be produced from it but the simple, the undistinguished – or it is assumed up front to be a manifold determinate; in that case one begins with a composite concept, precisely what human thought cannot bear. The requirement of science, the requirement of people, that unity exist in the many things and ethical requirements, would not be satisfied through abstract procedure seeking this unity in reason. For if it was contained in this, no multiplicity would exist. On the contrary, if the multiplicity which undeniably is present is to be produced by unity, then the world and the ethic cannot have a necessary law as cause.

This is not to deny that all the knowledge, including that of the just, is only gained through our capacity to perceive, which after all may be called reason. But static thought determinations, which is what abstract philosophy understands to be reason, are only capable of grasping in its determinacy a content that we already possess, and of hindering its loss or the confusion caused by its shading into something else – a mere negative use. Even active thought and knowledge (reason in a higher and richer sense), which does not exist in these hollow, isolated forms, is after all only a means of knowledge, not the object of it. This latter lies outside of us: the divine Spirit and His free acts, nature that He created, history that He directs, the Word that He proclaims, the goal that He sets for the world. The true, the just are therefore that at which reason in its activity arrives, not what it is; they are what is discovered *through it*, not *from it*. It sees the light and testifies of the light, but it is not the light and did not make the light. This is precisely what is wrong with rationalism: it turns the organ of truth into truth itself, and because of this, it thinks that by dismantling and examining this organ it has obtained the content of the true, which this organ was supposed to convey. Even Fichte, although apparently conceiving reason as active, creative, nevertheless seeks all knowledge in what it is, what the concept of self-consciousness abstracted from action contains as necessary characteristic. No one is so foolish as to believe that the corporeal instruments through which we receive and distribute food, actually *are* our food. Such a conception corresponds with rationalism's procedure. Reason ignores everything worthy of knowledge outside of itself and considers only itself as active in knowledge. It disdains the nourishment offered to it in order – as the result of all areas of science has shown – to shrivel up in itself.

Lack of Certainty for Pure Rational Proof

Reason as a principle of science, as was shown, does not contain unity, but neither does it contain any assurance of truth, and thus does not satisfy any of the general scientific interests. Kant shows the inadequacy of the ontological proof on which all systems of reason [Vernunftsysteme] are built. Namely, the concept of absolute being, whether thought of as a personal God or empty existence, does not yet contain the necessity of actual existence. It is not a contradiction with the notion of being that there be no being. Because he makes the mere law of thought into a standard, Kant here, in accordance with his general character as sketched above, overlooks the actual guarantee of this proof, which is the existence of he who philosophizes, and who, in accordance with the law of non-contradiction, indeed postulates existence generally. One could otherwise go even farther than Kant and ask: who guarantees the proposition of non-contradiction itself, which is intended to guarantee or not guarantee the ontological proof? Only someone real, existing, united with knowledge and thus knowing, could contain the proof for himself and for the existence of others.

Fichte brought this assurance, which everywhere is the basis, to awareness, in that he deals with it right at the start of his scientific doctrine. In this manner, the same progress is found in the relation to the guarantee of the assumptions as to the assumptions themselves. But if existence itself, which is to extend this guarantee, is also taken as principle, then it cannot guarantee the same. "As true as I am!" is a poor guarantee coming from a finite being. For there is no certainty with regard to the "I am;" it is not in my power whether or not I will be in the next moment. But everything that is built on this consciousness of existence as consequence, expires with it as well. In one of Homer's most famous statements, the truth of which impresses us above and beyond many others, Hector is horrified of the slavery that awaits Andromache after his death, but he comforts himself: this fate will not be – certain though it will occur – because he himself,

Hector, will no longer be. Abstract substance, logically postulated with my existence, cannot be *causa sui,* in that I myself am not *causa mei.* My life itself is only a thing of experience; it is mutable, passing; it requires the eternal for its foundation. Thought cannot be such, for it itself is a consequence of my being, not a mere deduction from it. I am its real presupposition, for which reason it cannot be my presupposition. A real existence outside of myself must therefore be assumed as the eternal, which grants the eternal guarantee to what is mine, and thus to the reality of my thought. Not that which logically follows from the concept of my existence as foundation is what is persuasive to me, but that which my entire being (as effect) professes in a real manner. A greater test and confirmation is not required by any human mind.

The method of natural law therefore runs as follows: precisely while I am a thinking being, such and such is eternally absolutely just. It can be argued against this, *firstly*, that if there is no other source of judgment [Entscheidung] than that you are and that you think, then one thing is as just as another. *Secondly*, even if certain results present themselves, they still would not have any guarantee of their eternal absolute truth. For in itself your thought has no reality, and you yourself possess only a passing, relative reality.

Contradiction of Content: The Basic Concept Required by Natural Law

This shows that the method of natural law which recognizes a multiplicity of ethical prescriptions and nevertheless derives them from reason, thereby contradicts itself. The same contradiction is involved in the *content* of natural law, which was already depicted and here can only be summarized.

Abstraction must adhere to two postulates as the bases of law: freedom of the individual, and a law of pure reason which restricts that freedom. These bases are, however, irreconcilable. If the law of reason is the principle of deduction, then it excludes freedom; if individual freedom is that principle, it suffers no restriction. There remains only the choice between logical despotism and individual arbitrary will. Both of these principles in their decisive opposition are demonstrated by Kant's and Fichte's systems. And the result was confirmed already by the basic conceptions: Kant, starting with logical necessity, was only able to deduce a non-prohibition, not an entitlement; Fichte, on the other hand, proceeding from the real I, only attained anarchy.

But apart from these all-round philosophers, the entirety of natural law doctors formed a third party consisting in unconsciously making either one or the other of these contradictory things into a principle. The contradiction in this is obvious and everywhere encountered. In this manner, Wolff, proceeding from the principle of freedom, maintained that there is no *societas* and no *imperium* without voluntary agreement. On the other hand, he derives the parental association from the rational prescription of childrearing, and the same with countless others.

The representative of this party is Feuerbach. He stands out among all other practitioners by his acuity, precision, and prudence; with him, natural law insofar as it is determined by a universal system of philosophy and therefore likewise determined by juristic requirement and judgment, attained the completion of its basic concepts. In the deduction itself, he everywhere remains true to himself, and when despite this he arrives at contradictions, these can only be rooted in the points of departure. His confession of faith in his critique of natural law therefore contains the mixture of Kantian and Fichtean standpoints (for the doctrine of law cannot do without both principles, even if pure speculation had the courage to give one up), and their irreconcilability is demonstrated precisely through the sureness of his train of thought.

Like Fichte, Feuerbach wishes to have the right of individuals as the principle of law, thereby separating this from morality; this is to be no mere negative permission but rather a "positively sanctioned" entitlement, a "legal capacity" [juristisches Vermögen]. But like Kant, he also wants to have practical reason as the principle of law; for legal capacity to be ethically sanctified and restricted, it must follow from practical reason and exist for the purpose of practical reason (morality). Both are undeniably demonstrated. But it is precisely through this that Feuerbach finds himself cornered at the decisive point: how can positive entitlement be derived from practical reason? Unable to hide the fact that such is impossible, he nevertheless takes refuge in the Kantian unknowability of things: certainly it must follow from reason, but the "how?" of it cannot be understood.[165] This is obviously an entirely false usage of the thing-in-itself. For how something that truly follows from reason follows from it is considered by

[165] *Kritik des natürlichen rechts als propädeutik zu einer wissenschaft der natürlichen rechte* [Criticism of Natural Law as a Propaedeutic to a Science of the Natural Law], p. 265.

Kant to be knowable, otherwise all cognition would have to be abandoned. With him, the incomprehensibility of the "how?" relates only to our real impression of the ought, not to what the object of the ought is, and in what manner reason holds it to be necessary. Nor should a withdrawal behind Kantian unknowability be able to provide any protection at the present time.

And so, Feuerbach's critique – the culmination of natural law – has no other result than what was expressed above: *natural law demands the positive entitlement of the individual, and demands that this follow from a law of reason; but how this is possible cannot be understood.*

The Institutions that Arise from this Contradiction

This contradiction in the derivation of general concepts might be acceptable, since this derivation is only of scientific interest. The problem is, those contradictory principles lead to contradictory results in specific institutions, and the statesman who pays homage to natural rights sees himself challenged everywhere by conflicting institutions. If one follows the freedom of the acting person, then such a person must be given the opportunity to bring about change, and the results of this action, which is to say, the inequality of the legal condition, have to be recognized: property, guild rights, political privileges, in short, all acquired rights of whatever kind. But in that case the unchanging equality of the law of reason has been violated. On the other hand, to satisfy the law of reason, every historically generated advantage must be abolished, not merely prerogatives of occupational group [Standes] or commerce [Gewerbs] but also unequal property and claims acquired through contract. For either nowhere or everywhere is the original equal opportunity of each to obtain the same rights as others a justification of the inequality that now exists.

Therefore natural law's watchwords, "freedom and equality," are a logical contradiction. They nowhere provide a positive decision; but it is certain that the one will repeal the other, simply in terms of the concepts. Freedom demands action, which is change, inequality. Equality for its part continually demands immutability, and excludes freedom and action. When one principle is followed this time and another is followed that time, then at least such a procedure ought not be passed off as being necessarily guided by reason.

Chapter 2: Real Examination of Natural Law

In an investigation which looks for its standard not exclusively in logic but likewise in human interests and their satisfaction, it is permitted to conduct a critique simply by highlighting the results which are decisive in this respect; and as we logically inferred the unsustainability of the results from the unsustainability of the principles, so now conversely, we may prove the untruth of the foundations from the repulsiveness of the results.

Dissolution of Morality into Mere Correct Thought

The ethic itself, not merely its specific content, is here derived only from thought, either from my concept as thinking being (subjective rationalism) or from thought as cause of the world (objective rationalism). Hereby the particular character of the ethic, which exists in an original real relation, is abolished. Morality can have no other value than consistency, and immorality is only a form of inconsistency, to wit, the logical contradiction between thought and action. This is clear to both Kant and Fichte, although the ethicists who do not follow a comprehensive system still consider the morality of their theory to be what their immediate consciousness considers it, something independent and unique. The source of the ethic – thought – is therefore violated much more directly by a false chain of reasoning than by an act that runs afoul of it; the former would be a much greater sin. One is reluctant to accept such a result, however surely it results from the foundation; yet a trace of this is found in Hegel's contention that it is mortal sin to view our knowledge as limited.[166] It can only follow from my concept that I *am* something, not that I *ought* [to do] something. For my thought has no real power over me; a drive such as contained in the ought is incomprehensible as a product of thought, just as is the trepidation that is linked to the ethic. Conscience is only comprehensible when two real beings are assumed, not merely ones that act but also ones that prescribe. It is even more obvious that thought-necessity as the general cause of the world excludes the ought entirely. For the ought consists in the one demanding while the other is capable of refraining; but what the law of necessity entails in every

---

[166] Hegel, *Enzyklopädie der philosophischen Wissenschaften im Grundrisse* [Encyclopedia of the Philosophical Sciences in Outline], §. 386.

specific case is unavoidable; otherwise, it would not be the consequence of a necessary law. Spinoza therefore openly and dauntlessly abandons the concept of the ought, of good and evil. And with Hegel, as will be shown, this philosophy actually makes a comeback.

Negativity of Ethics, Morality as well as Natural Law

But the content of the ethic which is derived from reason can have no other nature than a negative one. Reason cannot generate anything; it can only exclude. Regardless of whether its commandment prescribes actions or omissions, it is only oriented to the avoidance of what should not be done or what should not be omitted. The ethic is ready from the outset with a concept, and what is required is not that something arise and occur, but that the concept not be eliminated. What is to be done is what would be unreasonable not to do. All virtue is fulfillment of duty – non-transgression. Hence, the original independent value of the act receives no recognition; this is only derived from the consistency, the decisive thing being the agreement of maxims in accordance with which one acts, not the act itself. Every true positive virtue – love, faith – is an act and it is uninterrupted; it cannot be thought of as inactive. Fulfillment of duty, on the other hand, is in itself without action, for when no demand is made, this virtue is not for that reason suspended; and so when action is undertaken, because action is not its core, then the principle is the main affair, for the act is only the means of preventing its own non-existence. The ethic must therefore be solved as a mathematical example: it must be able to prove what is duty and what is not, and everywhere the duty is either fulfilled or not. After all, the fulfillment of duty, which lacks all positive intensive content, is not capable of augmentation.

Relation of Negative and Positive Freedom and Equality

But what every unbiased mind reveres as the pinnacle are positive virtues, which originally and in terms of their essence consist in action, endlessly striving and creating, which therefore cannot be found and exhausted by any finished concept. Who could find the essence of love, for example, from the concept of thought, or of ought? What are the actions that necessarily arise from the concept of love, or will real true love be content with these actions deduced from their concept? Where it exists, it always leaves thought far behind, and no moral philosophy should dare to dictate or even wish to know in advance what it achieves.

Every great act, every manifestation of the sense of heroism, of the truly God-filled mind, comes therefore as a surprise, and is accompanied by the feeling that it was not to be found *a priori*. For it is a new creation, as wonderful as creation in general. The slightest object outside of us, when we look at it seriously, fills us with the feeling of incomprehensibility. A wonderful sensation is contained in the "It is!" — "This is your father, your friend; this is what got you into this situation;" why this one? yes, why are you who you are now? And such incomprehensibility consists in the fact that being cannot be dissolved in thought, that it is not logically necessary, but its reason is in a higher free power. How incomprehensible must this power itself be, God, and the positive virtues that He wills, that are like His essence! They are of unfathomable depth.

It cannot be said of the personal God what Spinoza said: I know Him, or I know Him not; but rather, I know Him, but I could know Him infinitely more. So it is with the Christian virtues; one can practice them here, but one can practice them even more, they demand this, but infinitely more is not beyond their requirements. There is no limit to how much they can be augmented. Love and faith can always grow in warmth, in strength, in excitement, because life and act are not mere elements of their expression, but their actual essence, what is elevated in them.

But rationalism only wishes for what it can master. It therefore makes God into an abstraction of being, which cannot be lacking, and virtue into fulfillment of duty, the ethical value of which consists in the fact that its opposite would abolish thought. It can deal with this abstraction just as it wishes, it can fully comprehend it, dissolve it in its thinking, in that it made it from that; they are less mysterious and wonderful than a grass flower.

In this manner, all positive virtues must disappear from modern [der neueren] ethics. Love is reproached by Kant precisely as a motive contrary to reason (morality). Hegel tolerates it as a lower stage in which reason is interwoven with matter; the uppermost here as well is fulfillment of duty, unavoidably demanded by the logical process and which only occurs in its consciousness.[167]

Above all, *faith* must lose the acknowledgement that it pertains to the ethic.

---

[167] Hegel, *Enzyklopädie der philosophischen Wissenschaften im Grundrisse*, §. 447.

For it is positive in the highest sense, a positing, a synthesis, and the polar opposite of analytical thought. It looks nowhere to the mere exclusion of the possibility of another, in the way that analytical thought does, and thus in the mere positing of what one already had. Which, after all, makes it possible, even probable, that things should be different, for example, that Christ rose again, that we will rise again, is made into an object of knowledge, the purest act of will, with the power of freedom – thus not contained in what preceded, but primordial – with a creative act. Just as what gives and authenticates freedom is courage alone, not the anxiously calculated security which only recognizes a good outcome when a bad one is unthinkable, so also is faith, and not the logically necessary deduction. As positive as faith itself is, just as positively it is an ethical requirement. Only a free act could establish this requirement. It cannot be derived from any necessary law, in that such a law does not require any faith for its existence, and thus cannot require it, indeed makes it impossible, because in the end it is necessary to know what it contains and what it excludes. The ethical meaning of faith stands and falls with the God of Christianity. He can require it because He could also refrain from doing what He does, for which reason creatures cannot know, but can only believe that He will do this. But it is because He requires it, because He *wished* to require it, not because it was necessarily required by His existence and His concept, apart from His act.

So then, the excellence of natural law consists in excluding what contradicts the concept of law. This makes it the completed, absolutely just law. It is thus enduring when it can lack nothing, when it contains nothing else than the determinations without which law is inconceivable; whereas all positive legal constructions, from the highest to the lowest, contain much extraneous material which can change without the legal concept ceasing. The highest condition containing nothing but the eternal therefore has no other virtue than this: not having what changes or could change. As if, since the uppermost is eternal and unchangeable, everything that is unchangeable must be the uppermost.

This concept of law, the characteristics of freedom (*in abstracto*) and their restriction are finished and given from the start of human relations; nothing but them is needed to recognize and establish the highest legal condition. Nothing new, nothing higher is to be formed, only that which lies beyond this concept shall be removed, and not much insight is needed to complete for eternity the construction of the legal world, which after this cleansing is no longer capable of improvement. This doctrine of justice certainly excludes what contradicts the legal concept, such as true lawlessness of a person or anarchy, but no less so all the great, all the unexpected, which have as little to do with those two characteristics as love and enthusiasm have with the concept of duty. In the same way that positive virtues are banned from morality, everything is banned from law which cannot be found by assuming it away, which a living drive for noble designs produces. In this manner, the entire state edifice of the Middle Ages, this positive elevated work of art, is rejected *in toto,* without any further examination of its content regarding what might have been lacking here or there, but simply because it all could be imagined otherwise than how it existed here, without causing the concept of law to cease – because it is the product of a force which is able to form something new, and which reason cannot emulate.

The highest destiny of mankind at which Kant arrives is eternal peace, i.e., that there be non-war, non-disturbance. This is all that reason has to offer in place of a positive condition, the kind to which the Republic of Plato and the true Christian writers refer, even if only in isolated strokes.

Nevertheless, these purely negative requirements, when contrasted with mutable, incomplete conditions, have an affinity precisely with the highest positive ones. Because of this, at first glance and by the sound of it, opinion is disposed to agree with them. But regardless, they are absolutely opposed to these positive requirements.

By means of such an affinity, the notion of the *equality before the law* aroused general enthusiasm, and even now, after the extinguishment of this fire, no one would dare to conceal the fact that only this equality of men truly satisfies, and that the opposite of it surely arouses opposition. But it is not because this equality before the law is contained in the concept of man that it is obvious to all, but because the idea of man, his divine purpose, intends the same thing; and only in this way of requiring equality, not in the other way, does it possess this power of conviction.

Freedom issuing from the concept is only equal for all because it determines none; it is an equality of empty possibility. Where it is filled with content, acquires certain rights, becomes a specific freedom, it also becomes unequal. But the freedom to which end man is purposed by God [i.e., freedom according to the ideal] is positive, and in its reality and its content, which alone is its value, it is the same for all. It does not tolerate, the way the other does, differences in possession, enjoyment, spiritual knowledge, etc. The freedom of the Platonic nobility, burdened with no earthly care so as to pursue the divine – this positive freedom is the destiny of every person. The mass of people, occupied by worries about where the next meal will be coming from, directing their labor to common things – this is as contrary to equality in terms of the idea as the inability of a class of persons to acquire possessions, is contrary to equality in terms of the concept. This is only one example of positive freedom, which according to the idea is equal to all, because the full content of it cannot be described and exhausted before the fact, as the negative can, but is an affair of the future, an augmentation, the end of which is hidden from us.

One could argue that this positive equality does not lie in eternal justice: what do you care if alongside you a higher life develops, a higher happiness exists? It is enough that you have the right to be who you are. Can the perennial complain that it is not the fruit tree, or the pebble that it is not a diamond? But this argument is flawed. For no man is allowed to be what he is as long as he is not allowed to be what his idea is, and this is the same for one person as for another: to be the image of God. But in terms of this purpose, everyone must also have the highest right, and there is nothing higher than the highest. For this reason, the inequality which cannot be avoided in actual conditions, is justified in terms of the same idea that the positive equality of man requires as end. For neither mankind as a whole nor the individual corresponds to it, but one more so than another. For this reason it is fair for the perennial to be left to itself and the fruit tree tended, for the pebble to lie in the alley while the diamond graces the king's crown. The man must have a different right than the woman and the child, the uneducated worker in his humble activity a different right than the leisured landowner, to the degree that the vocation of sex, age, status or class entails it.

For its part, negative freedom is already a finished product, which every moment requires the concept of the thinking being to be in all human beings; whereas the ideal of man must first be cultivated, and elevated by God. So then, in terms of the concept, faith must already be removed from law, for the concept contains no specific religion and only entitles each equally because it entitles none. On the other hand, man in terms of the idea is a Christian. If this is truly achieved, then there is no difference in entitlement by virtue of faith, and each is entitled in the specific elevated manner that Christianity entails. But as long as mankind has not arrived at this, the unequal entitlement of religious parties is justified precisely by the equality of destiny. Maintaining positive equality will not be achieved by abolishing differences, because to do so would also destroy the content, the specificity of which is only given in such interconnection with the present unequal vocation. But the freedom and equality which requires no specific content only needs to eliminate this inequality to be established.

In terms of this negative principle, every variation in law either shows itself *justified* because it lies outside the sphere of equality, or else it must be rejected as *injustice*. The standard of the positive principle, for its part, stands between two extremes – the *imperfection* which is relatively justified in terms of time and relation, but relatively unjustified in terms of the end of things. It also distinguishes between such advantages which, according to the concept, can only be gained through the disadvantaging of another, which, depending on circumstances, are considered imperfect or unjust, and those which either do not shortchange others or do so only because of the limitations of given conditions, as for example the protection of landholding families to keep them from losing their luster or fortune, and to maintain an uninterrupted bond of memory over generations, or the right of the spiritual estate not to have to gain a living otherwise than by performing ecclesiastical activities. The former view now considers advantages of the latter sort with an envious eye and seeks to erase them as contrary to the concept. But the latter view sees in them the content of the positive, prospective equal freedom for all; even if it does not approve of one particular iteration, whether generally or in a specific instance. It does not aim to eradicate them, but rather to elevate the others to them. It does not aim to turn the nobility into citizens, but to make the citizens noble.

Thus, as a whole, the positive just law (as far as law can be spoken of in the consummated human condition) makes a claim to eternity, just as abstract law does. But it does not consider itself to be the uppermost because it is unchangeable, like abstract law; it considers itself unchangeable because it is the uppermost. It is itself a specific legal construction and its elevation is seen in its content, in the forces it generates, in the appropriateness to higher natures, to specific living beings. It declares the legal constructions of experience to be mutable, not because every specific legal construction must be mutable by its nature, but because all those specific constructions are not yet what they should be.

The distinguishing feature of the historical view of the ethic, therefore, is by no means proclivity for relative judgment or the past for the past's sake, but that its absolute is a future, a goal of things yet to come.

Destruction of Public Law

These are the consequences of the abstract character, in accordance with which only what is logically necessary has validity. Therefore they are unavoidable in every system of reason, regardless of their form and the more or less hidden manner in which they may be manifested. It is now necessary to give an overview of the consequences as they are evoked by the subjective principle in its immediate effect; for they are what distinguishes the development up until Fichte from what follows thereafter.

The subjective mainspring affected the moral view less in science than in life. In life, namely, the violation of the holiest relations began to be considered minor missteps; indeed, they even came to be considered permissible, if only they did no immediate harm. Science, however, did not wish to renounce moral dignity, and found a shield in logical necessity, which it set above man, under which, in this time of need, those relations could find shelter, even though only via arbitrary assumption; for the unconditional prohibition of divorce and incest, for instance, can as little be demonstrated by logic as by the well-being of others.

In the legal view, on the other hand, philosophy did not shy away from the results, if only freedom and the right of man were carried out as a principle of the laws. In its morality it had something to fall back on, and whatever it destroyed that was holy in law, it could always resort to the excuse that this was only removed from coercive institutions, not repealed entirely. Thus, consideration for the dignity and beauty of the state in its outward manifestation was consistently banished from the laws of its institution – blasphemy, suicide, perjury, where it did not endanger specific persons, even the murder of someone sentenced to death, who himself had no more right to his life, could not be considered a crime – marriage must be able to be dissolved arbitrarily, violation of marriage be thrown open. Every restriction in the disposition over things (even if intended by nature for generations, e.g., forests) or in the operation of trades for the purpose of general prosperity was inadmissible as such, regardless of accomplishment. The concept of the fatherland, the nation, in which people appear in non-voluntary association, has no place in this doctrine of law. Any aggregate of people can make itself into a nation [Volke] and no nation is a nation when they do not will it. The core of natural law as philosophical doctrine is not so much popular sovereignty as the sovereignty of individuals, and the sovereignty of the people as a whole over them has thereby ceased. No one is obligated by anything to which he has not freely subjected himself. Only what everyone happens to want is law, and if they do not agree, there can be no law.

This sovereignty of every individual *establishes* the state in terms of a contract, the existence and content of which requires unanimity. This sovereignty *rules* over it continually, for all power is valid only as the product of that unanimous decision, whether it is the power of a monarch, a representation, or merely the power of a majority vote. The king, the representation, even the entire people, to the degree that it makes decisions in accordance with a law of suffrage, are only delegates and officers of that original people, i.e., disunited individual persons. In the church, this view leads to the consummation of the collegial system, according to which the members' will is the law for the church rather than the church and its immutable content being the law for the members. These results, as already the principle, completely abolish the concept of public law. There is no more state, no church, no family, the law of which is valid; only the right of individuals, separately and in aggregate; there is nothing but private law. People are in the state, not to form unity but to secure their separate existences. Where, driven by necessity, those relations are recognized, it is not for their sake but because people come to an understanding about them. What looks like public law is only a voluntary transfer, and therefore a revocable one – private law. In this manner the ethic of the world perishes and the divine disappears from the earth. People are left with the burden of having to cultivate this on their own, while the sacred archetypes and the desire in their breasts may *never* correspond to an outward formation expressing them and lending visibility to their meaning. No human disposition could endure a world created in terms of such a doctrine. Those called to sanctification would have to rub shoulders with profanity; the living, with the emptiness and the negativity. And death from the non-satisfaction of yearning or from the boredom of monotony, is the punishment which the law of reason unavoidably imposes on itself, should it be in a condition to implement what it demands, and to maintain it for the duration.

The innermost untruth of natural law, which must strike every unprejudiced observer as soon as it is stated, is that it completely disregards the *inherent purpose of life relations*. Every human life relation bears within it its own particular purpose and thereby lays upon people a vocation to fulfill it accordingly, to give shape to it. This is the basis for the moral requirements that pertain to it, and also the requirements of its legal arrangement. For instance, the inherent purpose of marriage (the union of spouses for full life community), and not the reciprocal relinquishment of freedom among spouses, is that from which the entire legal formation of marriage proceeds: the obligation of faithfulness and community for better or worse, the prohibition on polygamy, incest, arbitrary divorce; the purpose of parental relations from which proceeds on the one hand paternal power, on the other the sustentation of children. The same holds true for every other human relation: property transactions, occupational groups, political groups, local community, state, church. This purpose of life relations is the principle of both ethics and law. All actual law indeed aims for this, and law is rational to the degree that it is shaped in accordance with these relations.

For natural law, however, this inner purpose of life relations does not exist, for it takes bare freedom and reciprocal recognition of the freedom of men as its standard. In that way, however, the true requirements of a rational law or a law answering to nature by necessity escape it. What God or nature wish to attain in and through every relation is not pursued; rather, only the uniform in everything, in order for men to maintain their freedom, with no one forced to do something he does not wish to do. For this reason, natural law is *destructive* in all spheres of life; for "destructive" means nothing other than the ruination of the order required by the nature of a relation. It is destructive to the family, for in accordance with its doctrine incest, polygamy, arbitrary divorce are liberalized; destructive to the social group, for the determining consideration is not the assured preservation of all but merely free laissez-faire. It is especially destructive to the state. It does not recognize the tasks which lie in the purpose of the state, to maintain a higher order over men, nor the organic distribution of position for its fulfillment, nor the authority and power which accrue to it automatically and originally precisely for this purpose; rather, it considers the state to be an arbitrary meeting of men for the mere protection of their freedom along with their necessary equal status, without any sort of power than what men freely establish in it. The entire business of natural law is indeed none other than to ignore the true objective life order, which lies precisely in the purpose of life relations, and to derive such an order simply from nature, or more accurately, from the freedom of man; the result can therefore be none other than the destruction of this order.

This purpose of life relations is the ground on which true legal philosophy takes its stand in opposition to the false philosophy of natural law.[168]

The Truth in the Motive of Rationalism and the Law of Reason

In his state, Plato violates the right of individuals; this kept him from attaining the ideal of beauty for which he sacrificed them. Here we see the opposite. Everything is sacrificed to human independence, and it destroys itself precisely through its exclusivity. For in this exclusivity it cannot acknowledge a free existence above it, and falls under the rigid necessity of its own forms of thought, which do not tolerate personality and freedom. Expressed in the language of the school: subjectivity as a principle necessarily leads to abstraction, and this in turn erases subjectivity. A motive that destroys itself cannot be the true one, at least in this form. On the other hand, a motive cannot be without truth which for several centuries held the faith of the best and brightest, and set the most outstanding minds in motion. This truth is now to be sought out.

What prompts man to resort to abstraction is the non-conscious and therefore haphazard character of the world around him. Awareness of the dependence of created existence is not lacking to man, but he cannot consider himself the creature of this motley being, lacking control of itself, as the world manifests itself. So Spinoza sees the unity and intelligence in his mind, and stands in amazement of and reverence for it, as if confronted with another being higher than himself. He must find it expressed in the world if he is not to despise that world. Because in actuality he possesses no power to change the world's manifestations, he considers the static, the immutable in his understanding, to be what has created and joined them. The course of development elevated this static intelligence into an active one. The result gained by the scientifically logical progression up until Fichte, is: *only the self-conscious is. Everything impersonal only has a purely derived existence and requires personality as cause. Only the personal is entitled and can be an end.* This philosophically establishes the right of the living over the dead, of those with understanding over those lacking

---

[168] Cf. Stahl, *Principles of Law*, §5.

insight and consciousness; it brings the true pure motive of rationalism to its final end.

But the mistake here is that it is still human personality – as with Spinoza it was the static law of reason – which is regarded as the sole existing and therefore as the absolute, or even the mere concept of personality, which then always leads back to what is human. From this comes the absurd result: the world – of which it is now understood that it is inconceivable except as the work of a self-conscious originator – can only be the product of *our* self-consciousness. In this way our faculty of thought, which is imparted and therefore only capable of registering, must assume the place of an original and creative faculty. The world itself – in that its shape is truly necessary and immutable *on our behalf* – ceases to be the product of a *free* intelligence *at all;* it must be asserted that the creation compels the creator. This is the negative gain of the orientation, the truth that results from the inability to implement the opposed attempt: the world cannot be derived from human intelligence, and another cause for it must be sought. In terms of the positive gain of this orientation, however, the cause can only be personal since nothing unconscious has causal existence. The deeper insight in the course of the newer philosophy therefore ensures against the divinization of matter, but no less against the divinization of the impersonal law of reason, with which it, misunderstanding itself, began, and from which the principle of acting reason cannot free itself, as long as it conceived as merely human or as reason *in abstracto.* This insight is the end of rationalism outside itself, at which point it must be abandoned, which therefore is not to be expected from its own process.

No less, however, did rationalism have a true motivation in the endeavor to comprehend the world in terms of the inherent, highly pronounced intelligence in it. God as the absolute intelligence built His creation not by accident but by intelligence, and should man, who is the image of God, even in the most degraded condition, not recognize this intelligence, even if only as a premonition and by approximation? The error lies in considering mere reason – formal thought determinations – to be this active creative intelligence, the product and expression of which is the world.

In the ethic, too, liberation from all created things, which as such are not self-conscious and not powerful, is the true motive of abstraction. Man cannot be the mere means for the state, as little as he can be the product of nature; through the dignity of personality, he stands over both. His happiness, his freedom, his act is what he should be, and the most perfected edifice of the state carried out without the knowledge and will of individuals has no ethical value. But over him is a personality whose purpose it is to fulfill his goal, whether it is aimed at individual actions or at the maintenance of enduring relations. Accordingly, instead of the rigid political virtue of the ancient world and the superficial profane virtue of most recent times – in terms of which one man is a god to another – the original virtue which has the fear of God as its center must take over.

But in ethics, as in theoretical philosophy, only human personality is laid at the foundation, and this rupture has brought about the horrors and emptiness of recent times. On the other hand, this liberation from the impersonal is behind the great political results, the enduring benefits and the ornaments of the age, which gloriously distinguish it above all others. Its epitome is humanity in the noblest sense of the word. It abolished torture and serfdom; it grants freedom of investigation and communication, freedom of aspiration to the highest as well as the lowest; it therefore guarantees the freedom of departure from church and state and the protection at least of private rights for every creed. It creates the tolerance which allows man to be accepted on his own merits, which recognizes his will, measures his capacity and therefore is mindful of the blindness of individuals or entire peoples in faith and deed. By contrast, how entirely separated by religion, state, class, was one person from another in ancient and medieval times, so that the one ceased being human to the other! And what outward persecution and inward contempt did the purest, most noble efforts meet with from those who thought differently! These gains are no longer contemplated with satisfaction because people became accustomed to them, and received them in the wake of great troubles; and indeed, there is no shortage of attempts recklessly to abandon them and to extinguish them. We see many taking serfdom under wing in order to be historical, and preaching fanaticism in order to be religious. The Christian religious parties, freed from previous partitions, prompted by self-interest to rapprochement, begin to do the opposite, to shut out one another in antagonism. Instead of free education, which favors open manly independence, people believe they need to reintroduce slavish discipline. But these efforts at reaction are by their very nature ephemeral and without consequence; public opinion opposes them; humanity will not allow what was purchased with such great sacrifices to be snatched away again. The fact that such humanity is a noble fruit of modern science in the manner of thinking as well as in public institutions will not be denied by anyone who is unbiased. In it can be seen the enduring value of the now-discredited subjectivity viewpoint, and if the destruction caused by the noted mistake forces us to seek a new doctrine which restores the ruined glory, then we only have to recognize such a one that at the same time secures that achievement.

The liberation of man from nature and the unconscious constructs of the ethical world therefore is the gain of Fichte's stage. The absence of something higher, such as human personality and the knowledge of it as something personal, is that to which this stage necessarily points, even though from this point philosophy took different paths, and in doing so left no stone unturned.

PART V: THE REVOLUTION AS THE FINALIZATION OF NATURAL LAW

Chapter 1: The Doctrine of Popular Sovereignty until Rousseau

The Relation of Liberalism and the Revolution to Natural Law

The great world-historical significance of the events in France at the end of the previous century, which we call *the Revolution*, lay not in the mere act of revolt, but in the coherent doctrine which was realized through that revolt. The Revolution is no mere act of violence and overthrow; it is a system of principles and institutions, a political and constitutional system. Indeed, for this system it is indifferent whether it is attained by "peaceful development" or by the spilling of blood, for the system itself remains the same. Even what is called *liberalism* in the technical, historically established meaning of the word – as opposed to what is understood in a mere linguistic sense as being the liberal manner of thinking and liberal institutions – is nothing other than this system of Revolution, either in its full energetic implementation or in a dilution that natural living conditions, external resistance, or its own sloth tend to bring on.

Liberalism, or Revolution in this sense, is the product of the principles upon which "natural law" is based. In the Revolution they appear in their final consistent accomplished manifestation, as in natural law they appear in their most subterranean foundation; in the former from their practical side, in the latter from their theoretical side. Natural law seeks the aprioristic explanation and justification of the state, while the Revolution seeks the aprioristic establishment and formation of the state. That is to say: the former makes the attempt to do away with the state in thought and deduce it purely from reason, while the latter makes the attempt to do away with the state in actuality and found a new one purely from reason, although both enact the rational state merely from the notion of freedom or the will of men. This explains why natural law is so compliant when it is confronted with reality; it can reconcile itself with any condition, and seeks to justify it by assuming a tacit agreement, in so doing satisfying its theoretical interest; the Revolution, by contrast, aims to break the power of reality, and destroys any institution that does not follow from its concepts of pure reason. For every constitution, the former provides the fiction that it was willed in order for it to consider itself free; the latter tolerates no constitution that was not willed and as such is not truly free.

The most eminent of liberalism's authors is Rousseau. With him the principle of older natural law is conducted consequentially to the point at which it issued forth in the complete doctrine of Revolution, needing only to be consummated. It therefore precedes the French Revolution, in the same manner that a physicist's explanation preceded the experiment. Nevertheless, he showed himself to be a poor physicist, for the experiment failed.

But natural law by no means developed into the teachings of Rousseau and the Revolution on its own; the practical turn and energy come from another source, the flow of which courses through modern history; its confluence with natural law first gave rise to the doctrine of the Revolution. This other train of thought is to be shown here.

The Defense of Rebellion in Consequence of Church Movements (Buchanan, Milton, Languet)[169]

The ecclesiastical reformation of the 16th century also took on a decisive political character, both with the Roman peoples and the Reformed bloc. In the first place it was taught regarding the constitution of the church that according to immutable divine order (*jure divino*) the Christian congregation, as the community of the saints, must have the supreme authority in ecclesiastical matters. In many countries, especially those in which state power resisted the Reformation or at least ecclesiastical autonomy, this was then extended to the point that the community of the saints, the people of God, was considered to have the supreme authority from God generally and therefore also for the civil condition, and therefore is authorized and even obligated to depose and even punish kings who resist God's commandment. This doctrine spawned powerful movements in Scotland and England, and in fact preceded the overthrow of the state in England. Despite deep-seated differences, this overthrow rightfully has been called the harbinger of the French Revolution. In this shape, in which the movement is fulfilled as a theocratic conception of the reign of the saints based on the inspiration of the Holy Spirit, on parallels with the Old Testament, it has yet to receive a scientific explanation. But from this movement there came, usually in defense of such explanations, an attempt to justify, by other means within the scope of the scientific learning of that time, that which the specifically theocratic conception had attained in life. These are the writers in the age of these

---

[169] [See footnote 3 on p. xvii for comments on Stahl's treatment.]

religious-political wars and uprisings, usually characterized as "*king opponents*" [Königtumsbekämpfer] (Monarchomachs), in particular Languet, [170] Buchanan, Milton.[171]

These writers have the same motivations of the mind, and their writings have similar demands and purposes. Languet as a French Huguenot wrote in opposition to the royal power that suppresses the Protestant faith;[172] Buchanan justified the cause of the Scots against the Catholic Mary Stuart; Milton conducted the famed defense of the English people against the accusation of Salmasius with regard to the execution of Charles I. But they also largely share the entire body of thoughts and rationales, except that Milton exceeds the others both in democratic coloring and in wealth of thoughts and mastery of depiction.

They initially combat the doctrine "that the prince is not bound by the laws," taken from later Roman law and used against the movement in a servile or slavish sense. Their own doctrine elevates the peoples over the princes: all power proceeds from the people and is transferred from the people to the king; therefore the people is higher and more powerful (*superior et potentior*) than the king; that is, when rule is exercised badly, power can be demanded again for the goal for which it was transferred, so that the people ends up with penal power over the king. They prove this first *by the nature of the case* (*lex naturae*), since power only exists for the purpose of the people, since a people is possible

[170] [Stahl credits Hubert Languet with authorship of the *Vindiciae contra Tyrannos* (see following footnote). Modern scholarship attributes this to Philippe du Plessis-Mornay: see the discussion in Franklin, *Constitutionalism and Resistance in the Sixteenth Century: Three Treatises by Hotman, Beza, & Mornay.*]

[171] Junius Brutus (Hubert Languet, †1581), *Vindiciae contra Tyrannos* [English translation: Mornay, *A Defence of Liberty against Tyrants*]; George Buchanan (†1582), *De Jure Regni Apud Scotos, Or a Dialogue, Concerning the Due Priviledge of Government in the Kingdom of Scotland;* John Milton (†1674), *Defensio pro Populo Anglicano*, 1651 [English translation: *A Defence of the People of England by John Milton; in Answer to Salmasius's Defence of the King*].

[172] Languet's liveliest thought is that when the king suppresses the true church, introduces "idolatry," the people are required to resist and punish the king, because God says, "whoever does not call upon the name of the Lord shall die the death" (quaest. II).

without a king but not vice versa, since the people precedes the king (so they all thought); then *from Holy Scripture*, the dicta that those who rule should be servants, that he who does not call upon the name of the Lord (even the king) shall die the death, likewise the Old Testament series of events, namely the election of Saul by the people; then the *example of the Romans* (especially with Milton), partly the dicta of famous men such as Cicero, Tiberius, partly the laws, namely the *lex regia*, by which the people transfer power to Caesar; finally from *the analogy with ecclesiastical relations* (with Buchanan and Languet) while already in the Catholic church a powerful party was of the opinion that the entire church (the episcopate) stood over the Pope, that a distinction needed to be made between the papacy and the person installed in the papacy, etc.

The notion that all power and majesty is originally held by the people and only derivative with the king is therefore already developed here.[173] But this notion is manifested in isolation, without connection to a general scientific conception of the state such as is the case with the natural law doctrine of Grotius and Hobbes. To wit, with all these writers the notion is lacking which attends Grotius' natural law, of the foundation of the state by contract, which first places human will principially above all authority. They do sometimes conceive of the relation between prince and people as a contract or covenant, but they do not derive the unification of the people, and their being constituted to form the state, from contract. Hence the basic idea of the higher power of the people over the king is not used to present the people's rule as a necessary and permanent constitutional condition, but merely to justify the isolated act of revolt. There is no question as to whether the people should retain and transfer power, and the recovery of power is everywhere referred only to the case in which the

---

[173] "Ut potestatem sic majestatem etiam populo adimere et in regem conferre studes, vicariam si vis et translatitiam, primariam certe non potes uti nec potestatem" Milton, *Pro Populo Anglicano Defensio, contra Claudii Anonymi, aliàs Salmasii, Defensionem Regiam*, ch. 7, p. 199. ["As you have endeavoured to take all Power out of the Peoples hands, and vest it in the King, so you would all Majesty too: A delegated, translatitious Majesty we allow, but that Majesty does chiefly and primarily reside in him, you can no more prove, than you can, that Power and Authority does." *A Defence of the People of England*, p. 168.]

king is at fault,[174] apart from which he is not denied a real and hereditary right of dominion. On the same basis, by the people who are to judge the king they understand the ordered arranged people, thus the lordships, governments, royal officials, in short the magnates[175] (the majesty [Ansehen] of which itself is referred back to a popular mandate), or the people in its naturally given unity, without being derived from the consent of individuals.

Connection of Natural Law to the Doctrines of Revolt (Sidney, Locke)

Hence natural law existed as a scientific theory of the state which undertook to change nothing in life, in particular not to unsettle the existing supreme power. And there existed likewise this doctrine of revolt, which proceeded merely in terms of a practical goal, to make the people judge over the king and an avenger of tyranny, without a scientific conception of the state. It was first Sidney and then Locke who joined together this practical doctrine of revolt and the scientific political doctrine of natural law, and thereby founded the system of Revolution which Rousseau brought to completion.

Sidney follows in the footsteps of those writers, in particular Milton, and combats the doctrine of a lawless royal power and unconditional obedience, in particular against [Sir Robert] Filmer, demonstrating from the nature of the case the superiority of the people to the prince, the freedom of men to establish their constitution and elect their ruler. To do this he appropriates the natural-

---

174 Even with Milton, chs. 6 and 7.

175 Hubert Languet, namely at the end of quæst. III: „Hujus vero foederis seu pacti (i.e., between prince and people) regni officiarii vindices et custodes sunt." ["The officers of the kingdom are the guardians and protectors of these covenants and contracts." Mornay, *A Defence of Liberty Against Tyrants,* p. 212.] As such, "those who have generally undertaken the protection of the kingdom; as the constable, marshals, peers, palatines, and the rest, every one of whom, although all the rest do either connive or consort with the tyranny, are bound to oppose and repress the tyrant; and those who have undertaken the government of any province, city, or part of the kingdom, as dukes, marquesses, earls, consuls, mayors, sheriffs, etc." *Ibid.,* pp. 212–213. Likewise quaest. II: "qui universum populi coetum repraesentant" ["represent the whole body of the people," p. 97]. Milton vindicated for England, in accordance with the existing constitution, the supreme authority of the plebs without special voting rights for the optimates.

legal deduction of the state and precisely in the form given it by his countryman Hobbes: how people are originally in a natural state of complete independence, and out of mutual fear erect the civil state, by contract.[176] But in terms of that living mainspring of kingship bowing to the people, he modifies this natural law theory and converts if from a contemplative to a revolutionary one. This occurs most decisively through his elimination of the tacit contract, which until then natural law had generally assumed for the existence of states. He accepts the first thesis of natural law, that the subjects of state power cannot be bound otherwise than by their consent; but he denies the second, that everywhere, and especially under a despotic constitution, this consent is granted or anticipated, and denies that the subjects are truly bound.

> Tho the right of magistrates do essentially depend upon the consent of those they govern, it is hardly worth our pains to examine, Whether the silent acceptation of a governor by part of the people be an argument of their concurring in the election of him; or by the same reason the tacit consent of the whole commonwealth may be maintained: for when the question is concerning right, fraudulent surmises are of no value; much less will it from thence follow, that a prince commanding by succession, conquest, or usurpation, may be said to be elected by the people; for evident marks of dissent are often given: Some declare their hatred; others murmur more privately; many oppose the governour or government, and succeed according to the measure of their strength, virtue, or fortune. Many would resist, but cannot; and it were ridiculous to say, that the inhabitants of Greece, the kingdom of Naples, or duchy of Tuscany, do *tacitly assent* to the government of the Great Turk, king of Spain, or duke of Florence; when nothing is more certain than that those miserable nations abhor the tyrannies they are under; and if they were not mastered by a power that is much too great for them, they would soon free themselves. And those who are under such governments do no more assent to them, tho they may be silent, than a man approves of being robbed, when, without saying a word, he delivers his purse to a thief that he knows to be too strong for him.[177]

---

[176] Sidney, *Discourses concerning Government*, ch. 2, section 1.

[177] *Discourses Concerning Government*, ch. 2, section 6.

With this train of thought, natural law, which is to say, Grotius' doctrine of the state contract, steps off of the stage of contemplation and onto the stage of action. It is not to be found in Grotius, Hobbes, Pufendorf, Thomasius, Wolff, Kant, nor even in Fichte. But it is to be found in Sidney and following him, Locke and Rousseau. The two main phases of modern legal philosophy can be distinguished as the natural law system and the revolutionary system.

Locke,[178] who through his doctrine of the separation of powers broke new ground in another direction, namely that of the construction of the constitutional system, in this respect only stands on the same ground as Sidney, albeit perhaps with a more refined execution. Like Sidney and in the same manner, he marries natural law theory (the "perfect freedom" of the state of nature and the establishment of the state on contract) with the ideas of combatting kingship. In this, though, he takes a step toward Rousseau, in that he expresses the notions which otherwise dawn already with Milton in a more specific fashion: royal power is nowhere actual sovereignty (supreme power), or could only be considered as such in a certain sense.[179] In the meantime, his entire conception is based on the notion that the king acquires a true right (even if not sovereignty in the strict sense) through contract and transfer, and therefore devotes an entire section, just as his predecessors did, to the justification of revolt against tyrants; that is the demonstration that in the case of abuse, the king can have the (thus truly) transferred power revoked again.

But in order to complete the doctrine of popular sovereignty, the step still needed to be taken by which the people does not transfer its power at all, the king does not acquire any right; that accordingly the entire concept of a revolt

---

[178] *Two Treatises of Government*. The peculiarity of Locke's natural law theory itself, based on his empirical standpoint, is of no influence in this regard. This will be discussed in more detail in the appendix to Book III [pp. 259ff.].

[179] To wit, the people as legislator is the "supreme power," but because the legislating assembly is not always active, the executive which likewise has a share in legislation may be called the supreme power, but only as the executor of the laws, § 149. In this way, Milton said of the English king (*op. cit.*, ch. 8), "neque enim ad leges ferendas sed ad custodiendas à populo latas constitutus erat" ["a King of England can of himself make no Law: For he was not constituted to make Laws, but to see those Laws kept, which the People made," *A Defence of the People of England*, p. 182].

drops out, since the dethronement of the king, even without a reason, is nothing other than the ever-authorized competence of the ever-legitimate sovereign, the people. Rousseau took this step.

The Jesuitical Doctrine

At the same time the doctrine of revolt was developed by the Jesuits, albeit from an entirely different standpoint. They taught, in the interest of the papacy, that the secular power is not from God, like the ecclesiastical power is, but in its specific form (*formaliter*), i.e., as regards the specific form of government and specific rulers, is from the people or the community (*a populo vel communitate*), and thus is not a matter of divine but human law.[180] It is the same notion as was expressed earlier by Milton and later by Rousseau. The former wrote, "power (*potestas*), not princes (*principes*), is from God," while the latter wrote, "it is not clear whether God wills that this form of government be preferred to that one, or that one should obey Peter rather than Paul, and this is what matters."

The conclusion is obvious: when people do not abolish the ruling authority in its entirety but only remove a particular king, who indeed as such derives his power from them, then they do not sin against a divine institution. In this selfsame spirit, in certain degree the Spanish Jesuit Juan de Mariana in the early 17th century went farther than even the French Revolution. He sanctioned the revolt not merely of the people, as decided in an assembly, but also when such an assembly is not possible (*si publici conventus facultas erit sublata*), in which case every individual is required to murder the tyrant, for where the possibility for citizens to gather is taken away, the will still exists to destroy tyrants, to punish the infringements of princes, etc. But this is not to take place by poisoning, partly because execution by poison is not a punishment practiced in Christendom, partly because this poses a threat to others besides the tyrant. In particular, the assassination of Henry III by a monk is praised.[181] To the degree that the doctrine of revolt was praised by the defenders of the papal system, it was

---

[180] Suarez, *Tractatus de Legibus ac Deo Legislatore* [Of the Laws and God the Lawgiver], book III, ch. 4. Cf. Stahl, *Der Protestantismus als politisches Princip* [Protestantism as a Political Principle].

[181] Mariana, *De Rege et Regis Institutione* [Of Kingship and its Institution], book I, chs. 6 and 7.

combatted by the representatives of Gallican episcopalism.[182]

Without a doubt, in this manner the Jesuits made an essential contribution to the undermining of royal majesty and prepared public opinion for the subsequent overthrow of the state. Nevertheless, their doctrine in itself had nothing in common with that of natural law and the Revolution, even though it corresponded with it in certain results and even in the manner of argumentation. For the latter put kingship under the pure human will of the people, while the former combatted it for the benefit of a theocratic power to which the people likewise is unconditionally subjected, just as princes are.

---

[182] Petrus de Marca, *De Concordia Sacerdotii et Imperii, seu de libertatibus ecclesiæ Gallicanæ* [Of the Concord of Priesthood and Empire, or the Liberty of the Gallican Church], book II, ch. 2.

Chapter 2: Rousseau

Inclusion of Doctrines Developed to this Point

With Rousseau[183] we find the gamut of notions as they developed up until him: the natural law doctors (Grotius and Hobbes), the defenders of revolt (Languet, Buchanan, Milton), finally those who drew upon both (Sidney and Locke): that men are free and independent by nature, and through contract establish the state for their protection and utility; that majesty and power are based solely on transfer, because no one in himself has them over his equals; that the people can reclaim the power that it has transferred, and may judge its king. All of this is only the inheritance that Rousseau received from his predecessors. If we inquire into what sets him apart, into the new and powerful principle that appears through him as the fulfiller of this development of thought, as representative of the world-historical catastrophe of the Revolution, then this can be stated in one word: the *inalienability of freedom*. Freedom was already the principle of development up until Rousseau; he was the first to make its absolute inalienability into a principle, and to implement it as such. This is the character and the epitome of his doctrine.

Accordingly, he first refutes Grotius' contention that a people can subject itself to princes by contract, indeed unconditionally, in the way that a man contractually can enter into slavery. To renounce freedom, he responds, is to renounce one's status as a man, to renounce the right of humanity, indeed its duties, and no alienation is permitted where no compensation or any equivalent is possible. With Grotius, the contract establishing the state had a civil-legal and therefore accidental nature; with Rousseau, by contrast, it receives a public and necessary character. It is the duty of men and of peoples to stay free; preservation of freedom is therefore a public necessity, in accordance with which the validity of the state contract is oriented.

Rousseau's Doctrine

The problem, however, arises from this principle: to find such a form of state association ("forme d'association") that *really does not alienate* freedom, but in

---

[183] *Du Contrat Social* [Regarding the Social Contract], 1762.

which everyone, by obeying the state, only obeys himself, and therefore remains as free as before. This form of government is then the one necessarily offered by nature, the only permissible one; any other is void, even for the slightest deviation ("moindre modification"). While Rousseau's predecessors considered a multiplicity of legal relations to be possible depending on the specific constitution, only one is manifested here as lawful and valid for all existing states. According to Rousseau, this form ("les clauses de ce contrat"), i.e., the solution to the problem, is now *the complete alienation of each member of society with all his rights to the whole community*. Rousseau's opinion that this truly solves the problem is based on the following:

First, the alienation must be done to *all*, to the whole community, not to a subject different from these "all," a king, a senate, a representative assembly; for in that case one does not alienate oneself with the alienation, because one remains an equal part of these "all" and gains as much as he gives up, or to use another expression, it is the *absolute reciprocity* through which freedom remains unalienated despite the alienation, for which reason social obligations are binding only for the sake of this reciprocity.

Second, it must be a *total* alienation without reserve ("sans reserve"), because the condition of equality ("condition égale") is achieved when each surrenders with all his rights, and only then does absolute reciprocity truly manifest itself. If a member of society retains something, an acquired right, he would stand over against others with it, and they would have divested themselves for the protection of that right while not receiving it back, in so doing truly relinquishing part of their freedom. Accordingly, the inalienability of freedom in this sense includes equality, and it is thus the *principle of equality,* which was lacking in Rousseau's predecessors, which he was the first to draw up and scientifically implement.

In this way freedom is not abandoned, and the coercion which is applied by the state contract is none other than the association *forcing the member to be free* ("on le forcera d'être libre").

Doctrine regarding the Basic Relation of the State Association and its Correlates

Through this complete alienation of all to all, a will of the whole association as a unity arises. This is the *general will* ("volonté générale") in which all individuals equally concur, but which stands above all individuals, as unity. It is the *sovereign*. Which is to say, power can befit no other subject than this will, which is the constant result of the collective wills as equally entitled and equally contributing. Sovereignty is inalienable from the collective whole; in this way, the inalienability of freedom is realized. People, state, sovereign, general will are therefore entirely the same thing.

Any other state constitution is therefore inadmissible. It is not admissible for a prince, an aristocratic body, a popular assembly ordered by census, to have sovereignty. Only the collective will of all is sovereign. And this means not merely that "it shall be, we must strive for it," but rather, "*it is*." This is the legal relation everywhere. What is different is invalid, is unjust. The general will is always and everywhere competent and is called upon to exercise its legitimate sovereignty against such usurped sovereignty.

Accordingly, the basic idea, and indeed the overall content of Rousseau's doctrine, is the inalienable and non-transferrable power or sovereignty of the people, i.e., the collective whole or the collective will. The correlates thereof are the indivisibility, unrepresentability, and unrestrictedness of this power to which the people are entitled.

The people have power which is *indivisible*. A branch of power, namely the executive, cannot be separated and transferred to the prince (in opposition to Montesquieu and Locke). For this would engender a subject of power; a will would obtain, even if only in a specific sphere, which is not the general will.[184]

The people have power which is *unrepresentable*. Delegates of the people cannot issue any laws, for they form something else than the general will, a will in which not everyone concurs equally. Laws which are not issued or approved by the people itself are not laws, and have no validity. There are therefore few states with true laws. The English people believes that it is free, but it is actually only free at the moments of parliamentary elections; when these are over, "it is a slave, it is nothing."[185] To this end, meetings of the whole people must be regularly held, called not by magistrates but by the power of the people, and as soon as the people is assembled, all majesty of the magistrate gives way, for when the

---

[184] *Du Contrat Social,* Book II, ch. 2.

[185] *Du Contrat Social,* Book III, ch. 15.

represented appear, the representative has no more meaning.[186]

The people have power which is *unrestricted*. It cannot be bound by basic laws ("loix fundamentals") for such restriction can only be based on contract, but the people (the sovereign) cannot contract with itself, obligate itself to itself contractually. It cannot be restricted by acquired rights, for everyone alienated those rights unconditionally. It can err about what is best for it, but it can do no wrong, for there can be no wrong that it does against itself.[187]

The thesis that the sovereignty of the people is non-transferable, indivisible, unamenable to representation, incapable of restriction, only provides various aspects of the single notion of inalienable freedom of men in Rousseau's sense. It is this which characterizes the basic relation of the state association.

Doctrine regarding the relation of government

But even in the further development of the state constitution, Rousseau's doctrine has no other leading motive and purpose, not for example the excellence of elements of government and the like, but simply and solely the preservation of the inalienable power of the people. That the mass cannot of itself and directly govern is a factual necessity that one cannot evade. Rousseau admits this: the sovereign people cannot be represented in legislation as the supreme deciding power (which establishes general rules for objects), but it can be represented by the government. This is the "gouvernement" and it can be a prince, a senate, aristocracy, national representation, etc. *Sovereign* and *government* are therefore two entirely different things. What is decisive for the inalienable power of the people is the relation between sovereign (people) and government (prince, senate), and on this basis Rousseau teaches that there is no contractual transfer of power, indeed no contract at all, but it rather must be viewed as the people, as sovereign, determining by a law the form of government, designating

---

[186] *Du Contrat Social,* Book III, chs. 13 and 14.

[187] *Du Contrat Social,* Book I, ch. 6. Certainly, Rousseau recognizes limits to sovereign power in the natural rights of citizens, their lives, their freedom. But they must sacrifice everything for what is important ("importe") to the community, and regarding this *importance* only the sovereign decides (Book II, ch. 4). It is not a sum of specified rights which the sovereign may not infringe, but abstract freedom the limits of which he establishes at will. This is the basis of state absolutism.

thereby the persons in a document (act of election). Both the law and the act of election are results of the complete power of the people and nothing else. The "gouvernement" does not hereby gain a power, a right, a contractual position vis-à-vis the people, but merely a task, a service, for which it is applied ("commission," "emploi"). The magistrate (king, senate) are mere servants of the sovereign people ("simples officiers du Souverain") who exercise power in its name, being its mere depositaries. The power can therefore restrict this power, change it, revoke it, whenever it wishes ("quand il lui plaît"), and vice versa, the magistrate (even the king) cannot resign, abdicate, for it is not his right but his duty, an affair of obedience to the sovereign and his law.

In this manner, all existing constitutions are to be accounted and juridically assessed. This is the irrefutable natural law, against which no positive law is valid; it is universal constitutional law. There is therefore no variation in constitutions. Rousseau does distinguish between monarchy, aristocracy, and democracy, but only as various forms of government, not as forms of sovereignty, and therefore not truly as different constitutions. For a true variation in constitution can only have to do with a variety of the subjects of sovereignty, not with a variety of governmental organizations, and least of all if it is revocable, and therefore only *de facto* and not legal. Which form of government will exist is an open question, a question of prudence and efficiency; indeed, Rousseau advises against the democratic form of government because it does not distinguish (*distingé)* between the sovereign and the government as it ought. But among all these forms of government the absolute democracy of the constitution, which the doctrine of the sovereign and irreplaceable people constitutes, remains immovable.[188]

Rousseau, then, distinguishes as do his predecessors (Locke and Montesquieu) between legislation – the affair of the people – and the executive or government – the affair of the "gouvernement" or the king, as the case may be; but in this he differs from all his predecessors in not giving the organ of this executive a real power or any sort of right, but treating it merely as an instrument of the entirety, without will or right. This means that there is no longer any need to justify revolt, as Locke does; the whole concept of revolt drops out. The people everywhere has only its own ministries, which it vests precariously; no legal

---

[188] *Du Contrat Social,* Book III, chs. 1 and 4, chs. 16 and 17.

relation is changed even if it dethrones the king, as little as the king changes a legal relationship when he dismisses his minister.

Doctrine of the Purpose of State Association

Finally, the objective that Rousseau sets for the effectiveness of the state is determined only by the principle of inalienable freedom, i.e. the same condition which is also unalterable in the association. This objective for him is the public good ("bien public"), not in the sense of the well-being of all according to their different situations and circumstances, but only the well-being of all in the condition equal to all; not the satisfaction of all the interests which differ according to the various interests, but only satisfaction of the interests which one citizen has just like another. Accordingly, he distinguishes between a general will ("volonté générale") and a mere will of all ("volonté de tous"). When among a people each, particularly each sphere, pursues its particular will in voting, the joint result is only the will of all; but when the people as a whole pursues the interest which is uniform for all, only then is the result truly (materially) the general will. But Rousseau does not give a guarantee for the latter and not the former, and does not seek one beyond the elimination of differences in legal status (namely all corporate entities), by which he expects to eliminate the diversity of interests.[189]

This is the point from which Rousseau would logically have to continue to communism. For in order to make interests uniform, it is not sufficient merely to eliminate the diversity of *legal* statuses; *any* difference in situation must be eliminated, above all, the diversity of *economic* situations. Moreover, in the general vote, there will always be an interest of the haves against the have-nots, and therefore there will always be only a "will of all," not a "general will."

In the main, then, Rousseau is a member of the school of thought scientifically inspired by Grotius — the system of "natural law" — and indeed, he brings it to finality, and pushes it to its extreme. He also belongs in particular to the Romanist faction of this school of thought, insofar as he conceives of the will of man merely empirically, materially, eliminating every remnant of a higher commandment, a necessity. In Kant's case, it is the freedom of others as a commandment of reason (a commandment of *homo noumenon*) that compels one into

---

[189] *Du Contrat Social,* Book II, chs. 3 and 4.

the state; with Rousseau, it is only the concern for oneself, one's own benefit.[190] Rousseau's own peculiarity consists in making the freedom of man into an absolute law, which does not allow the slightest surrender of freedom by freedom. This is his doctrine of the inalienable freedom of men, the immovable equality of the condition of all, from which is inferred the inalienable, unrepresentable power or sovereignty of the people. While earlier exponents (the defenders of revolt) understood the sovereignty of the people merely as a *potential* (latent) power which, when needed, erupts and puts an end to the tyrannical government, it is, according to Rousseau, a necessary and ever-present *actual* power; the people (the collective) cannot cease for one moment actually and completely to exercise it itself. The will of the people and therefore the will of the collective persons – collectively, but thought of in a thoroughly equal condition – is the source and lord of social order in inexhaustible actuality.

True, it was claimed that Rousseau had a higher principle in his "general will" than the mere collection of individual wills, because he distinguished this from the "will of all" ("volonté de tous"). But this distinction signifies, as already demonstrated, precisely the opposite, that the general will even in terms of its content does not entail a higher harmonic order, but only the abstract equal well-being of individuals, and in any case it refers only to the inner requirement of the voters, not to their constitutional relationship. In this regard, Rousseau speaks everywhere in the most decisive terms that the general will (the sovereign) can be nothing else than the will of all, i.e., in which all individuals concur in entirely equal fashion. Rousseau's concept does not have the least relationship to the general will of Schelling and Hegel. What Rousseau makes into the principle and the power of the social order is therefore only the will of man

---

190 "Sa (human nature) première loi est de veiller à sa propre conservation, ses premiers soins sont ceux, qu'il se doit à lui-même; livre I, chap. 2" [The first law of human nature is to is to ensure its own conservation, its first care is those, which it owes to itself; Book I, ch. 2]. "Comment les (his strength and freedom) engagera-t-il sans se nuire et sans négliger les soins qu'il se doit? ch. 6" [How will he engage them without harming himself and without neglecting the care he needs?]. If the basis of obligation of the state-establishing "engagements" are specified: "qu'en les remplissant on ne peut travailler pour autres sans travailler aussi pour soi" [that by filling them we cannot work for others without also working for ourselves]. Book II, ch. 4.

without a higher necessity, without a majesty [ein Ansehen] or a commandment over him, and it is the will of man *par excellence* in his selfishness, detached from every moral goal, from every harmonious life-formation to which he would have to aspire; therefore only human right, without human duty. What remains as content, duty, virtue is then again only man himself: the (sensory) well-being of man, the majesty of man, and accordingly the majesty of the people. Enthusiasm has no other object than devotion to the majority, recognition of equality, fraternity. The law of God and nature – for individual life, family, state, worship – all of this drops out, and the sanctity of the popular will is elevated to absolute power, it is religion, morality, justice. This is the spirit of Rousseau; it is the spirit of the Revolution.

But if this absence of true ethical content is disregarded, and Rousseau's doctrine is considered merely as what it pretends to be, a system of equal freedom (right [richtiger] choice) and equal satisfaction of men, which is to be fundamentally recognized and mechanically guaranteed, even in this character it demonstrates its untenability. Rousseau commits the tangible error where freedom and satisfaction are concerned, of considering the abstract unity of the collective (the mere result of voting) to be equal to the personalities of which it consists. He attaches, as is not otherwise possible, that abstract unity to law and power, for freedom and satisfaction are to be pursued for concrete personalities, and only make sense as the freedom and satisfaction of personalities, not as the freedom and satisfaction of a collectivity. The false calculation of reciprocity rests on this: if I, with an equal share in the vote, submit to a thousand votes, I do not give up my freedom, since arithmetically I made the same number of votes binding upon myself as the number that I made binding upon others; as if only the formal aspect, equal participation in the forms of decision-making, and not the material aspect, the content of the decision, were the decisive factor for my freedom and satisfaction. Likewise the false thesis that the general will can do no injustice while no one can do injustice to himself. If the collective can do no injustice to itself considered as an abstract unity, this is not to say that it cannot do injustice against itself considered as the concrete personalities of which it consists. The actual result of Rousseau's doctrine therefore is not the freedom (choice) and satisfaction of men, nor of the majority of men (for the same ones who, in the majority today, guillotine people, in the minority tomorrow get guillotined); but the freedom and satisfaction of the abstract law of the majority.

If Rousseau now believes that abstract voting must coincide with the interests of the people, at least of the majority, because everyone has the same right and thus the same condition, he should have gone further than he did. Namely, as stated above, he should have equalized economic conditions; but then that would not be enough either, since differences between health, labor power, beauty, intelligence, education, moral conviction, etc. would always remain. But that would also overlook the fact that people even in equal conditions strive to make these conditions unequal, to their own advantage; and equal competition gives no guarantee that what is unfair or unjust will not be implemented in voting.

Rousseau had to grant fully the inalienability of freedom. But true freedom neither includes the condition of immobile equality of condition (the English freeholder is free even though the landlord has a more favorable position, for his livelihood is free even though there are wealthier people) nor is it permissible to conclude that the inalienability of freedom leads to the sovereign power of the people. Sovereignty has never been granted to the people for them to yield it by alienation; from the start it pertains to the ordered state, to the constitutional authority; and sovereignty does not pertain to the "condition as man" as freedom does, nor does it pertain to the rights and duties of humanity.[191]

By the way, if Rousseau combats the irrevocable transfer of power to the king from the side of the popular mass as an inconsistency on the part of Grotius, he himself commits this very inconsistency, since he commits an irrevocable transfer of power to the popular mass from the side of the individual. It is in my "inalienable freedom" that I cannot irrevocably bind myself to the rest of the whole, and as Rousseau himself demands unanimity for the first establishment of the state, he would have to demand it for every future act, otherwise it would leave open the possibility of contract termination. If the ethical form of the community is based only on the will of the individual human beings, they must be able to repeal it when they wish. Popular sovereignty therefore not only leads to anarchy, but is anarchy.

---

[191] See the relevant sections of Volume II of this work for the more detailed elucidation of individual claims.

Verdict

Rousseau's presentation manifests the system of the Revolution in the strictest scientific train of thought. In life it dissolves into a series of individual postulates which nonetheless stand in indissoluble coherence. As is known, they are as follows:

Popular sovereignty – the collective mass of the people or the majority, as the case may be, is continually the supreme authority and power; all governments possess that power only by the authority thereof and therefore can be stripped of it, held to account, and punished according to the will of the people.

Democracy – just for this reason, the collectivity (all individuals) exercises the supreme power (legislation) truly (actually) and immediately (1793).

Freedom – the citizens in their freedom are not restricted except to the degree necessary to the equal freedom of others, hence not for the goal of public welfare, public mores, public faith; that therefore no restriction exist on the breakup of estates, on taking up residence, on commerce, on sects, consequently also on moral offenses (*Declaration of the Rights of Man*). This postulate was defended not so much by Rousseau as by Locke, the North Americans, Turgot and others.

Equality – in all public relations, differences in rights according to objective conditions (e.g., landholding), estate and vocation, corporate affiliation are to be abolished.

Rationality – what is rational, i.e., institutions recognized as rational by the respective majority, are to be established immediately and unconditionally, without regard for historical condition and traditional ways of thinking, without regard for acquired rights, the latter not only having to yield, but having no validity as rights in relation to the rational condition.

The *abolition of state religion* – the state is to be indifferent to religious confession, allow every form of worship, sanction none as public, give shape to life relations (e.g., marriage) without regard to revealed commandments, guarantee fully equal political rights without regard for differences in religious confession. But in this regard, Rousseau's doctrine deviated. On the strength of his deeper view of things, he recognized that the state cannot exist without a religious drive of mind, but, sharing an aversion to Christianity on a par with this entire school of thought, he arrived at the result: a religion must be invented and introduced by the state, which, however, only has the state as its purpose. This religion must be accepted by each on penalty of death or exile, and another may not exist in the state.[192]

These are the postulates that the Revolution undertook to realize; it is these which impel liberalism up to the present hour, even if, in the face of the existing power of kingship, it does not parade the extremes of popular sovereignty and democracy; and the consistent implementation of individual freedom is often abandoned in the face of the force of natural life conditions, especially where material interests demand it.

What has been said about natural law must, of course, apply in this way to this system, which is only the practical implementation of natural law. This system likewise has its being in tearing human freedom away from the higher power and authority over it, in dissolving the organically articulated state into an undifferentiated mass, in refusing to recognize specific differentiated life relations and their inherent purpose. Here as well, in the area of practice, this orientation misses its target. It makes individual freedom into an exclusive principle, but where a sphere once granted – acquired rights – is not protected, and where the sovereign people, or what acts in its name, maintains the requirements of freedom, either true or supposed, with unrestricted power, there individual freedom is not attained. As natural law oscillates between two foundations, individual freedom and laws of logic, without being able to hold a firm position, just so is liberalism as the living system between the two foundations: individual freedom and the common will. It bases itself first on the non-disturbance of the individual, as with Turgot, Bayle and many leaders of 1789, but then arrives at the impotence, even dissolution of the community; it then bases itself on the power of the unified people, on fraternity ("fraternité"), like Rousseau, Robespierre, and today's socialists, and then destroys individual freedom. The articulation of life relations in accordance with a higher order, the beautiful completed edifice of the moral world, eludes it everywhere, as does the internal standard for the freedom of the individual, for state power, for all the various elements of the human condition.

But even the progress of the public condition which we praised above as the consequence of natural law, is attained, as is self-evident, in the practical assertion of its principles, and indeed mainly by them. Indeed, it is the special fruit

---

[192] See the final chapter of the *Contrat Social* [Social Contract].

of liberalism that it not only influences the right and freedom of the individual, as does natural law, but also extends it to the people as a whole. The notion of the inviolability of individual nations [Völkerindividualitäten] is a glorious (even if often inconsistent) product of liberalism, which deduction via natural law would not have attained. The same is true of the requirement that the people itself actually act in the formation of its public condition. Natural law only extends to personal and civil freedom; the form of government by which these are protected, as long as this protection is secure, lies outside its sphere. Liberalism proceeds to political freedom, while the power to establish laws itself is an inalienable right of men. Here, however, we encounter the serious misunderstanding that the true demand of freedom and self-activity of the people, the right to preserve and co-determine its public condition, is converted into the false demand of popular sovereignty, i.e. the right primarily and exclusively to determine its public condition, and that the people themselves are not conceived as an articulated unity but as a mere collection of the masses. When the orientation is cleared of this murky addition, then that which is to be recognized as liberal in the true sense, in which the lasting fruit of this development of thought consists, will become clear.[193]

[193] Compare the relevant sections in Volume II of this work.

APPENDIX TO BOOK III: MATERIALISTIC LEGAL PHILOSOPHY

A contrast with the rationalist orientation begun by Descartes and completed by Hegel is formed by the one which is usually called "empirical" and which was exercised in England and France. In this case, "empirical" is used in a different sense than with Aristotle's legal philosophy as discussed above. With Aristotle, the expression refers to the object, the existing world of experience; here, by contrast, it refers to the subjective aspect of the means of recognition, to sensorial perception. With the former, therefore, "empirical" expresses the opposite of the ideal, i.e., of a fulfilled view, the content of which pertains to another, higher world transcending actual limitations; the latter expresses the opposite of rational, pure empty determinations and laws of thought, and thought generally. It indicates an orientation which regards substance and its sensorial impression to be the original and in this respect the only [thing], while the form of reason, indeed all thought, everything intellectual [Geistige] is considered to be the mere effect hereof. It is therefore more correctly characterized as the sensory, or, in its extreme form, the materialistic orientation.

Following the groundwork provided by Bacon, Locke's doctrine of human knowledge[194] laid the foundation for this orientation, albeit still in purely theoretical, contemplative areas. While the rationalistic doctrine derives all knowledge from reason (innate ideas or logical categories), Locke conversely held the view that reason in this sense (as originally innate) makes no contribution to our knowledge, but that all knowledge arises from experience, i.e., the influence of external material objects on our senses. Locke did not deny that we have innate ideas, categories of reason, axioms by which we think, but he considers them only to be an emanation of sense impressions. He considered the human mind or understanding to be a *tabula rasa;* the qualities of external things effectuate sense impressions in us, and these in turn effectuate images in that emptiness of the mind (e.g. tone, color, resistance). By combining these impressions and abstracting from them, the mind forms the concepts of behavior, e.g., from the sense perception of successive impressions, the mind forms

[194] *De Intellectu Humano* [*Essay concerning Human Understanding*].

the concept of time, from the sense perception that one impression begins to exist from another, it forms the concept of cause and effect. Thus, while rationalists regard reason apart from all activity as the source of all knowledge, Locke considers reason to be entirely without content, and its activity (abstraction, combination) constructs knowledge, indeed pure concepts of relation, from sense impressions. In this manner all knowledge arises through sensation, and reflection (this activity of understanding) is itself conceived as an inner observation, thus at bottom as itself a sensation, for which reason Kant characteristically said, "Leibniz intellectualized the phenomena, while Locke sensified the concepts of reason."

This function of reason is actually only passive; thought is a material thing that is set in motion by a material impetus. In line with this, the highest certainty for Locke is the certainty of sense impressions and thereby the existence of external things, while vice versa with rationalists these are entirely cast in doubt and only the logical form is considered to be certainly known. The implementation of this notion, the construction of all supreme concepts in terms of them is masterful, but Locke overlooks the fact that sense impressions, as he depicts them, are impossible without pre-existing concepts of reason. For example, to observe the succession of impressions, one must already have the view of time; in order to observe that one impression begins "as a result of" another, one must already have the idea of causality; for which reason, Hume on this basis rightly proceeds to cast doubt on the causal link, since the experience of one *after* the other never proves one *because of* the other. Indeed, this activity of reason – abstraction and combination, reflection – which he allows to proceed without any rational content in sense material, must have a law, and that would be an innate idea, a category independent of sense impression.

In the area of practice, this point of view now necessarily leads to the acceptance of satisfaction and, ultimately, sense satisfaction as the ultimate goal. When sense impression is the source and supreme truth of cognition, then it must also be the source and supreme rule of action. Locke therefore even denied that there are practical ideas that are necessary in themselves; virtue should be praised not because it is innate to us, but because it is useful, and accordingly it is characteristic of the great majority of English moral philosophers and the French who follow in this direction to accept satisfaction, well-being, happiness as an ethical principle, and to relinquish an independent value, an independent necessity of the good. Several of them, especially at the commencement of this theory, with a personally noble way of thinking, tempered the result of the principle so that it does not come clearly to consciousness, by teaching a satisfaction by the good, by charity, etc. But this gradually receded, leaving sense satisfaction as the center of ethics. In the same way, many gradations are conceived as to how one's own satisfaction (egoism) is assumed to be the basis (thus not necessarily goal and content), and to what degree, from the outset, common satisfaction is that basis.[195]

The logical conclusion of the sensorial principle fashioned into a comprehensive world-view is Mirabaud's "system of nature." For him there is no spirit; the universe or nature is only matter which functions according to its necessary laws. This is indeed the inevitable assumption, if Locke's theory of knowledge, according to which knowledge is only the effect of sense impression, is correct. Therefore there is no God, and the idea of such is an invention of fear or ignorance. Man is a totally material being; thinking is an effect of the material movement of the nerves of the brain; every thought arises only through the sense impressions of material objects. With the end of earthly life, human life ends forever, there is no survival except in glory, in the memory of posterity. There is no freedom of action, for every act is a necessary effect of attraction and repulsion. Good or bad depends on whether it leads to happiness, that is, to continuous sensorial pleasure. The most evil thing is religion, which, terrorizing through punishment, disturbs enjoyment in the present by holding out a prospective future.

The parallel in results of this consummately materialistic view with the consummately rationalist, hence logical-pantheistic view is unmistakable. Instead of God, there is a necessary lawful movement of its own unconscious

---

[195] The succession of sensorialist systems of morality and their various fractions, the presentation of which is not our task here, is done well by Erdmann in his *Geschichte der neuern Philosophie* [History of Recent Philosophy]. For the rest, a truth underlies these eudemonistic moral systems, by which in terms of the eternal order, the satisfaction of personality is no less an independent absolute goal as is the fulfilment of the higher (divine) commandment. The error lies in the fact that the latter is here made into a mere means for the former, while satisfaction is usually placed in the well-being of men in accordance with empirical-sensorial existence.

movement, let it be called matter, substance, logical law, idea; there is no freedom of man, no immortality. Even the rejection of religion as something immoral has its parallel in the pantheistic system, since Hegel declares Christian diffidence [Bescheidung] regarding knowledge to be the heighth of immorality.[196] By restricting human enjoyment, Christianity reaches as much into the heart of materialistic pantheism as it reaches into the heart of rationalist pantheism by restricting human pride of thought. Even so, the content of morality in rationalism, as is self-evident, is fundamentally opposed to materialism.[197]

As far as legal philosophy is concerned, Locke himself created no particular legal philosophy corresponding to his empirical point of view; rather, he took over the entirety of natural law, this result of the rationalist orientation which filled the minds of his time, and only modified it in certain points in accordance with his empirical standpoint.[198] Like the other natural law doctors, he made individuals in their isolation into the principle of the legal order, taught the original complete freedom and equality of the state of nature and the foundation of the state by means of contract, and restricted the goal of the state to the protection of individual rights. But in doing so he did not conceive of man rationalistically from the side of pure will, of abstract freedom, as they do; but sensorially, from the side of his entire sense existence. Accordingly, for the state of nature, i.e., prior to the establishment of the state by contract, he taught a law of nature which, from the outset, contains the entire individual empirical existence of man ("life, freedom, health, property"), not merely a general statement from which one and the other is gained by inference. In particular, he taught the immediate validity of property, especially in the state of nature. While all earlier natural law doctors derived property from contract, and Kant, who deviates from this, yet derived it from the mutual recognition of the will, and therefore also discovered the acquisition thereof in the expression of will (occupation), Locke deduced property from empirical lack, because without it, thus with common property, things could not be utilized. Accordingly, he attributed

---

[196] *Enzyklopädie,* § 386 and "Vorrede zu Hinrichs Religionsphilosophie" [Prologue to Hinrich's Philosophy of Religion].

[197] The positive midpoint of truth over these two orientations is discussed in Volume II, Book I [*Philosophical Presuppositions*], §§ 22, 29, and 37 of this work.

[198] See the *Two Treatises of Government.*

the acquisition of property to labor, as that by which goods are made to serve the needs of human beings, and not to occupation, by which the will merely expresses itself; and also recognized originally a limit to the acquisition of property in the possibility of cultivation and use for one's own needs. Unlimited acquisition of property only has meaning and purpose where trade and commerce, and money as means of exchange, exist; and all of this is first founded by contract.[199]

Finally, Locke taught that already in the state of nature, penal law can be exercised by individuals against those who violate natural law. This as well has immediate validity by virtue of that full empirical existence of men, and for their protection, and does not require initial contractual introduction, which would signify the consent of those who are to be punished. Indeed, the establishment of the state is itself nothing other than the renunciation by individuals of the exercise of this penal law which originally accrued to them, allowing it to be exercised by the community. For this reason, as he explained, state power is basically divided into two functions, the legislative and the executive; the former determines the laws the infringement of which ought to be punished, and the latter inflicts the punishment. Such penal protection for individual rights exercised by the collective instead of the individuals, and nothing else, now comprises the essence and meaning of the state. While the other (rationalistic) natural law doctors are filled with the *ideal*, that the human will (apart from any content and object) is the sole cause of human conditions, Locke is filled with the *real*, that man in his sensorial existence and, in particular, what is empirically the basis of it, property, is protected. For this reason the chief means for the former is contract, as that in which the pure will, absent any content, proves itself, while with Locke it is property which accrues directly to men, and the right which accrues directly to him to protect his own, by means of punishment and prevention. Locke's empirical point of view is also characterized by the fact that, with regard to the duration of the marital bond, he gave as reason for parents to remain together the education of the children, rather than cohabitation – not the only reason, but still the main one. Nor was he, as were the other natural-law doctors, at a loss to establish paternal power. It is precisely the

---

[199] Both relations (Kant's and Locke's) taken together yield the truth. See Volume II, Book III of this work [*Private Law*], §§. 22 and 29.

empirical existence of children which requires this power, while it is excluded by the idea of the children's will, which the others make into their principle.

In accordance with this point of view, Locke remained forever and fundamentally distinguished from Rousseau, although with regard to the doctrine of popular sovereignty over royal power, he is the final precursor to him. Locke is always firmly committed to the independence of individual existence within its certain, sensorially given circumference, which the community must serve; while Rousseau allows it to be submerged as an indistinct unit in the general will. The mere abstract (if only selfish) will of the individual can flow together into such an equally contentless general will, whereas the sensorial existence of the individual always remains separate. In Locke's case, then, it is not the common will on which the emphasis is placed, but the common law, the rule (standing rule) which protects individual rights, and the impartial "judge on earth" which in the event of a dispute decides on the application. This forms the contrast with the state of nature, according to which each individual gives the rule to himself, and also against the absolutism of the king, according to which he alone gives and applies the rule. It is a feature that very characteristically distinguishes the English from the French. Although philosophical abstraction kept Locke from defending the old laws and acquired rights as Burke did, he nevertheless advocated certain unbreakable laws and the safeguarding of a certain legal existence, not an imaginary share in a sovereign lawless collective will.

To this extent, the influence of the sensorialist point of view is expressed in legal philosophy as put forward by Locke. A logical and radical implementation of the same, in terms of its extreme form as materialism, is provided in the system of Bentham, which stands in isolation as an individual conception (particularly remarkable in its rejection of human rights and the other purely formal teachings of the rationalist system, to which he contrasts material well-being, utility), and furthermore the more recent French socialistic theories in all their factions: communism, St. Simonism, socialism.

The innermost focal point of these theories is none other than enjoyment as the highest and ultimate purpose of human life, and thus human community which has no other task and guideline than to provide the same, and the highest possible enjoyment to everyone. Rationalist philosophy of law accomplished the feat of juxtaposing human beings not under an ethical order commanded by God, but in terms of inalienably equal claims. But it only considered abstract freedom to be the content of these claims, be it free movement in the individual sphere as natural right, be it the equal participation in common rule, as is the case with Rousseau's liberalism. With complete truth it could be objected that little is done with this abstract freedom and abstract equality if, because of the inequality of possessions, the real situation of people differs: for the one, abundance, happiness, freedom, for the other, want, distress, dependence. The appropriate response is that if, because of the same nature of man, no one should be able to advance beyond the other in terms of power and influence, then no one should have any advantage in enjoyment of life, possessions, and education.

In the first edition of this book (1830), when we did not yet know anything in Germany about these socialistic theories, I made the same response to natural law.[200] If sense satisfaction is now regarded with clear awareness as the ultimate goal of things, a doctrine of the human community necessarily arises by which there is no other task for it than to provide means of pleasure by labor, and to distribute them in such a way as to make the pleasure equal. Pleasure-providing labor is the highest employment of people, and manual labor holds the highest rank. Pleasure is the fulfillment of the purpose of our existence, and what remains as morality, or rather as the appearance of morality, is the pursuit of pleasure without prejudice to the pleasure of all. Enthusiasm for equal pleasure is the only interesting factor in this materialistic doctrine, just as enthusiasm for equal participation in supreme power is the interesting factor in rationalist revolutionary doctrine. On the other hand, everything that constitutes the fulfillment of a higher commandment over man, the holiness of marriage, the administration of justice, the gathering and upliftment of the human mind for a kingdom beyond earthly pleasures, together with the preservation of the institutions of religion and education which lead to this, the attachment of a regard and a power which, as an organ of this higher order, of royalty or other authority, is to be revered for itself – none of this has any place in such an organization of pleasure.

What in the rationalist point of view is bare law stripped of its purpose in the moral world-whole, in the materialistic point of view is pleasure.

The socialism of Fourier and the distributism of St. Simon are not entirely logical, in that fortune [Schicksal], i.e., the greater talent for work of one person

---

[200] See p. 197 of that edition.

over another, or even justice, the greater effort being rewarded with greater enjoyment, leaves a field of unequalization which does not agree with their supreme axiom, the equal claim to pleasure of human nature. The same is true of Proudhon's doctrine which, while retaining separate ownership and acquisition, states that wages should be determined neither by the value of the product nor by the workmanship, but by the time spent on them. The consequential implementation of the standpoint leads to communism. Indeed, animosity to property must be the end-result of the materialistic orientation which began to germinate with Locke. For property is just a notion, a rational rather than sensorial phenomenon. If one removes the rational admixture from the property relation, nothing remains but pleasure. Consequently, in communism the whole idea of law is fundamentally abandoned. Not even the prudential justice of socialistic theory, stipulating that the more skillful and hard-working worker should have more, remains.

So these are the four slogans – down with Christianity, kingship, marriage, property – which the materialistic worldview has logically fulfilled in the practical fields of our day. The socialistic theories, and in particular communism, have gotten serious with materialistic philosophy (Locke, Helvétius, etc.), in the same way that the Sidney-Rousseau theory of the Revolution got serious with rationalistic philosophy (Descartes, Grotius, etc.).

However, this is only to mark this orientation in terms of its destructiveness — which undeniably, incomparably, is its dominant aspect. It destroys the kingdom of God, the moral order of life. But it also has a seed of growth, similar to the system of the Revolution. Freedom, the egalitarian freedom of men, is also a part of the ethical order, albeit not the only one, and its assertion was required in the face of the presumption of a single class and the oppression, even degrading oppression, of a numerous portion of the people. In the same way, material satisfaction and the distribution of necessary satisfaction for every person is likewise a part of the ethical order, and its assertion is also required, in particular in conditions of excessive abundance on the one hand and extreme deficiency on the other, even if it is not asserted here in the proper manner. Liberalism enabled the self-reliant, the propertied, to gain the recognition of their dignity and their due share in the shaping of the community; the socialistic theory aims at least to be a spur for the non-propertied to achieve the measure of life satisfaction that they deserve. In the same way that it is impossible now for the nobility to assume the position vis-à-vis the citizenry that it enjoyed before the Revolution, it will be impossible one day to waste children in factories, to let workers be worn down by overburdening them, or to leave free labor to its fate, without any public welfare provision.

For this reason, although the rationalist theory of natural rights and revolution, as well as materialistic social theory as a whole, must be confronted as a perverse and perishable doctrine, one may not deny the important aspects of truth, or indeed the true motives that they contain. It is necessary to seek to appropriate these traits into a truth-based comprehensive view of the human community. The positive gain brought by rationalist ethics and legal philosophy has been highlighted everywhere in previous chapters of this book. In relation to the socialistic theories, I have attempted this in the second volume, in which they are characterized and assessed in more detail. The significance and therefore also the elements of truth of the socialistic theories are however by the nature of the case less ethical and legal-philosophical than they are national-economic. Because of this, a history of legal philosophy is not the place for a more detailed presentation. It is justifiably reserved for a dedicated investigation and implementation.[201]

[201] See Volume II, Part I, Book III of this work [*Private Law*], §§ 31ff., and Part II [*The Doctrine of State & the Principles of State Law*], §§ 22ff. (Note to the 4th edition: a yet more thorough presentation of the social theories is now provided in *Die gegenwärtigen Parteien in Staat und Kirche* [The Contemporary Parties in Church and State].)

WORKS CITED

Alvarado, Ruben. *Calvin and the Whigs: A Study in Historical Political Theology*. Aalten: Pantocrator Press, 2017.

—. *The Debate that Changed the West: Grotius versus Althusius*. Aalten: Pantocrator Press, 2018.

Andlo, Petrus de. *De imperio romano Regis et Augusti creatione ... : libri duo*. Argentoratum: Rikel, 1603 [1460].

Aquinas, Thomas. *De regimine principum: libri quatuor*. Lugduni Batavorum [Leyden]: Ex officina Joannis Maire, 1630.

—. *Summa Theologica*. Trans. Fathers of the English Dominican Province. New York: Benziger Bros., 1947.

Bacon, Francis. *De dignitate & augmentis scientiarum libri IX*. London: In officina Ioannis Hauiland, 1623.

Bodin, Jean. *Les Six Livres de la Républiqu*e. Paris: Jacques du Puis, 1576.

Brutus, Stephanus Junius. *Vindiciae contra Tyrannos: sive, De principis in populum, populique in principem, legitima potestate*. Edinburgh, 1579.

Coccejus, Henricus. *Disputatio Juridica Inauguralis de Principio Juris Naturalis Unico, Vero, et Adaequato*. Francofurti ad Viadrum: Christophori Zeitleri, 1699.

—. *Positiones pauculae & generalissimae loco quasi postulatorum explicationi juris gentium & praelectionibus Grotianis praemissae*. Nova editio, revisa & aucta. Francofurti ad Viadrum: Joh. Godofredum Conradi, 1719.

Dante. *De Monarchia of Dante Alighieri*. Trans. Aurelia Henry. Boston and New York: Houghton Mifflin and Company, 1904.

Erdmann, Johann Eduard. *Einleitung in eine wissenschaftliche Darstellung der Geschichte der neuern Philosophie*. Riga und Dorpat: Eduard Frantzen's Buchhandlung, 1834.

Feuerbach, Paul Johann Anselm, Ritter von. *Kritik des natürlichen rechts als propädeutik zu einer wissenschaft der natürlichen rechte*. Altona: Bei der

Verlagsgesellschaft, 1796.

—. *Lehrbuch des gemeinen in Deutschland geltenden peinlichen Rechts*. Giessen: Georg Friedrich Heyer, 1801.

—. *Revision der Grundsätze und Grundbegriffe des positiven peinlichen Rechts*. 2 vols. Chemnitz: Georg Friedrich Tasché, 1800.

Fichte, Johann Gottlieb. *Beitrag zur Berichtigung der Urtheile des Publikums über die französische Revolution*. 2nd ed. [Danzig]: [Verlag Ferdinand Troschel], 1795.

—. *Das System der Sittenlehre nach den Principien der Wissenschaftslehre*. Jena und Leipzig: Christian Ernst Gabler, 1798.

—. *Foundations of Natural Right According to the Principles of the Wissenschaftslehre*. Ed. Frederick Neuhouser. Trans. Michael Baur. Cambridge: Cambridge University Press, 2000.

—. *Grundlage des Naturrechts nach Principien der Wissenschaftslehre*. 2 vols. Iena und Leipzig: Christian Ernst Gabler, 1796–1797.

—. *J. G. Fichte's ... Appellation an das Publikum über die durch ein Kurf. Sächs. Confiscationsrescript ihm beigemessenen atheistischen Aeusserungen*. Jena und Leipzig; Tübingen: Christian Ernst Gabler; J. G. Cottaischen Buchhandlung, 1799.

—. *The Science of Ethics as based on the Science of Knowledge*. Trans. A. E. Kroeger. London: Kegan Paul, 1897.

Franklin, Julian H. *Constitutionalism and Resistance in the Sixteenth Century: Three Treatises by Hotman, Beza, & Mornay*. New York: Pegasus, 1969.

Goldast, Melchior. *Monarchia s. romani Imperii, sive Tractatus de jurisdictione imperiali seu regia et pontificia seu sacerdotali... studio... Melchioris Goldasti Haiminsfeldii,...* Vol. II. Francofurti: Apud Joann-Davidem Zunnerum, 1668.

Grotius, Hugo. *De Jure Belli ac Pacis Libri Tres*. Trans. Francis W. Kelsey. Oxford: At the Clarendon Press, 1925.

—. *Rights of War and Peace*. Ed. Jean Barbeyrac and Richard Tuck. 3 vols. Indianapolis: Liberty Fund, 2005.

Hegel, Georg Wilhelm Friedrich. *Enzyklopädie der philosophischen Wissen-*

schaften im Grundrisse. III vols. Heidelberg: Oßwald, 1830 [1817].

Hegel, Georg Wilhelm Friedrich. "Vorrede zu Hinrichs' Religionsphilosophie." *Vollständige Ausgabe durch einen Verein von Freunden des verewigten: D. Ph. Marheineke, D. J. Schulze, D. Ed. Gans, D. Lp. v. Henning, D. H. Hotho, D. C. Michelet, D. F. Förster, Volume 17*. Berlin: Duncker und Humblot, 1835. 280–304.

Hobbes, Thomas. *Elementa Philosophica de Cive*. Amsterdam: Elsevier, 1647 [1642].

—. *Leviathan, or the Matter, Forme, & Power of a Common-Wealth Ecclesiastical and Civill*. London: Andrew Crooke, 1651.

Hoffbauer, Johan Christoph. *Untersuchungen über die wichtigsten Gegenstände des Naturrechts. Nebst einer Censur der verdienstlichsten Bemühungen um diese Wissenschaft...* Halle: Carl August Kümmel, 1795.

Kant, Immanuel. *Critik der reinen Vernunft*. 2nd. Riga: Johann Friedrich Hartknoch, 1787.

—. *Critik der Urtheilskraft*. Frankfurt und Leipzig: n. p., 1792.

—. *Critik der praktischen Vernunft*. Riga: Johann Friedrich Hartknoch, 1788.

—. *Grundlegung zur Metaphysik der Sitten*. Riga: Johann Friedrich Hartknoch, 1785.

—. *Metaphysische Anfangsgründe der Rechtslehre. Erster Theil von die Metaphysik der Sitten*. 2nd ed. Königsberg: Friedrich Nicolovius, 1798.

—. *The Metaphysics of Morals*. Trans. Mary Gregor. Cambridge: Cambridge University Press, 1996.

Linck, Anton Arnold von. *Über das Naturrecht unserer Zeit als Grundlage der Strafrechtstheorien*. Munich: Anton Weber, 1829.

Locke, John. *De Intellectu Humano Inquator Libris*. London: Impensis Aunshami & Johan. Churchill, 1701.

—. *Two Treatises of Government*. Ed. Peter Laslett. New York: New American Library, 1965 [1960]. First edition 1689.

Marca, Petrus de. *De Concordia Sacerdotii et Imperii, seu de libertatibus ecclesiæ Gallicanæ dissertationum libri quatuor*. Paris: Sumptibus Viduae Ioannis Camusat, 1641.

Mariana, Juan de. *De Rege et regis institutione Libri tres*. Toleti: Apud Petrum

Rodericum typo. Regium, 1599.

Milton, John. *A Defence of the People of England by John Milton ; in answer to Salmasius's Defence of the king.* Trans. Joseph Washington. [Amsterdam], 1692.

—. *Pro Populo Anglicano Defensio, contra Claudii Anonymi, aliàs Salmasii, Defensionem Regiam.* London: Typis du Gardianis, 1651.

More, Thomas. *De Optimo Reipublicae Statu deque Nova Insula Utopia.* Louvain: Dirk Martens, 1516.

Mornay, Philippe du Plessis. *A Defence of Liberty Against Tyrants: A Translation of the Vindiciae Contra Tyrannos by Junius Brutus.* London: G. Bell and Sons, Ltd., 1924.

Nettelbladt, Daniel. *Systema elementare universae Jurisprudentiae naturalis.* 3rd. Halae Magdeburgicae: In Officina Libraria Rengeriana, 1767.

Oldendorp, Johannes. *Iuris Naturalis Civilis et Gentium Isagoge.* Cologne: Ioannes Gymnicus, 1539.

Pufendorf, Samuel. *De Jure Naturæ et Gentium: Libri Octo.* Londini Scanorum: Sumtibus Adami Junghaus, 1672.

—. *De Officio Hominis & Civis Juxta Legem Naturalem Libri Duo.* Londini Scanorum: Sumtibus Adami Junghans, 1673.

—. *Elementorum Iurisprudentiae Universalis libri duo.* Hagae-Comitis: Adriani Vlacq, 1660.

—. *Of the Law of Nature and Nations: Eight Books.* London: Printed for J. Walthoe, R. Wilkin, J. and J. Bonwicke, S. Birt, T. Ward, and T. Osborne, 1729.

—. *The Whole Duty of Man according to the Law of Nature.* Indianapolis: Liberty Fund, 2003.

—. *Two Books of the Elements of Universal Jurisprudence.* Trans. William Abbott Oldfather. Indianapolis: Liberty Fund, 2009 [1931].

Rousseau, Jean-Jacques. *Du contrat social, ou Principes du droit politique.* Amsterdam: Marc-Michel Rey, 1762.

Selden, John. *De Jure Naturali et Gentium juxta Disciplinam Ebraeorum Libri VII.* London: Richardus Bishopius, 1640.

Sidney, Algernon. *Discourses Concerning Government.* London: [John Toland],

1698.

Stahl, Friedrich Julius. *Der Protestantismus als politisches Princip*. Berlin: Verlag von Wilhelm Schultze, 1853.

—. *Die gegenwärtigen Parteien in Staat und Kirche. Neunundzwanzig akademische Vorlesungen*. Berlin: Verlag von Wilhelm Hertz, 1863.

—. *Die Kirchenverfassung nach Lehre und Recht der Protestanten*. Erlangen: Theodor Bläsing, 1840.

—. *Philosophical Presuppositions*. Aalten: WordBridge Publishing, forthcoming.

—. *Principles of Law*. Aalten: WordBridge Publishing, 2007.

—. *Private Law*. Aalten: WordBridge, 2007.

—. *The Doctrine of State and the Principles of State Law*. Aalten: WordBridge, 2009.

Suarez, Francisco. *Tractatus de Legibus ac Deo Legislatore*. Coimbra: Didacum Gomez de Loureyro, 1612.

Thomasius, Christian. "Die Grund-Lehren des Natur- und Völker-rechts, nach dem sinnlichen Begriff aller Menschen vorgestellet." *Herrn Christian Thomasii Drey Bücher der Göttlichen Rechtsgelahrheit*. Hall im Magdeburgischen: Zufinden in der Rengerischen Buchhandlung, 1709.

—. *Fundamenta juris naturae et gentium ex sensu communi deducta*. Halae & Lipsiae: Typus & Sumtibus Viduae Christophori Salfeldii, 1705.

—. *Institutes of Divine Jurisprudence. With Selections from Foundations of the Law of Nature and Nations*. Indianapolis: Liberty Fund, 2011.

—. *Institutiones iurisprudentiae divinae*. Halae Magdeburgicae: Sumtibus Christophori Salfeldii, 1694.

Warnkönig, Leopold August. *Rechtsphilosophie als Naturlehre des Rechts*. Freiburg im Breisgau: Wagner, 1839.

Wolff, Christian. *Institutiones Iuris Naturae et Gentium*. Halae Magdeburgicae: Prostat in Officina Rengeriana, 1750.

—. *Jus Naturae Methodo Scientifica Pertractatum*. VIII vols. Francofurti & Lipsiae; Halae Magdeburgicae: Prostat in Officina Libraria Rengeriana, 1740–1748.

—. *Vernünfftige Gedancken von Gott, Der Welt und der Seele des Menschen, auch allen Dingen überhaupt*. Halle: Rengerischen Buchhandel, 1722.

INDEX

Abel, 43, 44, 55
abstraction, 23, 76, 77, 78, 82, 87, 98, 99, 101, 102, 120, 130, 175, 186, 209, 223, 231, 232, 260, 264
Adam, 55
Andlo, Petrus de, 51, 52, 55, 56, 57, 58, 60
Andromache, 217
Aquinas, Thomas, 47–51, 52, 53, 56, 57, 70, 141
Aristotle, 15, 16, 19–29, 31, 33, 39, 45, 51, 52, 56, 58, 59, 69, 70, 71, 72, 75, 87, 105, 133, 147, 259
  ignores progress in history, 33
Augustine, 43–46, 51–53, 56, 65
  reconciled Plato and Aristotle, 45
Bacon, Francis, 69, 70, 72, 259
Bodin, Jean, 69, 70, 72, 152
Buchanan, George, 238, 239, 240, 247
Cain, 43, 44
Calvin, John, 64
Calvinism, xvii, 64
Carneades, 139
Catholic principle
  reconciled with Protestant principle, 64–67
Charlemagne, 54, 55, 61
Christ, Jesus, 43, 53, 55, 60, 64, 66, 133, 224
church and state
  and right to resist, 238–41, 244–45
  Augustine, 45
  their separation the problem of modernity, 46
Cicero, Marcus Tullius, 39, 48, 240
Coccejus, Henricus, 160, 161
communism, 252, 264, 266
competence. *See* subjective right
  in Fichte, precedes law, 196
  source of law, 113, 200
Constantine, 54
contract, 119, 130, 153, 159, 220, 255
  basis for all rights (Kant), 197
  cannot be used to restrict the people, 250
  cannot be used to transfer sovereignty, 250
  chief means of rationalistic natural law, 263
  duty of subjects based on, 148
  justifies slavery (Wolff), 134
  lever of natural law, 128
  means of restricting freedom (Kant), 205
  only basis of legal institutions (Kant), 205
  social, 131, 149, 151, 206
  state, 206, 229, 240
    contradiction in, 132
    denied by Coccejus, 161
    Fichte, 199
    Grotius, 141, 144, 145, 147
    Hobbes, 150, 152
    Locke, 243, 262
    not akin to slavery, 247
    Revolution, 243
    Rousseau, 247, 248
    Selden, 160
    Sidney, 242
    Thomasius, 132
Dante, 51, 53, 54, 56, 57, 59, 60
Darjes, Joachim Georg, 97, 157, 159

Descartes, René, 62, 63, 69, 93, 154, 173, 259, 266
empiricism
  and Hobbes, 100
  Aristotle, 27
  Bacon, 70
  difference with abstract method, 87, 175, 187, 191–92
  legal philosophy, as opposed to rationalism, 259–67
  Locke, 259–64
equality, 50, 117, 118, 119, 128, 194, 201, 202, 220, 225, 227, 253, 254, 255, 262, 265, *See* inequality
  and freedom, logically contradict each other, 220
  before the law, 117, 225
    positive result of subjectivist orientation, 233–34
  mandated by concept of man, 117
  positive, 226, 227
  principle of in Rousseau, 248
ethic, ethics. *passim*
  (Judeo-) Christian
    filled with positive content, 222–25
    historical character of, 80–81
    will of personal God as basis, xix, 34, 94
  abstract
    destructive character of, 228–29
  Greek
    contains germ of rationalist ethic, xix, 34
    contrasted with rationalist ethic, 102
    subordination of the individual, 105
  historical, 227
Feuerbach, Paul Johann Anselm, Ritter von, 109, 113, 114, 126, 180, 219, 220
Fichte, Johann Gottlieb, 78, 79, 82, 83, 86, 89, 102, 111, 113, 126, 127, 130, 135, 172, 173, 174, 180, 181, 182, 183–202, 185, 189, 192, 203, 205, 209, 210, 211, 212, 213, 216, 217, 218, 219, 221, 228, 231, 234, 243
  radical subjectivism, 193
  subjective right as source of law, 113, 196
Filmer, Sir Robert, 241
Fourier, Charles, 265
freedom. *passim*
  annihilates existing institutions, 123
  contradictions are solved in the will of God, 131
  driving force of natural law philosophy, 117
  positive versus negative, 222–28
French Revolution, 126, 130, 148, 197, 201, 238, 244, *See* Revolution, the
Fries, Jakob Friedrich, 127
God
  and law, Jewish view of, 31–35
  bound by law in rationalist system, 168
  Creator, xvii, 81, 84
    rendered unnecessary by abstract philosophy, 85
  divine vocation as source of content of institutions, 215
  fear of
    basis of true ethic, 233
  of rationalism, 86
  personal, xviii, xix, 31, 34, 83, 84, 217, 223
  personal versus abstract, 81–82
  subject to natural law, 95, 97
    Kant, 175
government, forms of, 21–22

aristocracy, 21, 250, 251
democracy, 21, 251, 257
kingship, 21, 242, 243, 245, 257, 266
monarchy, 21, 56, 59, 71, 144, 251
oligarchy, 21
polity, 21, 22, 56
tyranny, 21, 241
Greek versus modern orientation, 105
Gros, Karl Heinrich von, 100, 203, 205
Grotius, Hugo, 62, 69, 71, 88, 89, 95, 96, 106, 107, 109, 127, 139, 140, 137–48, 149, 151, 152, 153, 155, 162, 175, 176, 203, 205, 240, 243, 247, 252, 255, 266
eliminated both Author and content of moral order, 147
in what sense founder of natural law, 146
Gundling, Nicolaus Hieronymus, 97, 155, 156, 158, 159
Hector, 217
Hegel, Georg Wilhelm Friedrich, 2, 79, 82, 83, 86, 94, 120, 135, 153, 186, 209, 211, 212, 213, 215, 221, 223, 253, 259, 262
Helvétius, Claude Adrien, 266
Heydenreich, Karl Heinrich, 112
Historical School of jurisprudence, 2, 65, 81
Hobbes, Thomas, 99, 100, 102, 133, 134, 149, 151, 152, 154, 155, 156, 240, 242, 243, 247
Hoffbauer, Johan Christoph, 99, 112, 119, 130
Holy Roman Empire of the German Nation, 47, 55
Homer, 217
Höpfner, Ludwig Julius Friedrich, 97, 134, 157, 159
inequality. *See* equality
actual, 126, 220, 226, 227
follows from freedom, 220
mandated by ideal of man, 117
of possessions, 265
of the law, 128
Jacobi, Friedrich Heinrich, 93
jus naturale, 49
justice. *passim*
Aquinas, 49
Aristotle, 23
commutative, 50
distributive, 50
Hegel, 11
Kant, 11, 225
Plato, 10, 13, 15
protective, 37
retributive, 37, 171, 198
strict, 14
Kant, Immanuel, xv, 51, 65, 76, 80, 82, 83, 84, 89, 94, 97, 99, 103, 108, 110, 112, 119, 127, 132, 134, 147, 148, 149, 154, 156, 159, 163–82, 189, 204, 263
categorical imperative, 176
kingdom of ends, 175, 177
maxim of coexistence, 179, 197, 205, 206
supreme principle of natural law, 204
transcendental philosophy, 173
knowledge
negative versus positive, 81
Lampugnano, Ubertus de, 53
Languet, Hubert, 238, 239, 240, 241, 247
law
coercibility
criterion for separating legality from morality, 156, 159
Greek
ahistorical character of, xix, 32
primacy of objective order, 37–

38, 105
separation from God, 32
human, 48, 244
in subjective slsense. *See* subjective right
Jewish view of
based on charity, 31–35
jus naturale, 139
lex aeterna, 39, 47, 96, 97
root of autonomous natural law, 94
lex humana, 48
lex naturalis, 47, 49, 95
lex permissiva, 112
moral, 39, 48, 110, 170, 175, 176, 196
natural. *passim*
binds God, 154
detachment from the will of God as prerequisite, 95
dissolves the bond between the world and God, 160
each system derived from an individual drive, 98
ignores the purpose of life relations, 229–31
modern, founded by Grotius, 146
reason as all-sufficient cause of, 96
root of its erroneous conceptualization, 47–48
subordinate role of God in, 97
transformed into law of reason, 179
nature of the case, 49, 239
of nations, 139, 146
permissive, 112, 113, 160
positive, 40, 48, 49, 121, 134, 140, 146, 251
theology as (Leibniz), 106
will of God as, 95
principle of
freedom as exclusive, 125
Germanic, 121
personal will of God as, 59
purpose of life relations as, 229–31
reason, law of, 82, 112, 114, 117, 171, 176, 179, 180, 182, 186, 195, 197, 198, 199, 200, 203, 206, 207, 214, 218, 220, 229, 232
natural law changed into, 179
Roman
abstract character, 121
and subjective right, 39
commitment to existing institutions, 122
comparison with natural law, 120–23
separation from morality, 39
legitimacy, 65, 66
Leibniz, Gottfried Wilhelm, 94, 95, 97, 106, 158, 173, 176, 260
liberalism, 237, 258, 266
does not recognize purpose of life relations, 257
implementation of the Revolution, 237
positive and negative effects of, 257–58, 267
Linck, Anton Arnold von, 180
Locke, John, 69, 241, 243, 247, 249, 251, 256, 259–64, 266
adaptation of English liberties, 264
adapted rationalist natural law to empiricist framework, 262
Louis of Bavaria, 54
Luther, Martin, 64
Machiavelli, Niccolo, 201
man
concept versus ideal of, 117

Marca, Petrus de, 245
Mariana, Juan de, 244
Marsilius of Padua, 51, 52, 57, 59
Mary Stuart, Queen of Scots, 239
Melanchthon, Philip, 61, 65, 72
Michaelis, Johann David, 60
Milton, John, 238, 239, 240, 241, 243, 244, 247
Mirabaud, Jean-Baptiste de, 261
Montesquieu, Charles de Secondat, Baron de, 71, 134, 249, 251
More, Thomas, 69–72
Mornay, Philippe du Plessis, 241
Napoleon Bonaparte, 201
nature-grace distinction in the medieval framework, 56–59
Nettelbladt, Daniel, 97, 111, 127
obligatio adventitia, 118
obligatio connata, 118
Ockham, William of, 54
Oldendorp, Johan, 62, 133
Plato, xiii, 9–17, 19, 22–29, 31–37, 39, 45, 69, 70, 75, 84, 94, 105, 151, 225, 231
    ignores progress in history, 33
property, xx, 72, 110, 119, 125, 126, 127, 129, 134, 141, 150, 155, 159, 185, 197, 204, 206, 220, 230, 263
    animosity to, result of materialistic orientation, 266
    communal, 215
    several, 127, 142, 262
Protestant principle
    reconciled with Catholic principle, 64–67
Proudhon, Pierre-Joseph, 266
Pufendorf, Samuel, 93, 95, 97, 106, 118, 119, 127, 153, 154, 155, 157, 161, 176, 178, 243
rationalism. *passim*
    character traits, 86
reason
    becomes source of truth, xvi, 216
    recognizes rather than produces content of the ethic, 215
Reformation, the, 61–67, 69, 72, 77, 238
    principle of
        against medieval theocracy, 61
        one-sided development by rationalism, 62–63
    separation of spiritual kingdom from external church power, 55
    sphere of individual freedom, 61
representation, political, 21, 150, 229, 241, 248, 250
    unrepresentability, 249, 253
Revolution, the, 63, 64, 65, 237, 238, 245, 247, 254, 256, 257, 266
rights. *See* subjective right, competence
    acquired, 118, 125, 129, 220, 248, 250, 256, 257, 264
        abolished by natural, 122
        sanctity of in Roman law, 122
    alienable versus inalienable, 130
    aptitudo, 109
    innate, 118, 119, 125, 129, 204
        jura acquisita, 118
        jura connata, 118, 119
    innate versus acquired, 118–20
    jura connata, 119
    jus quaesitum, 122
    natural, 133, 135, 220, 250, 267
        abstract character of, 120
    primordial, 119, 130, 133, 204, 205
        as unrestricted power, 197
Romulus, 44
Rousseau, Jean-Jacques, 134, 145, 148, 151, 204, 237, 238, 241, 243, 244, 247–58
    general will, 248, 249, 252, 253,

254, 264
reciprocity, 204, 248, 254
will of all, 249, 252, 253
Salmasius, Claudius, 239
Samuel, 53
Saul, 53, 240
Savigny, Friedrich Karl von, 2, 70
Schelling, Friedrich Wilhelm Joseph, xvii, xviii, 81, 189, 190, 209, 211, 253
Schiller, Friedrich, 176, 214
Selden, John, 160, 161
Sidney, Algernon, 241, 242, 243, 247, 266
slavery, 27, 129, 130, 133, 145, 201, 217, 247
sociabilist, sociabilistic system, 106, 107, 131, 139, 153
difference between Grotius and Aristotle, 147
socialism, 264, 265
sovereignty, 71, 72, 144, 150, 152, 229, 243, 249, 250, 251, 253, 255, 256
of the individual, 229
popular, 59, 144, 229, 243, 257, 258, 264
Spinoza, Baruch, 82, 83, 86, 87, 88, 103, 120, 132, 152, 158, 166, 167, 168, 172, 173, 187, 189, 198, 199, 211, 212, 215, 216, 222, 223, 231, 232
St. Simon, Henri, 265
St. Simonism, 264
state of nature, 100, 101, 105, 149, 152, 153, 203, 243, 262, 263, 264
Suarez, Franciso, 244
subjective principle, 38, 106, 173, 179, 228
driving force of modernism, 76–77
Fichte's radical subjectivism, 193
origin of its primacy, 59
precondition for Christian scientific understanding, 63
restricted by Kant, 179
unleashed, 62–63
subjective right. *See* rights, competence
absence of in Greek law, 36–37
as principle of law versus morality, 108–13
facultas moralis, 111
Feuerback, 219
source of law (Fichte), 113, 196
subjectivism
effect on ethics, 228–29
ends in subjection of all others' freedom, 201
subsumption, 58, 66, 118, 120, 134, 178, 204, 214
definition, 11
set aside by Fichte, 186
Sylvester, Pope, 54
theocracy, 35, 46, 56, 60, 61, 62, 65, 66, 71, 238, 245
theocratic principle, 60
Thomasius, Christian, 93, 95, 97, 100, 102, 103, 106, 107, 119, 127, 131, 133, 134, 154, 155, 157, 159, 205, 243
ecclesiology, 156
established coercibility as criterion for separating the legal sphere, 156
freedom of religion, 155–56
Tiberius Claudius Nero, 240
two swords, 53, 55
Warnkönig, Leopold August, 154
Winkler, Benedictus, 62
Wolff, Christian Freiherr von, xvii, 81, 95, 96, 97, 99, 106, 111, 119, 134, 157, 158, 159, 219, 243
Wolffian school, 94

The Recovery of Historical Law

TABLE OF CONTENTS

Preface xxv

Notes on the Translation xxxi

Book IV: Pragmatic Legal Philosophy 1

Part I: Modern Politics – Machiavelli and Montesquieu 3

Separation of Natural Law and Politics, and the Reason Behind It 3

Machiavelli 4

The Constitutional Theory of Locke and Montesquieu 6

Its Value and its One-Sidedness 8

Mechanical Protection of Popular Freedom and Government 10

Montesquieu's Scientific Greatness in General 14

Part II: The Relation of Constitutionalism to Liberalism 17

Agreements and Contradictions 17

The Constitutionalists of 1789 17

Sieyès 17

Constitutionalism during the Restoration: Benjamin Constant 19

The Doctrinaires 22

True Constitutionalism 25

Part III: Regarding the Origin of Law 29

View Regarding the Causes and Motives of Events and Legislation 29

The Influence of National Character and Its Use by Montesquieu 30

Ethical Result of this View regarding the Origin of Law 32

Opposition to this View: The Historical School of Jurisprudence 33

Book V: Speculative Legal Philosophy 35

Part I: Schelling's Philosophy 41

Chapter 1: The System as a Whole 41

Emergence from Fichte's System 41

Sameness of its Elements 41

Consequences of the Objective Use Thereof 43

General Shape of Schelling's System 47

Fichte's Real Principle and its Objectification by Schelling 51

Elevation of Philosophy 52

Disruptive Principle ... 54

Contradiction of this Principle with the System as a Whole ... 54

Unfolding of the Christian Viewpoint in the System Itself ... 56

Root of the Hegelian System ... 59

Chapter 2: Schelling's Legal Philosophy ... 61

Objective Will ... 61

The Ethical Organisms and their Process in History ... 61

Construction of the State and History ... 62

Inhibiting Principle in Schelling's Legal Philosophy ... 64

Anticipation of Hegel ... 66

General Character of This Scientific Period ... 67

Part II: Hegel's Philosophy ... 69

Chapter 1: The System as a Whole ... 69

Rationalistic Character ... 69

Foundational Notion ... 69

Philosophical Task and the Requirement of Dialectic ... 70

Outline of the System ... 73

Innermost Motive of the System; Origin of Its Logical Theory ... 76

Chapter 2: Hegel's Legal Philosophy ... 83

Its Basic Character; Delimitation of Its Object ... 83

The Entire Ethical Sphere: Abstract Law, Morality, Ethics ... 83

Construction of World History ... 87

Construction of Constitutional Monarchy ... 88

Chapter 3: Logical Examination of Hegel's Doctrine ... 91

Indeterminacy of Hegel's Dialectic in Itself ... 91

Fraudulent Acquisition of Its Results ... 93

Unfitness for the Reciprocal Action of Things ... 94

Its Application to Legal Philosophy ... 96

Particular Logical Shortcomings of Legal Philosophy ... 97

No Distinction between Reality and Mere Thought ... 98

Chapter 4: Real Examination of Hegel's Doctrine ... 103

Demise of Personality and Freedom ... 103

Pantheism ... 107

Relation to Christian Revelation ... 108

True Ethical and Political Results; Deficiencies Thereof ... 111

Separation of the System from its Results ... 116
Chapter 5: Hegel's School ... 121
Shared Pantheistic World-View ... 121
Difference of Ethical Position regarding Philosophy ... 121
Different Results for Religion, Politics, and World History ... 122
Desertion Rooted in Hegel's Own Doctrine ... 124
Part III: Regarding Speculative Philosophy and Dialectic ... 127
The One in the Many and the Mutable ... 127
In Our Conditions ... 129
In the World ... 130
Investigation into the Essence of Unity and of the System ... 131
Application to the Ethic and Law ... 133
The Connection between the One and the Many ... 135
The Capacity for Positive Knowledge ... 136
Speculative Philosophy ... 138
Dialectic; Plato, Hegel, Kant ... 138
Value of Dialectic ... 141
Hegel's Use of Dialectic ... 143
Part IV: Schleiermacher ... 149
Standpoint ... 149
Construction of the Ethical World ... 150
Law and State ... 154
Relation of the State to Science and Religion ... 156
The State Constitution ... 157
Verdict ... 159
Book VI: Historical Legal Philosophy ... 167
Part I: The Writers of the Counter-Revolution ... 169
Maistre ... 170
Burke ... 172
Haller ... 177
Adam Müller ... 182
Part II: The Historical School of Jurisprudence ... 185
Relation to the Scientific Treatment of Positive Law ... 187
In Relation to Legislation ... 192
In Relation to Legal Philosophy and Politics ... 194

Works Cited 199
Index 203

PREFACE

The second half of *The History of Legal Philosophy* picks up, logically, where the first half (Volume 1A) leaves off, at the utter failure of liberalism and natural law to engender a functioning social order.

It begins with pragmatic legal philosophy, which has the same root as the natural law theory, but which works in terms of an entirely different plan of action. The result is the mechanical constitutionalism of Locke and Montesquieu. Both of these are based on the presupposition that the law, along with all historical products, are the deliberate creation of men, and when they are not, it is because of man's shortcomings. For "just as both orientations originate in the motive force of human independence and self-activity, so they regard all historical phenomena as human products. The entire age virtually lacks the notion of how something could take shape unless people bring it about, consciously and willingly; that is, unless crude mindless coincidence is what caused it, which would redound to their shame, a sign of their weakness." This mentality, in turn, is the effect of science having "closed itself off to the divine spirit, which guides history" (p. 29).

The pragmatic approach to constitutionalism and politics originated with Machiavelli. Montesquieu was only following in Machiavelli's footsteps when he stripped out the ethical dimension, leaving the mechanical. A product of mechanism, his separation of powers doctrine is only a negative one: it can only restrict power, it cannot direct it. And without a directing philosophy, pragmatism leads to Machiavellianism. "If only man and the mechanical law direct events, only this alternative remains to him: either to make use of any and all means in accordance with this law, or to sacrifice himself, in this case his state. And if he does not desire, indeed is not permitted the latter, only the former remains for him – thus says Machiavelli. It is therefore clear that the phenomenon of Machiavelli does not need to be explained by special circumstances and intentions; it is simply the consistent implementation of the same principle that in general was held to be fitting." The only alternative to this is divine guidance. "If one leaves something of guidance to a higher power, then this whole kind of politics falls to the ground; if, on the other hand, one wishes to take care of everything oneself, then we inevitably arrive at Machiavelli's point of view" (p. 12).

Despite this, Montesquieu contributed to our understanding of the totality of legal institutions in terms of national condition and situation – climate, temperament, customs, etc. In this he went farther than his predecessors, Aristotle and Jean Bodin: "With them this is mixed with other things, but with Montesquieu this insight and the investigation conducted along its lines are manifest as the sole task of his book; this brings the basic idea itself more vigorously and penetratingly to consciousness, and yields an infinitely greater wealth of results than they were able to accomplish." (p. 14). He bases the various forms of government on various character traits, monarchy on honor, aristocracy on moderation, democracy on virtue; but he also recognizes that religion is more important than any of these (p. 15).

To escape the box of abstract thought in which legal and political philosophy was locked, what was needed was a sea change in approach. This was provided by Schelling, who performed the "Samsonesque act" of replacing the mechanical natural-law philosophy with the organic historical one. Schelling "lifted the temple of the previous philosophy off of its pillars and buried the whole army of enemies, himself included, under its ruins" (p. 58). Himself included – because he, like Moses, stood at the entry to the Promised Land without entering in. Schelling provided the materials to capture and further a historical understanding of law rooted in divine providence, but all the while he remained mired in a pantheistic rut.

The change is wrought through the medium of so-called speculative philosophy, which puts contemplative vision rather than abstract logic at the heart of understanding. As such, it "considers the world to be a free act of the personal God" (p. 138). With the help of speculative philosophy, Schelling and Hegel arrived at the concept of objective will and of the ethical organism, in opposition to hitherto dominant concepts of subjective will and radical individualism. The historical view starts here, as does the recovery of Christian philosophy (pp. 38f.).

Hegel did not take advantage of this. Despite the benefit of acquaintance with speculative philosophy, he remained mired in abstract thinking. In order to avoid the personalistic implications of speculative philosophy, he turned to dialectic and applied it in a new way. "But if abstraction insists on itself, sets itself up as the measure of things, and declares everything that it does not contain to be untrue, if it maintains that initial data, which is basically only obtained from the inner vision, and rejects everything else, thus casting vision itself as untruthful: how should it be conveyed? In sound minds, through the vision itself; for whoever is in agreement with himself as a whole believes consistently in the vision. But what of him who has given in to abstraction, and puts his trust in it? Through *dialectic!*" (p. 138). In so doing, he cast aside all the gains made possible by Schelling's approach. "Hegel was therefore compelled to give up all of Schelling's uniqueness: the primordial-real, act, life, creation. And so the palladium of Schelling's philosophy is lost, and all the dangers that threatened it at its creation had now to come home to roost. The world once again becomes inactive substance, the logical modalities of which are things; identity is disintegrated into oneness; the ought and individual freedom become a sham; and the goal of all living existence is its extinguishment into nothingness" (p. 59). The result was a lifeless assemblage of results, smuggled in by a fraudulent procedure (pp. 93ff.).

Objective impersonalism makes itself felt most directly in Hegel's predilection for government power.

> His doctrine is as little *ultraroyalist* as it is *ultraliberal*; but it is *ultra-governmental*. Everything should be accomplished through ordered (objective) power, the government, while the people accept this consciously and thereby freely; but the reverse may not also take place, whereby a work is accomplished out of the free, innermost personal drives (subjectivity) of the individual, of associations, the people, the estates, whereby the government only leads, sanctions or moderates, while the estates restrain or correct the government. He is an opponent of the free movement which emerges from the unordered and unprepared into order and clear shape, and no less the inviolable rights the holders of which must be brought into connection with the jointly beneficial, through inner conviction. All of this is the necessary result of the system as a whole, which everywhere stands only on the impersonal, substantive, logically necessary, and pushes personality (subjectivity) down into a dependent moment, in itself without content, the only purpose of which is to reflect those things (p. 115).

The free action of independent citizens cannot lead to order, but only to chaos. There must be a guiding substantial (i.e., objective) power to counteract the "subjective" power of an independent citizenry.

> Just as everywhere the substance posits the subjective moment only for its own purpose, in order for it to take it back into itself, just so does the government as the substance of the state hold the people and the citizens only as a means of realizing itself through their (seemingly free) labor. Hegel therefore prefers the princely power and even more so the civil servants, in which he finds represented precisely that substantial necessity of state upon which this security of the state mechanism rests, in opposition to the subjective (the people). Accordingly, for him, civil servants should not only be in government, but the assemblies of the estates should also be predominantly composed of civil servants, because they have the "sense of the state," the governmental sense (p. 113).

In other words, civil servants are the conscious part of the polity, or in modern street parlance, "woke," and as such they are the only ones capable of steering things in the right direction. De Jouvenel describes it well: "The motive force of society is the general will, which does all that needs to be done, whether or not the individuals who lack consciousness of the end are assenting parties. It is now, in short, a question of inducing in the body social a new efflorescence, the vision of which is possessed by its conscious members only. These latter form 'the universal class' in distinction to all the rest, who remain the prisoners of their own particularisms. It is, then, the business of the *conscious part* to do for the whole the necessary willing."[2]

Nevertheless, Hegel did manage to post some significant positive results. Primarily, this came in the form of reasserting the objective principle, by which marriage, the family, the state had intrinsic meaning restored to them, instead of being mere artifacts of individual contracting parties. "In this manner, Hegel victoriously fought the heresies that were widespread at that time: Kant's doctrine making the freedom of the individual and the mere consideration of the coexistence of people (maxim of coexistence) the exclusive principle of law and state, conceiving of marriage as a mere contract regulating sexual function,

---

[2] Jouvenel, *On Power: Its Nature and the History of Its Growth*, p. 50.

relegating it in all its ethical traits (prohibition of polygamy, blood disgrace, arbitrary divorce) from the legal system to mere subjective morality; Rousseau's doctrine of the sovereignty of the masses; Feuerbach's doctrine of punishment as mere psychological deterrence, that is, as a mere safeguarding of society; Beccaria's doctrine of the illegitimacy of the death penalty" (p. 112). Moreover, he restored objectivity to morality and ethics, lifting them above subjectivist confusion; and he restored the concept of the organic development of state power in opposition to the mechanical theory.

Schleiermacher likewise remained stuck in the received pantheistic framework. He too sees the world in terms of the unfolding process of reason. This process occurs in two dimensions, nature and the ethical world. Nature and reason are to permeate each other – reason being the impersonal world reason that uses individuals to realize itself, as with Hegel, albeit only realized in and through nature. Ethics take on an entirely objective character, so much so that, as with Hegel, individual fulfillment takes a back seat to objective manifestation. Reason subjugating nature is the focus. Yet despite this focus on objectivity over subjectivity, Schleiermacher makes room for personality. As such, "the peculiar implementation that Schleiermacher gives to the pantheistic-speculative standpoint is that, regardless of the objectivity of the scientific conception which it necessarily includes, the results predominantly stand on the side of subjectivity, bare individual human freedom. Certainly, the ethic for him is not the task and fulfillment of the individual, but of objective, world-forming reason, and therefore of the human community in which it is realized. But the way in which he arrives at the content of the ethic does not consist in higher orderings, but only in the development of personality" (p. 160). With the focus on personality, Schleiermacher takes a further step forward toward a more tenable position.

It was the Historical School of Jurisprudence that reestablished law and politics on the personal basis that a historical awareness brings when understood as the work of divine guidance.

> Precisely a deeper philosophical truth is that on which it stands in its ultimate foundation, unspoken and perhaps for most unconscious, and this is the recognition of living divine workings in history. From this comes the reverence for the previously existing, from this comes human reticence regarding the

> modification thereof, the looking to a higher power from which the most essential and the best is to be expected. Piety, according to its innermost motive, is that cautious nurture of history, the preservation of every peculiar institution, the awe regarding everything that has come about apart from our doing. Even the high and independent value given to the detail of positive-legal provisions in past and present presupposes a world conjuncture according to which it is not logical law but personality and freedom that is the primary cause of all that exists (p. 195).

The unspoken, perhaps even unconscious, nature of this commitment caused many to misconstrue the nature of the Historical School, as if it were a utilitarian effort, yet another iteration of pragmatism. It "only emphasizes one side of the law, its being the product of popular consciousness, and not to the same extent the other side, its being a higher power, the ethic over the people and the popular consciousness, which lays a requirement on the people, which measures and judges the people; and that therefore in the legal profession and in the legislator it sees only organs and representatives of the popular consciousness, and not organs and representatives of the law as such, as an independent higher power" (p. 196). Nevertheless, its openness to the work of God in history, its willingness to accept that work instead of succumbing to the temptation to assume it for man, is what distinguishes it above all else. "This cannot be emphasized enough: what is truly historical is for history not to be relegated to the past, but to see to it that uninterrupted becoming be recognized in it; and it is truly religious if divine guidance is not arbitrarily restricted to earlier formations, as if they were its unsurpassable works, but that the new future formations that it furnishes are received with implicit devotion" (p. 197). This understanding of history is what distinguished it from the Counter-Revolutionary writers, who looked too much to the past, as if repristination were an option.

Stahl closes his history of legal philosophy with the Historical School, which is fitting because this school served as the basis for his own legal philosophy, the subject of the second and final volume of his *Philosophy of Law.* There the themes of divine and human agency, higher law and positive law, duties and rights, custom and legislation, public and private law, constitutionalism and politics, provide the outworking of this truly Christian-historical legal philosophy.

NOTES ON THE TRANSLATION

The usual translating conventions are followed. Square brackets [like this] are used either to show the original text in cases in which the translation is not straightforward or unambiguous, or to provide interpolations for better understanding, or to provide supplementary material.

A note about the notoriously difficult words "Recht" and "Gesetz": as is well known, English has no direct counterpart to them. In one signification, they both refer to "law." Here they are sometimes used synonymously, sometimes not. This is similar to the Latin words "jus" and "lex," which confront the translator with the same ambiguity. "Recht" refers to law in the more elevated, transcendent sense, while "Gesetz" refers to law in the positive, man-made sense. This is usually referred to as the distinction between natural, or higher, law and positive law. But "Recht" can also refer to rights. Here, it is English which is unambiguous, German and Latin which are ambiguous. "Recht" in the singular I have almost always translated as "law"; the plural, "Rechten," always refers to "rights," and it is here so translated.

Other terms: "Politiker" seems to refer mainly to political scientists rather than politicians *per se,* and I have so translated it. "Ethos" is another ambiguous term. It refers to a specific ethical system or ethical framework such as is maintained by a specific entity, i.e., a people. The counterpart "Ethik" refers to the concept of ethics in general. Accordingly, I have translated "Ethik" as "ethics" and "Ethos" as "ethic," "the ethic." The former is general, the latter specific.

BOOK IV: PRAGMATIC LEGAL PHILOSOPHY

PART I: MODERN POLITICS – MACHIAVELLI AND MONTESQUIEU

Separation of Natural Law and Politics, and the Reason Behind It

It is a peculiarity of the modern era that its doctrine of state (natural law) and its statecraft (the preferred term for which is politics) constitute two completely separate sciences. This separation is the work of the mind that dominates science in this age. The ethic [ethos] is sought in reason, even though reason has no power over events and natural results: the things which external relations demand and compel have no connection with [logical] consistency, and act hostilely to it; therefore, it cannot be a matter for the ethics of the state to take this consistency into consideration. On the other hand, those who look to the natural results of actions and legal institutions to discover maxims for the real institutions and activity of the state are compelled to abandon what follows from this sort of abstract principles, or can see no reason to go back to them. Yet the times have no other source of the ethic to offer in its place; such a source at best is what is active, what fills the personality of the statesman, as if with an elevated goal. The single power from which both real effect and ideal goal simultaneously emanate has been discarded. Hence reason, which imparts ethical prescriptions, has no power over events; and nature, which guides events, is indifferent to ethical prescriptions.

For this reason, natural law and politics have no contact with each other and indeed are completely heterogeneous sciences. Natural law deals only with the derivation from general principles; it is rationality without regard for results in life. For its part, politics deals only with expediency, without examining the rationality of the end. The results of natural law, or liberalism – which is only natural law's practical form – therefore bear the character of rigid inflexible consequences, absolute commandments of justice; they are of a bare state-legal, not political, nature. The results of politics, by contrast, have the character of arbitrary external means and events. An organic science proceeding from the inner purpose of life relations would necessarily be the science of both reasonableness and expediency at one and the same time, but here this is replaced by an *abstract philosophy of law* on the one hand and a *mechanical statecraft* on the other.

Despite this separation, natural law and modern politics are closely related.

An investigation which only busies itself with observing what kind of result is attained by laws in terms of the actual nature of people, of their manner of acting and their destinies, is insufficient to realize the abstraction of all that is. Yet the principle of the new age must produce effects in this direction analogous to what it did with natural law. The next step is for the natural consequences of institutions to be investigated only in relation to subjective, arbitrary purposes. As such, modern political scientists [Politiker] observe the course of human events in a very different sense than did Aristotle. He sought to discover the law inhering in those doings, to find the will of nature in them in order to obtain the goal which it is to set for itself. The moderns, on the other hand, determine their goal by caprice and coincidence, or at the very least conduct no investigation to determine it, and the only thing they wish to learn from nature is how to use it for their aim. They do not wish to submit to nature in the way that Aristotle did, but rather to subordinate nature to their will. The Aristotelian method can be labeled *teleological*, the modern political scientists' method *pragmatic.*

Machiavelli

The one who took this orientation to an extreme is Machiavelli. His motto is actually "What is just is what leads to my goal." Montesquieu preserves his own honor and that of his nation from Machiavelli's shocking indifference to the ethical. Nevertheless, arbitrary choice in purpose and means is the essence of the orientation and therefore also permeates its scientific activity. Pragmatism often views what has a self-contained goal only as a means for something else. It even treats political freedom as a goal that states may set for themselves, not that they must set for themselves.

Machiavelli's *The Prince* launched the first epoch of modern politics.[3] It is a system of well-calculated and energetic but often despicable advice on the consolidation of princely power. Machiavelli knows only one thing to be reprehensible: the shame of being incapable of fulfilling a desire. There have been doubts as to whether his book was meant in earnest. But the character which permeates it is the same as in his *Discourses on Livy* and *History of Florence.* Even in the latter, treacherous assassination is never disapproved, but only the lack of

---

[3] Machiavelli, *Il Principe.*

decision and skill in its execution. At the time, Italy was completely destitute not only of nobler attitudes, but even of the ordinary virtues of justice and fidelity. In their place was enthusiasm: either not to be dominated by others, or to rule over others. Machiavelli's wisdom of state revolves around these two poles. In the way that in the *Discourses* all other considerations give way for the preservation of the republican constitution, so in this book they give way for this one tendency: the consolidation of princely power. He does not take the things of men as they should be, but – in line with his own statements – as they are. Or, we might say, as they were in the degeneration that surrounded him. He recommends that princes eliminate the descendants of kindred dynasties; investigates when it is good for him to keep his word and when not, what one who has come to the throne through crime, has to do to maintain it; and finds in Caesar Borgia his ideal of the wise prince. It is unjust for Schlegel and others to explain Machiavelli's political character from classical, namely Roman education. On the contrary, this manifestation is the result of the modern spirit, this arbitrariness of goals and recklessness of means is entirely foreign to the Roman world, the mentality of which is so unrelated to Machiavelli that he often misunderstands Roman doings. Even his artistic character as a speaker and historian is not Roman. He lacks the substance, the proud measure of the Roman *dignitas;* in its place he is distinguished by Florentine ardor and liveliness, act follows act, nowhere is there matter at rest, nothing fading, just as in the southern sky the objects are sharply outlined and day and night follow without twilight.

Machiavelli's doctrine has its deeper foundation, if not its justification, in the impulse to the development of the public condition of his time, and this also furnished it its great lasting effect. It was the time in which the fracturing of the nation into noble fiefdoms was ending, and a strong monarchy had to be established as the unified power of the state. Longing for this had to awaken especially in Italy, given its extreme decline due to the independence, oppression, and mutual feuds of the magnates. This is what Machiavelli aspires to, albeit not by permissible means. He occupies the same position in the theoretical field that Louis XI does in the practical. Accordingly, this was the first foundation of the new state edifice.

The Constitutional Theory of Locke and Montesquieu

Machiavelli's political system was followed by another which was more scientific because its object was not the practicality of the actions of rulers but the practicality of enduring civil institutions. Its founders are Locke and Montesquieu.[4] It is the so-called *constitutional theory*, a system favoring the people in the way that the Machiavellian favored the princes. Even so, they correspond very well with each other in terms of their gradational historical sequence, since actual state-building began with the concentration of power in princes and then progressed to the participation of the nation in that unitary power. Machiavelli and Montesquieu together give the picture of the modern state, albeit, in line with the general character of scientific conception in this period, only from its mechanical side.

Locke is the first inventor of the constitutional theory, i.e., the doctrine of the necessary division of the legislative and executive powers. He applied this on the basis of natural law and the doctrine of popular sovereignty. For he came to it by the notion that only the people themselves are entitled to give themselves laws, and that the king, in terms of his primary position, can only be an executor of the laws. For him, the doctrine is based less on mechanical calculation than on fundamental necessity; it is less political than legal-philosophical; and Locke is therefore just as much a predecessor of Rousseau as he is of Montesquieu. But because of this, on the political or mechanical side he did not bring it to Montesquieu's level of development and specificity; and though Locke exerted a powerful influence on the conception of the English nation regarding its constitution, and therefore on the constitution itself, Montesquieu after him determined the general scientific viewpoint on the continent and became the banner-carrier for a party of *constitutionalism* as opposed to *liberalism*. He finalized a system that functioned for a long time as the dominant political doctrine, as natural law was the dominant legal philosophy. It is therefore justifiable to lay this system, in the form that it took, at Montesquieu's feet.

Montesquieu taught that states, in addition to the general purpose of self-preservation, have a special ("particulier") purpose to which they set themselves, as for example the Romans conquest, the Indians religion, the Chinese public

---

[4] Locke, *Two Treatises of Government* 1680, second treatise; Montesquieu, *L'Ésprit de Loix* 1748, book XI, chs. 1–7.

tranquility, the Marseillais trade. In this way, a state can also set *political freedom* as a particular purpose; the English did this, and the principles of its constitution are those generally necessary for political freedom. According to Montesquieu, political freedom is the independence and security of the individual in the sphere that the laws grant him to be left undisturbed. It can therefore only be achieved by an institution which makes the abuse of state power impossible.

To this end, power must be distributed to different subjects according to their different branches, so that they keep each other in check ("il faut, que par la disposition des choses le pouvoir arrête le pouvoir"). Under this mutual restriction of powers, the individual remains secure in his legal sphere. The unification of the three powers, the legislative, judicial, and executive, destroys freedom, while their separation establishes it. The first requirement is the separation of judicial power, which already exists in all European countries. The other requirement, however, is the separation of legislative and executive power, and this is the innermost principle of the English constitution, on which political freedom there is based. Legislative power must be given to an assembly of representatives of the people, the executive power to an individual, a monarch, partly because only the people are entitled to legislate, and cannot do so directly themselves (here Montesquieu likewise crosses over to natural law theory), partly because an assembly is more suitable for consultation, while an individual is more suitable for active decision and immediate action ("résolution active, action momentanée"). Legislative power itself must be divided into two bodies with mutual rights of restriction: one is composed of delegates elected from all classes, the other of inheritance from the upper class of "those distinguished by birth, wealth, dignity," both in order to protect the privileged against the majority of the others, and to establish a new mutual restriction on power.

Now the executive power (the prince) can only effectively form a barrier against the legislative if it is given a negative part in the legislative, i.e., a veto; without such recourse, the legislative assembly could abolish it by passing a law. On the other hand, the legislative power can only effectively constitute a barrier against the executive by monitoring and ensuring the correct enforcement of the laws, not by prevention ahead of the fact – this would repeal all enforcement – but by means of subsequent accountability and punishment. But this would once again place executive power in complete dependence on the legislative authority, thereby making it incapable of being a counterweight to it.

The way out, the apex of the system, is for the holder of the executive power to be inviolable ("sa personne doit être sacré"); but his counselors must be accountable, and he must not be allowed to do anything without co-signature, i.e. the guarantee of a counselor. Hereby is the mechanism of independent counterweights completed. "Here," says Montesquieu, "you have the basic foundation of the government of which we speak. The *Corps legislatif* is made up of two parts, one of which inhibits the other by its reciprocal right of prevention. Both are bound by the executive power, which itself is bound by the legislative. These three powers ought to end up at rest and inactive. But as they are forced to move by the necessary movement of things, they will be forced to move in harmony (concert)."

The difference between Montesquieu and Locke is unmistakable. Montesquieu does not teach the absolute necessity of this constitution and does not deduce its basis from such a necessity; on the other hand, he emphasizes the mechanical effect of the separation of powers as an independent principle and converts it into a system. In terms of it, he assesses all forms of government, including the difference between monarchy and despotism, and uses this to derive a detailed constitutional mechanism which is not to be found to the same degree with Locke.

Its Value and its One-Sidedness

This doctrine has the great merit of having properly illuminated the mechanical side of the state constitution and, in particular, of the English constitution. It shows both the nature and peculiar condition of the various functions of state power when it highlights the truth that the separation of these functions and the competition of different elements for those functions confers the guarantee of freedom. Its great mistake is that it considers this mechanical side to be the main, even the only one. Montesquieu thus grasps the purpose of the state in a purely external and negative way. It is to him the mere undisturbedness of the individual, not any positive good, any glory in its own institutions and in life, of which it is the form, the bearer, and the patron, not fulfillment of the public condition; and accordingly, state power comes into consideration only in terms of the aspect of its abuse ("lorsqu'on n'abuse pas du pouvoir"); it has no other task than its own neutralization. Above all, however, it recognizes in the elements of the constitution only the mechanism of mutual restriction, not its living organic significance, the significance of kingship, of landed aristocracy; it thereby halts at the separation of powers, without likewise finding a bond of unity.

The English constitution, from which this theory is deducted, does not consist in such mechanistic elements and does not contain such a division of power. The king is not an individual who is drawn from the crowd simply for the purpose of procuring the implementation required for the current resolution and for restricting Parliament. On the contrary, he is the head of the dynastic family which historically assumes the elevated position over the people, and is the personal bearer of the majesty of state order. The peerage is not a mere counterweight to the popular representation, but is itself a natural popular element of a peculiar political significance. Similarly, in the English constitution the legislative and executive power are not *per se* separated and only externally welded to each other by the royal veto. Rather, they are originally one in the sovereignty of the king, and the equal participation of Parliament only holds for this one function. Indeed, in reality, according to the English constitution there is no mere veto by the king for legislation. This would presuppose Parliament alone legislating (statutes, not mere bills), which the king, like the Roman tribunes, could only inhibit. The real relationship is that the king gives the laws, but only with consent, or, as established by external form, gives them only when proposed by Parliament. The "Assent" is a positive sanction of the law, not a mere veto. It is undeniable that Parliament actually determines the law, but factually it no less determines the executive and the government; factually it can hardly tolerate a veto by the king. In England, state power legally is unified in the king and factually is predominantly undivided in Parliament.

Rousseau rightly said of Montesquieu's division of powers, that it is similar to dividing a man up, giving one the will, the other the mind, the third memory. Montesquieu's successors consistently pushed the merely mechanical character even further. They eliminated the remainder of a natural-aristocratic element and wished to establish two similar chambers apportioned only by chance or election, and they eliminated the substitute of organic unity, the imposition of executive power on the legislative by means of the veto, and wished for a prince who is a mere executive. So was it later taught by many, and so was it introduced in some ephemeral constitutions of the Romance countries. However, the power of conservation which lies in the truly constitutional arrangement, especially the English one, is mainly based on its organic character; each of its natural elements has its center of gravity and its measure in itself precisely according to its nature; it asserts itself thereby and limits itself like the others. On the other hand, in the mere mechanism as constitutional theory teaches it, no element, since by nature they are all alike, has a natural necessity to take its proper place, for which reason it strives to displace the others. A mutual struggle for extermination arises, which comes to an end with the sole domination of one element (the Council of the Five Hundred, the Executive Board, etc.).

Mechanical Protection of Popular Freedom and Government

In this way, the political science of this period has a negative purpose as rationalism has a negative principle, and in the way that natural law allows the human condition to be determined by its rule via the logical law, political theory does via the mechanical.

This way of thinking has therefore become widespread in recent times. Constitutions need to be set up in every respect in such a way that those in power not only will be enabled to carry out their tasks, but will not be able to leave them unfulfilled; freedom must not be left to anything, but everything must come to fruition with inevitable necessity. The motive of such theories is obviously a mere lack of trust and confidence. Men, those in power, are unreliable – their will may be good, but it may also be bad. Security calls for a power over them that can rule over this will. The question now is, what power would that be? An age of faith seeks it, without neglecting precautionary measures, in honor, ethical reserve, the fear of God, as Joseph says: "Fear not: for am I in the place of God?" [Genesis 50:19, KJV.] Likewise, it seeks this in the power present in the world which directs events and provides security where no deliberation is sufficient. But if man isolates himself from the great conjuncture of things and from his true center, he only maintains his security where such a law helps him which itself cannot be otherwise, or cannot function differently, than it is, the assistance of which cannot fail to materialize.

The mechanical law is the only remaining refuge. As such, not only the determination of natural conditions is considered to be subject to it, or armed forces, money, trade relations; but human nature as well and its vital motivating factors, the mathematical calculability of which is assumed. From such a source comes the European balance of power, which is conceived only mechanically (without taking into account and acknowledging the individualities of peoples given by nature) and the machine-like calculation of security in the state. Therefore no one people should be able to subjugate another; no power in the state should be able to overstep its boundaries; and no help to this end should be needed from Him, with regard to whom there is no certainty because no one knows His plan, so that the help from Him in whom one has to put his trust, may be disregarded; rather, the institutions should suffice which, by nature without consciousness and choice, make such subjugation or transgression impossible.

In the same way that rationalism seeks a foundation of the world and a connection of things with it which are not merely there, like God and His action, but which cannot not be there – being itself, and what is logically contained in being – this politics seeks an institution in which one no longer needs to have trust, but in which everything for which one wishes will exist and will occur, because it cannot not exist, cannot not materialize. With natural law, it is only man and the logical law which determine law and ethics; here it is only man and the mechanical law which effectuate events and results. In this respect too, pragmatic and abstract legal philosophy share the same lot; both wish to liberate man, and both, because they still wish to liberate everyone and therefore have to seek a bond, something dominant over them, come to subject man to a rigid and will-less law, which in the case of abstract philosophy is the necessity of reason, in the pragmatic the state mechanism.

Plato explained the task of man by the task of the state; for us it is more natural to proceed in the opposite direction. The institutions of security in the state constitution have the same value as the precaution of the individual. Now there is a wide gap between the man who despises the use of lightning rods because the outcome is God's, and the man of Jean Paul's ilk,[5] who does not leave the house without carrying a lightning rod with him. The distinguishing thing is not just the degree of precaution. The former does not disturb the activity of

---

[5] [Apparently a reference to Claude-Jean Veau Delaunay (1755–1826), who demonstrated a telescoping lightning rod for the use of those, such as farmers, who operated in open fields. Michael Brian Schiffer, Kacy L. Hollenback, and Carrie L. Bell, *Draw the Lightning Down: Benjamin Franklin and Electrical Technology in the Age of Enlightenment* (Berkeley, CA: University of California Press, 2003), p. 190.]

life, for he who hopes for things from higher assistance knows not to sit idly by instead of getting on with things. But the anxious care that wishes to calculate everything, takes the best part of the strength and activity which should be directed towards a higher vocation, instead of being expended in such concern. He who gave this vocation would assume the care and concern that one thereby neglects. One needs to trust in Him. Lack of that trust, causing one to fail to take up one's vocation in order to protect oneself, makes one a disgrace. And because others evince no need of such help, it even makes one a laughingstock.

Likewise with states. This calculation of powers in the state and governments vis-à-vis one another, and the quest for a distribution whereby they prevent each other from abusing one another according to the laws of nature, is a gain and an honor of the new era. But this negative side of life should not be turned into a positive one. The constitutional mechanism should be a barrier to state power, but it should not positively determine the activity thereof. No guarantee that what is right and appropriate will everywhere take place should be expected from it. A wide sphere of freedom must remain, for which trust in the government, not safeguards against it, is required. The awareness that all human calculation is deficient after all, should everywhere keep ignoble arrangements from being chosen, even if it seems that only ignoble ones can ensure success.

This applies equally to the government against the people as the other way round. If only man and the mechanical law direct events, only this alternative remains to him: either to make use of any and all means in accordance with this law, or to sacrifice himself, in this case his state. And if he does not desire, indeed is not permitted the latter, only the former remains for him – thus says Machiavelli. It is therefore clear that the phenomenon of Machiavelli does not need to be explained by special circumstances and intentions; it is simply the consistent implementation of the same principle that in general was held to be fitting. If one leaves something of guidance to a higher power, then this whole kind of politics falls to the ground; if, on the other hand, one wishes to take care of everything oneself, then we inevitably arrive at Machiavelli's point of view. The same detachment from the living God that necessarily leads to Spinozism in philosophy leads to Machiavellianism in politics. Both appear at the inception of the orientation, in such a manner as to be heralded immediately in both spheres with all decisiveness. The later representatives of this orientation, despite being their successors, called them heretics for no other reason than because they knew what they wanted and had the courage not to tremble for the results to which the path leads, once embarked upon.

Montesquieu's doctrine in its own way attempts, as much as these do, to remove ethical impulses from the relationship between prince and people, and to establish them merely from mechanism.

Modern history shows both the true side of this negative policy and its noxiousness when made positive. To it alone is due the formation of states by which they deserve the name, in terms of which the order of the whole permeates all of the parts, and finds in itself an enduring guarantee against accidental individual arbitrariness. But since it was made a true goal, it has also violated requirements which it should only serve. In this manner the individualities of nations have been sacrificed to the system of the balance of power. The honor, right, and freedom of citizens has been compromised by secret police, house searches, violations of postal confidentiality for the sake of the mechanically secure execution of government regulations. Conversely, the popular party where it came to power, in order to keep the king from abusing power, left him completely powerless. Above all, the view has even become widespread which holds that morality, openness, and honor have to betake themselves from political relations, and that the only important thing here is to investigate and outwit one another.

Politics has thus become alienated from the generally human; for, as Plato says, it is not possible for the same nature to love the truth and the lie. The voice of the simple man, who suffers damage from this, could only be countered by arrogance: did he not understand that such petty considerations as truth and humanity do not come into consideration against the great interests of states, i.e., against a mechanism of security? The statesmen look down on the cramped, sterile forms of school philosophy with contempt; but the teachings of politics of that time were no less mindless and uncreative. This is necessarily the result if politics is guided only by the effort to secure itself against every imaginable possibility. The very outcome itself shows that the balance of power, the constitutional mechanism, the house searches and all the dishonesty and pretense do not achieve what one wishes. The mechanical laws guide real events as little as the logical categories give us knowledge. However, a people can be assured of a just legal control of the state even if it does not have the utmost mechanical means of protection (arbitrary refusal to pay taxes, absolute ministerial responsibility); on the other hand, a noble government does not need to forge fear, to move in secrecy, to violate the right and dignity of man; rather, it can trust in the rightness of its cause and go to work honestly and openly. In truth it is not that one trusts in the good cause to protect him, but that God will assist him, which is why a cause which is good even exists, and why he takes it up in the first place.

Montesquieu's Scientific Greatness in General

Montesquieu added another achievement regarding scientific legal knowledge in addition to constitutional theory (the developed insight into the mechanism of state power). For he took the results of laws and the suitability of means into account, not only in relation to the establishment of state power and for the purpose of political freedom, but through all areas of legislation and for all the purposes that states confront in history. He provided a complete system of statecraft. In this he led his legal-philosophical and political considerations, which only generally dealt with principles or results without regard for specific conditions, away from this indeterminateness, to consider the legal institutions (the "laws") in connection with the entire condition of a people: the condition of the land, the climate, temperament, customs, education, religion. In so doing he followed the path trod by Aristotle and then Bodin. With them this is mixed with other things, but with Montesquieu this insight and the investigation conducted along its lines are manifest as the sole task of his book; this brings the basic idea itself more vigorously and penetratingly to consciousness, and yields an infinitely greater wealth of results than they were able to accomplish. Among these results, his doctrine regarding the *motive forces of the various forms of government* stands out: the motive force of despotism being *fear*, of monarchy being *honor*, of aristocracy *moderation*, of democracy *virtue*. While not defining these motive forces sharply and clearly, he maintained them correctly and decisively; from them, he derived both maxims for government and institutions for every kind of constitution that are true and profound.

The motives of fear and moderation need little further explanation. By honor, Montesquieu understands not ambition but rather the peculiar self-esteem that has flowed in the Germanic peoples to this day from distinction of birth and from the service of the prince. It is an impulse of the mind whereby one acts only in terms of one's own honor, one's high vocation, and in particular as a bond with the prince as the center of all distinction of birth and all consecration of service. Maintaining this through custom and institution is indeed the nerve of the monarchy down to the constitutional era. Even now this motive should not cease, especially among public servants, even if, as far as content is concerned, service to the king and service to the community now are identified with each other. The deepest moral sense of this Germanic character trait is, moreover, the high esteem in which both the general ethical and the particular social vocation are held, with which one sees oneself, one's own personality, as united, so that one cannot forgive something against the former without forgiving it against the latter and vice versa; this trait exists in either a true or a degenerate form depending on whether the vocation is made to serve personal satisfaction, or the person serves to maintain the sacredness of the vocation and position. In this, its true form, it should not now be expunged from the nobility, but rather be made into a common good of the nation. Something like this has been realized in France.

According to Montesquieu's explanation, *virtue* as the driving impulse of democracy means love for equality, or, we might add, love for the law that applies equally to everyone. Satisfaction in the steadfast application of the law (*lex est res dura inexorabilis*) and strict compliance with the law, the renunciation of personal privilege and jealousy of the privilege of others, is the spirit upon which democracy is based. Virtue in the true and general sense, purity of morals [Sitte], is not meant in the first place; but the concept also mixes in here, both in Montesquieu and in truth; for such strict submission to the rule of the community is not very compatible with immorality, but presupposes a condition of the soul that also subjects itself to the rule in private life. That is why democracy has much more difficulty existing without the virtue of the people in the true sense than does aristocracy or monarchy. In general, in democracy, the character of the people must replace what guarantees the strength of the form of government in monarchy. Living Christianity furnishes a higher force for preservation for all forms of government than do these four motive forces, as Montesquieu himself explains.[6] However, it must be added that the various forms of state

[6] "Les principes du Christianisme bien gravés dans le coeur, seraient infinement plus forts que ce faux honneur des monarchies, ces vertus humaines des républiques et cette

always keep their peculiar requirements and thus also their peculiar moral individuality; therefore, the Christian mentality will not abolish, but instead transfigure, the motive force of honor in monarchy and the strict legal order in democracy.

This entire point of view, broached for his time anew by Montesquieu, is an achievement of even more general and insofar greater importance than the constitutional theory. Indeed, with him the latter shows itself only to be a part of it. This is the reason for Montesquieu's immortal fame. In this he is the precursor of the deeper historical recognition represented in our days by the Historical School of Jurisprudence, speculative philosophy, and other aspirations. And yet, his bias toward the pragmatic view, whereby everything that has been or shall be created, is created as a means to an end, prevents him from conducting the insight he gained to all its profundity, as will be shown in Part III of this book [pp. 29ff.].

---

crainte servile des états despotiques" [The principles of Christianity, well etched in the heart, would be infinitely stronger than this false honor of monarchies, these human virtues of republics and this servile fear of despotic states]. In his *Zerstreute Blätter* [Scattered Pages] (III, p. 305), Göschel has meaningfully emphasized this passage as the one in which Montesquieu points beyond himself and at the same time describes the true relationship of Christendom to those motive forces.

PART II: THE RELATION OF CONSTITUTIONALISM TO LIBERALISM

Agreements and Contradictions
Natural law, and thus its latest iteration, liberalism, is the legal-philosophical doctrine of the age, while constitutionalism is its political doctrine. Both stand on *the same foundation*, freedom and the entitlement of man. But they run in completely opposite directions, the former as a doctrine of rationality or justice, the latter as one of expediency, for which reason they arrive at totally contradictory results.

The Constitutionalists of 1789
Constitutionalism, taking consequences into account, wishes to divide power because the masses in their sole rule even destroy their own freedom; liberalism, operating in terms of the consistency of the absolute and equal authority of man, desires the exclusive and undivided domination of the masses. In the Revolution, therefore, they together overthrew the old monarchy – the victory of the principle of subjectivity over objective authority – but then they found that a fight amongst themselves was unavoidable. The former demanded the mechanism of the two chambers and the royal veto, the latter an undivided and unrestricted national representation. The legal-philosophical doctrine of the age prevailed over its political doctrine. In the face of the furious rush of liberalism, the maxims of constitutional theory were dashed, and the two chambers, the king's veto, and finally the king himself, were defeated. Liberalism then undertook to carry out Rousseau's teaching in its entirety. Only after the fall of the regime of terror was there a return to the mechanism of the separation of powers, yet not in the original Montesquieuian sense, but in Sieyès' sense.

Sieyès
If you take the worst, most fallacious aspects of the doctrines of Rousseau and Montesquieu and join them together, you get Sieyès' political system. Sieyès takes Rousseau's idea of the general will, which despite its formation by individual wills lays claim, albeit wrongly, to a unified will, strips it of its unity and composes it only of the majority of individual wills. Numbers are therefore

Sieyès' supreme principle, and everything of political significance is decided as if it were a math problem. If you ask what significance the nobility and clergy should have in the constitution, he answers: they make up 1/90th of the French nation. If you ask whether the king should have a veto, he replies: the king is only one of twenty-five million Frenchmen. The same treatment is given to Montesquieu's alternating restriction of powers, which still had an organic admixture and also consisted of real, if only artificially formed, powers: Sieyès conceives of this exclusively mechanically. The elements that are to be restricted must originate from completely identical material, namely the total mass, and must also remain completely identical; they therefore must not become permanent bearers of power, but only momentarily be given a countervailing competence. He then rejects the royal veto and the aristocratic chamber, but (as he already says in his writings about the third estate) wishes the people's representatives to be divided into two or more chambers, mutually restricting each other. He makes the so-called executive power completely dependent on the legislative, and all positions must be of a temporary nature, dependent upon ongoing choice. This combines, at least in theory, the doctrine of a mechanical self-restraint of power and one of the undivided absolute rule of the masses, but the result achieved by this self-restraint is unsuited either to restrain mass rule or to maintain itself.

This spirit engendered the subsequent constitutions of France up to the Empire, none of which proved viable. The most striking caricature of Sieyès' principle is the draft constitution he presented to First Consul [Napoleon] Buonaparte. In this constitution a Great Elector ("Proclamateur-Électeur") stands at the head of the empire, unbounded and unaccountable, representative toward the outside world. He forms the government (Council of State and Ministers) of candidates proposed by the people; but he himself has no part in the government. Legislation is initially divided among three bodies: the government that has been formed, the people's tribunal, and the legislative authority. The first two have to propose laws and defend or combat them, while the third decides between them. Finally, a constitutional jury will be appointed as the fourth, which, on appeal by the government or the tribunal, can quash the verdict of the legislative authority. All these authorities are equally chosen from among the masses and by them, for a short period of time. By the way, such a Great Elector, who expends six million in income, composes the government from popular candidates, configures it outwardly, and otherwise is not allowed to interfere in anything, is the purest representation of a constitutional king that liberalism can conceive.

Constitutionalism during the Restoration: Benjamin Constant

When the Restoration reestablished the monarchy in France, it was necessary to go back to Montesquieu's constitutional theory. However, political doctrine focused mainly on a situation that Montesquieu did not go into, the decision as to the constitution's center of gravity. This concerned the relationship of executive power to its counselors and thus to the legislative assembly to which they are accountable. In terms of Montesquieu's merely negative point of view – public authority should not abuse its power – it seemed sufficient to keep the king from doing anything without the ministers who are accountable. But life demands that public authority not only not be abused but that it be used, that governance take place; the question then arises as to who should rule, the king or the ministers, the one who is independent of the people's representation or the one who is completely subordinated to it? In other words, should popular representation be a factor in legislation and a guardian of the laws, or should it determine the entire government? This was the point that Benjamin Constant above all others took up. He wished to unite kingship, which had become an inevitable fact, and freedom, i.e., the rule of the people, and unify them by making the king into a power, but only a balancing one, not a determinative one.

In line with his predecessor Clermont-Tonnerre, Constant's doctrine is: one must distinguish *royal* power from *executive* power; the latter may be the attribute of the ministers, but the former is the attribute of the king and is supported by religious remembrances and traditions ("par des souvenirs et par des traditions religieuses"). The executive is concerned with the actual government, while the royal is a neutral power, everywhere balancing, deciding between and tempering other powers. Hence the king's role is to dissolve the chamber as the legislative power, to remove the ministers as the executive power, to correct, by pardon, the verdicts of the tribunals as judicial power. It is also his responsibility to reject the laws, in so doing to maintain the existing state of affairs. On the other hand, everything else, the drafting and submission of laws to the chamber, the enforcement of the laws, the administration, etc. is a matter for the executive power, the minister. These must not be mere passive instruments of the king, for which reason they must be viewed as independent holders of power. The excellence of the state constitution and the depth of its insight are based on this fourfold set of powers.

As far as this conception in itself is concerned, it is another mechanical view of the constitution. Instead of recognizing the power of the state as an original unity which in its development in terms of the various functions obtains the participation of manifold elements, here it is composed of four independent powers; in a sense, the mechanism of power is already finished with the legislative power of the people's representatives and the executive of the ministers, with only the balancing royal added. From the outset, it is a misguided idea that religious traditions should be combined with royal power of this kind. These only connect with kingship as sovereign, the authority set over the people, not with kingship which is the fourth of four necessary gears. Religious traditions could just as well be linked to the other three, and indeed, in this view, most of all with the representation of the sovereign people.

But even mechanically, this view is not feasible. The supreme majesty and the real government, which in terms of their nature are one, cannot be separated in this way. Royal power should decide about war and peace, executive power about the entire inner government, i.e. the ministers; the king should have the power to accept or reject the laws deliberated on by the chambers, the ministers should have the power to propose laws to the chambers without the king by virtue of their executive power (what kind of royal power is that, when ministers propose laws without its consent and authorization!); the veto is to follow from the nature of royal power and from the nature of executive power, the latter in particular recognizing the unenforceability of a law, and yet it obviously cannot accrue to the ministers but only to the king.

Indeed, the whole idea that those who are responsible for power should be exposed to arbitrary dismissal at any moment, and definitive dismissal (not just in the way of delegates who by dissolution of the chamber, are subject to new confirmation) at that, is unsustainable. Likewise, the notion that a mere balancing neutral power, which in fact originally appoints ministers, cannot supervene to remove them or to refuse unsuitable ones. Although ministers, as Constant demands, should not be passive instruments, it does not follow that they are bearers of their own power. Admittedly, the king is also a balancing tempering power; but that is only the effect of his being sovereign and thus pervading all elements and functions of the state; an original and positive influence is also inseparable from sovereignty. If this influence and thus sovereignty is taken away, royal power cannot exercise this balancing power. As such, most of these attributes are groundless. In terms of theory, then, Constant's conception is a deterioration from Montesquieu's; he turns it into something overly artificial and unnatural.

But if one looks at the ultimate practical result, such a separation of royal power from the executive, while pretending to strengthen the kingdom, in fact weakens it; the main thing is that the executive power is detached from the king and transferred independently to the ministers. According to Montesquieu's doctrine, executive power accrues to the king and the minister should only make use of it by exerting a negative influence on it; according to Constant's doctrine, it accrues in itself and originally to the ministers, and the king only has the negative influence of tempering it. The sum is this: "le roi regne, mais il ne gouverne pas" [the king reigns but he does not rule]. Certainly, Constant opposes the extreme teaching of the Revolution from Montesquieu's point of view: he wants a royal veto, an hereditary chamber of peers, and the like; hence he would like monarchical forms, as in England. But he would like to eliminate the royal power in its positive activity, as in England, and even more so, because he seeks to put in principle and within strict limits what in England is only *de facto* and therefore less pinned down.

He too always stands on the basis of popular sovereignty; he corrects Rousseau only in relation to the scope, not the subject of that doctrine. Sovereignty should have its limit set by justice, and this too can only be found in individual rights; but within this limitation it should accrue to the people, not in the original way of constitutional authority over the people. This, then, is Constant's stated confession. But what he does not say – whether he does not intend, I cannot say – is that the executive power that he attaches to the ministers actually becomes, not a power of the ministers, but a power of the chambers to which they are responsible, and that in themselves the ostensibly counterbalancing acts of the king (veto, dissolution of the chamber, etc.) are only exercised subject to the assistance of a minister and therefore subject to the omnipotence of the chambers, insofar as they have the voters on their side; and therefore, in this separation it is not several powers that are established, as with Montesquieu, but only one single power, the electorate in France. Constant combines constitutionalism and liberalism in such a way that from the former he only takes the forms, while from the latter he realizes the substance. The position of royal authority in England, based on custom as it is, and which can be modified in accordance with the king's aptitude, is fine for that country. But there is no reason to require this position universally for any well-constituted state, and on the contrary, it is generally bad to set it in stone, in principle and in law. But to see in this a union of kingship with popular rule, i.e., the maintenance of kingship, is deception.

The Doctrinaires

Another and better attempt under the Restoration to reconcile the liberal and constitutional system with kingship is contained in the doctrine of the few men to whom the term "Doctrinaire" was given. It originated with Royer-Collard and was developed by Guizot. In its own words, this small group based itself on the Revolution or the new France as against the Counter-Revolution and the Old Regime. That is, it wishes for equality before the law and the dominant power of the middle class, and desires "Gouvernement répresentatif," government which is orderly and open to the influence of the whole nation, by contrast with the state in which nobility and clergy and especially the court determine the government and exploit it to bolster their superiority over the other estates. That is why it represented all the institutions which are based on free movement in social conditions and in the communication of ideas, but above all it sought, like the other factions of the new France, a free and true representation, in which the Chamber of Deputies really gave expression to the opinion of the numerous middle classes; as Royer-Collard describes it, "vérité des élections" [truth in elections], while the institution under the Restoration only had "de fausses élections, de faux depútés" [false elections, false deputies].

Now it is already a correction of the liberal system that the Doctrinaire school does not base free representation on the abstract principles of universal equal entitlement, thus pushing it to excess; that it does not require "political equality" (equal competition in the exercise of state authority) like it does "civil equality" (abolition of privileges). Rather, it links up with the real natural elements of the popular condition, emphasizes the importance of trade, the importance of small landowners, etc. for the state and therefore strives for the influence and the internal organization of the middle class. Furthermore, it is an even more thorough correction of that system that it recognizes as the aim and fulfillment of the public condition not the rule of the will of the people (majorities), any more than the unrestricted royal power by virtue of divine law, but rather the rule of reason, of justice, of law ("la souveraineté de la raison, de la justice, du droit"), and in this sense combats both the sovereignty of the masses and that of the individual, and asserts a higher bond over man.

However, none of this is a peculiarity of the Doctrinaires; these principles, albeit to a lesser degree, are shared by other insightful and moderate representatives of the new France, such as Constant. What makes the Doctrinaires' teaching unique is its *commitment to "legitimacy"* and its *peculiar conception thereof.* By legitimacy they understand a right of the king which is based neither on popular will nor on divine institution (the latter being the legitimacy of superstition), but is founded in itself and has its roots in history. Just as the people and every single citizen have their freedom as a right, so must the government have its position as a right.[7] That would yield a reciprocity ("réciprocité") of rights. What the entire constitution, the entire system of the public condition, should have in all its components, is therefore the character of legality; this is what legitimacy is based on, this is what is held to be its concept. But all law has its beginning in power and in simple factual conditions; it only grows into law through history. As such, royal power, which was originally only *de facto*, thus based on strength, became a legal power, i.e., attained legitimacy, only through history, specifically through the extended lapse of time. This is no less true with regard to the freedom of the people, which also initially arises *de facto* (hence mostly as anarchy) and only matures in history into rights, into true freedom. It is therefore also important to prove that the French people have always had

[7] "C'est, qu'il ne suffit point à la société, que le droit se rencontre dans les citoyens; elle a besoin, qu'il réside encore dans le gouvernement. C'est peu, que chaque homme possède et revendique ses libertés comme un droit légitime, si le pouvoir qui commande aux hommes, n'exerce aussi un droit légitime à leurs yeux" [It is not enough for society, that the law is encountered in the citizens; it also needs it to reside in government. It is a small thing that each man possesses and claims his freedoms as a legitimate right, if the power which commands men does not also exercise a legitimate right in their eyes]. Guizot, *Du Gouvernement de la France,* ch. 7.

rights and freedoms; freedom that arose only yesterday is not true freedom. In doing so, the Doctrinaires incorporated an historical element that is foreign to the other factions of the new France, and Burke's influence on the doctrine cannot be ignored either in this or in the idea of the "sovereignty of reason." Now then, because long duration is required for legitimacy, this doctrine later had to be content with a quasi-legitimacy for Louis Philippe; but, in accordance with its principles and with the truth, it warranted that Louis Philippe became king *because* ("parceque") and not *although* ("quoique") he was a Bourbon. So while according to the liberal view kingship exists only as a discharge ("emploi") of the people, and according to the constitutionalist merely as a mechanical device, so according to the doctrine of the Doctrinaires it exists as an independent entitlement based on historical grounds. Royer-Collard (February 10, 1820) also advocated a certain degree of independence for the king in the exercise of government, in particular the election of ministers. Guizot, of course, demands the decisive influence of the middle class for this as well, but his assertion is not so sharp and determined as to rule out a moderating understanding.

In this way the "new France" (or the "Revolution") is to gain the legitimacy which was denied to it because of misunderstanding and because of the false position of legitimate kingship. Revolution and legitimacy in the sense in which they are taken here are indeed perfectly compatible. The usual accusation against the Doctrinaires, that they maintained an unsustainable happy medium, is therefore unfounded. Rather, the doctrine is a great correction of false opinions and a great step forward to true recognition; and yet it is by no means complete. Above all, it mainly lacks the scientific development and integration of its principles. The term "doctrine," which it accidentally received through Royer-Collard's frequent use of the word, is by no means the most apt for it. By virtue of its dual interest, it is certainly not carried away by party passion, but must seek its measure everywhere by intelligent consideration; this may be called doctrinaire. But it has much less doctrine, i.e., metaphysical or any sort of principled foundation and rounding off than any party of France, whether liberals, constitutionalists, or legitimists. In particular, the doctrine takes kingship as a given, as something which as such must have its right; yet it has no answer as to why kingship exists, and what the ultimate reason for it is. That is not enough, because from the bare principle that every position in the public condition must be regarded as a right, one could also conclude a legitimacy (i.e., an inalienable position) of ministers. The doctrine only accords kingship its legal and historical significance, not its ethical significance, by which it is to exist as an authority over the people; its specific sanctity and reverence cannot be explained or assured by the mere recognition of a right and its historical condition. Indeed, royal authority then appears to be of entirely the same sort as any other, like property owners, citizens; and it was therefore necessary to express the requirement of lengthy historical existence, which is inherent in legitimacy and derives from its deepest moral meaning (submission to the higher divine disposition),[8] as a general principle for all rights. This doctrine can therefore satisfy the intelligent; usually one must agree with its practical applications; it is the most benevolent and sound now available in France. But it does not vouchsafe the deeper moral and above all religious basis of the state constitution, at least not on scientific grounds.

True Constitutionalism

Kingship is not just a *mechanical* institution, but an *organic* institution; it is not just an external *historical-legal* institution, but an *ethical* institution. The king is the authority over the people according to the moral order (which in its deepest foundation is divine order). He is therefore the bearer of the one indivisible state power, which nevertheless unfolds from this center into its branches, and in this development gains other equally powerful bearers; he is sovereign. This is the basic relation of the political condition; the religious intimacy of the bond links up with it; it is the bond which Constant tries in vain to gain for the mechanical *pouvoir royal*. This does not contradict the many gradations of constitutional arrangement (the trueness of charters) and in particular France's current constitution. It is not contradictory that the sovereign power of the king, which is a given over the people, be connected with the people's own right of co-rulership; *this co-rulership of the people with the king is the true essence of constitutionalism* as opposed to both the liberal and the constitutional theory.[9] It entails that the principles and goals according to which the people are to be ruled, are to be determined by the people, in line with their freedom, together with the king (through a formal and direct participation in the

[8] See Vol. II, Part II [*The Doctrine of State*], §. 74.

[9] See Vol. II, Part II [*The Doctrine of State*], §§. 53f., §. 96, and chiefly §. 149.

legislative function and indirect influence on the government sanction), and that this maintenance be overseen and shielded vis-à-vis the royal government by organs responsible for this. The constitution can be understood, and participation in the individual functions determined, from these simple and natural elements of the state, the *sovereign king* and the *free people*, and not from the abstract mechanism of power. Such co-rulership can be of various extent, either a significant subordination to royal power, as in the German constitutional states, or an actual preponderance over royal power, as in England and France. This distinguishes the constitutions in revolutionary and non-revolutionary states. Yet it must never fundamentally diminish the foundation upon which it rests, the original royal regard that preceded it, nor reduce the kingship to the function of merely carrying out the will of the people or equilibrating among other powers as a supervening power.

This is the only view that naturally and unconstrainedly explains the real constitution as it developed in England: the royal sanction of the laws, the veto (more correctly, the requirement of the royal assent for a bill to become law), the appointment of ministers, and the specific regard for kingship. It alone guarantees a real union of kingship and national freedom and can therefore satisfy the sentiments of both parties, while the merely mechanical treatment of kingship always only sees one side, the freedom of the people. In this view, to be sure, the people's representation must have an influence, a greater or lesser one depending on the country concerned, on the choice of ministers and on the principles of the government; but this is not the sole decisive influence as it is according to the liberal-constitutional theory. There are two wills, the royal and the popular, both applicable, which moderate and correct each other: the royal must measure itself against that of the people; if it is constantly at loggerheads with the latter, it cannot survive; but the popular will must be restricted by the royal; the king not only has the free administration on the basis of the principles determined solely by the people (public opinion, chambers); he has an equally important part in determining those principles. A synthesis [ein Drittes] results from this, as is everywhere the case where independent forces oppose each other harmoniously, while in accordance with the constitutional-liberal theory the king merely fulfills the popular will, or at most exercises a supplementary, moderating influence in the case of division in the popular representation, not to assert his will, but the actual popular will. In that case, however, the relationship between king and ministers is not that of two powers, one executive, one neutral and balancing; rather, it is the sovereign who alone has the power with his constitutionally necessary organs, which however are not mere "passive agents" of the sovereign, because they have a constitutional obligation, a conscience, an honor, and because insight and expertise are represented in them which have no automatic or necessary connection with the royal quality. Neither the original and positive influence of the king nor the independence of the minister can be lacking, and the measure of the one and the other will always depend on personal endowment in insight and character, precisely because indivisible cooperation is required.

The theory of the English writers, still basing themselves on Locke, is just as mechanical as Montesquieu's. But in England this is less harmful because the constitutional positions themselves are precisely identified and confirmed everywhere by history and origin, and the parliamentary form and language, far from corresponding with this mechanical conception, instead express a true organic kingship, and do so to a higher degree than actually exists. By contrast, in France and Germany, where the constitutional positions are still in the process of being determined, pure doctrine is what counts.

PART III: REGARDING THE ORIGIN OF LAW

View Regarding the Causes and Motives of Events and Legislation
Although the natural law doctors and the political scientists disagree with each other in their view of the ethic, they agree on the origin of actual law. Indeed, just as both orientations originate in the motive force of human independence and self-activity, so they regard all historical phenomena as human products. The entire age virtually lacks the notion of how something could take shape unless people bring it about, consciously and willingly; that is, unless crude mindless coincidence is what caused it, which would redound to their shame, a sign of their weakness. Science has closed itself off to the divine spirit, which guides history, even though this is what human freedom moves upon as its foundation.

Now it is natural to think of the human mind as always having been what it is in one's own time and environment. This lends credence to the idea that the mind is not formed by history, but on the contrary is the sole formative factor on history, as opposed to the notion that the mind has changed its character during the course of ages. In line with this, the deliberations and viewpoints such as are manifested in our day, under our conditions, are attributed, if not to everyone, at least to the leading men of other ages, and their deeds and arrangements are so arrived at. It is admitted that here and there the legislators of antiquity were biased by the prejudices of their time; but this only affects individuals and is precisely their weakness. On the whole, the sentiments with which they were surrounded, in terms of which they made their laws, only acted on them as raw material; they had to take the prevailing way of thinking into account, otherwise they could not achieve their purposes; in no way was it their own archetype, did it determine their own judgments and will. The manner of thinking and the kind of intentions they had when they actually put legislation into practice, is viewed as being like ours in the present, instead of in terms of their own times. They are put outside the nation and operate from that remote location; they nevertheless operate the levers.

Thus Machiavelli has the Romans, the leaders of the Senate and the people, reflect in the manner that they might reflect as wise men such as himself in his own state, free of their Roman character. In this manner, Moses could not have considered sacrifice, priesthood, blood vengeance to be what he should be striving for, what should exist for its own sake. He only paid tribute to this institution, which he himself probably recognized as unreasonable, as being the opinion of his nation, because only in this way could he achieve his other great purposes. The fact that food is unclean, that a year of celebration might include divine worship, was never his own faith, but only prescribed as a religious commandment in order to ensure the best health, fertility, and whatever else is considered to be a suitable aspiration for a wise man. Lycurgus did not consider surrender to the state, the alienation of every single right and possession, to be right and necessary in itself; he only used it to provide his Spartans with the ever recognized goal of states, military strength. Luther himself, in the view of the enlightened, may not have believed in Christ and the miracles; his recognition of the Gospel was only a means of giving the first impetus for the Enlightenment, which at that time could not yet be introduced from the ground up.

With respect to the actual origin of events, the pragmatic exaggeration as described above, which leaves nothing at all to exist for its own sake, is therefore how things are generally understood; for only in this manner can the historical phenomena be explained from this point of view. There was no other way to understand the origin of the Homeric chants than to ascribe to the poet some moral purpose, some useful teaching, which they were intended to prove. This is the method of recognized historians. It is the reason that even Montesquieu, with his rich historical knowledge, while he correctly observes the consequences of the law, often just as incorrectly assesses the reasons for its origin. He, too, entertains a biased view as to how a motive and goal that dominates people without their having chosen it, produces institutions; everything is said to have been embraced only as a means for something or other by conscious choice. He treats the originally Germanic motive force of honor, the family fideicommissum associated with the oldest legal views, as if introduced to preserve the monarchy; he treats the inviolability of the king in England as an instrument for his mechanism of state; he treats the special chamber of the peerage, the highest privilege of all because it grants greater participation in government, as a mere shield to protect other privileges from being infringed.

The Influence of National Character and Its Use by Montesquieu

It is true that great emphasis never ceased being placed on the national character, on the influence which it has always had on the legislation, and, of course, even more on the influence it should have. And the universal verdict is that it is mainly Montesquieu who is the repository of observations and maxims of this influence. Montesquieu also says that the laws should suit one people in such a way that it is only a particular coincidence if the laws of one people also suit another. But look at his view of national character! For him,[10] the national character of the French is that they love conviviality and cheerfulness, like to joke and chat, and communicate easily, that they are lively, at times reckless, even rude, that they are brave, generous and open. The characteristic trait of the Athenians, which makes them similar to the French, is their gifted nature, in terms of which they applaud and joke about the most serious matters. The Spartans, on the other hand, are dry, grumpy, and closed.[11]

So what great influence can such qualities have on the law? Even if the descriptions are more or less complete, at best they can explain individual provisions. So, one always has great expectations of the influence of the national character, because that accords with the theory; but when it comes down to actual demonstration, it evaporates. It is then quite natural that in this age of science, the true concept of national character is completely lacking. The isolation of men from one another prevents it. For now the nation is not seen as *one* mind; rather, the way in which the people who belong to it show themselves in isolated individuals is what appears to be the national character. The orientation, the particular ethic of the nation, which is only effective in its entirety, is thus necessarily lost, for example, the pursuit of the comeliness and symmetry of the state, of empire [Weltherrschaft], of the articulation and gradation of estates. For no one can have such an aspiration from and for himself; he is only seized by it when it exists in the nation. What remains after the detachment is nothing but those merely dormant properties of temperament or intelligence that are no longer directed at a particular object, e.g., liveliness, apathy, wit. Therefore, even according to Montesquieu, it is only a chaos of random things "that help to determine the way of thinking and acting, climate, laws, state maxims, ancient examples, manners and customs, religion (the particular content of which is of course also here considered to have arisen coincidentally). From all of these

---

[10] Montesquieu, *L'Ésprit de loix,* book 19, ch. 5.

[11] *Ibid.,* ch. 7.

we get what we call a national character."[12]

But the national character in the true sense is what the nation recognizes and desires as the supreme goal of its general aspiration. It is the nation's total disposition, its moral certainty. It effects all the significant phenomena of life – *virtus est actuosa* – and from it, therefore, proceeds law as a whole. This goal and this judgment were not taught it by accidental circumstances, climate and ancient customs; they are directed to it by a guiding intention. *National character is the divine vocation of a nation.*

Ethical Result of this View regarding the Origin of Law

The view of the actual origin of law as here characterized is of the greatest consequence for ethics. If, after all, all institutions are genuinely created by the deliberating human spirit, then this spirit must also be entitled to cancel them out and put others in their place. Prudence may well be required to conserve them for some purpose, especially in order to ensure reverence and strength for all institutions, thus also the suitable ones, by habituation to their uninterrupted existence. This is how Aristotle treated the question of whether imperfect laws should be left standing, so as not to weaken the idea of the sanctity of all laws, or whether they should be modified in pursuit of the general natural urge to perfection. And from this perspective he probably exhausted the pros and cons that flow from it. But it is not reverence for the laws on the part of the agent himself that prevents him from changing them. It is only the endeavor to instill that reverence in others; and he is no longer prevented if he believes that others will maintain their reverence regardless, or if he can bring them to obey without it. Also, it is only reverence for the law *in general* that comes into question here, not reverence for *particular* laws which happen to exist in the here and now, which have developed in history. Particular laws as such cannot have sanctity on those terms, because no one has cause to bow down and worshipfully reverence the things which made them: the prudence of others, the climate, and the character of the land.

Now then: Because every orientation has fully to run its course for it to become fully known, all reticence against change and abolition vanished, and governments even began experimenting with legislation. In this, the two aspir-

---

[12] *Ibid.*, ch. 4.

ations which emanated from the same origin, which were animated by the same spirit but were shunted onto different paths, became united: the natural law doctors and the political scientists. In terms of ruthless transformation, they are one and the same; they deviate only regarding the goal they pursue. For the former, it is the realization of their abstract deduction; for the latter, it is either arbitrary, partly secondary goals, or fixed uniform ones, and generally the mechanical security of the state and each of its indispensable functions.

Opposition to this View: The Historical School of Jurisprudence

The Historical School of Jurisprudence forms the opposite of this view of the actual emergence of law and of the ethical relation to what exists. This, as matters now stand, is its peculiarity; and this must be regarded as the first expression by which the historical view in the philosophy of law has shown itself to be effective.

BOOK V: SPECULATIVE LEGAL PHILOSOPHY

When we first become aware that we are headed in the wrong direction, we usually turn back; and when destruction has come to an end, we tend to rebuild. The abstract orientation delivered all sacred bonds over to arbitrariness, initially only those invisible, mysterious ones which only faith can reveal with certainty – man's immediate relations with God – but eventually the relations that are interwoven with physical life, which are constantly present, and for which reverence is not weakened even with those who are not as introspective. Just as the sense of the emptiness and iniquity of such a state came to life, so did the insight into the untruth of the way of thinking which led to it.

These relations exercise a power over man that binds him both ethically and factually, and cannot be derived from his will. Even though an attempt was made to justify the relationship between spouses by contract, it proved impossible to do so with the relationship between parents and children. And the family in general not only exerts its influence on those who have entered into or belong to its bond; every third party is touched by it and must recognize it. In ancient times the family took blood revenge and demanded blood money; nowadays, he who insults a woman has to answer to her husband; the rank, the place of jurisdiction, the place of residence of the woman depends on the man. There is no question here of mere internal moral duties; for the determination of the plaintiff, of the court, is by its very nature something external and legal. But these provisions, whereby every marriage has a legal influence on all fellow citizens, would seem an injustice against them if their rationale was sought in the agreement of the spouses. Nowhere is it allowed for someone to enter into a community of legal status with a friend. Thus, the family itself must have a right, regardless of the rights of the people who make it up.

An equal right must also be accorded to the state. It might be based on tacit consent with a better semblance of truth [than the family], for the citizen can enter into or withdraw from the state without physical effect. There are not here, as in the family, various relationships – husband and wife, parents vis-à-vis children – which, through their peculiarity and their immutable distribution, remove any thought of arbitrariness. In fact, the relationship between those in power and those who obey might be changed at any moment. But for mere tacit consent to be considered a reason for citizenship, a right of the state would be presupposed by which the citizens would be obliged to declare their position regarding it. The citizen should be made aware that he might abolish the bond, and how. In fact, however, everyone sees himself encircled by the state already at the first awakening of his consciousness; he is already chained to it with many bonds, enjoys rights without having done anything to gain them, and has taken on liabilities before he knew of and wanted them. And how, finally, is it that the state, i.e., the contracting persons, can close off the territory and forbid land ownership to those who withdraw or refuse their consent? Even the external power by which the state becomes and is, stands in the way of any attribution to human will. This eternal construction, which counters the ravages of time with indestructible duration, would be impossible for human wisdom to implement or maintain. If a person who knew nothing of the state were to be shown the movements of popular life storming in countless directions, in constant opposition to the state – since all the interests of the individual are against it and its order – he would believe less in the possibility of the state than most now believe in the eternal kingdom. This coercive power of the state, through which it exists, which requires no human will and against which the human will can do nothing, testifies to a greater will inherent in it, higher than the human will.

With this insight into power and law, which are themselves inherent in ethical relations, a new period begins in the general opinion of what is just. The political writers who combatted the Revolution asserted this in a practical way, calculated for success and effectiveness in public events. In German legal philosophy it appears with a purely scientific interest in the *concept of objective will*, in *ethical organisms*, which owes its origin to Schelling's system and also distinguishes Hegel's natural law from the earlier versions. This is the beginning of the historical view. For now a cause besides man and his thinking is recognized as the basis of the ethic and of rights; it was only necessary to consider this cause as acting and self-aware. And yet this did not happen all at once. Rather, the will and the right of the family, of the state, still appear here as people's personal will and right, instead of as a will-exercising ruler over them, which makes their existence not only to be something on behalf of people, but absolutely necessary. Because of this superhuman and yet inactive power, glittering merely through its being and its form, our legal philosophy had a close relationship to the Greek during this period, as also expressed in Schelling's admiration for the Platonic Republic and for the Greek constitution.

Nevertheless it also differed essentially herefrom. On the one hand, it has the advantage that it carries the germ of the historical within it, and Schelling therefore forthwith draws the progression of state formation into his system. On the other hand, however, to the degree that it remains unhistorical, it is so because of the requirement to derive determinate, particular existence from a pure unfulfilled cause *as something necessary;* the divine freedom that guides and alone determines historical movement, which the Greek view simply lacks, is here therefore still positively shut out. *Speculative philosophy,*[13] which signals the great change in science, is still in its first iteration *pantheistic philosophy,* although it contains the germ of and the transition to *historical,* to *Christian philosophy.*

---

[13] [See p. 138 below.]

PART I: SCHELLING'S PHILOSOPHY

Chapter 1: The System as a Whole

Emergence from Fichte's System

"I want to extend myself to yourself!" This is the first step Schelling took to emerge from Fichte. Fichte's system was able either consistently to make the thinking individual into the All, or arbitrarily to accept as many worlds as there are human beings, and let them exist in disconnection. Schelling therefore adhered to Fichte's conclusion whereby material things outside of us have no being but are only [figments of] reason;[14] but actual active reason, which Fichte made into the ἓν καὶ πᾶν [one and all], is made by Schelling into universal reason; and where Fichte turned the individual I into substance, Schelling turned the absolute I into it. This in itself forms the world and thus all individual "finite, empirical" I's, without itself being an I. Fichte's doctrine of consciousness is then transferred to this all-I in all its aspects. It is crucial to pay attention to this replica of human consciousness to bring clarity to Schelling's first writings. Schelling himself could scarcely have an idea of the universe he depicted, except by means of this model.

Sameness of its Elements

Fichte's I, in terms of its nature, thus by necessity posits a not-I opposite itself; this is its acting real side, and it does not exist prior to this act. In the same way, with Schelling the first act of the absolute I (God) is the real: this = the absolute power of God, absolute action, absolute necessity.

The other aspect of Fichte's I is that it observes an act (the object), distinguishes itself therefrom regardless of whether it precedes (theoretical) or follows (practical) the object – and that is its ideal side, the seat of freedom. With Schelling this corresponds to the other aspect of the Absolute, by which it is

---

[14] "The only basic prepossession, to which all others are reduced, is none other than that there are things outside of us." Schelling, *System des transcendentalen Idealismus,* p. 8. [English translation: *System of Transcendental Idealism,* trans. Peter Heath (Charlottesville, VA: University Press of Virginia), 1978.]

ideal, primordial knowledge, absolute wisdom of God, freedom. But in both moments it is only the one substance (here the absolute, there the individual self), which is active, which is what does the effectuating, which is the being in both – and that is the identity between subject and object, with Schelling in the universe, with Fichte in self-consciousness. There is no object in the old sense, namely no mere being, no thing; rather, everything is action, expression of a force that is itself spiritual, therefore homogeneous with the cognizing spirit. For Schelling, however, this force is outside of man; consciousness only arises through the permanent opposition of their original, simultaneous effect in subject and object. [15] It is therefore universal reason which, according to Schelling, makes itself into an object through action, to then, as thought, observe it (subject-objectification). As object, however, it makes itself into multitudes, into particulars, in things, in individual human beings, as Fichte's I does in his ideas; while insofar as it remains a subject and differs from the object – as knowledge – it is always one and universal (identity of the universal and the particular). For although it is only in the individual human being, as an empirical self, that it really knows and cognizes, this cognition as such is something universal, and everyone has that certain sense that his knowledge is not his as an individual, therefore is not arbitrary, but is the effect of a universal truth, and therefore is necessary.

Instead of the microcosm, the macrocosm is thus restored, and the law observed in the former is transferred to it. A world returns to existence which does not bear within itself the primordial illusion of believing that which it itself is, to be something outside of it; rather, for the individual self, what appears outside of him, is indeed so. Nevertheless, the possibility of conceptualization, out of which this system also first grows, is salvaged.[16] Kant did not arrive at this, because he regarded reason as static and therefore completely separated it from what is real. Fichte gained this through the identity of self-consciousness with that which also acts. Schelling asserted this by the identity of his Absolute, which likewise unites that act of consciousness in itself. In Schelling, the thing

---

[15] *Ideen zu einer Philosophie der Natur,* p. 186. [English translation: *Ideas for a Philosophy of Nature,* trans. Errol E. Harris, Peter Heath (Cambridge: Cambridge University Press, 1988).]

[16] *Ibid.,* Introduction.

and its concept are as little one and the same as they are in Fichte; instead, the substance, the subject is one and the same, even though the things [it produces] by acting are the same as the knowledge [it gains of those things] in observing its action, just as according to Fichte, the conceptualizing I and the I which distinguishes itself from what it conceptualizes, are still one and the same I. By putting the identity of human consciousness back in the universe itself, we keep from denying the object, yet without abandoning the bond between it and our conceptualization. From this point forward, the question as to how conceptualization is possible is put to one side, while the question of the existence of being is restored in importance.

Consequences of the Objective Use Thereof

This universal impersonal reason must necessarily constitute specific things and individual personalities, like Fichte's I does with its conceptualizations. Therefore, reason is alone; and all that is, is only reason. As with Fichte, the task of philosophy is to find the world of experience from reason, yet not as a mere conceptualization, but as a something real; not to show why I have to think it, but why reason outside of me has to form it. In order to solve this task, Schelling finds the means in the two series or potencies that form Fichte's I, the real and the ideal. What appears there as a process of consciousness here becomes the process of the world. Both potencies, which are equally absolute, neither of which exists without the other, are conceived as living, acting in a manifold penetration in which there is a continual ascent from the predominance of the real to that of the ideal – the process of potencies. Man, personality is itself only one stage in this process; for the absolute, which exists only as both real and ideal, is already effective in this duality before it reaches this stage, even in the lowest natural products. For Schelling, therefore, the object and the real are no longer the same as they were previously; for there is no object in which the ideal side is not already there; in things themselves there is already divine (universal) reason, without which specific bounded things could not be, and could not be recognized by us as the bearers of universal reason.[17] But the process of potencies does

[17] There is absolutely no danger in Schelling's system of spirit becoming corporeal, as the name "natural philosophy" might lead one to fear. For in this process, nature itself

not stop at people; the relationships among the many people and the real events in the world, since they themselves cannot be anything other than the effects of that universal reason, must likewise be explained by it. It has to be shown how the absolute had to be, with the same necessity by which *this* (specific, existing) nature had to be, as well as the state and *this* (specific, existing) history, as it really took place. Every thing, every relationship, every event, all that is or that even exists as a thought, can only be the result of this process. Here, first of all, the real world becomes the output of philosophy, not only in its entire extent, as with Fichte, but also in its own coherence. This gives rise to those now well-known and generally cultivated sciences as branches of philosophy, of which Schelling had no idea: philosophy of nature, philosophy of religion, philosophy of mythology, of revelation, etc., i.e., not what one hitherto would have understood under this term, and is still presumed by the unphilosophical public today – a consideration and judgment about the truth or untruth of positive religion, about the empirical causes or the moral value of historical deeds and events – but the demonstration as to how, in accordance with the world-forming potencies that philosophy has ascertained, history proceeds precisely in these events and deeds, how the religious consciousness of the human race has to go through precisely these religious conceptualizations in necessary processes, thus these forms of worship in succession.

Therein lies the mighty transformation of philosophy expressed as the contrast between speculation and reflection. The essence of speculation is to recognize each individual in the totality of all being and then in its absolute cause and its absolute significance, while reflection has as its object only the individual in relation and connection with other individuals, hence only derivative causes and relative significance. Reflection seeks an external individual cause for a physical phenomenon, e.g., air pressure for the viscosity of water, but this leaves to one side the question as to why water is not as impervious to air as other bodies are, etc. Speculation, on the other hand, explains this from the absolute significance of water, that it is the portrayal of the infinite in the finite; accordingly, on the one hand, every part must be the same as the whole, and on the

becomes something, if not knowing [Verstehenden], yet reasonable [Verständigen], bearing reason in itself. The danger is the reverse, that what is real is lost, becoming a mere impression of thought forms.

other hand it must portray finitude [Verendlichung], and this portrayal is viscosity. For a historical event, e.g., the Revolution, reflection seeks the individual empirical causes, which in fact are both inexhaustible and lead in turn from one to another. Speculation explains this from its absolute significance in the totality of history;[18] a moment must arrive at which the ideal (reflection, will) overcomes the real (the historically extant); this moment is the Revolution. It is therefore absolutely necessary, and those empirical causes are themselves only the outflow of this absolute necessity.

The same thing applies to purposes as to causes. Reflection considers an institution of nature or human society, e.g. marriage, to be a mere means, e.g., for reproduction, and thus raises the wider question: what is the end that this purpose, reproduction, is to serve, why should there be a myriad of human beings, and why are the conditions of nature such that that purpose can only be achieved by that means, why has nature not established other ways? Speculation, on the other hand, seeks the absolute necessity of this institution (the division into sexes, mating) as this purpose (the multiplicity of people) in the totality of creation: the demiurgical principles must finally present themselves personally as genders, and the bond, the unity thereof, must show itself as creative. Reflection moves within the framework of the chain of causes and intended purposes. But the chain of causes and intended purposes presupposes the existence of nature or the world as specifically what it is; it does not explain why and to what end it is precisely what it is. Speculation undertakes to demonstrate the absolute coherence. The means to this knowledge of the absolute significance of things is precisely that process of potencies (later with Hegel, the dialectic process). Just as it is the supreme and sole cause of everything that is and that happens, it must also be the sufficient source of explanation and knowledge of these effects.

But what is highest in creation and history, or as one might say from a vulgar point of view, their final purpose, is, according to Schelling, *art.* For it is the highest simultaneously real and ideal activity, that is, the most perfect effectiveness of the primordial power, the essence of which is to form products by such a penetration of the two potencies. For his part, Hegel, since he recognizes the pure determinations of logic as the world-forming power, logically sees art as a

---

[18] Cf. Vol. II, Part I [*Philosophical Presuppositions*], §. 14.

subordinate level, and hence science as absolute perfection, while Schelling, who recognizes the world-forming power as originally really working, just as consistently recognizes its highest expression to be art. He therefore makes the artistic character a requirement for that supreme achievement and the innermost essence of things. The purpose of the state is to be a work of art; history in its innermost essence and its highest meaning is a work of art; and it is the real historian who can present it as a work of art. Science itself in its highest perfection must appear to be an artistic reproduction.

But with the full recognition of the object, the difficulty removed by Kant arises again as to how change in the world can be conceived, everything being reason and necessity. It was no longer possible to deny time and change without giving up the gain whereby reason is active, and objects are recognizable and thus amenable to deduction and even reason – in short, all the progress since Kant. Change had to be recognized; the only way out was to assume that it was contained in the unchangeable in an unchangeable way, letting the one be many in terms of its nature, and considering change or progress to be the necessary way of existence. Time and space are therefore not subjective forms here, but are real beings, forms which the absolute must assume in its processes, its necessary modalities. But they are not true as time, as change; rather, the true, unity in time is eternity, i.e., *timelessness*, "aeternitas," not "aeviternitas."[19] So the absolute, the in-no-way-determined [das nichts Bestimmtes], is the true, the original and the ultimate in the midst of all the change of things and events. The ought consists in nothing but the return of the particular I to the absolute, the indeterminate.[20] The whole world, thus, with all its forms of time and change, act and event, is in itself borne as the one immutable, timeless reason, necessary even in its change.

But the ability to perceive the timeless in time, to perceive in movement and act the one in the truly many, the totality in the particulars, is *vision* [Anschauung]. This is therefore the organ of philosophy. It is an *intellectual* vision, because what is to be beheld is not the things that have already become fixed and sensorially determined, but the actions of the primordial forces themselves. The representation based on it, showing how the mutable is contained in the

---

[19] *Vom Ich als Princip der Philosophie* ["I" as the Principle of Philosophy], pp. 57, 59.

[20] *Ibid.*, pp. 55, 57.

immutable in a timelessly necessary way, i.e. the scientific method that this system requires, is called *construction*, a designation which is modeled on geometry, and which is to indicate the contrast with the logical method from the law of non-contradiction. Because to find from construction signifies to find from the totality of a figure. As such, it is an absolute, something that cannot be substantiated further, that obeys its own law and includes a multitude of parts, a whole that is already originally structured. It is contrasted with the proof according to which a higher statement is premised and the statement in question is placed below it as separate from it. Fichte's method is also construction in this sense; self-awareness is a totality, which contains all products as integrating parts, according to its own laws, which do not exist outside of these products. But the Fichtean construction is based on the view of consciousness, the Schellingian on that of the universe.

General Shape of Schelling's System

Schelling laid the logical foundations of his philosophical edifice in his treatises on the absolute I, on transcendental idealism, etc. His lectures on academic study then drew the outline of how the parts fit together. To be sure, the innermost driving force of the system, the creativeness, the real expression of ideas as a world principle, find expression in his treatises and discussions on art, but the real implementation of the system initially began with nature, which is where the designation "natural philosophy" comes from. Here we can see the conception that through the two potencies of the real and the ideal, and the unity thereof, he can create all of nature in all its stages and forms. The unity of both, the bond (copula),[21] he in turn sees as a power, indeed as the center, as the actual creative force. In what is connected, this bond expresses its own nature, which consists in identity. It can also be called the infinite love of itself, the infinite desire to reveal, to will, to affirm. The world is only the imprint of this eternal infinite self-will. In nature, this bond is on its one side (the real one) *gravity*, as that which binds all things, which makes unity in allness by pulling everything

---

[21] [The *Oxford English Dictionary* provides this definition: "copula, *n.*: *Logic* and *Grammar*. That part of a proposition which connects the subject and predicate; the present tense of the verb *to be* (with or without a negative) employed as a mere sign of predication." https://www.oed.com/view/Entry/41288, accessed March 26, 2020.]

into the center; on the other side (the ideal), *light* (principle of light), as that which likewise unifies things, while it is present, completely present, as a whole in each of its parts and each object which it inheres. By virtue of gravity, things are one on the outside, united in one point, while by virtue of the light principle they are one on the inside, mutually present amongst themselves (similar to the omnipresence of clairvoyance). This also yields *space* and *time*. Space is the form of things without the bond, the negation of the bond, and the bond (as gravity) is the negation of space (the attraction of the center negates space). It is precisely in this manner that gravity also sets time, because by pulling things into the center it sets things in motion, and time is set by this movement. Gravity and light are the two principles which, in their opposition and again their penetration, form nature. Thus the imprint of gravity in its own realm is the solid, the inflexible, the earth (here each part is finite, closed for itself, relatively differentiated from the other and polarly opposite to it); the imprint of the light principle in the sphere of gravity is the air (here the whole is contained in particulars, each part absolutely from the nature of the whole); the identity of both is imprinted in water, which is why water has viscosity from the principle of gravity (principle of finitude) and the presence of the whole in parts from the principle of light. The light itself as such acts on this whole sphere of gravity (these three elements) and unfolds the bud of things to behold itself in them.

In the same manner of construction, the basic forces of nature (magnetism and electricity) are obtained, like their formations themselves: organic nature, plant kingdom, animal kingdom, finally man, in which the contrast of the two principles (light and gravity) presents itself as an opposition of the male and female sexes, where it is then demonstrated that unity (copula) is the creator, the new existence having come from the connection of the sexes. But even in man that eternal bond (light and gravity, infinite and finite) has only a fleeting expression; in the end it must set its perfect and imperishable expression; this happens through the structure of the world and the divine all-absorbing stars. But what is God in this extension of nature? He is just the one in all, the all in one, the all-copula. To demand proof of His existence is folly; who can ask about the existence of His existence? We perceive Him as a double potency in the alternation of our lives, in sleep and waking, where we one moment are given over to gravity, the next to light. But the all-copula is in ourselves as reason; our spirit gives testimony of this. Regarding God, we are not concerned with an external and supernatural "thing" (Schelling completely ignores the assertion of a supernatural person), but with the immediately near, the only real thing, to which we belong and in which we are. There is no boundary, no here and now, to distinguish, because such does not exist. Immanence and transcendence are equal and empty words here, since this true view cancels the opposition and everything flows together in it, into a God-filled world. So God is nothing else than the world soul giving birth to this creation, force emerging from and flowing back into itself. He is eternally creating nature.[22] Here pantheism appears at its most florid (comparable to the passage in Goethe's *Faust:* "Who dare name him?"),[23] just as with Hegel it appears at its most dessicated and abstract.

Schelling's system entered a new epoch, however, when it was carried forward by the material from nature to man himself, and thus to the other side of the philosophical problem, history. It began with his treatise, *Über das Wesen der menschlichen Freiheit* [On the Nature of Human Freedom]. The problem of this treatise is not just what is contained in the title, freedom, but more profoundly the creation of man and the history of the human race; namely the existence of a being with consciousness of God, and with freedom, and thereby at the same time with the possibility of evil; and it is to explain (demonstrate the necessity of) the particular types of consciousness of God as shown in history in its various epochs. He solves the problem in its essentials by means of his

---

[22] Cf. in particular Schelling, *Von der Weltseele... nebst einer Abhandlung ueber die Verhältniß des Realen und Idealen in der Natur* [Of the World Soul... in addition to a treatment regarding the Real and the Ideal in Nature]. This too means: gravity is the "*entire God*" to the degree that it is expressed as unity in diversity.

[23] ["Who dare name him? and who avow: 'I believe in him?' Who feel—and dare to say: 'I believe in him not?' The All-embracer, the All-sustainer, does he not embrace and sustain thee, me, himself? Does not the heaven arch itself there above ?—Lies not the earth firm here below?—And do not eternal stars rise, kindly twinkling, on high ?—Are we not looking into each other's eyes, and is not all thronging to thy head and heart, and weaving in eternal mystery, invisibly—visibly, about thee?—With it fill thy heart, big as it is, and when thou art wholly blest in the feeling, then call it what thou wilt! Call it Bliss!—Heart!—Love!— God! I have no name for it! Feeling is all in all. Name is sound and smoke, clouding heaven's glow." Goethe, *Faust: A Dramatic Poem,* p. 153.]

previously developed system. It is a real potency in God that makes up the material of all existence, through which the independent creature is possible – the "dark ground," the "longing in God," "nature in God," which is differentiated from his creative power (the spiritual ideal potency of God); in this, the ideal potency in God, the divine spirit, forms the shapes of beings (according to the principle of gravity and light). The perfect imagination of the spirit in this dark ground yields man; he is therefore in the center of creation, he has the consciousness of God, because here the spirit has fully reached its development [Durchbildung] or imagination [Einbildung] in the material. But man also carries that dark ground, the other potency, in him; he is woven from these two divine powers; therefore he has the opportunity to surrender to the former, to let it work in him, and so to fall prey to the matter from which he is raised, and that is evil.[24]

The succession of religions, however, is precisely the divine process itself. God realizes Himself only in man, but He realizes Himself in a varied relationship, a sequence of stages of His own powers, which sequence of stages is precisely mythology. This explains Schelling's exorbitant claim that the mythological gods had reality. This does not mean that Zeus, Venus, and the like lived as individual beings with the history that poetry ascribes to them, but that at that time God was really nothing other than a power of the kind that the God-consciousness of that time (mythology, apart from poetic fashioning) conceived of Him. Quite naturally, the mythological consciousness is only the mirror, or rather it is itself the only realization of God, i.e., of the world powers at that stage. God then Himself is subject to a process; the history of God-consciousness is the history of God, just as nature is His history. That is why Jakobi rightly accuses this treatment of teaching a *developing God*, and Schelling does not actually reject it, but rather confirms it, by replying in his *Denkmal Jakobi's* [Memorial to Jakobi] whether the God of the Old Testament is not quite different from the God of the New? The problem begun here already contains the one which is the subject of Schelling's recent endeavors: mythology, revelation, i.e.,

---

[24] The explanation of how the individual human being decides freely in the individual case and yet a necessity of action is given by the specific nature, the character of this human being, is of no interest here. See Vol. II, Part I [*Philosophical Presuppositions*], §. 41.

the innermost history of the human race.

If one analyzes this system in its first beginnings and in its established statements, one might consider it to be just as sterile as the earlier ones. It still has the old requirement of rationalist philosophy, according to which everything exists in terms of a necessary law and cannot be thought of any other way than it is.[25] For there it is still an empty substance, the ἓν καὶ πᾶν; and two movements thereof, likewise without content, create the world. It must then come as a surprise to find, in the implementation, spirit – something which the earlier philosophy of reason lacks – and an abundance of ever newly generated thoughts, while the earlier philosophy only carries out the one thing, which is its basic view, in ever-recurring application. Spirited treatment and a dead system do not come together by chance. To make the former explicable, the latter must carry a living germ within it. *And this is the principle of the real, the principle of act.*

Fichte's Real Principle and its Objectification by Schelling

Even Spinoza, as realistic as his doctrine seems to be, has no true principle of the real. The reality of its substance is in fact derived first from its concept (*causa sui*), and therefore is itself only a product of pure thought. For him, then, the world-conjuncture [Weltzusammenhang] is not even a physical one, but merely mathematical. Fichte was the first to use the only reality accessible to rationalism – the act of the subject – and so unconsciously took the first step towards overcoming it. Schelling retained this real element for his absolute, which distinguishes him from Spinoza. For him, pure substance is not a being, nor a thing, but a pure ability [Können], nothing but positing; the way in which the modalities are contained in it is not a complete understanding of itself, but a (still necessary) production, a relationship of living forces. With Schelling, analytical statements become theoretical.[26] Kant's question: how are synthetic judgments possible, i.e., how does reason *contain* things outside itself, here becomes: how does the pure primordial act come to do something specific, which

---

[25] Schelling rejects the argument from empty categories from the start; nevertheless, for him, everything particular is still contained in the universal in a necessary, lawful way and must therefore be able to be discovered from this law (*a priori*). The universal needs the particular to exist.

[26] *Vom Ich als Princip*, 2nd ed., p. 81.

is no longer pure act? It is thus recognized that synthesis is only possible in action. Even the term "system of identity" could be exchanged for "system of action." For the act contains the unity between the active and the modality in the activity; but besides that, there is no identity. Mere being, that which does not act, can only be completely the same vis-à-vis another, where every two [Zwei] is excluded, or it can be only two, only another. With Spinoza the identity of the concept and the thing is only asserted; with Kant it is given up; only with Fichte and Schelling can it be perceived, while with Hegel it again becomes incomprehensible.

However, this real principle only attains its true effectiveness if the creative action is no longer that of man, of whom it is certain that he cannot produce anything that is independent in itself and for itself. Only now does the real element of its product (the object) get added to the real element of the act (the subject). Fichte had only picked up the dead object; here first is it brought to life.[27] Creation no longer has the human individual either as its center or as its originator; the consideration of the relationship of things to me (I first confront myself with people, then with things, then with a body, etc.) is dismissed. The primordial force of creation itself is the center; how it works in a real way, that is, according to its own conditions, must be seen, nature and history must be understood in *their* context, in *their* sequence of time and level; the explanation of things from our empty categories of reason must be abandoned.[28]

Elevation of Philosophy

In this way, philosophy is able to absorb all the richness and vitality of creation. Nature is no longer a mere means for rational subjects to deal with each other in terms of their rights, as with Fichte; it has its meaning in itself, and not just that of the expediency that Kant ascribes to it, but as an expression of the divine (e.g., light is the manifestation of the essence of spirit in the corporeal, which is why it exists). This is the objectivity of Schelling's system, by which, to

---

[27] *Ueber das Wesen der menschlichen Freiheit,* p. 420.

[28] *Darlegung des wahren Verhältnisses der Naturphilosophie zu der verbesserten Fichte'schen Lehre,* pp. 35, 36. [English translation: *Statement on the True Relationship of the Philosophy of Nature to the Revised Fichtean Doctrine: An Elucidation of the Former,* trans. Dale E. Snow (Albany: SUNY Press, 2019).]

the degree that it leads the discussion, rationalism ceases. The same is true regarding the pragmatic view. The world, nature, no longer stand in opposition to reason. Instead of the two rulers, blind chance and rational man, history now has a single ruler which is neither of these, the power of the absolute and its evolution. If events are necessarily part of the world process, they cannot be the work of human calculation and choice. The particular stage that each age occupies in this process determines its ethic, and the ethic determines the aspirations and actions of individuals. The world, which is an objective act, i.e., the creation of a real force outside of myself, takes on a completely different form than that which owes its existence simply to my conception. For the acts of my consciousness are arbitrarily or in fact randomly stirred by the continually appearing objects; without the continuous progression of the shapes thereof, they can or must break off at any moment. On the other hand, the products of the world, when they come from an action apart from me, constitute an uninterrupted stream of this activity — a *becoming.*

These two traits, objectivity and becoming, are the peculiarity of Schelling's system, which is why it should be called the philosophy of time. For even the most celebrated poet of our age is not only characterized by the objectivity that is praised in him, but also by this other trait. One of the beauties of Goethe's novels, which absolutely no other work of poetry has shown, is that becoming is depicted in them in the same way as reality. We see a passion in the first bud, we see it grow and grow, finally to displace everything else. To us it is the same with every stage and nuance in life: it seems as if it had always existed like that, yet when we look back we see that it has become, and yet find no transition... where? and how? And with the same invisible growth, the conditions, the relations around them change as well. The feeling of eternal and necessary existence, but at the same time their temporal emergence and transformation, accompanies us in the same way as in our own situations and fortunes. This never-ending growth, this lively becoming, also dominates Schelling's view, and his system is an incessant struggle to depict it. The same trait is a peculiarity of Savigny in his sphere, and shows him to be the founder of the historical view of law, although other essential traits hereof were dealt with earlier and more exhaustively by others. With this elevation of philosophy, the requirement of artistic character had to arise; for art is a replica of the spirit that is active in creation. Hence, Schelling is the first to make this demand and, in modern times, the only one to meet it.

Disruptive Principle

With this great advance in philosophy, however, a deficiency becomes all the more palpable in another respect. It comes naturally through this first step of the system: the absolute is no personality. The I of the world already is, already gives shape to all of nature, before it really becomes an I. *Before* it differentiates itself from its objects – thus not, like Fichte's consciousness, *at the same time* as this differentiation – it makes nature, and consequently itself is a non-being. It never becomes personality. For the self-consciousness of the creature is not the personality of God. The I who says, "I am," is not God, and reason, which is *everything*, as such, can never say: I am. The emergence of human personality is itself only an abstraction that proceeds in universal impersonal reason, and is known only from the product thereof, not from the being who undertakes it.[29] This is the feared pantheism of this system, not in the sense of immanence, but in the sense that God has no self-consciousness distinguished from the creatures. In this way, philosophy has returned from the human consciousness as the cause and center of things to the universe; objectivity has been gained; but the personality of the unconditioned has not yet been acquired.

Contradiction of this Principle with the System as a Whole

This was a natural way station for philosophy. It could not suddenly jump from man to God; first, the world had to be given the life that had been taken away from it. But there was also a need for this in the rationalistic requirement that everything must be found from out of the human spirit – the unrestricted comprehensibility of the true. As long as one insists on this, one assumes that the cause of the world is what it is in the consciousness of the thinking person, and entirely so; how else could it be aware of its effects? But now the freedom and choice that I find in myself is not the cause of the world; if it were, I could make it otherwise. This freedom is only mine and has no influence on it; what I find in myself as universal, on the other hand, is only that which is necessary, the law. For the freedom of God, if He has such, is precisely that which is not shared; His personality must remain His property, we can never become Him.

---

[29] *Ideen zu einer Philosophie der Natur*, pp. 130–140.

It is only by His voluntary communication that we can know what He wished for and wishes in the decision which exists only in Him, and only as far as that communication goes. Therefore, if through our thinking we are to find the absolute, the world-conjuncture, then the same must not be a free thing, it must be *the* universal, which is also found entire in us, that which of necessity effectuates – impersonal reason.

This assumption is therefore necessary in rationalist philosophy, but it is by no means inseparable from the basic principles of Schelling's system, if one disregards rationalist philosophy; on the contrary, it contradicts the essence thereof. Through it, everything that heralds itself as a special characteristic, as a higher gain in it, is transformed into mere sham. They are no longer act and creation if everything had to come from a preceding necessity. Becoming itself is not becoming, if nothing else was possible from the beginning, if it is not in its innermost depth also a *history*. But this is not the case if God, instead of being the free author of it, is subject to it, if His own existence is a mere becoming rather than a dealing. To be sure, our interest, the sense of truth, demands a necessity in everything created; but that only amounts to independence from our choice, the mastery of another intelligence, while in this other case, necessity would in itself be becoming, it would be so for God. The freedom of the individual and of the ethic, which are maintained from the very beginning of the system with astonishing strength against the crushing weight of pantheism, would have to be abandoned, just as the goal of the ought would have to be placed, not in a positive union of personalities in which both exist, the divine and the human, but in the extinguishment of all personality, against the basic view that real production and its infinite increase is the goal of the primordial force.

The supreme truth of this system – that living forces form the universe – cannot be maintained and conducted without being united from the outset in a personality. For philosophy must have a reason for the fact that these forces penetrate precisely at such and such a stage, form such and such a product; it cannot be a matter of chance. If this reason should only be necessity, if such be the nature of these forces which they cannot relinquish, then their vitality, their character as a force, would cease; they would become mere substances which must be brought together as ingredients to yield a product. To be sure, the product contains both the real and the ideal; but its determinateness is still something other than the universal nature of these forces; it is their particular application, and why is it precisely such in each instance? To create something other than itself is the essence of the living force. If this did not happen according to freedom, then from the start it must have already been what it would create. It is necessary that the tree is root, trunk, and leaves; but that the seed yields the tree is a miracle, a creation and a matter of freedom, even when not its own.

Yes, one must ask further, since Schelling has the entire universe emerge from his absolute and sees it as a revelation of the absolute: what is this absolute in itself, before it has revealed itself in the world and things; and then there is nothing but the abstract: the non-differentiation of the real and the ideal, the subject and the object. And already this alone makes it is incomprehensible that such an empty, content-less, spiritless absolute should become known to itself in such a richly fulfilled world, that this richness of manifestation could be the self-realization of emptiness. This is the impression that runs through all of Schelling's writings: a plethora of life (of stimulating ideas, profound inklings) in the implementation; but when it comes to the ultimate reason, it ends in the barest abstraction, in which everything dies again. One is touched by the current of these figures; but if you climb up to the source, from which you wish to find refreshment, it has dried up and you cannot understand how such a current could flow from it. There are two different people in the system, a presentient poet who sings about divine things, and an abstract philosopher who skeletizes the universe.

Schelling gave rise to the notion that can be regarded as the innermost characteristic of pantheism: individual life manifests itself as a negation and deprivation of the universal. We will come back to this in the portrayal of the Hegelian system.

Unfolding of the Christian Viewpoint in the System Itself

So it is in the nature of this system, which recognizes as the unconditional neither the subjective activity of reason nor any static determined power, to pass over to a personal, freely determining God. A creative principle is therefore the postulate that Schelling makes from the beginning. In his very first writings he treated the potencies with complete freedom; he established no law by which they had to be penetrated in order for them to produce these formations and none other, no more, no less. Yes, one might even say that he treats them with poetic license. There is no order and necessity of progress; often the most particular connections become decisive links. Thus for him the divine all-incorporating stars comprise the end of creation, toward which the progress of man is guided, instead of the other way round; thus time is classified as a product of gravity in the system; thus the church is merely a surrogate of the lost democratic form of the state, etc. This freedom become arbitrary above all with Schelling's successors. While the Kantians subsume, while Fichte, according to Jakobi's parable, knits his I with his not-I, one can say of Schelling's school that it *throws dice* with its potencies, with which, however, it has been all the less successful because this *game* requires the *luck* of the genius. This arbitrariness was part of the experiment with the numerical ratios, just as the witty manner which, in the joy of having been freed from the old logical constraint, is delighted in the most random combinations, whereby something sounds good and seems to makes sense – but something else, something contradictory, makes just as much sense. The otherwise genuinely witty Adam Müller is likewise infected by this manner, when he tries to explain the thoroughly distinct relations of public life by reference to his war against the elements, his relationship of one over two, comparison of man and woman, youth and old age.

There is also a steady advance in Schelling's system, whereby the personality of God receives more and more dominance while rationalist philosophy is abandoned to the same degree, so that the beginning and the end no longer correspond. First it says: "There is nothing except reason, and in reason is everything,"[30] etc. By contrast, in the sequel: "The whole of nature tells us that it is by no means there because of a mere geometric necessity; it is not just pure reason, but personality and spirit.... Creation is not an event, but an act. There are no results from universal laws, but God, i.e., the person of God, is the universal law, and everything that happens, happens by virtue of the personality of God, not according to an abstract necessity that we, let alone God, would be able to bear with in action."[31] "They say: God must be superhuman. But if He wanted to be human, who would object?.... So I can't tell Him in advance what He should be. He is what He wants to be. So first I have to try to investigate His will, not

---

[30] *Zeitschrift für spekulative Physik* [Journal for Speculative Physics], vol. 2, issue 2, p. 2.

[31] *Ueber das Wesen der menschlichen Freiheit,* p. 482.

prevent Him in advance from being what He wants to be."[32] The treatise on the nature of human freedom is an epoch in the development of Schelling's system, both in relation to the subject matter and to the doctrine.

Finally, however, during the long hiatus that has intervened in Schelling's literary activity from this treatise until now (1854), the change in the basic viewpoint has come to a decisive breakthrough. It was perhaps decided in part by Jakobi's attack, perhaps by the formation of Hegel's system, in which Schelling could see for himself the result of his pantheistic viewpoints; but certainly and mainly through the material itself. Since Schelling, in the course of his work, no longer had nature but religious consciousness as the object, he, being interested in explaining the object and therefore never able to foist ready-made forms onto the object with the ruthlessness of Hegel, could no longer insist on the old aprioristic deduction and premise of an impersonal cause of the world, which he too had initially proclaimed with complete determination. Thus, in his lectures of 1828, Schelling described the systems of rationalism from Descartes to the present day as of a *merely logical* as opposed to a *historical* character, in the sense in which it was explained above,[33] that is, assuming I understood him correctly.

This is indeed a *Samsonesque act*, with which he lifted the temple of the previous philosophy off of its pillars and buried the whole army of enemies, himself included, under its ruins. In Schelling's latest doctrine – judging from the little which has come with certainty to public notice – the guiding motive is nothing else than the great object of explaining the human consciousness of God in its development. Nevertheless, he brings the levers of his original system to bear on this explanation. Just as the powers of the real and ideal, gravity and light, and the copula meet us again in the treatise on human freedom under changed names like dark ground, longing, and the like, so are they now hard to miss in the potencies being-can, being-must, etc. But just as certain is Schelling's definite confession of the personal God, who Himself is not subject to the development of god-consciousness, but stands eternally above it, and to the facts of revelation as factual non-allegorical truth. Whether that earlier basic view, which Schelling does not give up, is compatible with this recognition of a personal God and His real acts, which are supposed to be creation and revelation, is a

---

[32] *Briefe an Eschenmayer*, p. 91.

[33] Book III, Part I [*The Rise and Fall of Natural Law*].

judgment which cannot be made scientifically, as long as we do not have Schelling's latest doctrine in authentic communication.[34] In any case, Schelling's system in its *a priori* pantheistic form could not be finalized as mere rationalist philosophy.

Root of the Hegelian System

On the other hand, starting with Schelling's standpoint, Hegel maintained and implemented that conflicting rationalistic element – the rational necessity in the world and thereby the impersonality of God. Hegel was therefore compelled to give up all of Schelling's uniqueness: the primordial-real, act, life, creation. And so the palladium of Schelling's philosophy is lost, and all the dangers that threatened it at its creation had now to come home to roost. The world once again becomes inactive substance, the logical modalities of which are things; identity is disintegrated into oneness; the ought and individual freedom become a sham; and the goal of all living existence is its extinguishment into nothingness.

---

[34] Note to the fourth edition. It must be remembered that these words were written at the beginning of 1854.

Chapter 2: Schelling's Legal Philosophy

Objective Will

The idea of the *general* will – not the composition of individual wills, but an immediately absolute, purely objective will, standing over all individuals – is Schelling's first achievement in the philosophy of law.[35] It corresponds entirely to the absolute I as a principle of theoretical philosophy, and emerges from Fichte's individual will in the same way. As this latter relates to Spinoza's substance, the former does to Kant's reason or man in himself. Namely, reason is static, ready-made, while will is active. However, this general will, like Kantian reason and the absolute I, is a mere abstraction; another step had to be taken to conceive of it as will determined in its various stages, rather than as mere general will. This led to the formation of the system, the construction of the universe from the two activities of the absolute.

The Ethical Organisms and their Process in History

The objective will (the absolute), in the gradational penetration of these activities, now turns into various shapes, the archetypes of moral duty[36] and the legal connections which, precisely because they emerge from this world process, are totalities, i.e., ethical organisms. Just as that upward process of creation in nature necessarily created the various kingdoms, genera, and species, so in the moral world did it create the structures of the family, the state, the church. The different shapes that these assume in history, i.e., in succession, are likewise only the work of the production, in terms of law, which generates forms side by side in nature. Thus the state is the organism of freedom,[37] or the "harmony of freedom and necessity"; therefore, its true nature is: all that is necessary, likewise happens freely, and all that happens freely is at the same time a necessary thing.

---

[35] Schelling, "Neue Deduction des NaturRechts [*sic*]" [New Derivation of Natural Law] in Fichte's and Niethammer's *Philosophisches Journal*, vol. 4, issue 4, and vol. 5, issue 4.

[36] *Vorlesungen über die Methode des akademischen Studiums* [Lectures on the Method of Academic Study], p. 146.

[37] *Ibid.*, p. 226.

But the state is the expression of this harmony in the real – it is namely a spiritual (hence a free) life in a standing, externally fixed form, that is, in the real, expressing itself necessarily – .while the church is the expression of the same in the ideal, it being an external formation and community on the basis of the spiritual (subjective), of knowledge and belief. The state is also the highest representation of the identity of the universal and the particular (the one and the many), because here the single public order joins together an aggregate of particular wills. But the different ways in which these moments, the one and the many, interpenetrate form the history of the state, the history of the world. In the ancient state (the republics), unity and diversity were in direct (absolute) connection, the multitude knew itself as a state from which it could not detach itself, and the unity of the state, the state itself, in turn existed only in this diversity, the people. The unity (state power) that prevailed was nothing more than the many who obeyed. In the modern state, on the other hand, this identity is abolished; unity stands as a monarch, who is not at the same time many, and it stands in relation to diversity, the people, in which everyone feels again to be an individual. Unity rules over diversity as separate from it, therefore in "abstract form," while on the other hand diversity, by opposing unity, disintegrates into detail and ceases to be the vehicle of the generality. The modern world therefore needed the church, which represents this unity in the ideal (subjective), as a replacement for the loss of true unity (identity) in the state. "The concept of monarchy is therefore essentially intertwined with that of the church." Both are effects or surrogates of the lost true state.[38] The contemporary state is therefore a disagreeable one, in that private law and public law (subjectivity and objectivity) have broken away from each other. For this reason, current jurisprudence is not based on the application of ideas, but only on empirical acumen.[39]

Construction of the State and History

Thus, from the point of view of this system, law manifests itself according to its absolute coherence within the totality of all world relations, and also appears

---

[38] *Ibid.*, pp. 229, 230.

[39] One discovers here not only the manner but also the basic ideas from which Hegel's legal philosophy and philosophical construction of world history originated.

as a necessary manifestation of world-forming reason. Just as these are determined in the stages of their potencies as nature, as human beings, as world history, so also as law and as state. Legal philosophy therefore has to "construct the state from ideas," i.e., it must visualize and demonstrate how the absolute must necessarily create law and the state in general, together with its particular institutes and their historical forms, as well as how, in themselves as well as in these various configurations, only the one, universal, and absolute is expressed. With this treatment, the entirety of previous natural law, in form and content, drops from consideration. The formalism of subsuming reason-less relations under a universal abstract rule of reason, in which a single relation ("isolated fact" [Einzelheit], e.g., that of freedom) is arbitrarily extracted in order to "warp the remaining mass in terms of it," no longer comes into consideration; instead, the relations and their rules arise, in particular and inseparably, as a single product of the idea. Ethics is no longer derived from the concept of man; instead, the primordial power and its real production generates the things, the people and the ethical laws, and it creates them together, the free person for the law, the law for the free person: "For all of life consists only in mutually restricting forces." The contradictions and problems of deducing freedom and two kinds of law from reason disappear; for this primordial power produces totalities of relations containing both, in which, in accordance with the two basic forces, opposites must also permeate each other everywhere.

By grounding law in a higher than human existence and will, objectivity was restored in legal doctrine. The institutions [Anstalten] are no longer there merely for people, but have a higher meaning; they are not based on what purpose people might have, but on the archetype of what they are supposed to represent. Hence the requirement for the state to be a work of art, for beauty of public life, great, sublime institutions to exist for their own sake, not in order to satisfy any individual as the final purpose thereof. The state has a right to be the state. Logical consistency, which used to be recognized as uppermost in both positive law and the law of reason, is duly subordinated.[40] The living play of forces, the manifold way in which these two powers, the universal and the particular, freedom and necessity, penetrate each other and thereby create a wealth of forms, is what should be. By virtue of its inner content, morality ascends from

---

[40] *Ibid.*, p. 228.

the limited standpoint of the isolated fact, the dutiful, the "I ought to do this!" to something total, the recognition of something universal over man, who himself comes into consideration as a mere part thereof; to the requirement of a "God-like attitude, to become one with God."[41]

Ethics was given this objectivity and vitality from the real world-generating principle of the system, and in view of the necessity of the times, it would have found not only entry but also permanence and general comprehension, if that general inhibition did not also extend to ethics.

Inhibiting Principle in Schelling's Legal Philosophy

The system establishes itself on the standpoint of the primordial power. But as long as it does not make full use of divine freedom, it does not yet have the creative power to consider man as the center in his sphere, in the way that God Himself confers this on him. That is why action and knowledge appear to be of equal value here;[42] for this is how they have to appear, where one only refers them to the absolute, only appreciates them as *its* representations; even though human-related action, the product of choice, is specifically higher than knowledge, the involuntary, as is confirmed by the general consciousness. When, therefore, earlier natural law is effectively absorbed in morality – namely, everything is aimed only at the action of the individual – here morality itself bears the color of law, it approaches the Greek ethic, which aims to ensure that certain phenomena exist in the ethical world. Every duty comes from an idea (product of potencies), which the act has to represent;[43] its purpose seems to be less for it to be an act than for it to be a representation. The original vitality, however, would thus sink back to the mere representation of such a life. The state as "public morality" would no longer differ from the morality of man in its innermost essence, but only in degree; for the decisive factor – here the conscious sentiment, hence dependent on choice, which must be given afresh at any moment; there the established rule, which is itself unconsciously expressed in a public construction – this decisive factor rescinds itself if both are merely

[41] *Darlegung des wahren Verhältnisses der Naturphilosophie zu der verbesserten Fichte'schen Lehre,* p. 10; *Vorlesungen über die Methode des akademischen Studiums,* p. 145.

[42] *Vorlesungen,* Lecture 1 and at the start of Lecture 6.

[43] *Vorlesungen,* p. 146.

considered the necessary expressions of the world-generating forces.

It was therefore necessary for progress that the primordial power itself be considered to be desirous of free, creative, individual independent existence and that it set a standard for actions in accordance therewith. But if one appropriates and develops those viewpoints that only, as it were, scratch the surface in Schelling's doctrine, one arrives at Hegel's results, according to which morality is only a chapter of natural law, which is achieved not by the act of men, in the *fulfillment* of duty, but in the study of the absolute, in the *existence* of duty.

Another consequence is that the state not only does not have man as its purpose, but has no purpose at all outside itself. It is its own highest purpose, just as it belongs to the existence of the absolute in a *necessary* way. In that case, the question no longer can be posed: "What does God (the Absolute) intend with the state?" as little as: "What does He intend with nature?" or "what does God intend with Himself, what is God there for?" He is in a certain stage of nature, in a particular state, and cannot be anything else than that. The state, the church, which are desired by a personal God, are certainly divine, but are not themselves God; they are directly higher than man; insofar as He desires them, man must submit to them; but they are not the finally willed, for the image of God, the personal man, must be higher than that which is not like him. And it is conceivable, indeed it is to be expected, that one day He will no longer desire the state, and will discontinue the temporary submission which at bottom is paid not to the state but to the person of God. Yet if God is not the creator of becoming, but is Himself subject to becoming, then He is the state, and the state is God in a certain modality. If it now demands man's incontestable subordination, it must be a higher form of God than man himself, and the fact that it is something impersonal is not only not a disadvantage, but a decisive advantage. In the state, God has given up the personality and self-awareness that He as the Absolute did not originally have; He has returned to Himself.

In the end, there is no need to prove that the abstract – universal, particular, unity, diversity, freedom, necessity – does not yield the state, any more than that nature results from the abstractions of the real and the ideal; and if Schelling accuses the legal philosophers of distorting the natural relations of things, the accusation affects him no less, if in a different way, for one cannot do more violence to the institutions of world history than what is done when Schelling portrays the church as a surrogate of the lost ancient constitutions of the state, in terms of the viewpoint of the identity of unity and diversity. After all, that certainly signifies an "isolated fact warping the remaining mass."

This characterizes the aberrations included in this system and which emerge even more strongly in the subsequent philosophical doctrine. It itself could not completely fall victim to them because it had a better element in the original real [thing] which it held onto, through which it was preserved. The principle by which it relates to the others is only the basis on which it found itself because of the manner of its emergence from Fichte, and from which it arises. I should not be accused of arbitrariness because I am inconclusive in my depiction of Schelling's doctrine; the correct view demands that no aspect and no viewpoint [of it] be considered closed and static. There is incessant growth in this system, and its structures therefore should only be regarded as the germs and buds from which the flower and fruit wish to emerge. Every assertion here is not that which it initially proclaims, but that for which it strives.

Anticipation of Hegel

The easiest, most convenient way for philosophy to take would have been to go from the I of Fichte to the I of God; that is, if it did not have a higher purpose to fulfill, namely, to grasp the immanence of the world in God. For this, God had first to be contemplated in the world, so that He then would be recognized over it, but still be seen in it. Schelling's constant endeavor is to bring the omnipresence and omnipotence of God ever clearer, ever closer to the spiritual eye. The beginning of his system is therefore, to borrow one of his own images, the dark ground which is the longing to give birth to God. One therefore cannot regard this beginning as true only for its own sake, nor can one form a judgment or even a conception about it apart from the longing for that to which it wishes to give birth. For "it does not *have*" this longing "but *is* it." If you inhibit the living, forward-moving development, what you thought you were holding onto is no longer what it is. You cannot keep the youth a youth; you have to either let him become a man, or you make him into a corpse.

In this sense, I have deliberately emphasized here the side of Schelling's doctrine from which Hegel's system derives its origin. Schelling himself later no longer dealt with law and the state. But a much richer, livelier, more intimate, and – the highest designation – a much more human legal philosophy than appears from the lectures on academic study was to be expected from the writer of *Über das Wesen der menschlichen Freiheit;* if in this treatise as a whole an all-changing step is not made, then at least this statement makes its appearance: "The will of man is the divine outlook on life, shut up in the depths, which God saw when He summoned the will to nature. In him (man) alone, God loved the world."

General Character of This Scientific Period

The rule of the impersonal is a necessary way station for Schelling's doctrine; but it is also a general characteristic of that period. The aesthetic school put it like this: Art and beauty are there for the sake of art and beauty, not so that they can satisfy or uplift people – a most striking contrast to the concept which hitherto prevailed, whereby every work of art was measured based on whether it could move people to do their duty. With those who make it their business to take things to extremes, it has even become fashionable to make one's utter perdition into something universal, an idea in which those who do not know who they are, find the purpose of their existence; to renounce personal immortality and to portray the desire thereto to be petty, selfish, and weak. Seemingly a grand disposition, but in reality an unnatural and incredibly great folly. It is based on a deification, not of nature, i.e., of the sense-oriented, but of impersonal thought. But when we take a closer look, we see that the oh so unselfish and sublime worshipers of this god nevertheless, at least in the eyes of most judges, hardly surpass Socrates or the apostle Paul, who laid claim to a limited or petty selfish immortality and a loving God.[44]

Most writers of that time, some of them the luminaries of our literature, were accused of mysticism. This is to confuse the meaning of this word, for there is no necessary association between devoted faith and incomprehensibility. Those writers are sometimes incomprehensible, mystical, but are not for that reason believers, and are incomprehensible to the extent that they are not believers. Life, creation, wealth, freedom dominate consciousness and purport to be the product of the impersonal primordial force, absent knowledge and will.

---

[44] When I wrote this in 1829, such pantheistic reversal and exaggeration was still in its faintest beginnings. It was limited to the school, and those who confessed it rather sought to conceal their confession. Since then it has developed and strengthened in fearful degree. It has become an orientation in the nation and is sported in stark nakedness.

What follows from this fundamental viewpoint can never be comprehensible. Rationalism had given up God and the world; this period took hold of the world again with admiration and enthusiasm, but still without God. All of the productions emanating therefrom thus speak to a deep holy presentiment, but some of them are only murky billowing waves, from which light and clarity can arise only when that one and only supreme Word is spoken. What is said here also applies to several of the traits in Schelling's earlier writings, which are illuminated only by what followed them: No one understands except through a lengthy process of familiarization how the absolute effectuates bodies, effectuates the workings of nature,[45] effectuates human connections; how the identity of the one and the many destined the Greeks to be a republic, the Germans to have vassal armies. But it can be made clear to the simplest that God effectuates the workings of nature in an absolute way, and not just by deriving one thing from another; and that He desires harmony in history whereby the external destinies of men and peoples correspond to inner striving, so that not only what has empirical causes must occur, but also what pertains to the completion of that total work of art according to its ideal, hence what it itself directly (absolutely) effectuates, must occur as well.

---

[45] *Darlegung des wahren Verhältnisses der Naturphilosophie zu der verbesserten Fichte's-chen Lehre,* pp. 35ff.

PART II: HEGEL'S PHILOSOPHY

Chapter 1: The System as a Whole

Rationalistic Character

Hegel's basic stipulation is the universal rationalistic one: "The entire progress of philosophizing as methodical, i.e., as necessary, is nothing but the positing [Setzen] of that which is already contained in a concept." In this process, thus "through analysis," everything that is comes about.[46] Accordingly, free action cannot be the cause of the world. All things are such that cannot be lacking or be otherwise than they are, indeed cannot be thought of otherwise than they are. If one maintains the standpoint of Schelling's earlier system, one inevitably ends up with Hegel's standpoint. The real principle, the act must be abandoned as that which does not result from the determinations of thought, and thought must be preserved as the one and only. But in that case it is not possible to return to the earlier stages. A real world beyond this reason cannot be assumed, as with Kant. Reason cannot be regarded as the reason of the individual, as with Fichte. Nor as the reason of a higher, freely acting being; because the basic requirement opposes this. The only thing left is to understand reason not as the reason of any being, but as impersonal thought, and to declare it to be the All of things [das All der Dinge], the god apart from which there is nothing – this is Hegel's consistent objective idealism.

Foundational Notion

For Hegel, reason as the unconditional is *pure* thought, i.e., without an intended object, without a content other than its own general forms and determinations, e.g., the notions of being, nothing, existence, something, limit, quality, quantity, cause, effect, judgment, conclusion, etc. It is *substantial* thought, i.e., without a thinking subject. Substantial, namely, is that which does not take on its properties, but which has properties which adhere to itself as solid,

---

[46] *Encyclopädie der philosophischen Wissenschaften im Grundrisse* [Encyclopedia of the Philosophical Sciences in Outline], 2nd ed., §. 88.1. The original has "ganz analytisch" (entirely analytical), not "durch Analyse" (through analysis). The meaning is the same.

irrefutable, finished, of which one can only say: it is so and so, not: it voluntarily makes itself into this or that. The opposite of substantial is the actual (subjective), the character of personality. Substantial thought is therefore such that does not *think*, but *is* mere thought. This thought, then – without subject and without object, the epitome of all pure determinations of thought as a system – is the unconditional, one and only, God. But it is also the universe; the entire outfitted [erfüllte] world, as it is, must be given with it according to its own laws; the world is only the analysis performed by this thought. Logic is God, pure before the creation of nature and the finite spirit, implemented after the creation thereof.[47] The pure forms of thought are therefore the independent, the causal; everything else is caused by them, or rather follows from them. "The necessary forms and specific determinations of thought are the highest truth itself."[48] In this way, all real, independent existence is regarded as a mere manner of appearance of those empty logical relations, and vice versa, these relations, which exist only as forms, qualities of a being, and as something that is effected by it, are made into the only thing that is real.

Philosophical Task and the Requirement of Dialectic

It is obvious that the universality of the task, which Fichte already set for Schelling with regard to philosophy, continues for Hegel's system; it only has a different coloring. He too must present the whole universe from reason; he too must regard time and events only as an immutable, necessary modality of that timeless thought; but if in Schelling the world manifests itself as a life of the Absolute, as a product of forces through real motion, it in turn appears here, in the manner of Spinoza, as its modifications, as what is grasped in thought without any other than logical movement, analysis. Schelling's task is to demonstrate how reason (the original real and ideal) had to *produce* nature and history, while Hegel's task is to demonstrate how reason (pure thought) had to *be* nature and history.[49]

---

[47] *Wissenschaft der Logik* [Science of Logic], vol. I, "Einleitung" [Introduction], p. XIII.

[48] *Ibid.*

[49] Therefore, when in the *Encyclopädie,* §. 244 it says: "The idea decides, the idea releases itself," then this is an empty saying. As if it were given a choice and as if it reflected, as if it could take things into consideration before it became human.

But solving this task shows the difficulty: how can this pure thought arise from itself, become different from what it was originally, namely a system of filled instead of empty thoughts (nature), a self-thinking, personal being instead of mere thought (human being)? How does it come about that completely pure thought even comes about? For where we seek unity, we find only a multiplicity of determinations; the unity of Kant's apperception, of Fichte's active consciousness is given up, there remains empty, motionless substance; how does this become complete, pure logic?

In order for the one to become many, it is absolutely necessary to have a movement and thus an impetus to this movement. For this task, Fichte had the I, which is always active by nature. But Hegel negates the will and personality as originating; these, which alone could be the impetus for movement, shall only be engendered in the sequel thereof. The same error (namely, to deny the real in the real) that put him in this difficulty also grants him a remedy for it, and this is the perpetual motion machine of his *dialectic*. Let it be the law of all thought: every conception and every thing is not only itself (abstract moment), but also its opposite, and thus negates itself (dialectical moment), just as it posits a third, which is its unity, i.e., their mutual negation as the truth of both (speculative or positive rational moment), e.g., being – nothingness – becoming, or law – crime – punishment.[50]

The fact that some conception *prompts* the thinker to present another notion opposite to it is insufficient to proceed further, should one not have the inclination to follow this invitation; it is absolutely necessary that it itself *be* the other. In order to let mere thought think itself up without a thinker, all synthesis must be nothing other than analysis, and the analysis of whatever conception, be it the most empty (of pure being), must yield the most complete synthesis (the entire universe); for that which is not already contained in that emptiest, simplest determination, given that no act adds or shapes anything new, could not manifest itself outside of that determination. Therefore being might just as well be nothing; "Law is injustice, fraud."[51] But no one could resort to such an assumption, which Hegel needs to advance just one step, unless he has denied everything real. This dialectic is necessary from such a point of view; but

---

[50] *Encyclopädie*, §§. 79ff.

[51] *Grundlinien der Philosophie des Rechts* [Elements of the Philosophy of Law], §. 87.

only from this point of view could it be accepted. One can only believe that what is posited in fact precludes itself, when one has no conception of what "*in fact*" is, when one views the merely thought-of as something that has being. Because only in fact, i.e., in reality, is the opposite excluded; as mere thought, it can exist side by side, even be mutually conditioned. The finite excludes the infinite and itself continues to subsist; by no means does it negate itself. The same is true of being, nothingness. But the finite is put forward with the infinite: if I think the infinite, I necessarily think the finite as well, as something that is not present, that does not exist, even though I still think it. If one now treats empty thought without real existence as a being, nothing stands in the way of saying: the conception posits and contains its opposite and thus negates itself; everything that *negates* itself – because it must be *thought* of together – is that which *exists* together, intertwined.

First of all, therefore, according to the laws of logic, every conception is just as much its own negation and the positing of its opposite, and the latter in turn is its own negation and the positing of the former – *dialectical moment*. However, this does not directly express either of the two opposite conceptions; on the contrary, what it directly expresses is that it be it itself, and not its opposite – *abstract* moment – only the contemplative thinker finds this reversal in it. According to Hegel, a third conception is therefore necessary, which directly expresses this negation of self and positing in opposition to self. Becoming, for example, *immediately* announces that nothingness negates itself and posits being, and vice versa, that being negates itself and posits nothingness (for where there is becoming there is not yet being, but during that period, still nothing). This third is thus the unity of both, which already exists outside of it, but first *appears* in it, *posits itself as such and announces itself*. It is no longer mere negation, like the dialectical moment, but a positing; the mutual transition itself is posited here as the truth of both – *the speculative or positive rational moment*. According to the requirements of the system, this must also be the case with the analysis of the first two; because otherwise philosophy, in its methodological progression, could not find there to be such a connection between the two, and even less, of what sort.[52] In this speculative moment as well, we are not referring to a conception or thing in which the two opposites *exist*, but only in which

[52] *Encyclopädie*, §. 88.1.

they both have to be thought, which presupposes the conception of both, e.g., punishment contains law and crime in itself, and therefore is their unity posited as such.

Outline of the System

In such manner does Hegel's system progress. Namely, this third conception, which was obtained from the first by connecting with the contradiction contained in it, must now as this third itself contain a contradiction, negate itself and lead to a new unifying conception, until finally there come about all the determinations of thought, the universe, nature, man with all his faculties, functions, connections, the events of history as they really happened, in short everything that is, and that is thought of; which then demonstrates that all of this is already contained in the conception of pure being, cannot not be, if only that conception is, and must necessarily be found as it really is, if one only analyzes that empty conception according to the eternally constant laws of thought (dialectic).[53]

First of all, the epitome or totality of the pure determinations of thought is unfolded in this way, which however – according to the basic assertion of the system – are the actual and sole essence of things – *logic*. Logic therefore includes not only what were previously presented (especially with Kant) as forms of thought (categories), i.e., as the means of human (subjective) understanding (quality, quantity, modality, etc.), but everything that underlies the nature of the real external world, albeit stripped of anything concrete, real, e.g., life, gender distinction (strangely enough, in pure logic a gender distinction for nature!), knowing, willing, the good (a will, a good, prior to personality and subjectivity!). Furthermore, then, logic does not depict the rules of human (subjective) thinking, but rather the relations of thought which things bear in themselves, the types of the world, from which, however, the world emerged by itself without the help of an act, or if one wishes to so express it, by the rules according to which God (pure impersonal thought) thinks, the thinking of which forms (or rather is) the world. For this reason, the determinations "concept,"

---

[53] "In this way the system of concepts has to be formed and to be completed in an unstoppable, pure way, that takes nothing from outside." "Einleitung" to the *Wissenschaft der Logik,* p. XX.

"judgment," "conclusion" do not appear here as functions of the human spirit (this is only a subordinate moment), but as supreme world relations. Because of this character, Hegel also describes his logic as an *objective* logic by contrast with the subjective logic that existed from Aristotle down to him. In particular, the "*concept*" is the center of the whole system; it is in Hegel's worldview roughly what God is in the Christian. This "concept," which effects all things and events, is not (as one would otherwise vulgarly think) the concept of an object that precedes it; on the contrary, it is from it that the object first emerges; it exists prior to all objects, as a pure category relation. It is the totality of pure determinations of thought and (by virtue of that dialectical law of non-contradiction) at the same time the necessity that these pure determinations of thought have to be realized externally in particular things. This is why there is also the unity of the universal and the particular. In terms of the viewpoint as a whole, this necessity is the very cause and the innermost center of the world. Together with this necessary-realization-in-an-object, it is the *idea*.

This entirety of the determinations of thought, which as such are *intertwined* with each other, demands according to the laws of dialectic that they be of opposing character, namely *separated* in *space and time* – this is *nature*. All of nature is therefore nothing other than the reprint of those determinations of thought in this external field. Therefore: it is "the idea in its otherness." It is not, say, reality that constitutes the specific character of nature in contrast to pure thought, for this pure thought is supposed to be real, indeed the actual reality; rather, it is merely the separation-from-each-other in space and time that constitutes it. From nature, thought (idea) returns to itself as spirit, first of all human (speculative moment of logic and nature). Spirit (personality) is the unity of the idea (that totality of thought determinations) and nature. Namely, in nature the idea has become external, has negated itself as idea (since it is a separation-from-each-other), retains its natural existence as spirit (human being), but in turn negates the same by being able, as idea, to abstract itself from all natural existence by means of man's thoughts, whereby man can prescind even his own natural existence. It is not self-consciousness as such, which is in every act as totality, which as primordial existence cannot be explained from another – it is not this then that Hegel considers to be the essence of personality or spirit, but the possibility of abstraction; and the culmination, the supreme mark of personality is therefore the possibility of suicide.

Spirit itself, however, immediately again goes through dialectical development. First of all, it is the spirit of the individual, *subjective* spirit, personality, the I, which has the world and other personalities over against it, as an opposite, because it excludes, and which is why Hegel calls it "abstract" personality, in the sense of the "abstract" moment of dialectic; then the opposite of that, spirit expressed in overall human existence (the social institutions and the epochs of world history) – *objective* spirit; and the unity of both: the inclusion of this objective spirit (thought expressed in institutions and history) in the human (subjective) spirit – *absolute* spirit. This final realization of the spirit has three stages: the incorporation of the thoughts and feelings on which, thus, the world is based – *art* and *religion* – and finally the absorption of the same in thought itself – *philosophy*. In art and religion, because of prejudice in the material and subjectivity, the true nature of the unfolding God has not yet been recognized. For what the religious sentiment worships is really nothing else than this architecture of determinations of reason which are depicted in nature, law, and the state; but in its limitation it dresses the same with quite different conceptions, such as the person of God, love, providence. Only in philosophy is this eliminated and logic recognized as the true God. The highest realization of God *in Himself* [an sich] is therefore the state and its gradual development, the history of the world; the highest realization of God *for Himself* [für sich], i.e., where He comes to self-understanding, recognizes the law according to which He has become all of this without realizing it (thus only substantially), is philosophy. It is the end and the goal of creation.

Hereby has God, the All-Being, been completed. From this the entire thought-complex becomes clear. It is not empty being, with which science had to begin methodically, which is the actual principium, but rather this (impersonal) world spirit, universal being, which is expressed in world history and recognizes itself in philosophy; and dialectic is its own law and essence, according to which it is all of this, from the emptiest imagination (nothingness) to the fullness of the world, and yet in all moments the same All-Being, which is "spirit that remains with itself." The living motive of the system is none other than to eliminate the personal otherworldly God and to make the world comprehensible in itself, without God. The power of which the poet sings[54]:

[54] Goethe, *Faust: A Dramatic Poem,* p. 22.

In the tides of life,
In the storm of action,
I am tossed up and down,
I drift hither and thither.
Birth and grave,
An eternal sea,
A changeful weaving,
A glowing life—

... this power, which is nothing in itself, but consists only in eternal birth and eternal return, is to be made comprehensible. Schelling, who aspired to the same, understood it as a process of potencies; absolute indifference is for him God, who then unfolds in these two demiurgic forces and thus gives birth to the world as real and ideal, gravity and light. But there is always something left that cannot be understood, cannot be solved in terms of thought, the "dark ground" that does not get incorporated. That is why Hegel considers this power to be purely logical. So he takes all the general determinations that he abstracts from the existing world (quantity, quality, mechanism, chemistry, life, gender, organism, knowledge, willing, etc.) and clumps them together as a "concept" or "idea," which is now the center and union of the universe, from which the corporeal and spiritual world emanate and in which they are taken up again, and in such manner that the emanation, like the retraction, are themselves only a logical progression.

Innermost Motive of the System; Origin of Its Logical Theory

From here, the innermost origin of Hegel's dialectic becomes clear. Schelling returned to Spinoza's basic view: God is the universal, the world substance, world reason, albeit not as a rigid substance but rather as an eternal process. Accordingly, God (the universal) is not outside of things, does not have a separate existence in Himself; only by being things, is He. Conversely, however, particular things have no actual being either, but are only the process of world reason, i.e., a constant positing and negating – (flow) – of universal being. God is only as the things, things are only as God. The universal is the particular, the particular is the universal.[55] All individual existence and life then appear as a negation, namely as the negation and limitation of the universal substance (the world soul, world life), which in turn gets negated, must return to it. The pain in all individual life is precisely the robbery that it commits against universal life, and reconciliation is precisely its return to this, its cessation as an individual life. The personal creative God not only posits His creatures but also preserves them; for Him they are positive, for He does not require their abolition in order to be. The pantheistic God has His being only in things; in order not to lose it to them, He must take it from them again; they are a negative for Him, He can only grant them the existence of a moment (moment used in its double meaning), no enduring existence, otherwise they are, and God has ceased to be.

This is Hegel's basic view, the belief from which he proceeds. But it is his job to make it comprehensible and to present it as something necessary. He does not find this accomplished by Schelling; he finds that Schelling accepted it too arbitrarily and immediately. In Schelling's case it is an immediate vision, in which the All-Being negates itself in the particular, and negating itself, returns to itself – the union of universal and particular. For all of this, Schelling has no proof except precisely the vision of the universe itself, which he invokes – no analysis, no logical deduction. This is what Hegel's well-known saying refers to: with Schelling, spirit "appears to have been shot out of a gun." For this reason, Hegel sets himself the task: the same result should result logically as a necessary one, it should not be laid down as an axiom or made dependent on a special gift of immediate philosophical vision, but should be obtained scientifically. To this end, he gives the Spinozist-Schellingian worldview a method, i.e., he invents *a*

---

[55] For Schelling, therefore, the statement put forward by Spinoza also applies: "omnis determinatio est negatio," every determination, every particular is limited, but God must be unlimited. The particular things as the determinations of God are in this respect really a limitation of God; but for all of them, they are again and again negated in the universal, are only appearances, products of the process. Since only the universal, which goes through the world-forming process, is the permanent, the real, it is determined and limited in itself, and yet it is the infinite, unlimited. This is called (especially later on, with Hegel) *positive* infinity. By contrast with the *negative* or "*bad*" infinity, which only prevents the finite (or finitude) from the start and denies it, positive infinity instead develops the finite, but takes it back forever into itself.

new logic, opposed to the previous one, upon which it is to be grounded. This and nothing else is his *dialectic*. Until then, logic was based on the *principle of non-contradiction*, i.e., the exclusion of the opposite. From this follows the very opposite of that view: the universal is not the particular, the particular is not the universal, the ideal is not the real, God is not the things, the things are not God. That is why the reverse must hold true; true logic must rather be based on the *principle of the unity of opposites*. In order that, as that worldview asserts, the universal world substance itself be particular things and be able to take them back in itself, albeit as posited, the logical law must not be anything other than that every conception (every logical one) is at the same time its opposite, and a third, in which it negates this opposite in itself. Hegel's dialectic was obviously not found in a logical way, for along this path it would not have occurred to anyone to claim that precisely the contradiction is the truth; it is driven by the pantheistic worldview in its Schellingian iteration, which Hegel found ready-made; it has no other motivation than to make comprehensible how the All-Being is at the same time the particular, the infinite is at the same time the finite, in short how the impersonal (in itself indeterminate) world power can be things without ceasing to be itself. From this motive Hegel found his dialectic, and in this worldview, which for him was established beforehand, he found its certainty. But once he contrived it for this purpose, it naturally immediately became an independent, supreme logical law, for it must be such if it is to support that world view as the true logic; and so he uses it not only for that basic relationship of the world-conjuncture, but also for everything particular; it becomes the all-determining method of his system, so that no result is now considered scientifically discovered and recognized in its truth which did not result in this dialectical way.[56]

Accordingly, it may also be clear how futile it is to attempt to establish in Hegel's philosophy the premise of a personal transcendent God, or to eliminate the denial of such a God. The meaning of individual passages comes up for discussion here, and Hegel was very careful in expressing himself on this point. Yet the whole system has no other meaning than to make the world comprehensible without a transcendent God; and the core of the system, the peculiar dialectical

---

[56] Cf. Hegel, *Vorlesungen über die Geschichte der Philosophie* [Lectures on the History of Philosophy], vol. III, pp. 662, 683.

method, was invented solely for this purpose, and becomes pointless when a personal God is smuggled into it, given that the universal (God) is not His opposite, is not things, but is completely independent of them, never automatically passing over into them; the infinite is not the finite but lies beyond it, etc.

Even if the dialectic was invented only to justify the Spinozist-Schellingian worldview, it does change that significantly: the pantheistic character remains the same, but the inner relation of world-forming power and its structures becomes different. By undertaking to logically deduce Schelling's basic view, thereby dissolving it into purely conceptual determinations, Hegel removed the real element in it. According to Schelling, the principle of the world is originally both real and ideal, and from the outset the universe has its center only in the unity of nature and thought; indeed, the real appears as the first (*prius*), which is then transfigured into the ideal. With Hegel, on the other hand, the principle of the world is mere thought, and it is precisely this mere thought that is the center of the universe. According to Schelling, the effectiveness of this principle is real, it is the interwoven action of the potencies, while according to Hegel, it is merely logical. With Schelling, things arise when thought overcomes a real power in matter; with Hegel, when a logical law is implemented. Schelling's system is based only on the identity of those distinct opposites, the unity of world power and its individuation, the unity of nature and spirit, while Hegel's system is based on the abstract doctrine that opposites are one after all.

With Hegel, therefore, rationalism has reached its limit and been finalized. For a start, only thought remains as a principle for him, indeed as the only reality; there is no real world recognized beyond it, as with Kant; no thinking subject, as with Fichte; and no original real nature of the absolute, as with Schelling. Furthermore, in the earlier systems, this thinking itself is already manifold, the individual determinations of which do not turn and follow from something else by necessity. One might ask, for example, why do I have not only the determination of quality, but also that of quantity, of limit, of becoming, of one, of many? If thought wishes to abstract completely from everything from which it can abstract, it must also be abstracted not only from the person of the thinker, but even from its own *specific* categories; for it would still be possible for thought to exist that did not have this or that category (e.g. dimension, shape, appearance, one or the other); therefore none of them is necessary *a priori* to thought. If it frees itself of all content in this manner, completely hollows itself out, only one thing remains: its *pure function*, by which it is thought, e.g., differentiation (opposing itself) and connection. Hegel's dialectical movement contains nothing else; these two abstractions of thought activity, opposition and connection, are the principle with which he begins the system and builds it up, without any other means. Because one cannot say that with him someone or something moved in this form of differentiation and unification and in this manner created the world: not the idea, complete pure thought, because this itself is first formed by it – perhaps empty being or nothingness? So it is obviously the empty movement itself that does everything, and instead of saying "logic is God," Hegel should more correctly have said, "the logical law of the three moments is God." In the entire system, everything has the appearance of logical necessity; chance, unreasonableness itself are only necessary = reasonable forms of reason; according to the law of opposites, necessary thought must also oppose itself as a coincidence and unreason. The entire universe appears here to be made from determinations of thought – without any other ingredient and just so that any and every thing can be resolved into the emptiest thought determination of being. This is the finalization of the systematic construction and the complete feasibility of the definition demanded by rationalism.[57] Hegel does protest against all definitions, but in fact only because of the form they were given by others, and because of their incompleteness; he must acknowledge the correctness of the definition which brings any concept or thing back to nothing through the dialectical movement, in accordance with the rigor of a mathematical equation, as for example in this definition of injustice:

Injustice [Unrecht]=dialectical moment (opposing movement) of law [Recht]
Law=speculative moment (connecting movement) of the will of the individual and substance

Will=	Individual=	Substance=
speculative moment of feeling and thought	speculative moment of logic and nature	being

etc., until finally pure being appears again in all columns. Everything is then

[57] See Book III, Part I [*The Rise and Fall of Natural Law,* pp. 75–89].

broken down into its elements, all the way down to being and the determinations: dialectical and speculative moment, which are themselves the simple elements – that is the definition.[58]

Like no other, Hegel is faithful to the rationalist task and never violates the canon. But this also shows how the requirement of rationalism inevitably leads the infinite richness of life to appear to be the eternal return of one and the same form of thought. This system is therefore also the most prejudiced by subjectivity; of all treatments, it is the most artificial, even though it claims objectivity, i.e., impartiality of method, as anyone who but opens a book from this school must be convinced of. Hegel says of himself with enormous gravity, that he is only following the matter and its own development, and so should at least sometimes be understood by those who do not know his method, since the matter itself is not completely foreign to those who are otherwise intelligent and educated. But because Hegel in fact ignores the essence of things and only places his subjective scheme in them, it is natural that someone who does not know this scheme does not understand anything about what has been said; on the other hand, anyone who knows the scheme, often learns nothing new, but only does the business of someone who decrypts a letter of known content in ciphers by knowing the key. To conceal this monotony and inner lack of life, the presentation usually applies the most exaggerated terms, attributing everything which is due only to the living, to the unconscious, to abstractions, with emotion, praise, blame, even indignation – a manner which naturally gives rise to the most revolting distortions among Hegel's students.

---

[58] A Christian philosophy would, of course, have to attribute everything to the will of God. But the self-conscious Creator would appear first, rather than empty being. And then, God's will is such that He can desire one thing here, another there, while the law of the dialectical movement is always the same.

Chapter 2: Hegel's Legal Philosophy

Its Basic Character; Delimitation of Its Object

It is obvious that the character of legal philosophy must be completely different with Hegel than it was in the period from Grotius to Kant. The question used to be: what should one choose in order to do what is right, assuming that one can accomplish the higher will through one's own activity, whereby, in order to accomplish that will, one must try to ascertain it by reflection. With Hegel, on the other hand, the god realizes himself in his logical movement. Nobody should be concerned that the right thing is done; the only purpose of knowledge is to see what happens regardless; knowledge follows rather than precedes an action, which thereby becomes an unfree action. What *should* be (the rational, the necessary), *is;* to understand it as something necessary is the only task. This is the viewpoint which objective rationalism must have, as already shown in Spinoza's representation above. This is expressed in the famous dictum: "What is rational is real, and what is real is rational."

The area covered by Hegel's *Grundlinien der Philosophie des Rechts* [Elements of the Philosophy of Law] is not, as the name suggests, law and the state alone, but the entire moral universe: law, morality, state, world history. What is common to this area is acting individuals bringing a necessity of thought (determinations of reason) into existence.

The Entire Ethical Sphere: Abstract Law, Morality, Ethics

Just as the universe emerges in the first place from *subject-less thought*, i.e., that which is neither the thought of man nor of God, but thought pure and simple, the pure determinations of thought found in our minds; in the same way, this ethical universe also emerges from the *subject-less will*, not the human will as in Rousseau, not the divine as in the Christian viewpoint, but from the will pure and simple, the pure moments of will as found in all wills, from the will as a concept. Accordingly, law, morality, the state, all ethical regulations and institutions, have no other reason and purpose than to realize this subject-less, impersonal will, and no other content than the pure (formal) moments that can be found in all wills and from which the concept of will is abstracted. The period from Grotius until this point builds law on the will of the individual; Hegel builds it on what he calls the objective will. But this is not really objective will;

it is not the actual will of a higher power over man; rather, it is nothing else than the abstraction of his own will. So the mechanism of will is broken down into its moments, and this is to result in the construction of the ethical world. Hegel's procedure is no more than to show this mechanism (formalism) of the will in the treatment of the will of the individual, i.e., by abstracting from our decisions, and then immediately to transfer what has been found here to ethical institutions as a parallel or analogy.

If we observe the will by prescinding all specific decisions, i.e., the *act of will pure and simple,* what is found in every decision, it contains, according to Hegel, the following moments, which anyone can test against his own consciousness.

1. The I, abstracted from any possible content, posits itself as pure I, as an absolute possibility, absolute ability – moment of universality. (It should not be overlooked that by the I, Hegel does not yet mean the I of an individual, full self-consciousness, but the concept, the impersonal world power, which here posits itself in the individual as absolute ability, as still entirely content-less possibility.)

2. This universal indeterminate I posits a determinate content, object, over against itself, i.e., drive, inclination, purpose, principle – moment of particularization. However, this is by no means the I choosing some such, but that such content and subject is presented to it; it is challenged to make a certain decision, and this is portrayed (because based not on the individual I, but the pantheistic All-I) as an act, a positing of the I itself.

3. It decides. This is the unity of those two moments; for the I, in grasping the particular decision (selecting the *specific* from among the infinite possibilities), is at the same time aware that it itself is always that *universal* ability. With the decision, the All-I (the concept) has posited itself as an individual, as the I of the decision-maker. (As if that universal ability was not already an ability of the individual).[59]

---

[59] Cf. vol. II, Book I [*Philosophical Presuppositions*], §. 39, p. 117. The essence of freedom, "concrete freedom," consists according to Hegel in the unfolding of these three will moments. We would call this abstract freedom. To wit, Hegel abstracts entirely from the question of what causes A. to make the definite decision M., B. to make the definite decision N. For him, concrete freedom is "willing" in general (the formalism of the will).

Through these functions, however, the concept of the will is merely realized as the will of a human being, as a subjective act of will, and therefore only as the uniform form for a varied and random content of innumerable such acts of will, good and bad. But the concept of the will [Begriff des Willens] has to be realized purely as will-concept [Willensbegriff], in a permanent objective existence, so that these three functions, of which it is made, are at the same time its content, indeed its only content.

This is done through the construction of the ethical order, which breaks down into the three moments: *law* (*abstract right*) or the right of personality, i.e., property and contract; then *morality*, i.e., the moral demands on individual persons (well-being, happiness, charity, the good as an end and as a motivating force); finally *ethical life*, which Hegel understands to mean the permanent bonds and orders of the human community: family, civil society, the state, and the progression of world history in terms of its own inner law. These three great relations of the ethical world (law, morality, and ethics in this sense) are nothing else in their innermost essence and content than those three moments of the will function. Namely, in abstract law, property, the moment of mere ability, of the universal, is still completely indeterminate because property is nothing other than being able to undertake anything, to will and to pursue nothing definite, but rather the absolute empty possibility (just like the I before it is proffered any invitation to act); that is why Hegel does not recognize utility or satisfaction as an essential element of ownership, because that would already be a definite purpose, but only ability. Morality realizes the second moment, in which the will (i.e., the subject-less will as a world power) sets an object or content against itself (as above, inclination, drive, etc., so here utility, well-being, happiness), but not yet as decided, but merely as demand, therefore here as ought. The existence of the requirement, not its fulfillment, corresponds exactly to that second moment of the concept of will, and the essence of morality is therefore simply the ought and the "coincidence" of fulfillment. It is the call to do something in particular in the face of that indeterminate ability to do anything and to be determinate on nothing. Ethics [Sittlichkeit], i.e., the social institutions, is the realization of the third moment; here the will (always the subject-less will as world power) does not merely oppose to itself the particular content (as I) as a requirement, but actually makes a decision; because family, civil society, and state are not just requirements and goals, but are existing institutions, always real existences. These are the ethical determinations that have become "nature," an external existence, an "existing world." The essence of these institutions is therefore not the fulfillment of their higher requirements (free devotion and sacrifice), but their existence independent of the choice of the individual.

This is Hegel's basic view of the construction of the ethical world. But into these three spheres, which he establishes in this manner, he interweaves another thread of development. Law (in that broader sense, or the ethical world) is namely substantial will (law of thought, conceptual necessity), which comes into existence through subjective will (the people). These three spheres therefore express not just the way in which the concept of will is explained as a function of decision, but also the way in which it is explained as a relation of substantial and subjective will. They contain the unity (indeterminacy) of the substantial and the subjective will – then the division or opposition thereof – finally the positing thereof as differentiated and yet unified.

In abstract law (private law) consists the unity, undifferentiation thereof. For here initially, the substantial will (law [das Gesetz]) only wants what the subjective will wants. What the individual wants with regard to his limbs, his property, his claims – this is therefore also the lawful. The ethic here confirms the will of the individual, which only wills on the behalf of the individual, and excludes everything else.

Morality is the diremption of the substantial and the subjective will. The ethic here requires the subjective will to yield, and the requirement stands as an external (not-I) over against the individual. Morality is therefore the opposite of law; for the general, the necessary, and the will of the individual are united in the latter, but opposed in the former. Crime indeed is already a contradiction of law, but not so completely as morality is (*sic*); for with crime it is merely *one* single will that opposes the general will, but with morality it is the *concept* of the individual will itself which emerges as the opposite of the general will. Therefore, with crime the contrast between law and the individual is accidental, while with morality it is conceptual. That is why law is also morality; for I (according to dialectical law) cannot have the notion of the unity of those two moments (substantial and subjective will) without at the same time excluding their opposition, and therefore conceiving of it; and this opposition, as has been shown, is not otherwise conceivable than in the concept of morality.

Ethics (family, state, etc.) are the differentiation between those two moments, and at the same time their union. Family and state are demands on the individual and at the same time the satisfaction and protection thereof (both duty and right); they stand over against the individual as an ethical structure external to them, and yet are only realized by them, and in them; they are only the totality of individuals. Individuals already pertain to the concept of the state and the family, and on the other hand they recognize that their innermost essence is not themselves as persons, but rather substance, impersonal thought, logical necessity – this is the state.[60] In the state, therefore, the law is likewise choice, i.e., dependent on people's voluntary compliance, and yet it has an existence independent of their choice, namely, it always continues as a rule whether or not they transgress it. Ethical life [Sittlichkeit] is thus the highest moment of the ethic, and is no longer mere task, but is already fulfilled. What ought and what is, here coincide.

Construction of World History

The same logical process that forms that foundation of the ethical world is necessarily repeated at every stage. Thus (abstract) law is its opposite, injustice and crime, and the unity of law and its opposite is punishment. Ethical life is the family; its opposite is several families, civil society; and the unity of the same is the state. The state initially posits itself directly as a state – *internal constitution*; it immediately posits itself over against other states and in relation to them – *external state law*; finally, it posits itself as a unity of the state and the many other states (i.e., as all states, all national spirits) – *world spirit*. This in turn unfolds its epochs in the dialectical process – that is *world history*. This is how four world empires emerge: The first is the oriental, the substantial stage from which only superhuman will (God, religion) rules, and the human being (subjective will) merges into it entirely without any rights; but the former itself lacks any true content and any realization in this world. The Greek Empire is the next step in the division. Here the subjective will has already separated from the substantial will into own existence and entitlement, but yet completely devoted to

[60] *Encyclopädie*, §. 514. Of course, only the philosopher has this awareness of being substance, as clear knowledge; but everyone is imbued with it, since their sense of having to obey is nothing other than this consciousness.

this existence, everywhere referring only to it; this is the ideality, the rhythm of Greek life. The Roman Empire is the complete division of the substantial and subjective will, in that the patricians (an oriental priestly caste), representing the substantial will, merely sanctify the given religion and caste constitution as supreme, in total insensitivity to the people and their needs, while the plebeians simply assert their subjective human needs and rights, regardless of a higher bond. As a result, both moments become spiritless, and their ultimate separation and opposition in Roman history is the pain of the world, which requires reconciliation in Christianity. (Hence, it is not the opposition of what we ought to do and what we want to do, which runs through the history of all peoples, it is not sin and its consequences, death and so on, which demands reconciliation, but the opposition of those two moments, an objective legal order and subjective entitlement as contained in the Roman constitution and history.) The Jews are the people prepared for this reconciliation, and it is provided when Christ as God-man unites the two moments of the substantive and the subjective. The idea of Christianity or this reconciliation, however, is objectively realized only in the fourth, the Germanic Empire. Here the higher objectivity of the state and the constitution, with their well-developed architecture of rational determinations on the one hand and the highest subjective freedom and entitlement on the other, have come to full unity, which finds its final completion in modern (constitutional) political development. (So here lies the realization of Christianity, in the construction of the social world, and not in the sanctification of the Christian and the Christian community, the promises of the future world, the transcendent kingdom of God.)

Construction of Constitutional Monarchy

As far as the state constitution in particular is concerned, dialectical development leads from the concept of power to constitutional monarchy. First of all, power has the moment of universality (to issue rules) – legislative power; then the moment of particularity (to mediate these rules and to execute them in particular concrete circumstances) – governmental authority; finally the unity of both – princely power, in which both are centered. The princely power should not provide any sort of content to the laws or measures taken, but only the final, formal decision (yea or nay! the dotting of the i); it in turn therefore represents the third moment in the concept of the will, the decision which has already been preceded by the content (drive, inclination) as another moment and in which the will is posited as individual I. That is why it must also pertain to an individual I, a personality, subjectivity (monarchs). The government as subsumption is discharged by several, namely, civil servants. Legislative power is discharged by the prince, as the absolutely decisive power; and at the same time by the estates, so that what in itself is of general import, is necessary, can at the same time be seen as general for itself, i.e., that of which the multitude (the "many") is conscious. This subjective moment is a determination of the idea developed into totality; herein lies the necessity of the estates-oriented constitution.

Chapter 3: Logical Examination of Hegel's Doctrine

The nerve and the secret of the Hegelian system is dialectic. It forms the context in which everything in it manifests itself; it is the only path of real knowledge; what is not known in this dialectical development is not known in its truth; indeed, this is the way in which the real production of things takes place. The question of the truth of Hegel's doctrine is therefore simply based on the question as to whether or not this dialectical law is really the true logical law, whether or not it really is the world-producing and world-preserving power.

It is by no means true that a conception includes or posits its opposite in itself. To exclude, or to involve as excluded, is not to posit, and therefore it cannot be said that the conception is at the same time its opposite, or that it postulates the (real) existence thereof. Thus the infinite is never the finite, and the existence of the infinite does not postulate that there is also the finite. So pure being, even if it is not definite being, is never nothing, it is always specifically a position, even if the emptiest, and requires filling, and therefore is not the eternal opposite and the bare opposite of anything. But even the connection of opposing conceptions, by which they, at least in thought, mutually condition each other through mutual exclusion, applies only to contradictory [kontradiktorischen] opposites, not to contrary ones [konträren]. If it can be said of being and nothingness, finite and infinite, right and wrong, that they mutually postulate themselves as conceptions, the same cannot be said of logic and nature, of law (entitlement) and morality (ought). If, e.g., I imagine thought (spaceless and timeless logical relations), this conception does not at all compel me to think of a physical world at the same time.

Indeterminacy of Hegel's Dialectic in Itself

But the greatest logical weakness of this dialectic is its utter vagueness. For the terms "opposite" and "unity" in which it moves are used and applied in a wide variety of understandings. The opposite which it claims every conception (or thing) postulates is sometimes the contradictory, sometimes the contrary, sometimes just a different example. For example, the finite postulates its contradictory opposite, the infinite, whereas the family only requires other families or the majority of families; the transition from the finite to the infinite is based on the fact that with the one, one also has to think of the other, while the transition from pure being to nothingness is based on the fact that one has as little benefit from pure being (in terms of result, utility) as from nothing. Likewise, the unity of the two opposites (speculative moment) is sometimes of the kind that both are only thought of in a third, sometimes that they are actually connected in such, sometimes that the one annihilates the other. Thus, for example, becoming as a unity of being and nothingness negates nothingness in favor of being, which only then is to arise; punishment as a unity of law and crime abolishes crime in favor of the law, which is to be restored; on the other hand, princely power as the unity of legislative and governing power preserves them both, and the world spirit (world history) as unity of the various states and various national spirits negates them one after the other. The reproach with which Hegel reproaches his opponents,[61] that they stop at an abstraction of unity instead of thinking of a specific manner of unity, is no less true of himself. The unity of opposites (dialectical moment) consists only in the fact that the one involves the thoughts of the other, *regardless of what sort*, and the immediate appearance and operation of this unity (speculative moment) consists only in the fact that in a third, both need to be thought of together, *regardless of what relation* it might be.[62] How could such a chameleon of logical law contain the true logic? Above all, a logical law which is to be the supreme and at the same time the sole cause of things, should necessarily be firmly and sharply determined within itself. Otherwise the whole world is based on the coincidence of whether the law is understood in one sense or another.

The motive behind Hegel's dialectic provides sufficient explanation for this indeterminacy. As has been shown, it was first conducted to support the Spinoza-Schelling worldview, hence to deduce the identity of the universal and the particular, the ideal and the real; for this very purpose, however, in order for it to be regarded as a logical law, it had to go much further, namely to assert the identity of the opposition *per se*, and to derive all results from it. In this way

---

[61] *Encyclopädie*, §. 573.

[62] "Everyone has a conception of becoming and will admit that it is *a* conception; furthermore, that if one analyzes it, the determination of being, but also of the absolutely other of *being, nothingness*, is contained therein; furthermore, that these two determinations are undivided in this *one* idea; so that becoming is therefore the unity of being and nothingness." *Encyclopädie,* 2nd ed., p. 103 [§. 88.3].

Hegel is forced to understand this law of the unity of opposites in the most varied and vague way, so as to be able to incorporate all of the concepts and things into the same.

Fraudulent Acquisition of Its Results

Accordingly, if this dialectic is a delusion in itself, it is no less so in relation to its results. In this finalization of rationalism, its incapacity is also most evident. Nothing results from this bare movement of opposing and connecting, unless that which is opposite, with which a connection has to be made, is not already given somewhere else. Because it was demonstrated that the lines which abstraction is able to draw on its own are unable to express fulfilled, bodily life, Hegel now, by means of his postulate of the opposite, also draws lines transversely. But the living source can as little be molded into a network of threads than into a simple series. Nature, for example, is for Hegel the idea (pure thought) in the form of its being-another. Now nature is surely another than pure thought, and in case it is really just thought, it is thought in a form other than its own; therefore, it is its opposite. But the opposite of pure thought still is not nature; the latter includes *specific* being-another, that by which nature is *this* nature, and it is not contained in the concept of pure thought, neither in that of temporality and spatiality, nor of atemporality and aspatiality; but is completely independent, and from it dialectic, having first received it, then goes and delimits the category of the opposite of thought, for in fact, dialectic could never have derived nature from this category. All definite existence is therefore neither logically postulated by its opposite, nor is it *merely* the opposite of this other. The same thing with man, who according to Hegel is the unity of nature and logic, in whom nature and the determinations of thought are inseparably linked. Apart from these two, the concept of man, if one analyzes it, does not exist; but the system of thought determinations and nature connected to one another into a unity, still for that reason (as Hegel concludes) does not = human. One will not yet discover what man is from these two and the necessity of bringing them together. That which is specific to man, through which he is – self-consciousness, personality – is something besides the preceding data and the dialectical rule. Nature, spirit and everything of that sort is therefore not found in the "pure course that takes in nothing from outside," as is claimed.

Unfitness for the Reciprocal Action of Things

The first step of the system, "becoming," was taken in this way. Becoming is not just a thought relation common to being and nothingness; it is a peculiar movement and positive activity, of which nothing in the conception of those two is to be found. However, such a connection in a third is not logically necessary at all. I could halt at empty being and nothingness, keep observing how they mutually negate each other, and always keep saying that they are the same – what is the point of a third? The third moment is only logically necessary because there happens to be becoming, because there happen to be people, and because the logical development is dashed if it does not suit reality. That in this way a new positive content is introduced by means of its relation to the initial or already present determinations, even though such content does not result from this relation, is not contained in it, and cannot be found from it, that is, that such is given to be a product of the dialectical movement, which that movement was unable itself to *produce*, but merely placed *side by side* in terms of its scheme: this is the sophistry of this system. It is the above-mentioned sophistry of rationalism in general, only in a particular form. Fraudulent acquisition is always more difficult to prove in the later stage than in the earlier, because there is a larger stock of such false gains from which the new one has to be distinguished. Such an ever-expanding usurpation of thoughts and realities creates the work that flabbergasts: thought, from its emptiest beginnings, works up to formations in which there is talk of splendor and glory, of will and act, feeling and love.

According to this dialectical law, everything is to arise by the negation of the negation; that is the secret of creation.[63] But the negation of the negation will never be able to produce anything unless preceded by an authentic position which was first negated; and empty being-nothingness is not such a position. To have its negation and to negate that negation, is the liberation and exaltation of all existence; but it presupposes existence. Faith is stronger after overcoming doubt, the freshness of life more joyful after surviving illness. But what could faith be after overcoming doubt if it had not itself been something before? If it not only needed doubt to be elevated, but even to exist? If the original position (a truly real, fulfilled existence) voluntarily posits its negation and overcomes it

---

[63] *Encyclopädie*, §. 82.

and produces a new one with creative power: then a world is formed. But should the synthesis be such that its product is necessarily given with the foregoing, i.e., should it also be analysis, then its product is always – nothing.

If, accordingly, Hegel's dialectic is not able, as it claims, to engender real existences, it is not in the least able to engender the interaction of these existences in the real world. For wherever a law of thought, such as here the dialectic, is said to be positively productive, inflexibility is inevitable; things can only be considered in the direction that the logical train demands; the wealth of relationships which every living thing has on all sides, by which it interpenetrates and is interpenetrated, is lost to science. This inflexibility prevents it from shedding light on the immediate connection between what was produced later in the intermediate stages with what was produced earlier, or whether there is any connection at all between them. How in particular is the following to be seen: in the earlier phase, there is the relationship between cause and effect, the necessary causal nexus of events;[64] in the later one, all events appear as the logical consequences of the course of world history. How is it that the logical and the causal connection yield the same product? For example, the concept of beauty requires that the Greeks, as representatives of it, fragment into manifold tribes;[65] how is it that propagation of the forefathers, and the migrations determined by external events and needs, according to the law of cause and effect likewise proper in itself, have brought forth this diversity of tribes precisely in this nation? Or, with regard to the French Revolution, which had to occur because of the will-moments which were logically contained it – if we go back and calculate how in terms of the causal nexus of all previous events, all motives of the individuals, all accidental events – how it is that here too the calculation lines up exactly? Why does it not transpire that either an unloaded shotgun goes off to satisfy the logical consequence, or conversely, that an Orange,[66] whom the idea would have shot, remains alive because the powder got damp? What is it that gives the logical process command over the causal nexus?

One could now try to maintain this dialectic simply by considering it as the

---

[64] *Encyclopädie,* §. 153.

[65] *Grundlinien der Philosophie des Rechts,* §. 356.

[66] [A reference to William the Silent, Prince of Orange, who was assassinated by pistol in 1584.]

form of the world, the content of which is given to arise elsewhere. The only question then would be: if the dialectic did not make things, what did make them? and as long as this is not answered, it could not even be decided whether it is the true form. On the contrary, if things are not made *by* it, there is no reason to assume that they were made *in accordance with it.* The true system of the world, however, would have to show how the lower stages are contained and connected in each higher stage; but it would still regard this higher one as a new creation, not just a product of the lower one according to the necessary logical rule. Neither would it acknowledge a sequence of steps in Hegel's manner in which, as in military rank, one concept follows the other; instead, the most varied of activities, a connecting on all sides, where every string strikes a thousand strings. However, Hegel's assertion of his dialectic is not that modest. His system is based on it being not just the form of the world, but the only cause of its content; and if there is any content that does not necessarily have to be what it is now by virtue of the dialectical movement itself, he would have to give up his doctrine.

Its Application to Legal Philosophy

The fraudulent acquisition which encumbers the dialectical method generally, naturally also affects its entire implementation of natural law; for the latter takes no step without the former. It is untrue that an institution demands the existence of its opposite, and that what is issued as the unity of opposites is at best not only this but something outside of it that is not affected by the course of the system. For example, the family, which contains the arrangement of the relation of reproduction, even conceding everything else, is yet something other than the mere product of the concepts of unity and the opposition of ethical necessity and individual will; otherwise, this relation of reproduction would have to be contained in those factors. But it is these concepts alone which must result in the systematic development of the essence of the family, and must form it completely. As with the previous version of natural law, in which everything that is supposed to follow – be it because it is specifically desired, or because reality demands it – is proven by the fact that it does not contradict itself, so also with Hegel's natural law, because the function of opposing and connecting occurs in it. In truth, however, the entire content of previous natural law gained by virtue of its own merits is "that which contradicts itself does not exist"; while

Hegel's is "there are things that contradict each other, and they are connected." To speak, in the former case, of what specifically does not contradict itself, or in the latter case, of what things exist which contradict themselves – neither has the means to do so. But if something specific is to be deduced where in actuality nothing specific can be deduced, then of course what is deduced depends on one's predilection. Therefore, arbitrariness prevails even more in Hegel's natural law than in the previous natural law. Hegel reproaches Kant for the fact that communal property can just as well be inferred from his merely formal law as can private property, but the same applies even more to Hegel's formal movement. Why, for example, is injustice and crime the dialectical moment of law, instead of another's right; on the other hand, why is the dialectical moment of family, of state, not non-family, non-state, but several families, other states? It would be perfectly in accordance with the dialectical method to substitute the following instead of the progression which Hegel chose: The opposite of the state is the unstate, i.e., a *band of robbers.* This would have demonstrated the necessity of this concept and of this matter in the world order, and that is indeed essential; for the moment of crime as the opposite of law does not contain this rational architecture of crime. But now the speculative moment [the synthesis] has to be sought for the state and the gang of robbers, and as such, what presents itself is the *predatory state.* The predatory state cannot be thought of without these two concepts; in its thought the thoughts of the state and the gang of robbers play inexorably into one another, they always pass over from one to the other. The predatory state is therefore the unity of state and gang, and thus the truth of both, just as punishment with Hegel is the unity of law and crime, and thus the truth of both.

Particular Logical Shortcomings of Legal Philosophy

So the entire deduction of natural law is based partly on that ambiguous tendency of the dialectical law, partly on the fraudulent acquisition of the results. But it still has its particular logical shortcomings. To begin with, one factor is the same, the superhuman will, the purest abstraction, the naked negation of the human. In itself it has no content; it only receives such after there is something human which it can negate. This superhuman will is therefore in one moment a mere requirement, in another an institute, in a third an event, in a fourth the idea of the person of God and the like, etc., and yet it is always the same, namely, it always has the criterion: not to be human and yet to have a relation with human beings. Furthermore, the construction of the ethical world, which Hegel carries out from the analogy to the three moments of the act of will, does not correspond in any way to this. For in the act of will, the I, which is conscious of being able to do anything, is also *the same* as that which directly makes the decision; in the construction of the ethical world, on the other hand, the universal ability, which is supposed to be realized in the right of personality (property), is an ability of the individual, and the decision (the realization), which should be realized in ethical life (family and state), is in any case a decision of substantial will. Nor do the individual moments correspond. For example, the universal ability in the act of will is actually unlimited, indeterminate, objectless; whereas the (abstract) right of the person or of property is an ability only within certain limits and in relation to a certain object.

No Distinction between Reality and Mere Thought

The fraudulent acquisition of real results separates Hegel from the entire rationalistic development. But what is peculiar to him is that the logical does not appear as a mere means, as it does in the vulgarly rationalistic view, but as the thing itself, as the actual essence; as a result, what is actually real is necessarily denied reality. This falsehood of treating what is merely thought of as something actually existing, runs through the system as a whole as well as in particulars, and constitutes its peculiar character, which is also the reason why most people do not understand it; because a sound and sincere sense has no inkling of this way of thinking.[67] Because of this, nothingness, the lack of all reality, appears here to be a reality, like being; it is an involved, acting person, indeed, a world-generating potency. Creation does not just start from nothing (*terminus a quo*); rather, nothing is itself the motion-initiating drive (*causa per quod*).

The negative determination is richer than the positive, because it contains the positive and something besides, namely, its negation.[68] Freedom of the will

---

[67] This character of Hegel's philosophy reminds us of Baron Münchhausen's post horn, which blew its own notes [see Rudolph Erich Raspe, *The Surprising Adventures of Baron Munchausen,* ch. 7].

[68] In the "Einleitung" to the *Wissenschaft der Logik,* p. XX, Hegel declares this even of

consists in the fact that in the decision, what has been decided is posited as thought at the same time as its opposite (the possibility of everything else); the real power of the decision, that I can choose between A and B in a specific case, is left out of consideration; whether my decision is effected by chance, by a law outside of me, or merely by me is not even investigated; it is enough that while the one thing occurs, all other possible things are thought of alongside it. So there is always the possibility of the other as thought, even if, because of, e.g., predestination, it should be impossible for such truly to come into existence – and that is freedom.[69]

Those remarkable, indeed incredible transitions by which the system progresses stem from this. Indeed, the most varied and even contrary things are presented as the mutually complementary stages of the world-forming process, in terms of their kinship in some such specific logical relation that achieves nothing less than the exhaustion of their essence. Thus, for example, the death of the individual forms the transition from *life* to *cognition* [Erkennen],[70] for in the death of the individual the universal (the genus) has already taken the particular back into itself; but this takes place to an even greater degree in cognition

---

the combination of two into a third, e.g., punishment is richer than the law. For the same reason, however, he will have to maintain this about immediate negation.

[69] *Grundlinien der Philosophie des Rechts,* §. 5ff., in particular §. 15, note. Hereby Hegel only gains the empty idea of an impersonal, substantial will, a will that does not want, but is only will. If, in any institution, a certain meaning (as if willed) is formed, and if, according to the nature of the institution, there is no actual possibility for its existence or this meaning to be negated by man, although such a possibility must yet of necessity be thought of along with it, then this is a substantial will. That is to say, here all the requisites are present which Hegel attaches to the will: a specific realized content and the possibility of another, provided by imagination. The peculiarity of the will, the will itself, and the real choice, which that being cannot have, is not even required. The state, for example, has a certain meaning. So someone must have willed it. Not man, of course; nor the personal God, for He does not exist. Hence, impersonal thought. But impersonal thought, one would think, could not have willed this, because it itself has no choice. However, according to Hegel, choice does not pertain to the will; what does pertain to the will is the existence of the thought of the possibility of the other.

[70] *Encyclopädie*, 3rd ed., pp. 395, 66 [§§. 222, 30].

(thinking) where the universal (the rule of thought) not only takes back a particular existence into itself, but the particular existence as such (the object), the universal. That is why life in nature, death in nature, and cognition form the systematic progression. In the same way, the *proof* forms the transition from cognizing to willing;[71] for in the proof the mind does not accept the object as something that is directly given, but as something necessary, thus brought about by thought (that is, subjective activity). In willing, however, the object is finally accomplished only through subjective activity (i.e., through thought). That is why cognition, proof, willing form the systematic progression. In the same way, as already explained above, crime is the transition from law to morality. Although it is usually believed that crime is much further from morality than from law, this shows that it is actually much closer, even bordering on that; for in crime, the individual will already set itself, as opposite, over against the substantial will, the law, which it now does fully in morality, since here, in terms of concept, a requirement is in conflict with something that ought to be done.

As well, as has already been shown above, there lies in this annihilation of all true reality the root of the self-deception apart from which his dialectic would have proved impossible from the outset.

For this reason, however, Hegel does not merely say what is untrue, as did the earlier rationalists; rather he absolutely destroys all truth; his doctrine not only gives reality to non-being, but denies it to all being. The dialectical law, namely, is the sole content of the system, it is carried out by creation, supposedly *generating* it, but in fact coming upon it and *destroying* it. Everything that exists, nature, history, art, religion, is strung together according to such a scheme; each is denied the truth in terms of the particular thing that it is, and only the abstract relation – in which it forms an opposite of another or combines in itself the conception of two others – is declared to be the truth of it. In this way, all reality is positively and consistently eliminated. Hegel therefore never justifiably arrives at a real world. His dialectic moves from pure thinking to nature, because the former has to negate itself and posit its opposite. Reality, independence and causality cannot now be what is characteristic of this opposition, that is, of nature, because all this was already granted to pure thought itself. All that

---

[71] *Encyclopädie*, 3rd ed., p. 405 [§. 190].

remains is temporality and spatiality.[72] But what can determine that this temporal and spatial nature be accepted as a truly existing, real one, and not merely one that is thought in terms of time and space, as in dreams we also have nature extended in time and space, which, while it lacks what is essential to nature – reality – still it contains all the requisites of Hegel's nature. Hegel's objective idealism is no less a mere dream world than is Fichte's subjective idealism, but beyond that, it has no dreamer.

So no ethical institute is granted the right to be itself, to have existence for the sake of its own content; only its one-sided, external relationship with another, its schematic relation according to that dialectic, gives it existence and meaning. For Hegel, morality cannot have its essence and purpose in its commandments being *fulfilled,* but rather that they exist as *tasks.* The family, the state, have their meaning only in this: God beforehand posited Himself as will, then as ought, and now a third is dialectically necessary, in which both must be thought of. The figure that emerges when one does not consider law, morality, and the state in their entire fulfilled existence, but only in the one abstract relationship by which in law a conformity of the ethic with my will, in morality an opposition, and in the state both (although by no means in the same relationship) must be thought of – this figure is the sole cause of their existence, and their content should only be determined by such. Similarly, another philosophy holds the numerical relationships in which things oppose each other to be the cause and the innermost essence of them. In this manner, one might assume that only the various figures which, recent discoveries tell us, are formed by the vibrations of sounding bodies, are the real meaning of a great piece of music. It follows as a matter of course that all those who consider the institutions and events themselves to be something, and take upon themselves the responsibility of investigating their particular nature, and therefore do not busy themselves with the empty game merely to discover those categories in them – for example, Savigny, Neander – all those are poorly appreciated by this school. It should not be denied that such logical figures as well as numerical relations really run through the institutions and events of the ethical world. But the beauty of creation is that every production fulfills innumerable aspects at the same time, and what is new and freely created takes its place alongside what is given in a

[72] *Encyclopädie,* §. 247.

recurring course, as if inevitable. Art follows this example, which is why free poetry progresses in a regular rhythm. But who wants to derive the content of poetry from meter and rhyme? And the rhythm of the world wishes to be more elevated, richer than the figure of the three moments, or of the Tetras. One cannot assume that the artist, who alone possesses the true mastery of his material, is content with such drab monotony.

Chapter 4: Real Examination of Hegel's Doctrine

Demise of Personality and Freedom

If one examines Hegel's teaching on the real side, i.e., to what extent it satisfies the innermost requirements, the immediately known convictions, and the deepest longing of the human heart, the verdict at all points will lead back to the one center of decision: *in the pantheistic system, personality and freedom perish*. Substantial thinking is the beginning and the end, the alpha and omega, while personality is only a way station, only the means to bring that impersonal to its existence, to its distinguishing itself from itself. The individual and his satisfaction is therefore nowhere a lasting moment, a final purpose; it is only posited in order to return to the substance. Accordingly, the happiness of the people and the pursuit of their well-being are regarded as a subordinate moment, as that which is not yet truly moral; immortality is given up; on the contrary, the idea of life is realized and is freed precisely through the death of the individual.[73] (But nobody wants to accept the continued existence of the universal, the world, to which we belong as part, as his own immortality.) Freedom is not where the individual can choose, but where he cannot choose, where a rule is implemented without his will; the law of thought, not people, should be free (i.e., its implementation not be dependent on people). It is not people who act in history, as our previous historians thought, but the logical law of the three

[73] "In *death*, the genus proves to be the power over the immediate individual. But hereby the *idea of life* has *freed itself*, not only from some particular immediate *this*, but from the first immediacy of life in general; *it* comes hereby to *itself*, to its truth; herewith it comes into existence as *free genus* for itself. The death of the (merely immediate) individual particularity is the emergence of the spirit." *Encyclopädie*, 3rd ed., p. 395 [§. 221, addendum]. This is said in relation to life in general, not specifically about human life; but precisely because it applies to life in general in terms of its thought, it must also apply to human life. Moreover, the same assertion, especially with regard to man, refers particularly to "*abstract* personality." Because this means: if I know myself as I, and the All as another (opposite) of me, I (or rather the world power that posits itself as my I) am in the untrue moment, I therefore have to be negated as I, I must be my other, the All outside of me, and not as something like sentiment of devotion, but in terms of existence (the world power enters into the moment to negate me again as I).

moments. The corrupt intentions and motives of apparently acting people do not diminish their luster, if only what is required by this law is carried out through them.

Therefore, those who regard such subjective stains as stains are called psychological valets (most of them, of course, rightly), apparently to protect human greatness, but in fact to deny it; although man is treated as conscious being, he is also treated as an organ of the logical process, who does not act on the basis of his own determination.[74] It is not man who knows himself in the family, the state, in philosophy, in God, and the living God in him; rather, the system of thought determinations, the thought of the family, the state, and the like, knows itself in people; one might say, the mirror views itself in man. The purpose of legal institutions is not to satisfy personality, be it human or divine, but on the contrary, to abolish it; reason posited people in order to be able to negate them again, so as to give itself content. Here it is not at all the act which fulfills the ethic, but mere existence, by being expressed in institutions and rules that do not know themselves, that are violated by people, but which in general continue to exist as rules and institutions. "Substantial" ethical life is higher than personal and actual ethical life, that is, the expression of thoughts and laws in the involuntary action (achieved through coercion or threat of coercion) of people is higher than the inwardly good and sanctified will, and the voluntary act, of people. The worst state is therefore a more elevated phenomenon than the most accomplished man, for its concept contains a richer development of the conceptions of the universal and the particular. That the logical law of the three moments (the god in his intension) now also spreads out everything it contains, and that we finally know (philosophy) that the entire fullness of the forms is nothing but that law, or more precisely, that the law itself knows this about itself – this is the final goal of things. Hegel's doctrine tells the hungry and thirsty when they feed and refresh themselves: "The world spirit does not want your refreshment!" It says to the lover, the enthusiast, the devout: "The world spirit does not want your feeling, your exaltation, your happiness! Rather, in these processes and sensations the movement of opposing and connecting is expressed in the most varied and developed way, and this is what they ought to be about, this is their truth!"

---

[74] *Grundlinien der Philosophie des Rechts,* p. 121 [§. 124].

It is true that we Many are only truly what we are for the One. But this One is God; what He is, is determinate, is true in Himself beforehand, and for Him we are something true and permanent. According to Hegel, though, this One is empty indeterminacy. It itself is nothing, and we are nothing for it but its untruth; in the end, for it to realize that this is the case is its only purpose.

Although personality seems to have great significance in this system, it is a necessary moment in the development of the world law, and Christianity itself is praised for having secured the right of individuality. A personality that exists only through a logical process and therefore ultimately only for it, does not really exist as a personality. For this reason, it is not aimed at the real, specific personality, at me and you and him, but at personality *in abstracto*, which is an eternal moment, like the thought of the universal itself. This is realized as long as there are people; even if the individuals and the sexes there die, it never dies. The many people in the state have their right to be represented, which is why representative constitutions are rationally necessary; but not so that A and B and C, all who really live there, are represented, but so that the category of plurality has its external organ. The fact that we often do not maintain our right in the state is not an imperfection of our states. Yes, our right is guaranteed to us *in abstracto*; the recognition of the right of the individual is expressed in the standing laws and delineated by the exercise of the law and the avowal thereof; the rationality of our states therefore leaves nothing to be desired. The relation between A and B in the matter of X is only a random one, and just or unjust treatment in such a matter cannot depend on it; on the contrary, it is even rationally necessary that reason should also be random, like its opposite, so that *not* every case is decided justly. Aristotle raised the question as to whether good laws or good rulers are better. His investigation is guided by the yardstick of better decision-making in individual relations; his goal is thus the particular case. But for Hegel, this question already disappears; for nothing depends on what is in it for the specific relations and people involved.

The dissonance that cuts through the world in only too real a manner, here appears merely to be something abstract, and finds its solution in abstraction as well. Not that we, specific people, in certain cases want something else than we should, as the apostle says, "I do not do what I wish, but that which I hate, I do," that all existence points to a state of perfection, which it struggles vainly to achieve in the sweat of its brow – this is not the dissonance of the ethical order, according to Hegel. Rather, it is that the will and the ought exist at all – that there are two such conceptions. How can reason, this indefinite One, be will and also ought, and yet must be both, since it is everything? This dissonance is due to the fact that we are separated from God, and our will and aspiration is different than His. But with Hegel this contradiction of act becomes one of logic: a person, a personality exists, and yet reason (God) is impersonal universal thought. As a member of this school expressly put it: that an I exists, is sin.

Just as this philosophy finds contradiction where it does not exist, namely in the fact that there are various conceptions, so it also finds solution where it is not, in the fact that the various conceptions can be combined into a third. All of humanity is waiting for the restoration of the condition in which human and divine existence are in harmony. As Christians, we have the confidence that the day of perfect redemption will come. Then our nature will be purified, such that we will not want anything we should not want, and we will be allowed to do everything we want. Just as we are born of God in terms of our nature, we will also be from Him in terms of our actions, in will and deed. This is the condition the occurrence of which can be doubted by anyone who does not have faith, but which he must nevertheless recognize as the only true solution. In Hegel, on the other hand, the unity of God (impersonal thought) and of man, of ought and of will, again lies in the fact that some new concept is found in which all these must necessarily be thought of, whereby the one passes over in the other. The concept of the state is inconceivable without willing, ought, permission, without the thought of something universally necessary and of individual persons, and none of these conceptions is conceivable in terms of its concept without the other; in this manner, the state is the solution to the contradictions. That individual people often want something completely different than the state wants, that those people have a great deal of want, may, and ought left over which is not fulfilled and determined by the state, is of no importance; it is enough that there is an institution in which conception all of these other conceptions necessarily present themselves. The mere fact that I am part of creation and that therefore it pertains to my concept as I pertain to it, is no consolation for the fact that I suffer, get sick, and die. So even if reason, by making itself into the logical construction of the state, contains people as a necessary material, this is no reconciliation of the pain that comes from the fact that the existence of people differs from the one that rules them eternally (which in truth is not the state), or even for the fact that their wishes and desires often and typically differ from this rational construction, the state. No human heart which knows what it wants and does not consider the "vanity of a particular knowledge" to exceed the blessedness desired by all, will be put at ease by this solution. If, therefore, Hegel boasts that he no longer considers that universally desired redemption to be something otherworldly, but instead has made it this-worldly, has drawn it into the present, then one can only concede that if he were right, he would have robbed us of the prospect of coming salvation, but by no means that he prepared us for a present one, or even showed us one.

Pantheism

From the start, Hegel was accused of *pantheism*; for his part, he never stopped declaring that this accusation was unfounded, even nonsensical.[75] The assault is so often claimed and so often denied that repetition of it already seems tasteless; but that would leave this philosophy to hold the field, while it for its part seems to overlook those who make this claim against it, and those who do make this claim seem to have misunderstood it. It is therefore necessary to examine both what is meant by the allegation and what is meant by the rebuttal. The reproach does not in any way touch on Hegel's explanation that there is nothing but God, that all things are from Him and in Him; the more one is a believer, the more likely he is to concede this. Rather, the reproach applies to the impersonality of God: the criticism does not refer to the claim in philosophical systems that God is the All, but rather, that He is *only* the All. They do distinguish God from things; the substance as such is not the modalities; the concept of the universal is in each thing, but things are not the concept of the universal. However, God is separated from His modalities only by abstraction: in terms of fact and reality, no existence outside of them is left to Him. The philosopher distinguishes Him from the world, but He does not distinguish

---

[75] *Encyclopädie,* §. 50 und §. 573. I already gave these explanations about the pantheism of Hegelian doctrine and its position vis-à-vis Christianity in the first edition of this book, during Hegel's lifetime, before the publication of his philosophy of religion. Through the latter, it has become generally known and recognized that, according to Hegel, God only comes to consciousness in man. I only found confirmation in the later published works of that which was already entirely clear to me from the earlier works.

Himself from it, He is conscious of nothing: "here I am God, without being a specific creature," since He is not conscious of Himself *as* God at all. Hegel allows this reproach to be lodged to a degree against the earlier pantheists, namely Spinoza, but not against his own system, because the former stand by the determination of God as substance, while he leads God up to spirit. In this manner Hegel believes that he has saved God's personality and has eliminated the accusation of pantheism. But this spirit, which is the final stage of God, is personal only insofar as it is the finite spirit, the consciousness of people. According to Hegel, the personality of God consists in the fact that personal beings are among the All of things that are God.

This fact also shows that this is where the dreaded consequences of pantheism really crop up. The God who is them all, but is nothing outside of them all, is just as well evil. Therefore, in this system crime and sin are moments that necessarily arise and just as necessarily must be negated, not in any other way than as nature, indeed as law, morality, even religion. As perishable, they are all necessarily also crime; as enduring, they are all untrue, even religion. Only this one thing remains: the dialectical movement and the knowledge that only it, philosophy, is. Only between this and everything else, the ephemeral, is there a significant difference; otherwise there is none. Hegel would have to understand the proposition that he puts at the head of his natural law, "the real is the rational," in this completely different sense: "the just is what results from the emptiest thought determinations in terms of the law of three moments – everything that is conceivable" (at bottom, of course, nothing at all).

Relation to Christian Revelation

However, Hegel does not merely set up a pantheistic system, he also pushes to the extreme the abuse that began in philosophy prior to him, whereby his doctrine, which is directly opposed to Christianity, is passed off as an expression of Christianity and is stated with great emphasis to be in agreement therewith, so that the [supposed] truth of his doctrine is all the more fortified by the authority of public faith.

It goes without saying that for Hegel, religion cannot know how philosophy relates to it, but that philosophy alone knows how it relates to religion;[76] for

[76] *Encyclopädie,* 2nd ed., p. 520 [§. 573].

religion is only the way station, and to that degree untrue, through which God finally comes to be philosophy, where He can see what it is He actually was after with His earlier stages. So one should not be surprised if something is passed off as Christian doctrine that is unworthy of the attention of any Christian, indeed any human being, much less to be considered the content of his faith, which on the contrary gives up as an untrue form that which every believer reveres as essential. To appreciate that Hegel's view is Christian, one only need differentiate between speculative thinking and the forms of conception and the reflective understanding.[77] But there is a difference between these forms: universal thought says, I am never you, he, it. And Hegel's thought says, I am you and he, God is initially only It, then He becomes you and me, and we become all, and He is, *as* God, thereby still also only It. Hegel's philosophy thus [supposedly] has the means to grasp the most profound thing of Christianity, the Trinity.[78]

First of all, God is the essence, the substance in all existence; in this respect He is God the Father, the Creator. He is of course only the Creator in terms of the untrue conception of cause and effect in general; in truth, He is in this first moment the abstraction of the universal, of being, in which every specific existence is analytically contained. But in terms of the most appropriate translation of philosophical language into popular, this abstraction is the same as God the Father, the Creator of heaven and earth. The predicate "*almighty*" should not be taken in the ordinary sense, namely, as being able to do what He wants. Rather, the philosophical sense is: who can do what He must do, or more significantly, who must be what He is – *who can do nothing*.

The thought determination (God the Father) now demands its opposite, particularity and diversity, i.e., the whole world, nature, individual people. This is the dialectical moment of the universal substance, popularly expressed as the Begotten, the Son of God. But the universal is itself particular, the latter is analytically in the former, as with all opposites – in this consists the unity of God the Father and the Son.

That in the whole universe the conceptions of universal essence and particular definiteness are united into one in every single thing and thought, that in every being neither particularity can be thought of without universality nor vice

---

[77] *Encyclopädie,* 2nd ed., p. 518 [§. 573].

[78] *Encyclopädie,* 2nd ed., §§. 566ff.

versa; this is the unity of both, which is posited and documented as such – "the Holy Spirit," which is present in the world. This is the mystery of the Trinity, the truly intended content of the symbolic Christian narrative, now made completely plain and easy to understand. To have made it so plain is the consequence of Hegel's great discovery, the praise of which almost entirely fills the preface to his *Encyclopädie*.[79]

Hegel accuses the confessors of the revealed religion of being confessors of the unrevealed, to wit, not revealed because of their claim that one cannot know anything about God, while Hegel adheres to the revealed religion according to which God in all His moments becomes known, because he infers that God does not enviously withhold the knowledge thereof.[80] As if a Christian ever claimed not to know anything about God; as if everyone who believes the gospel revelation and hopes for a more complete revelation in the future does not also acknowledge the absence in Him of this supposed envy. The difference between faith and Hegel's philosophy is not that the former does not accept revelation but that it accepts a *voluntary* one, while Hegel accepts an *unavoidable* one. The Christian personal God, the Creator of heaven and earth, i.e., who made them and could have left them unmade, who is what He is, even without them – He who wishes to grant His creatures the highest blessedness, imparts to them His knowledge because He wishes to do so, not because He has to, and therefore does so in the manner and to the degree that He wishes to. God is therefore not unknown to the Christian; but as long as this voluntary revelation is not complete, he cannot fancy that he knows the entire world plan, that he knows the future or even the past, the causes and intentions in terms of which everything has happened – a conviction which he shares with those who are revered as zealous and thorough researchers. Nevertheless, he will have sufficient cause to praise his God as being *without* envy, for what He has already imparted to him.

With Hegel, however, revelation is necessary; it is not the act of God, but

---

[79] One might therefore ask Hegel what interest he might have in whether Tholuk is only concerned with the suffering of Christ or also with His resurrection, for what Tholuk understands by these two is for Hegel equally untrue. Or what interest can it have for him if Tholuk finds difficulties in the Christian doctrine of the Trinity? Doubt as to what Hegel means by the Trinity probably as little occurred to Tholuk as to anyone else.

[80] *Encyclopädie,* 2nd ed., p. 513 [§. 564; Stahl lists p. 492].

His nature; this god is not even there, indeed he cannot even be thought of, if he does not reveal himself. Abstract substance, whether it likes it or not, is at the same time that which has taken on all its moments and determinations, besides which it would not be "logically real"; this includes consciousness-raising in all its moments by an individual, i.e., revelation. As little as one will thank the circle area, that it is not only the total conception of the circle area but also the individual radii, the center, the periphery – as little can one thank this god for revealing himself, which is to say that he is God, if the knowledge revealed here would be worth being thankful for. Obviously, the predicate of lack of envy cannot be given to he who could not withhold his gift, who only learns that he has given it when it already has been given, namely when he has entered the moment of philosophy. For without having become the consciousness of individual human beings (to whom he grants his knowledge), this god himself does not even know what he is, nor even that he is. For a god compelled to revelation cannot withhold one jot or tittle. As one must say, he has to be what he is, therefore also, he has to *reveal* what he is. For this reason, philosophy must know everything that God is; nothing can be hidden from its perception, for what is not revealed in it – beyond which God no longer brings forward – is not. A plan of God of which it is not aware would only tautologically be a plan of God of which God is not aware, for it alone is the self-knowing God.

True Ethical and Political Results; Deficiencies Thereof

What has been exposed both by myself and by so many others since then, has demonstrated the complete untenability, both logical and real, of the Hegelian system.[81] On the other hand, Hegel scientifically and ethically did promote the knowledge of the age in extensive areas, completely independently of his system as such, by virtue of his personal mental gifts, and by means of deep and fruitful thoughts.

This applies particularly to ethics, legal philosophy and politics, for which Hegel rendered tremendous service. His objective (substantive) principle of

[81] These chapters of the second edition which are particularly intended to critique Hegel's doctrine, for the most part only collect together the arguments which were already given in full in the first edition, but which were incorporated in various places in the two previous chapters.

reason led to the recovery of the regard for the ethical power over people and institutions which that principle calls for. Family and state have their purpose in themselves; they are not merely a means for the individual (indeed, pantheistic exaggeration even sees it as their purpose to negate individuals as such), and they also have their necessity, the reason for their validity, in themselves, rather than being based on the will and contract of individuals. In this manner, Hegel victoriously fought the heresies that were widespread at that time: Kant's doctrine making the freedom of the individual and the mere consideration of the coexistence of people (maxim of coexistence) the exclusive principle of law and state, conceiving of marriage as a mere contract regulating sexual function, relegating it in all its ethical traits (prohibition of polygamy, blood disgrace, arbitrary divorce) from the legal system to mere subjective morality; Rousseau's doctrine of the sovereignty of the masses; Feuerbach's doctrine of punishment as mere psychological deterrence, that is, as a mere safeguarding of society; Beccaria's doctrine of the illegitimacy of the death penalty. In the same way, in the field of morality, Hegel showed the principle of those conceptions to be individual conviction, noble intention, empty [inhaltlose] arbitrary enthusiasm, and above all the interest of unethical genius by which great individuals stand above the other order of men, and genius bears the standard and law of its actions in itself. To all of them he opposed the ethical seriousness of the law and its objective power above all subjectivity. Even now he would oppose the deification of the flesh, the exaltation of the bond of sensation and passion over the honest, the cult of genius and all such phenomena of our time, to the same effect and with the same energy.

In particular, Hegel also significantly promoted insight into the state constitution and its elements, in particular the appreciation of constitutional monarchy. To the constitutional theory with its mechanical separation of power, he opposes the unity of state power as princely power and its organic development. No less did he combat Haller's private-legal feudalist doctrine.

The main criticism in relation to its political results is the lack of all *higher sanction* and the lack of all *historical principles.* Just as he gives up the living God and His order, he also lacks what alone can give the political truths that he really teaches their confirmation and surety. Mere logic, the concept, the laws and determinations of thought found in man do not grant holiness or power, which then binds the hearts and fills them with fear and reverence. Indeed, they do not even provide a solid result. In accordance with their mobility, which is their nature and attains its highest elevation precisely in Hegel's dialectic, they can be used just as easily everywhere for the opposite result. Thus his doctrine carries in it no guarantee at all against its being led back of itself to all the solutions of the Revolution from which he once liberated it, as experience has shown.

Furthermore, just as the human condition is based on a purely logical development of the concept and is the free act neither of God nor of man, just so does Hegel pay no attention to what comes about through an act: positive inherited right and the acquired rights based upon that right. In this, his doctrine, in itself and from the outset, stands on the same ground as the Revolution. But positive right and acquired rights do not emerge from the logos; they are the work of history, of human acts up to that point. Because of this, they have no place in his system; indeed, he has the most determined aversion to them. This explains his distaste for the English constitution, the main characteristic of which is the sacred maintenance of established law and acquired rights; likewise his distaste for Roman history, his partisanship in favor of German sovereigns as opposed to the positions and claims that stem from the [confederal] German imperial union.[82] His own constitutional ideal therefore also excludes all self-founded, self-organized, and self-asserting rights of subjects, estates, and corporations. For him, every constitution is blameworthy in which such rights exist, in which the common advantage must gradually be wrested from them and in fact issue forth from their assertion, every constitution in which there is a real power of resistance. Rather, his constitutional ideal calls for an institution by which government should be implemented from a single point with logical, mechanical consistency, whereby the substantive necessity of the state should only *apparently* be opposed by these personal (subjective) rights, without any real power of resistance, and in fact infallibly bring itself to completion by means of them.

Just as everywhere the substance posits the subjective moment only for its

---

[82] Cf. Hegel's "Über die englische Reformbill" [Concerning the English Reform Bill] and "Verhandlungen in der Versammlung der Landstände des Königreichs Würtemberg, im Jahr 1815 und 1816" [Proceedings in the Assembly of the Territorial Estates of the Kingdom of Würtemberg in the years 1815 and 1816]. Cf. also Vol. II, Book II [*Principles of Law*], §. 9.

own purpose, in order for it to take it back into itself, just so does the government as the substance of the state hold the people and the citizens only as a means of realizing itself through their (seemingly free) labor. Hegel therefore prefers the princely power and even more so the civil servants, in which he finds represented precisely that substantial necessity of state upon which this security of the state mechanism rests, in opposition to the subjective (the people). Accordingly, for him, civil servants should not only be in government, but the assemblies of the estates should also be predominantly composed of civil servants, because they have the "sense of the state," the governmental sense,[83] which is to say, they do not represent any separate personal rights, but only government activity, the substantial state as such. Indeed, even the popular representation in general is only there to ensure that the government activity, which in itself could just as well be provided by the prince and his officials, also includes the moment of subjective participation and acquisition. The other primary significance, that the representation of the people should provide a guarantee and protection for the real rights of the people and individual subjects, he not only ignores but virtually rejects. There can be no more striking similarity in form than that between Karpzov's church-constitutional doctrine and Hegel's constitutional doctrine. According to Karpzov, within the sphere of the church, the clergy has the *internal* power ("postestas interna"), i.e., to determine the content of decrees, the prince the *external* power ("potestas externa"), i.e., to provide naked sanction to these decrees, and the people have the power of approbation, although whether they also have the right of reprobation remains doubtful; at the very least, it is not assumed.[84] For Hegel, within the sphere of the state, the civil service has the internal power, by means of which the logically necessary content of the government should take precedence; the king has the external power, the merely formal decision (the yea or nay, dotting the i), and the people in their representation have the power of approbation, while rejection or resistance is doubtful, or at least the occurrence of it is never assumed.

Accordingly, it should be clear to everyone that Hegel does not push popular

[83] Hegel, *Grundlinien der Philosophie des Rechts,* §. 310; "Verhandlungen in der Versammlung der Landstände des Königreichs Würtemberg."

[84] Cf. my *Kirchenverfassung nach Lehre und Recht der Protestanten* [The Church Constitution according to the Doctrine and Law of Protestants].

freedom very far. Neither does he teach actual despotism, i.e., arbitrary government, government in terms of caprice and arbitrariness, above all under the pretext of divine authorization of the prince to such personal discretion. His desire is for reason to rule, what is objective and necessary to occur; this was the view of wise men at all times, among whom neither a Rousseau nor a Filmer can be counted. But for him this reason is logical formalism, and as far as the institution through which it is to come into existence is concerned, Hegel is predominantly on the side of rule from above as opposed to building from the bottom up and from inside. His doctrine is as little *ultraroyalist* as it is *ultraliberal*; but it is *ultra-governmental.* Everything should be accomplished through ordered (objective) power, the government, while the people accept this consciously and thereby freely; but the reverse may not also take place, whereby a work is accomplished out of the free, innermost personal drives (subjectivity) of the individual, of associations, the people, the estates, whereby the government only leads, sanctions or moderates, while the estates restrain or correct the government. He is an opponent of the free movement which emerges from the unordered and unprepared into order and clear shape, and no less the inviolable rights the holders of which must be brought into connection with the jointly beneficial, through inner conviction. All of this is the necessary result of the system as a whole, which everywhere stands only on the impersonal, substantive, logically necessary, and pushes personality (subjectivity) down into a dependent moment, in itself without content, the only purpose of which is to reflect those things.

But with all that can be criticized in Hegel's political viewpoint, he greatly purified and promoted the insight into the basic form of the moral and civil order, by promoting a higher (substantial) ethical order and by recognizing the freedom and entitlement of people in indivisible unity as its essence.

This entire point of view, through which Hegel towers so mightily over the ethics, legal philosophy, and politics antecedent to him, was obtained by Schelling; Hegel carried out what Schelling creatively instigated and had already expressed in its basic features. It is nevertheless the implementation as such, and the independent and peculiar way in which it was done, which constitutes an invaluable achievement. In this, Hegel has an advantage over Schelling in that Schelling mostly only gives general ideas and individual applications that he just presents, which seem suitable to clarify and confirm his ideas; his ideas flash back and forth, while Hegel develops these ideas through the entire object. Often, one is unsure as to how Schelling's doctrine comports with the most important objects of science and social life (e.g. logic, constitutional monarchy), but with Hegel one is almost always sure. This gives him a huge advantage not only in dissemination, but also in greater circumspection and assurance.

Separation of the System from its Results

One should not find a contradiction in the fact that Hegel's system is combatted as absolutely unsustainable, and yet its great achievements are recognized in many scientific fields, particularly in legal philosophy. It is a mere prejudice to think that everything which proceeds from a consistent thinker also stands in indissolubly coherent relation. As little as the facts of nature and of social life, which are presented in Hegel's system just as if they arose solely from it, really are a product of the system and stand and fall with it, just as little is this the case with the better ethical and political appreciation of such facts which Hegel draws from the more mature educated opinion [Bildung] of his time, as well as from his own reasonable judgment. This is confirmed by the fact that similar appreciation is also found among other contemporaries who are not at all devoted to Hegel's system. Hegel's mighty predecessor, who took the decisive step in philosophy from subjectivism to the recognition of objectivity, ought not to be considered in this respect because with him the ideas that characterize the change are embedded in the context of a philosophical system which is the least akin to it. But did not Schleiermacher, Savigny, Walter bring to light the ethical meaning of marriage at the same time as Hegel, as opposed to the earlier profane view? Was the objective power of the state by contrast with the doctrine of the state contract and popular sovereignty, the significance of punishment as justice and not as mere protection of society, not also asserted by Burke, Adam Müller and other writers of the Counter-Revolution, was not the substantial unity of the people also asserted by the Historical School? Did not the more intelligent appreciation of world history, especially of the Greek and Roman epochs, not come from the new school of philology, and regarding the Romans in particular, from Niebuhr? I emphasize this, not to infringe on Hegel's merit, as he is and remains one of the movers and shakers of the times and its turning point, but only to prove that all of this has neither its origin in Hegel's dialectic or other philosophical principles, nor is it conditioned by his pantheistic worldview. I emphasize this to justify my opposition to Hegel's philosophical system as an absolutely erroneous and pernicious doctrine, and despite many and weighty moral and political truths, I reject Hegel as one of its first or foremost representatives.

It is precisely the period of philosophy under Schelling and Hegel which has given rise to vacillation, ambiguity, and general confusion. A deep, rich spirit runs through this development, one which destroyed the shallow forms of the older manner of thinking from the ground up, but which is not easy and convenient to grasp, like the other was. It may therefore be permissible once again to gain an overview of what this has brought about.

The great motive that inspires this development is objectivity and historicity. Hereby was recognized the untruth of abstraction which can only grasp the static, the unchanging. The task of philosophy was thus expanded from the reason of man to the universe. Earlier philosophy opposed the world to reason, tacitly assuming chance in history and nature. Here everything appears as the intelligent work of the one world power, so that science is not science unless it knows itself also in this universal context, unless it takes up each into itself as something made by that power. The pragmatic view, which regards events as the work of arbitrary human intentions, and the subjective-rational, which ignores them, drop out at the same time. This task of looking for meaning in what appears to us to be accidental and contingent, of considering the whole of history, the whole of creation as a great work of art, links up with the peculiarly intellectual treatment which distinguishes Schelling. It consists in striving to see everything from the center, as God Himself sees it. Hence the magical power of his presentation, hence the astonishing things in his viewpoints, the demonstration of a connection, rhythm, and an artistic meaning which, when taken from the individual point of view, of necessity must disappear. Schelling basically says of the manifestations of the world what Homer said of his heroes: "This is what they were called by men, but that is what they were called by the immortal gods."

The sense of necessary submission to something higher permeates ethics. Ethical duties, legal institutions no longer derive their significance solely from their effect on the well-being of people, but rather from their inherent splendor, i.e., from what they are for the divine spirit that created them according to its purpose. Once again there is true public law, inviolable sanctity of the authorities, and the consciousness of universally true ethical requirements that are independent of haphazard conviction.

But a perverse satisfaction destroyed the gain promised by the truth of the motive. Together with the goal that this orientation powerfully pursues, it is caught in the old bonds: it still sets the requirement for mere logical connection. In this way, that superhuman existence becomes impersonal; that this nevertheless likewise acts, that there is history, is contradictory. Hence, life and act and history must once again be lost in a rule of thought, and destruction must be sought for what should be achieved by the new turnabout. Life, freedom, personality and history become the mere products of the mechanical working out of a formula. Even the universality of science extends only to ruination, since now, being lifeless, it no longer lets life exist outside of it, but draws everything into its standstill and death. The truth whereby every new product of creation weaves preceding creations into itself, becomes the untruth that there is basically no new product, the new stage is already contained in the former and only needs to be taken from it analytically, there is no creation and no free guidance of things. If this view were to be maintained, one might doubt whether overcoming the pragmatic view could be considered a gain. For when the freedom of God is given up, it is still more comforting to see the world governed by human freedom than by laws that know nothing and want nothing. Pragmatics – coherence through action and intention – should not have been abandoned. Instead, divine pragmatics should take the place of human. Objective rationalism does not tolerate this. Hence Spinoza, in his frankness, already declares: God has no understanding and will, and, since he claims that man cannot sin against God, he carefully guards against the expression, "divine predestination," as something he does not recognize. Hegel's view is no different here; in order to prevent misconception, he should refrain from using the expression "plan of Providence" to refer to his process of history.[85] For it is precisely the peculiarity of his view that nothing is foreseen, but that everything is known only afterwards, after it has happened.

In the ethic, such unconditional submission becomes that of the empty thought form. This, itself unfree, cannot tolerate a free existence outside of itself – hence the demise of the individual. It is nowhere itself the goal; that god

---

[85] *Encyclopädie,* 2nd ed., p. 492 [§. 549].

always only wants itself, and man only for its sake. The rigidity of abstraction, which used to make man egotistical, now makes God so, if, indeed, one can subjoin that predicate of self-conscious mind to this abstraction. The ethic itself in its consummation no longer consists in free action, in an uninterrupted creative act; hence it can never become individual, and can never demand specific action. Rather, it consists in an architecture of thought determinations that bears in itself the fixed arrangements of life. Ethics is thereby in the strictest sense *materialized*. Finally, in this kingdom of thought determinations, everything that should and could be there, actually is there. For where there is the freedom that what should be does not really exist, then it is not possible for everything to be the product of a necessary process. So this state of the world must be seen as what ought to be, as the realization of all high things; the prospect of blessedness, of an exuberant glory beyond reality which cannot be made out of thought determinations, which cannot be analytically taken from being, collapses, and insight into this dry mechanism is the only compensation for its loss. In addition, there is the delusion of having solved those problems which have so far been overlooked by Providence: human freedom and its relationship to the eternal world plan, and the like; in that the process of thought, as it forms these conceptions and raises the question, is consistently held to be the solution, and the knowledge of the logical figure in which the thing appears, is consistently held to be the essence of the thing itself.

Finally, speculative philosophy makes the deepest and truest things of the natural and ethical world-conjuncture, which are completely closed to vulgar rationalism, its center: the need and the reality of a reconciliation of man with the power that is above man (the objective, substantive, and the subjective). But even of this supreme truth, it only has the shadow. Instead of the reconciliation and unification of living personalities, the divine and the human, through living action, it is content with the reconciliation of logical moments and their merely conceptually unified depiction.

Chapter 5: Hegel's School

As is well known, Hegel's school is divided into two factions. The older one adheres exactly to the master in everything, in doctrines, forms, sympathies. The newer one (the "left wing"), on the other hand, takes a completely different position. The accusation of atheism and radicalism is now being raised against it from those outside, and the members of the other faction also accuse it of apostasy from Hegel's doctrine. The reply to this is that the substance of the indictment in the main was expressed by Hegel himself, whose name is expressed with awe, and to the degree that this is not the case, it is the necessary consequence of his doctrine, which he had not yet recognized himself or had been reticent about expressing; here too, therefore, it represented only the necessary further development of Hegel's philosophy. So the question is, how does this later faction of the school relate to the master?

Shared Pantheistic World-View

Hegel's *pantheistic worldview* is entirely of a piece with his successors. The denial of the personal otherworldly God, the denial of personal continuity after death, the stripping away of the hereafter following the here and now is the center of the system. Admittedly, Hegel observes a certain delicacy; he does not announce these results with emphasis and ostentation like the disciples do; he does not wish to put all the attention on them, which would make public opinion decide between philosophical and vulgar (religious) ideas, but instead tries to divert attention from them. But regardless of this, they are found in the same potency with him as with the later followers, and indeed not hidden (*implicite*), but completely unfolded (*explicite*), clear, specific, unmistakable, self-conscious. In this main point there is no difference between Hegel and his later school. We trust that this was put beyond doubt by the overall description of the system above, and is also confirmed by these newer successors themselves, through countless individual references.

Difference of Ethical Position regarding Philosophy

But on the other hand, Hegel took a completely different *ethical position* in his philosophy than did the later faction. His entire life-orientation, just as with Schelling, ran against the principle of subjectivity, individual will or individual spirit, which wishes to determine the world and the design thereof instead of recognizing that they stand over it. Hegel therefore had a deep reverence for what is given (objectivity), for what exists prior to human reflection as a value-preserving and world-ruling institution. To comprehend it rather than to destroy it and see another put in its place, was his aspiration. He has reverence for the existing historical constitution and sovereignty. He has reverence for the immovable moral rules of human action. All this is to him the work of power which exists in itself and in its formations over human beings, even though it is only in man that it comprehends these formations and raises itself to consciousness.

This ethical motif, the core of the man Hegel, has been completely renounced by the disciples. This is the dividing line between the two, and is the evidence for the accusation of apostasy against the master. This even affects the position regarding the doctrine that they have in common with him. Hegel namely comes to pantheistic results from (supposed) scientific compulsion; he would willingly give it up with joy, if he did not at the same time have to give up the scientific insight into the world that he thought he had. The disciples, on the other hand, are drunk with joy at these results; they would sacrifice the scientific system to them if that were necessary. The system is no longer the main thing; their whole doctrine is only a dithyramb to the non-existence of God.

Different Results for Religion, Politics, and World History

Such a difference in the ethical core and the innermost life-orientation could not remain without influence on the content of the doctrine. Hegel's teaching contains a *sure objectivity*, the acknowledgement of a power and effect over man, which the disciples have given up. This holds for religion, politics, and the position vis-à-vis world history.

Certainly in Hegel's view, religion is not the working of the true God, who is outside and above the world, but the working of an (objective) world power. By contrast, it has become the confession of a part of the later school that religion is a mere *anthropological production*. Man puts his own personal qualities (sense orientation, feeling, heart) outside of himself through an act of imagination, thus forming his deity and holding his own product to be a power outside himself. So religion is a mere product of (subjective) human weakness, albeit a lawful [gesetzmäßigen] weakness residing in human organization, not the necessary expression of the (objective) world reason (idea) which in religion unfolds its own (not human) meaning and content, in terms of a certain stage. Man's prayer is not a union with this (albeit impersonal) power of the universe; it is nothing other, says Feuerbach, than a dialogue of man with himself. Accordingly, Marheineke rightly accused this teaching of losing the richness of the idea and sinking back into the triviality of the old vulgar rationalism with its psychological explanations. Of course, if religion is not the work and witness of the living God, it is ultimately a matter of indifference for general human interest whether it is the necessary exposition of an idea or the mere process of the functioning of the human heart, just as it is a matter of indifference, if my prayer does not reach the merciful God, whether I am pleading to the world substance that is unconscious of itself, or I have an edifying dialogue with myself. But it is not without significant practical consequences for the public condition. In Hegel's view, maintaining religion as a public institution is always a requirement, since it is a realization of the world spirit. In Feuerbach's view, it is the other way round: the requirement is to annihilate this mere illusion of human self-deception in general.

The state order, according to Hegel, has a prestige and a dominion over the people. It is the substantial will of the world power, which posits itself as a prince, as an official, as a body of the estates, to which the individual man and the mass of human beings are to submit, hence its struggle against popular sovereignty and revolution, the July Revolution [of 1830] no less than the Revolution of 1789. The later school turns this "general" will into the will of the people in Rousseau's style, albeit with some remnants from Hegel's construction of the state. The popular representation, which according to Hegel is only supposed to appropriate the content of legislation and administration emanating from the prince and government, so that it exists as acknowledged, becomes the main, even determining, power of legislation and administration. Along the lines of Hegel, the prince is indeed recognized as an essential member of the constitution, as the "formal head"; this is Hegel's doctrine, in which the prince does not determine the content of government himself, but rather confirms a content given elsewhere, dotting the i. But what the prince merely has to confirm, the i which he has to dot, is, according to Hegel, a necessity in itself that develops out of itself and has its representative in particular in the civil service; for the later school, it is what the masses want. Therefore they fraternize with liberalism, which Hegel combatted, and sympathize with the July Revolution, and even say that Hegel no longer grasped the historical significance of this because of the new moment it added. It was always Hegel's basic doctrine that the state is above the people; it is, on the other hand, the aspiration of the disciples that the people be above the state. For them, this is what comprises the "Protestant state," and to the degree that this is not the case, they consider it the Middle Ages.

For Hegel, world history is the objective God, substantial reason. It is the world spirit first in itself, in terms of its immanent necessity in the formations of empires, and only then becomes for itself, that is, it understands itself in philosophy. Man, philosophy, therefore never have the vocation of making history from themselves (*a priori*); the world spirit makes it; they only have the job of understanding it from out of themselves (*a priori*), to reproduce it in their thoughts. History and its product are thus everywhere given. This is the positivism that the disciples reproach, this limitation of philosophy to the mere comprehension of what has become, outside and before it. They, on the other hand, believe that philosophy, and themselves as the bearers of philosophy, are called to start the world anew and even to give shape to it, as was seen in France in the previous century, in the *siècle philosophique*, the *siècle des lumières*. According to Hegel, the world spirit is first in itself, then it becomes for itself; but the disciples demand that it be the other way round: it should first be for itself and only then in itself.

Desertion Rooted in Hegel's Own Doctrine

This relapse of the younger school into all aspirations of the old principle of subjectivity is not an accidental occurrence, it is the fault of Hegel's doctrine itself, and so was inevitable. To wit, it is due to the fact that his *objectivity is only apparent*. What he assumes to be the objective world-forming power outside of himself is nothing other than the epitome of the determinations found in his thought; in fact, it is only his own I and its product; it is therefore quite natural that his successors take other moments from this I and use them in the same way: just as he objectifies the logical categories, Feuerbach explains the anthropological properties, etc.

If Hegel had real objectivity in his system, a real power outside and above man, no such relapse would have been possible for his school. A personal transcendental God could never be dissolved into a mere psychological creation of man, but a god which consists only of human determinations can be nothing else than them. A truly objective authority in the state, which by virtue of divine sanction is above the people, could not be dissolved again into the will of the people, as could a "substantial will" which is nothing more than the moments in the concept of will. If Hegel had founded world history on divine guidance, it would never occur to his school to rebel against it in a revolutionary manner. But the logos that they made in accordance with Hegel, they possess just as well in themselves; it is nothing other than their own thought determinations. So they have it and all its means; why shouldn't they also take over its work? If man can so fully grasp the world spirit as Hegel has, if he breaks it down into its moments and sees how these, in their unfolding, had to produce history in exactly the same way and not otherwise, how should he not have the ability himself to take the place of the world spirit? What stands in the way of him consciously making world history from now on, who hitherto unconsciously made it? He thereby elevates God to a higher level, the level of conscious world production! Hegel's reverence for everything that exists objectively, which has come about apart from him, is ethically quite honorable; but it is scientifically inconsistent. If it is thought determinations that make up the world, which first come to consciousness in man, then it is the more elevated and therefore the more necessary that man bring forth history; for the god who comprehends himself is necessarily higher than the one who still creates unconsciously.

It is also remarkable that the disciples often put what Hegel sees as the main thing, his logic, *in the background*. It is inanimate, unsuited to act on the masses, to intervene in the shaping of the world. So what do they have in common with the master when they throw away the key to his system, and oppose him in such important results and positions in life? Nothing else than the pantheistic worldview and the pretension of the speculative standpoint, i.e., the pretention of insight into the absolute coherence of the world! It is evident from this that the power of Hegel's doctrine does not consist in the correctness of its logic. Rather, its power lies in the depth of the speculative problem, because even if this is not really solved and cannot be solved, the insight into the task itself is already a great advantage over other scientific standpoints; for the rest, it consists in the pantheistic worldview, which already in itself is nowadays on good terms with other circles, but which appeals in general to the orientation of the times, because it opposes religious revealed faith.

PART III: REGARDING SPECULATIVE PHILOSOPHY AND DIALECTIC

Since Fichte, philosophy has expressed its aspiration to be speculative philosophy. The outset already shows that this must be related to the active principle as first taken up by Fichte. Together with this endeavor, the high value of dialectic, which Plato represented as the most difficult and most elevated science, is once again recognized, and the Hegelian system is built exclusively on it. It is therefore possible to see which impulse actually led to it, and since this dialectic does not satisfy, to see what true speculative philosophy is, what true dialectic is, and how what is now understood to be such relates to them. But allow me to link Fichte's and Schelling's results with my applications thereof into a whole, using a thread of my own; and indeed, an examination which does not in the least have dialectic as its purpose, may also begin dialectically.

The One in the Many and the Mutable

We find absolutely no simple thing in the entire real world, no thing such that nothing more can be said about it; and yet this many is not without unity, to which it pertains. As little as such a simple thing really has being, just as little can we think of it as real; for what cannot be, is not conceivable as having being. For the same reason, multiplicity without unity is not only not real, but also inconceivable. If we tried to think of one or the other of these, we would end up with the purest nonsense. Plato concerned himself with this in his *Parmenides*. The apparent contradiction is therefore that the one must be a multiplicity, and the multiplicity must be one.

We also find change. Namely, things take on determinations at different times that cannot exist at the same time, and yet remain the same things, e.g., a person is healthy and sick, sad and happy, and is always the same person even though health and illness are mutually exclusive. Likewise with space: the same person stands in space A and space B at the same time. How is such a change and alternation conceivable? *For one thing,* one might think that the healthy is something very different than the sick, the joyful than the sad, the one in A than the one in B, and it should no longer be said that it is still the same person. *For another,* one must indeed leave one condition in order to get to the other; where is one during the time of passage from one to the other? No matter how much I divide space, I can only jump from one point to the other, just as when I pass from health to illness. Just as I find myself in space A and B at the same time, am I not absolutely split by it? So in the case of change, it is by no means an interruption in which the one ceases and the opposite begins, but God, as Socrates says in the *Phaedon*, has intertwined the ends of opposite things. And if that were not the case, the changing thing could no longer remain the same thing; but all connection between it in the previous and in the present state should cease. There is an uninterruptedness, coherence between the mutually excluding, but how is it conceivable without contradiction? Because the opposite cannot be one and the same at any point; at the point where one is, the other should no longer be; in other words, there can be no coherence! So the questions are: how can something have several determinations at the same time and still be one? And then: how can something change, i.e., take on determinations that are mutually exclusive in different times or spaces, such that the coherence between its opposite states still remains? The solution can only be that one and the same subject always remains amidst the multiplicity and change of predicates, one which is only one and never becomes another, which as subject can never change.

It is therefore necessary to seek such a subject which by its very nature is something apart from its predicates – these rigid characteristics of being – and thus is free of them. Only such, while it contains the many predicates, or assumes them one after the other, can remain unchanged as a subject, regardless of them. For if it were only its predicates, it should always become another, since these become others. But the predicates are connected in that they exist through the same subject; yet they are kept apart, since the one is not the other, but the subject alone is both. Now then, the properties of subjects can change relatively, i.e., there are countless such, some of which subjects may be free of, others not; but only one subject is absolutely free of every particular property, and that is the self-conscious, the personal. Personality is the magic of unity, which no change destroys, which can go through all possible states and still remain the same, which connects these states themselves through the unity of self-consciousness. I can do anything and become anything, and yet I do not cease being me. The only thing that I cannot become by remaining me is you and he and it; I can neither be so at the same time nor one after the other; this is the absolute contradiction. And in the case of a transition from I to you or it, if that were possible, there would not be uninterruptedness as above, but an infinite gap: where the you or it begins, the I has already ceased, and yet there is no point in which that transition could now be found; hence the transition is as little conceivable as the unity of the transitioning with its earlier being. The notion of reincarnation, or immortality without reminiscence, is already a contradiction in terms. That we can think of a transition from one state to another, the change of one thing to another, but not of a transition from one person to another, is the sure proof that it is the subject that alone connects the opposite. So it cannot be affected by the change of states, it has a determinacy apart from them that always remains the same; however, it cannot change this or give it up. This determinacy by which the person is *the* person, is not to be regarded as an attribute, because an attribute is just that which does not pertain to the person, to the subject. I, you, it are not attributes, and "I am I" is not a sentence. The person is always only a subject, while on the other hand, everything else is only a predicate; where it appears as a subject, it is personified in the particular relationship. This specificity of the person cannot be defined; not only can it not simply be broken down into rational categories, it cannot be brought into any equation at all, because nothing apart from it is equal to it; it can only be pointed out – "there it is!"

In Our Conditions

The change in our conditions and the multiplicity of the determinations falling to us simultaneously are therefore conceivable only through personality. But what about, first, the change in impersonal things, which can still remain the same regardless of that change; beyond that, how is it conceivable that several personalities, between whom there is no transition, can belong to one and the same world? It is the same way with the universe as with each individual. If this is multiple and changeable, the mutable in it must also fall to a subject that exists independently of it. If only the self-conscious is such a subject, unity in it can only be the personal God. It is inconceivable for substance to be unity; for it has no determinacy, no reality other than its modalities; unless it is those particular modalities, it does not exist. If one says: "all of these modalities are," there is no need to say: "the substance is," for only in the former case, not the latter, is anything actually said. So here all determinacy is only in the predicates, while on the subject side, nothing remains but pure, empty indeterminacy, the abstraction and negation of determinacy. Now nobody would like to say, "empty indeterminacy (Hegel's being in all existence) is animal, plant, stone and the like; consequently they are interconnected." Nor would anyone like to say: "It is always this empty indeterminacy which, remaining the same, passes from one to the other; therefore, change is comprehensible." According to such a system, then, there remains an aggregate of things which is unthinkable without unity and without which there is no unity.

In the World

It is otherwise with the assumption of the personal God. His will is the stuff of the world; just as He creates everything only out of free decision, so, since He can also leave everything uncreated and still remain God, is He a subject in the universe which is not individual things; but He is who He is, even apart from them, which thereby have their unity in Him. But each of His thoughts and intentions turns and forms a smaller one in this great unity, by combining an aggregate of determinations into one product. So even something which is not itself a personality can nevertheless be a subject free of predicates, by dint of what pertains to it; namely, it can change its determinations and still remain the same, as long as that intention remains in it. The tree can bloom and wither and still be a tree. But the seed is not the tree, nor is the tree the seed, and yet they are not different; it is the divine intention, which is already in the seed of the future tree.[86]

There is unity among various people only because they are not persons in the

---

[86] If one imagines the ideas in this way in God, the conflicting sayings of Plato about them are reconciled and justified. The ideas have produced the world and are therefore real; and yet again they are what is common to many specific things. The ideas are immutable, while the things that are modeled on them are evanescent. The ideas are the highest, they alone are what is high and truthful in all things; and yet not even the meanest, the most disgusting thing is without its idea; for there is nothing without the intention of God, who relates it to His total intention in creation. That all of this, which a living philosophy must comprise, is incomprehensible if one thinks of the idea as independent, apart from God, or above all as concepts of reason, as with Kant and Hegel – requires no further discussion here.

highest sense, as God is. Because only the Almighty, who is not bound by any determination but gives and takes them according to His will, is free in the absolute sense. But we are bound by many determinations given us by God; that is why in a derivative sense we are persons, but originally, and with reference to Him, only predicates, which He accepts according to His will and to which He gives freedom according to His will, vis-à-vis their own properties as well as themselves. He alone is the bond between people and generations. It is therefore understandable how we gradually come to consciousness and do not consider ourselves to be another person; we even consider the completely memoryless state of our initial childhood – basically the It [das Es] – to be *our existence.* It is the Creator's intention, the idea of our existence, which connects these states. But it is inconceivable that God Himself first arrived at His own consciousness; for the one who is not yet conscious of what is his, and the one who is conscious, would be beings just as separate as the I and the Thou; where their connection is, by which one can say that it is always the same God, cannot be seen. So in all of creation, as in our existence, existing diversity and change is only conceivable through a subject free of all qualities, i.e., through a personal God.

Investigation into the Essence of Unity and of the System

However, this only explains unity in the conditions of the world, not the unity peculiar to Him. The person is already a manifold: being, knowledge and the like, and yet also a unity, just like the world; it therefore includes the same contradiction. Is the personal God the only conceivable unity of the world? What is the unity in God? Empty substance being simple, this question can no longer be posed with regard to it; but the confessors of the personal God must speak of it. It is important to determine exactly *in what unity in general consists.*

In order to unite different things, it is necessary that there be something in one thing that is also in another thing, and indeed not only when it connects with the other, but in each for itself, as it exists. The concept of the animal is in the horse, in the lion, in each for itself; the notion of being is in all things; this is why there is a unity of the same. But there is no concept of a pile of stones in individual stones; therefore the pile is an aggregate, and not their unity. Nevertheless, the statue for itself is not in the limbs of the statue, the tree is not in the leaves of the tree, but regardless, the statue is the unity of its limbs, the tree the unity of leaves. Why is the pile of stones not the unity of stones, but the tree the unity of leaves, even though there is as little of the tree in the leaves as there is of the pile in the stones? Only because the notion of the whole tree, the whole statue, is in the individual leaves, in the individual limbs, and without this notion they would not be these leaves, these limbs. If we could imagine that the leaves could exist without the tree, then the tree would not be their unity. Unity of this kind, as already stated above, always presupposes an existence beyond the unified, the notion and power of which unite it; it is therefore not in itself, but an external one. But one thing is certain: that which is the unity of the diversity, must exist in each individual and not only crop up when the other is added. So it turns out that where unity really exists, the individual – since it could not be what it is without that unity – is drawn from it, not the other way around, as if unity were formed from the individuals. This is what distinguishes the system from the aggregate.

But it may be that only in some relations, the individual does not exist without that uniting [factor] – that is, unity fills only one sphere of it, not the whole; in that case, this is merely partial unity. Above all, this includes formal unity. For example, the concept of the animal is in every particular animal; but each animal also has an existence to which this general concept does not extend, as when the animal is sick, the concept of the animal is not sick. Nevertheless, in the world and in God, we are not looking for a partial unity but a continuous one. So there cannot be something that is not fulfilled by that unity – which we actually find in personality. In every one of its acts, every condition, every predicate, the whole of self-consciousness, which is its unity, is contained, and not in individual relations but through and through, hence not like the concept of the animal in individual animals. If a member of mine is sick, then I – the whole, the unity – am sick; if my power of thought is busy with something, I am busy with it. Self-consciousness, however, is in the individual limbs, states, actions of the person in a completely different way than the tree is in the leaf. This is because the tree is only a whole derived through the personality of another; it therefore can be dismembered and the consciousness of the higher still maintains unity. In particulars, it is not the whole itself but only the notion, the relation to the whole, as held by the higher. Personality, on the other hand, is the original whole; here no dismemberment is possible; in each part unity must be present not only as notion and relationship, but really, not its effect, but itself. So this unity has the self-consciousness that it is already fully in every part, in every state, in every act, and not just conceived, like the tree in the leaf, but real, not just in a relation, like the general concept in the individual things, but fulfilling the whole existence of the same. The former distinguishes internal from external unity, the latter distinguishes living from formal unity. The ultimate antithesis to the aggregate is therefore the person. It is the most consummate system, the protosystem, and there is no system but it. Every system in science, every unity in art is only externally, through the thought of another, that which the person is internally, through himself. We only strive to make everything systematic, because God is personal.

This is why external unity cannot be the highest, the beautiful higher than the good, the state more than man, and formal unity even less so. Kant was correct, that man must act systematically; yet he should act, not according to a logical consistency, but a higher consistency, in the way that we commonly express ourselves without being clearly aware as to what this higher consistency is, and why it is higher. They are considered great who put their entire existence and personality into every act; this can be found in the presence of mind, energy, serious concentration. But he who puts the innermost of his personality, the particularity of it as it is in God, into every act and every thought – though he thereby violate every logically derived system of principles, he is the most perfect, the most systematic person.

Application to the Ethic and Law

The state is also to be a unity, it is outwardly to represent what God is inwardly, the unity of personality. Hence the Platonic state, in which a living spirit is present in all members; which is why Plato everywhere implements the analogy between the justice of man and the state. Now the construction from the concept of law leads to formal unity, not to this image of the primordial system. That is why it is fair to say that Germanic law is more systematic than Roman law. Germanic law has a living unity; the aspiration of the entire nation is always active in every institution and fills it. Roman law, on the other hand, is merely formal; individual rights as far as content is concerned are torn from the state and are joined together only by abstract criteria. Formal unity, although it is the one that cannot exist for its own sake, is easier to see everywhere, and is believed to be the real one; however, as has been shown, it does not correspond to the prototype, and for this reason it never vouchsafes the satisfaction that it initially promises. It resembles the devil's gold in fairy tales, the love of which brings one to sacrifice the best he has, only to find out that it was not gold but only dust and sand.

It is a self-contradicting attempt, however, to construct the living unity, the person, from series, acts, potencies, e.g., as an activity proceeding from and returning to itself. Because then, in the outgoing activity that has not yet returned – as distinguished not timewise, but logically – there would still be no personality; it would then become a mere aggregate. True, that is, universal, all-ruling, living unity, is thus vouchsafed only by the personal God. The opponents of this have no unity in the world; if they now accuse us of having unity in the world but none in God, while the latter has an advance from the former, then both are untrue. That there is unity in the personal God has been shown here; but it can likewise be shown that in the impersonal foundation of the world, although appearing to be simple, nevertheless there still is no unity. To wit, in order to form the world from it, an impulse to particularity, a law of movement must be added to it from the very beginning; but this is something outside of it, it being merely matter. There can only be one substance, says Spinoza; but the law according to which it must assume its modalities is a second substance outside of it. Thus Hegel also begins his system with pure being and at the same time with the dialectical law. Each for itself, on the one hand substance, being, on the other hand the law of particularization, the dialectical movement and the like – each for itself is not God, and the God of all, who alone is God, is not in one or the other for Himself. If both now together form the god, they do not form him in the way that my being and my thinking together = I, but as a bunch of stones together = piles of stones. There is a force, a primordial will, which sets being and thought in motion, and without which neither the one nor the other could be. But what would be the higher thing here over being and its law, which unites them? Not will, not self-consciousness; a concept, then? But this would only come about through those two. If one can put two such things together, neither of which has in it that which forms unity, then one can do so with anything. If God reduced to the simplest can be an aggregate, the whole world can be as well. As one says, "those two together are God," one might more conveniently say, "all things together are the world." So this is the result: only personality forms a unity in the multiplicity that it takes on, because it has a determinacy independent of that multiplicity. But it is also true that only personality is a unity in itself, because the whole that it is, is really in each of the many individual things that it contains, and it is completely pervasively present in them.

The Connection between the One and the Many

One could say, however, that this only postpones the logical contradiction, rather than eliminates it. For we have here a multiplicity which is already originally a unity, and yet multiplicity and unity are contradictory concepts. It is therefore yet to be seen what kind of connection there is between the many and the one, how the former is connected with the latter, hence how the many are connected one to another. The various determinations cannot accrue to the one in such a way that it be them; the copula does not have the meaning of = ; moreover, the counterpoised determinations, being equal to the subject, should also be equal amongst themselves. But they cannot befit it in such a way that they are equal to a part of it, such as: this library is the works of Homer, Sophocles, Plato; moreover, the one would only have a joint existence by virtue of these provisions, making it an aggregate. So these determinations must have a relation to the one by which it is the same, and yet is not, that is, it can exist without being them; such a relation is only the *act*. Indeed, the subject has determinations, precisely for which reason it is, but then again is not, since it would be the same subject without this act. Act is freedom, and freedom is the innermost essence of personality. Every act, in its concept, is a creation, and creation is conceivable only as a free act. For through it the self-conscious will receives determinations which by no means already belong to its being, which are therefore something apart from it – a product. In this manner, the world is separate from God: not that it is independent of Him, or that it could be if He did not will it again and again at every moment; but by the fact that God is God without being the world, that He created it without having to produce it. The true system is not that in which multiplicity is contained in the one – logical unity – but that in which multiplicity is created by the one and controlled by it – real unity, the unity of act.

The *Republic* of Plato also pursues this unity. This is how every unbiased person imagines things; it does not occur to him that there is a contradiction in our concepts, that the one should not be able to accept the many, and the like. How does science come to discover such contradictions, which are not at all tangible to mankind? Simply by not recognizing the bond that alone links the separated, the contradictory – the act. It wishes to maintain everything in a state of rest; to dissect what each is, not to watch what such freely generates outside of itself; science wants a non-creation. So there remains only the one relation of being equal, whether in whole or in part, between the subject and the predicates. It is thus incomprehensible to it how the one can also be a multiplicity, how the contradictory can be united, the separated joined. It assumes that there is no creation, no act, no freedom, and therefore finds it necessary that creation, act, freedom be contradictions, supposedly in themselves, in truth only in their presupposition. It asserts that what it cannot find from itself, is not; but this claim is not the result of its investigation, it is the starting point.

The Capacity for Positive Knowledge

The capacity of the spirit to experience the act is *vision* [Anschauung]. This, in turn, is itself an act; it establishes a consciousness that was not yet there. Opposed to it is analytical thinking, which only examines what is already there, but which would have nothing to investigate unless this creative knowledge provided it with material; for even our own forms of thought can only be experienced through inner vision. This analytical thought, as it cannot discover its initial data from itself, cannot itself discover the subsequent data, nor the connection between them; all of this, because based on will and action, is only taught by vision. This alone is the capacity to know the truly existing, the definiteness. *It* is the knowledge before all outwardly experienced history, through which alone this history can be taken up and appreciated. *It* is the power of the mind to know *a priori,* and it has this because it is one being with God, because it is created in the great harmony of the world, as it were through sympathy with nature and events. But what the spirit knows *a priori* like this, it knows as something that is, not that has to be, with the confidence of faith, not the necessity of mathematics; and it knows this not as one thing from the other, but as total fact. This capacity is also capable of knowing future things, as is proven by men with a living spirit, and would prove itself even more if current educated opinion had not cut the connection between man and God, though which alone such things can be known. This creating power of knowing, however, is a special gift which does not already lie in the concept of knowledge, which, like any positive force, is vouchsafed more to one person than another; from this comes genius, enlightenment, the gift of divination in small and great, for itself and for the whole.

Now rationalism has conferred such power on the rules of thought which are the same everywhere. Therefore, what is known in accordance with it must be known as something necessary, for which reason the truth must be knowable and demonstrable to one person as well as to another, if only he is human. It was shown above with regard to ethics that, according to the abstract view, the good either exists or does not exist, and no increase in it is possible, just as the freedom of men, which is inferred from the concept, either exists or does not exist. If the human capacity for knowledge *in abstracto*, that is, what cannot be prescinded in thought from this capacity, extends to the knowledge of the general categories and logical laws, then every human being must be capable of all possible knowledge, and we should be able to comprehend one thing as well as the other; there can be no difference in the objects of knowledge, so that one person, for example, would require a higher power of the spirit than another, since the spirit is not at all capable of increase in this negative sense. Hence the objections to the effect that Christian doctrinal positions, such as regarding the Trinity, are absurd. That God is triune is not in any different way a logical contradiction, than that generally the one is the many, that in God there are at the same time many people, even only unconscious things, all of which nevertheless are not Him, and yet cannot exist apart from Him, or that I think of many, different or opposite things at the same time. Rationalist philosophy, if it were to make the attempt, would have to deny the latter just as well as the former. With the latter, however, it is prevented by the vision that is given to every human being, which is not the case with the former.

It is indeed everywhere the same power to produce something outside of self and yet to be it, not to allow it to be torn from itself, which makes possible the Trinity, the freedom of our will in spite of divine omnipotence, the existence of a tree as a tree (according to Schelling, the reality of the thoughts of God), our self-consciousness and unity. But the latter is the least expression of this creative power, the former the highest. If we now know every creation only through that which corresponds to our vision, which like the former is a thoroughly positive force capable of infinite enhancement, then everything depends on the degree to which we have been given the power of vision, which decides which act of divine existence we can still comprehend to some degree. And there is nothing contradictory in the fact that with the same spirit which is sufficient to contemplate the activity of our own consciousness, or even the existence of a world in God, we have no vision of how we are free and yet dependent on God's help, or how the Redeemer can be the Son of God and yet God Himself. Rationalism will have to admit this, just as it understands that, in order to know and comprehend only the most insignificant fact, its negative capacity of knowledge is insufficient, but rather that the positive capacity of vision is required, for which, once it is admitted, no limits on increase can be set on that basis.[87]

Speculative Philosophy

Already as a matter of words, *speculation* is the same as vision.[88] Hence, *speculative philosophy* is that which considers the world to be a free act of the personal God. This, then, has been the impulse of modern philosophy since Fichte.

But if abstraction insists on itself, sets itself up as the measure of things, and declares everything that it does not contain to be untrue, if it maintains that initial data, which is basically only obtained from the inner vision, and rejects everything else, thus casting vision itself as untruthful: how should it be conveyed? In sound minds, through the vision itself; for whoever is in agreement with himself as a whole believes consistently in the vision. But what of him who has given in to abstraction, and puts his trust in it? Through *dialectic!*

Dialectic; Plato, Hegel, Kant

Dialectic is talking about one thing as if it were another [Hinüber-Reden in

---

[87] The entire investigation here conducted does not in the least claim to be exhaustive. I am well aware of the new questions to which this everywhere gives rise, and I have not even indicated the boundaries for arriving at a solution, or from whence such might still be sought. The subject is too rich for me to go more deeply into it, since it does not form part of my actual occupation. It was only a matter of emphasizing the main points indicated by modern philosophy which have a decisive influence on ethics and legal philosophy.

[88] [The *Oxford English Dictionary* provides this definition: "speculate, *v.*: To observe or view mentally; to consider, examine, or reflect upon with close attention; to contemplate; to theorize upon," with the caveat, "Common in the 17th cent.; now *rare* or *Obsolete*." https://www.oed.com/view/Entry/186112, accessed March 26, 2020.]

ein Anderes]. Abstraction must be shown that with regard to what it thinks it is holding, it is on the contrary talking about something else, that is, it is contradicting itself. Hereby is that which abstraction wishes to deny, the act, taken out of the picture, and abstraction is left to go where it likes, which ever results in self-contradiction – this is what dialectic is based on. [For example:] I think the infinite. This is not my act; it therefore = me or a part of me. Now, with the same thought, I also think of the finite; in this manner, I am in the same relation to the finite. Thus the finite and the infinite must be the same. All the known fallacies turn on this, e.g., the she-dog is yours, the she-dog is a mother; ergo, the she-dog is your mother. The various meanings of the copula, which it can obtain solely through the relation of action, being active, vanish, and what remains is =, as a result of which that conclusion is correct. Just so the fallacy from the uninterruptedness of the transition (2 sheep are not a flock, are 3, 4, 5 ...?), the contradiction of which can only be alleviated by the fact that someone acting connects the opposite, who sets the sharp boundaries or else keeps it in suspense by his decision, whether determined or hesitant.

This is how the Platonic dialectic initially works with concrete objects. If one analyzes bravery and distinguishes it from fearlessness and boldness, one finds that this is only possible through their relation to virtue. So to maintain the notion of bravery, this relation must be included. If there is no relation of act, then of necessity bravery = virtue. Abstraction, therefore, although it wishes to maintain each for itself, is precisely compelled to say of different things that they are the same. In the case of such specific objects, it is now easy to prove that nothing can be kept separate. But this becomes more difficult with purely abstract concepts, and the most decisive one here is, of course, the concept of simplicity itself. If it is shown that abstraction cannot even maintain this, and through its analysis necessarily lands in another, then it is completely defeated.

This is achieved by Plato's most ingenious dialectic, which he conducts in his *Parmenides*. In doing so, he undertakes it in such a way as to refer this concept [simplicity] to existence, to underpin it with reality. As long as Parmenides asserts the one to be a mere determination of thought, he seems to be able to completely fend off the determination of the many. He is forced to introduce the latter only where he wishes to think of the one as being, as real. Now he arrives not only at the questions: where, when and how is this one? but the notion of existence itself is a second, next to it. This seems to me to be the key to

Plato's *Parmenides.* The solution to the contradiction is by no means that opposite determinations are the same: waking is sleeping, pleasure is pain, the finite is the infinite, the one is the many; but rather, that the one, being, is everything and, in acting, produces. Thus, the highest task of dialectic is to show in the pure concepts themselves the impossibility of inactive maintaining, by the contradiction that arises from it.

In this, however, it still had to achieve a consummation which is lacking to the Platonic procedure. This consummation was gained for it by Hegel, and this is his great achievement for science, which he diminishes only by putting it to wrong uses. Plato, as was demonstrated, allows abstraction to maintain the pure concepts as such; the contradiction only comes out if one relates them to reality. Yet even apart from this relating, they still contain reality – unless the free-acting person is assumed. For this maintaining a determination is itself an act, which abstraction must not make use of if it does not wish to allow free action, creation of the world, and thus its own inadequacy for knowledge. To posit being, nothingness, in thought, is something that has been done, that has happened, and that could also have been avoided. What keeps the infinite from the finite when one operates in pure abstraction is only one's own act: it gets posited, and only in this way does it exclude the infinite. Therefore, if in pure abstraction we still think correctly, this happens no differently than by personalizing this abstraction, unconsciously attaching a will and an act to it, thereby excluding the opposite. But the infinite must also be thought of in the finite; the former is in a relation to the latter that cannot be removed from the analysis of its concept. The difference in relations which action produces – and therefore necessarily the difference between positing and excluding – is now abandoned, from which follows: the finite = the infinite. Negation itself in terms of its concept is an act; if you give up action, everything that is can only be the same. On the other hand, however, the same abstraction, which is here compelled to =, intended the opposite: the finite is by no means the infinite, and if there is one, the other cannot be, because this would be a transition, a change.

Hegel shows this dialectic, through which even the pure concepts negate themselves if they are not held onto by a will, with the strictest consistency; his only mistake is that he considers it to be true, as shall be shown below. Kant's dialectic also proves what has been said here: Hegel demonstrated that the antinomies in supreme concepts, which Kant pointed out, are not eliminated by his denial of time, since they are logical contradictions. "Everything presupposes a cause unto infinity, and yet one of them has to be the first!" This will not change if I think away time; for the concept of cause and effect, or even just ground and consequent, still remains, and without time, the ground precedes and the consequent follows. Kant truly should have denied change, for then he would have solved the antinomies. But there would also be nothing left for him than the absolutely simple, which is only one determination from eternity to eternity, that is, nothingness. Thus, like Hegel although with a very different intention, he showed the contradiction in the pure categories of reason that leads one, if one pursues it, to the opposite, and yet reason intends everything to remain what it is. But the vision of living activity really solves the antinomies, e.g., the antinomy of the finite and the infinite in space.

Value of Dialectic

Certainly from childhood everyone is troubled by imagining the infinite. "Above these stars, this sky, there are again stones, again sky, again space and so on and on, where does it all end?" The incomprehensible, the contradictory comes from conceiving of the stars, the sky, space as independent, as-such, simply there. It does not bother us at all if in our thinking we think of a certain great heaven and yet can always think of an even greater one, all the way into the infinite, if we only stick to the knowledge that we *form* it within ourselves. Nor does it bother us that we ourselves are closed and limited by our being, and nevertheless are unlimited in the power to form another than ourselves, a non-determined, non-existing thing, in our thoughts. So it is confusing when we think of heaven outside of ourselves and yet infinite; for in that case the infinite, the unlimited, which consists precisely in indeterminacy, should be there, and therefore have determinacy. We will therefore undisturbedly imagine it if we think of the universe as the uninterrupted act of God – in accordance with the activity of our imagination. In that case, both behave correctly, both infinity and the finiteness of space. The former consists in the fact that God *can create* more, and more expanded, things; the latter, in that He *has created* and *maintains* a determinate, that is, a limited space. The infinity of the world is thus the possibility, the freedom, the omnipotence of God; but the finite is His decision. It is only from this living relation of freedom and determinacy that the relation of the logical determinations of finiteness and infinity can be understood; Hegel therefore takes precisely the opposite path, since he wishes to make freedom of will and decision comprehensible from these logical determinations. What Schelling already hinted at in his letter to Eschenmayer, and later explicitly stated, that true philosophy must lead to an insight into the logical conditions, rather than such an insight first producing a true philosophy, proves itself.

The self-contradiction by which that weak transition is passed off for the true one, is therefore in no way the intention of the dialectic. In fact, by pointing this out it will lead to the knowledge that such a procedure is not the proper one. It goes to work everywhere as abstraction does, as if there were no free action, and it therefore dares not expect a true result by itself; it can only expect that it will lead to nonsense, thereby proving that everything in the world exists by free action. It therefore has only a negative value, it heals by abstraction the one who is caught up in abstraction. It is, as Plato says, the medicine of the mind; but from medicine one can only demand that it alleviate the disturbance, not that it itself performs the functions. Plato is therefore wrongly reproached for the fact that his dialectic always gets stuck with the negative and achieves no positive results; that is precisely its virtue. Dialectic must prepare the way for speculation; but it itself must not, as happened with Hegel, replace speculation, or be considered such.

With his dialectic, Plato of course does not wish to refute (as might seem from my description above) the absolute and scientific abstraction of all content, prior to any knowledge thereof; but he does wish to refute the practical abstraction, which stops halfway, to which one abandons oneself who is caught up in any passing phenomenon, as if there were nothing more than this. For us, too, dialectic has this practical use besides its scientific one. It is an abstraction, for example, to be caught up in the present; therefore, dialectic has to cross over in discourse from the present into the future, as it does into the past. In doing so, it purifies judgment and aspirations, and merits consideration, in line with Plato's wish, as the art and insight that befits the wise man. This dialectical power is what comprises the value of classical education. But even here, dialectic does not invent or discover past times; it only shows the finiteness of the present. Vision, experience, tradition characterize classical antiquity, and to appropriate it in its particularity is not the place of dialectic.

Hegel's Use of Dialectic

Now Hegel has an untrue view of the world-unity, which is why his dialectic takes a wrong position, such that even what is true in it becomes untrue.

The fixed and correct point from which it proceeds is: unity in the changes of the world can only be movement; what is untrue is the abstraction that maintains everything at rest and excludes transition. But real movement, which is the free act of God, is something Hegel cannot establish according to his standpoints, for which reason he takes refuge in a logical movement, which in truth is not a movement because it shows what is generated to be immutably contained in the being of the generating, which therefore never comes out of itself. The god who is supposed to connect the multiplicity – being – has no determinacy apart from it; it is only the assemblage of individual predicates. He does not connect them by his act; hence, the only way they can befit him is a whole or partial =. Hegel cannot say: God is the same in His essence, different in His actions. Because the different things are not His actions, but His essence, that which the analysis of His concept yields. So if there are different things, then God Himself, who is all of them, is already different in His essence; in what way should He, or should things, be one? For this reason Hegel has never been able to explain to what extent opposites are one, and to what extent they are really opposed. For he says that to the abstract understanding, they are opposed, but to reason they are one. Now this cannot be regarded as an explanation of the matter, for it only signifies that Hegel calls his conception of opposition "understanding" and his conception of unity "reason." It is not shown by what right and to what extent reason, contrary to understanding, can be considered one.

Hegel negated the act. There remains to him, as with all abstraction, only the dilemma: either multiplicity is entirely disjointed, or it is one single thing. Now older systems said, "nothing is equal to its opposite." This is true; but if one does not recognize the act, it follows that "there is no unity between opposites, no unity in the world." Hegel proceeds in the opposite direction: "there is unity in the world." He does not recognize the act; it follows, then, that "the opposite is equal to itself." That is the point of falsehood of his dialectic; the non-activity, which true dialectic presupposes only in order to prove the necessity of coherence through action from the contradiction that results from it, this non-activity, is foreseen by Hegel's dialectic, because it itself believes therein. It shows on this assumption that everything flows over into its opposite, and this with evidence hitherto not perceived. It should have followed from this that the only thing that can ensure the existence of each, the only thing that can posit each, must really be the free act. But if it does not do this, then it must maintain as a permanent result what should have served to restore it from the nonsense of the prerequisite. The crisis is its curative.

Hegel made dialectic, which can only be a negative principle, which by its nature is destructive, into a positive principle; and the result can therefore only be destructive. He stops at this destruction, instead of proceeding to that alone which protects against it, the All-Preserving, who says: let there be, let there become, let there remain! According to Hegel, the negation of each conception for the sake of the other is not the final result; but what he passes off as such is nothing other than the clearly documented fact that only this mutual negation and interweaving has permanence and truth. But the conclusion, which follows from both premises, repeats the question of which, regarding those premises, Hegel is unable to answer: regarding the two, to what extent are they one, to what extent are they different? To what extent is, e.g., becoming the same as being and nothingness, to what extent is it different from them? It should be nothing but their analysis, so they must be the same as it, and yet they must not be the same as it; it should be something new.

Thus, by denying the personality of God and His free act, Hegel no longer has unity for the variety of things, for what consistently unites them; he has to assert that amongst themselves they are the same; and then he must turn around and not admit this. For this reason, his entire system is a ghostly exchange, in which the figures get entangled, get swapped, are the same and different, no one knows how. For this reason, it is eternal movement without rest, i.e., a crowding of predicates without subject. He can say of nothing, that it is; everything arises and perishes, or rather appears and disappears. The only thing that could be said to be here is non-existence, transition itself, the abstraction of movement. This is the "*spirit forever staying with itself*," which is repeatedly invoked in the progression of the system. And this eternal hunt cannot stop until it arrives where there are no more predicates, at nothingness, at the tranquility of the graveyard, as Hegel himself declares in the memorable passage with which he closes his *Phenomenology*. In recent literature there may not be two more closely related phenomena than this dialectical play of Hegel and the products of Hoffmann's poetry. Here, too, the figures play into each other, the real persons are the fantastic ones, and the fantastic persons are the real ones, and yet they can only be one or the other. They suddenly turn from one into the other; it is impossible to pin them down. An eerie power plays its game with us, and we are powerless to see through the smoke and mirrors. Plato considers dialectic to be the highest science, because it lifts the soul from the mutable to the one, the immutable. But Plato had no idea that eternal change itself should be the only unchanging thing.

It is therefore impossible to seek the unity of that which, according to Hegel's system, is the ground and the moving part of the world, because it is still the empty indeterminate, so that no subject can exist apart from the various predicates. Now one might wish to seek unity in the end rather than in the ground of this world, in what is ultimately brought about by movement, as we rightly say: the unity of all phenomena lies in God's final intention. But this does not fit the impersonal god of Hegel; for he did not have the intention in the beginning; instead, in the beginning there is unconscious law-pursuant unfolding, and only at the end is there insight into it. The end of the building, philosophy, of course now contains all the moments that preceded it, and so Hegel passes this off as the unity of the world. He can only do this, however, by generally deluding himself about the unity which science seeks, about that which distinguishes a system from an aggregate. It has been shown above that the difference is this: In the system, the one must be present as such in each part, whereas in the aggregate it is not in the individual part, but only makes its appearance when all are together. In the system, the whole precedes the parts, while in the aggregate it follows them.

Now what Hegel passes off as unity in the entire execution of his doctrine is always only the unity of the aggregate, never the unity of the system. For him, the connection of two conceptions into a third is the unity of the same, e.g., becoming is the unity of being and nothingness. If this is to be a systematic unity, then the notion of becoming, already as becoming, should be present in the notion of being, as my intention is entirely present already from the beginning of my act and therefore forms its unity, or my personality, the feeling of my existence, is already in each of my limbs, by which alone they are these limbs. But in the conception of being as such, the conception of becoming is precisely still prevented, it is not present in it; only through the development of nothingness and its joint correlation does becoming arise. Being, as such, remaining being, thus does not contain becoming, in the way that my act as such contains my personality; rather, only through its surrender, by the addition of something else, does the notion of becoming enter the scene, as the notion of the heap of stones is not yet present in the individual stone, but only comes up when other stones are added. Being and becoming are thus a mere unity of the aggregate, if one does not have a subject above both that unites them, in which, then, it is not becoming that is the unity of being and nothingness, but rather that such a subject is the unity of all three.

This is exactly the case with the final unity, philosophy. It was created by the run of all the moments; but it, philosophy, the insight that everything is only dialectical movement – is not contained in any of the moments, but only arises when they all have come together. And here, too, these moments still exist apart from it, e.g., philosophy is not in the state, in the family, while the dialectical movement is; yet the insight into this movement is not, and it is not the beginning but the end that is to be regarded here as unity. The intention of the personal God is in all things, in each individual, and is therefore its systematic unity. On the other hand, philosophy in Hegel's system only arose through the totality of all moments, without having already been present in each individual as such, nor by being in every individual now. The conclusion of this system is therefore also a mere product of its parts, like the heap of stones, rather than the all-pervading unity. It does not grant unity to the foundation of it, because it is nothing but its phenomena; nor to the end, because it is not present as what it is in the individual phenomena.

Speculative philosophy is the recognition of movement. Just as for Hegel this movement really is not act, so for him is speculation not vision, but the pursuit of a logical (dialectical) movement. Dialectic thus takes the place of speculation. For this reason, it must show not only the transition from one conception to another, but it should find the conceptions, the things themselves, like vision can. The empty movement of separating and connecting must then form the world, and the logical mechanism, which dialectic was supposed to abolish, enters the scene in its place, in a different way.

It is considered to be Hegel's achievement that he objectified the dialectic. If one is to understand by this that he treats dialectic as an art, which is not supposed to play a deceptive game, but rather to show true living mobility, then such treatment was already provided by Plato. What distinguishes Hegel from

Plato is that it is not only *mobility*, but *the movement itself*, which is to provide him the content. This then is not objectification of what is initially merely subjective, but rendering positive what is only negative in Plato. And it is not the achievement, but the untruth of this dialectic. The true achievement thereof was outlined above.

PART IV: SCHLEIERMACHER[89]

Standpoint

Schleiermacher's world-view originated from Spinoza, was initially conveyed by Fichte but finally settled by Schelling, in the same way that Hegel's was, and in some respects even more so. For him as well, it is reason as an objective impersonal world power which, in its self-realization, in its processes, forms the All-Being, both nature and the ethical world. As well, this process for him consists everywhere in an unfolding of original identity into opposites, which always therefore mutually condition each other: the unity of being and knowledge, of material and spiritual being, of the universal and the particular, and their necessary opposition – all existence is based on this. It is the task of science to show the process by which reason is realized as nature and as ethical world; it is therefore only one, even if it unfolds in different aspects, and that one is absolute, even if it has not yet been completed in time.

The aspect that Schleiermacher chose to treat is not nature, but the ethical world. In this, he again distinguishes two aspects, ethics and history, which relate to each other like force (or essence) and appearance. To wit, the universal laws of reason, according to which reason is realized through human action as personality, legal condition, state, social mores, church, are ethics; but the entirely concrete way in which reason implements these universal laws in space and time, is history. A philosophy of history of the kind which Schleiermacher would draw up, would have a different character than the one drawn up by Hegel. For Schleiermacher, it would simply be the application to an individual subject of the principles obtained as ethics; for Hegel it would be the application of a principle that stands above ethics itself, which has an even higher form of expression in world history than in ethical laws. For Schleiermacher, world history is the terrain of the entirety of ethics, which is already complete prior to it; for

---

[89] *Grundlinien einer Kritik der bisherigen Sittenlehre* [Elements of a Critique of Received Ethical Doctrine]; *Grundriß der philosophischen Ethik* [Outlines of Philosophical Ethics]; *Die Lehre vom Staat* [The Doctrine of State];"Über die Begriffe der verschiedenen Staatsformen" [Concerning the Concepts of the Various Forms of State].

Hegel, world history is one sphere of ethics, alongside and to a certain extent superior to the other ones.

Construction of the Ethical World

Now the essence of ethics according to Schleiermacher is the *unification of reason and nature, so that they permeate each other*. Reason here, as we always have to keep in mind, is not the reason of a personality but the impersonal world reason, which, however, has personality as the necessary exclusive organ for its realization (as with Hegel). For Schleiermacher, however, it is not, as in Hegel, the epitome of certain moments of thought, but, more faithful to Schelling's view, it is still an indeterminate element that only becomes determinate through its opposition to nature and its imagination in nature. In itself, it is only absolute indifference, the oneness of being and knowing, in which no determinate being and knowing has yet been distinguished. If one thinks of reason before the ethical process in which it is permeated with nature, it is a mere principle, without concrete content.

Since the realization of ethics is reason as world power, ethics has an entirely objective, and what is more, an entirely impersonal character. In terms of its causal force, it is not primarily a law for human beings but rather the law inherent in reason as a world power, and it is fulfilled hereby ineluctably; that is why Schleiermacher rejects the manner of conceiving ethics from the point of view of "*ought*," because that would be a law that exists for the individual and whose realization depends solely on the individual's fulfillment of it. In fact, this relation with human beings is only a subordinate aspect of the true ethical relation. In the same way, ethics are not aimed at people, as with the achievement of their perfection, but only at that impersonal world power, its most perfect penetration with nature. The perfected action of man is therefore only a secondary moment; the actual moment is the realization of the ethical forms: the existence of gender difference, the family, the nation, the state, the social condition.

This is the basis for distinguishing three areas in ethics, which are nevertheless one: goods, virtues, duties. By ethical *goods*, Schleiermacher describes what reason wishes to accomplish, its ultimate purpose, the forms of the ethical world, which embody their permeation with nature, such as, e.g., language, art, property, legal transactions, family, state. The *virtues* are the qualities and powers of man, by means of which reason effects these forms and maintains them in their true manner, as love, wisdom, perseverance, prudence. Finally, the *duties* refer to the individual actions required for the realization of the goods, the respective relations of the individual to the whole of the ethical world. Clearly, the concept of ethical goods is by far the most important of the three aspects of ethics; for it determines the other two, which are there only for it, each is adapted to it. However, goods are not to be understood as a satisfaction of human beings, as the expression might suggest, but on the contrary they are only intended for world-forming reason, the realization of its forms; the satisfaction of man is only a secondary moment and by no means a necessary one. Schleiermacher therefore also distinguishes happiness as a completely different concept from the ethical goods, and moreover expressly declares that virtue does not grant happiness, but only worthiness for it. In the same way, the highest good for Schleiermacher is not God as a personality above the world and personal unity with God; it is only the totality of those individual ethical goods: family, state, sociability. The relation to human personality and to the divine occur necessarily in the pantheistic viewpoint, and there remains only that which lies in the middle, the ethical form of the world as a cause and purpose in itself, which people serve merely as means and tools. Hegel's view in this is essentially the same. The whole course of his legal philosophy aims to substantiate what Schleiermacher calls the goods (property, family, state, etc.), only that he sees virtue and duty (love, etc.) partly themselves as a sphere of ethical goods (morality), partly, like Schleiermacher views them, as a mere correlate of certain ethical goods (e.g., the family) , but without presenting them separately. For Hegel, too, the ought is not the basic essence of ethics, but only one of its spheres or modes of appearance, and indeed a subordinate one.

Just as the nature-subordinating process is not a process of individual reason but of impersonal universal reason, so is there no absolute beginning or absolute end to it. Namely, this subjugation of nature is everywhere already a given, from which the process starts, and it never completely ends. The existence of man is already such an interweaving of nature and reason. (As will be shown below, as consciousness he is the symbol of reason, and as acting being he is the organ of reason.) This interweaving, which reason has effected directly or impersonally and, to that degree, one might say physically, already presupposes ethics. This is concerned with how reason, by means of human beings, that is, by means of personally conscious beings, accomplishes the further permeation of nature. On the other hand, there will never be a condition in which a natural object exists that is not already fully appropriated for reason. It would have been consistent if Schleiermacher also reckoned what he calls the presupposed unity of nature and reason to ethics, since he relates ethics as a whole not to the individual but to reason as a world power. At the least, given his point of view, just as with Schelling, there can be no generic difference between the former and the latter. Reason accomplishes everything according to inherent laws and as a necessary process, not from the point of view of an ought. In the treatment of ethical goods, Schleiermacher actually deduced the existence of language and memory from his ethical process, no less than property and the state.

In accordance with this, good and evil are not positive opposites. Evil is merely the non-intermingling of reason and nature, thus only a non-good, since nature in itself is also what ought to be. Indeed, since ethics is only an infinite process, has no beginning before which it would not have been realized, and no end at which it would be fully realized, good and evil can denote nothing other than to what degree a natural existence already has entered into the ethical process, is permeated by reason, or to what degree it has remained outside of that process, to be permeated only subsequently. Good and evil are merely a relative and fluid relationship, and evil is not a direct opposite to good, but merely denotes a lack, a not yet.[90]

The permeation of nature and reason in which ethics consist or through which ethical goods come about, takes place through a dual function, the inculcative [anbildende] (organizing) and the descriptive [bezeichnende] (knowing, symbolizing), i.e., in such a way that reason turns nature into its *organ*, and in such a way that it turns nature into its *symbol*. It makes nature into its organ by there first being created some external existence in nature, which now turns and serves reason in its purpose of subjugating nature. So the first inculcative act of reason is the human body, because this, despite being natural existence, now serves reason as a tool; in the same way, all external existences and configurations of the ethical world are the expressions of inculcative activity, as for instance property, legal transactions, family, state. They are natural existences

[90] "The contrast between good and evil means nothing else than the juxtaposition in each individual ethical area of what is posited as the interweaving of reason and nature, and what is the separation thereof." *Grundriß der philosophischen Ethik*, p. 26.

through which reason achieves its realization by acting on another nature it has not yet permeated. On the other hand, it makes nature its symbol by appearing in a natural existence as knowing, self-comprehending, so that natural existence is the bearer of reason. As the human body is the most original organ of reason, so is consciousness (first the senses, then the understanding) its most original symbol. But this also advances further; in religion and science, the symbolizing activity of reason manifests itself in its world-forming process, as its organizing activity does in the family, nation, and the state. The former is form-giving, the latter is the consciousness-raising of what has been given form. Through the former, one might say, reason enters into nature, and through the latter it returns to itself. These are the two poles that form ethical configurations. Thus, from the inculcative activity of reason emerge personality itself, property, legal transactions, family, people and race, the state, etc.; on the other hand, the symbolizing activity engenders thought, language, art, science, religion, hence also the scientific association and the church.

This opposition of the two ethical functions, the inculcative and the descriptive (form-giving and consciousness-raising) is intersected with yet another. By imagining nature in a process and a development, hence not as All-Reason absorbing All-Nature, individuality and particularity arise. In particular, human nature splits into a plethora of individual beings. Nevertheless, as reason it remains the universal, and itself is complete only through the totality of the individuals into which it has split. Ethics is therefore constantly reciprocally conditioned by particularity and universality, separation and community. The concept of the person itself is none other than this: universal reason has given itself an existence as a particularity in a natural whole, which is now just as much an independent center for itself as it is a part and relation to the community or the entirety of the realization of reason. The reciprocal conditioning runs through both spheres, that of inculcation as well as that of knowledge. The whole realm of consciousness (symbolizing function) has a side of particularity or non-transferability and a side of community and communication. Emotion belongs to the former, thought to the latter. What has arisen in the individual, so that it can be communicated by him to others, exists in language and memory (since, according to Schleiermacher, memory should have no meaning for ourselves, but only for the purpose of communicating to others). In the same way, the entire sphere of inculcating or form-giving has both of these sides. In absolute opposition, they appear as the body of the individual and the body of the earth. The former is the organ only for reason in the individual, the latter is only for reason in the community; the former cannot be communicated, the latter cannot reach anyone separately. Everything else is relative, and the opposition manifests itself as ownership and legal transactions, acquisition and exchange, as domestic law and hospitality.

Particularization does not strike Schleiermacher as merely the positing of many individual copies, but as the positing of quite different individualities. What is specific to every existence, or, as he puts it, the necessary conceptual difference of each existence from the other, is for him a supreme physical-ethical postulate. This applies both to the people themselves and to all the relations in which they act. Because reason, although it is completely identical in itself, insofar as it uses nature as a symbol or organ in order to act on another nature, i.e., is permeated with nature, must differentiate itself like nature does.[91] However, Schleiermacher does not give an answer as to why, in every existence, nature is something different, indeed something specific.

So there is a twofold opposition and accordingly a quadruple polarity from which the ethical world is formed, from which the ethical forms (in fact, we may generally say "the forms") of human existence arise.[92]

Law and State

According to this system, then, *law* is the ethical relation of individual beings to each other in terms of *transactions,* i.e., the particular acquisition and shared possession of the external objects of the earth. It pertains to the inculcating sphere of reason, the action thereof upon external objects; and in this contains that dualism of community and separation of individuals, but in such a way that community materializes only as an ongoing transition from one

---

[91] *Grundriß der philosophischen Ethik,* pp. 40, 41.

[92] The same four categories can actually be found in Hegel as well; Schleiermacher's inculcative and descriptive functions roughly correspond to Hegel's in-itself and for-itself, and Schleiermacher's universal and particular correspond to Hegel's substantial and subjective. Except that here too Hegel does not set up the two polarities separately, but rather has them permeate each other; so that the subjective becomes the means of the for-itself.

individual being to another (as contractual relation). Accordingly, Schleiermacher, like many others, understands law to be private law, mine and thine. For this reason, mere contractual relation does not lead to the state, or in other words, the state is not a mere relation between individual and individual. Instead, the state is the community of people as such for this inculcation or subjection of nature.

The essence and purpose of the state is namely the *process of developing nature,* which proceeds from the mass of people as a unity, namely through the unity brought about by what is peculiar to that specific people [Volkseigentümlichkeit]. This process of developing nature, which characterizes the essence and purpose of the state, involves putting external objects to use for human intelligence and its purposes, and putting human facilities to use, but only to the degree that they serve the subjection and enjoyment of nature. It contains "gymnastics, mechanics, and agriculture" in accordance with the broader meanings Schleiermacher attaches to these expressions. As the subjection of nature by man in its entirety, the state necessarily encompasses the subjection of nature which proceeds from the individual and which is communicated in turn to individuals, i.e., transactions and property, or in short, law. The state contains the law, but not, as in the older view of natural law, as a mere relation between individuals, to which is added the community merely as a means of protecting it, but as a relation among individuals that is supported precisely by the relation of human community. The people subjugate the soil, produce and increase the means of human satisfaction through the orderings and institutions of the overall public stock; and only on the basis of this total production do the transactions take place among the individuals for themselves, the ethical form of which is law, and the state then protects and maintains transactions (exchange) as well as individual entitlement (the side of non-transferability as well as of the community).

This is undoubtedly Schleiermacher's point. Thus the sphere of the state is the rule of the human race over nature and the distribution within it on behalf of this rule, namely the position of individuals vis-à-vis the whole and one another for this purpose. On the other hand, man himself as intelligence lies outside the sphere of the state. For one thing, knowledge, as far as it comes into consideration in this regard, does not only serve to subjugate nature (speculative knowledge as opposed to technical knowledge), and so to that degree is not the object of state rule. Nor is feeling, and especially the highest level thereof, religious feeling, hence religion, the object of state rule. These two are a matter for particular associations separate from the state. This whole process of natural formation, which is the essence of the state, has its rational meaning – is true subjugation under reason – only if it emanates from the people, as connected by a type of discerning and developing activity, which reveals the peculiarity and personality of the people. This revelation of popular peculiarity in the subjugation of nature is the real, ultimate purpose of the state. Initially, the people exercise this process automatically in an inferior manner, as a horde. The state is given in the manner in which the people orders itself to this end, namely, in the manner in which ruler and subject arises. The criterion of the state is therefore a relation between magistrate and subjects.

Relation of the State to Science and Religion

As a result of the state being limited to the process of developing nature, two other associations have automatically arisen that likewise are required to realize reason: the scientific association (school, university, academy) and the church, the former for the community of thought, the latter for the community of feeling. Both together form the opposite of the state, because they are taken up in the cognitive function, while the state is taken up in the developing function; they wish to achieve a result on the inside of man or reason, the state on the outside, in nature.[93] But they are opposed to each other, because in this area of conceptualizing activity the scientific association represents the side of commonality, i.e., of thought, while the church represents the side of particularity (that which a person has for himself, cannot be transferred to another), i.e., feeling. The means of realizing itself, of establishing a community, is therefore language, for the scientific association as an expression of thought, and art, for the church as an expression of feeling. Just as religion and the church repose on the side of peculiarity, so is the difference between religions, at least in their higher level (rational religions), based on peculiarity, and the error, the origin of fanaticism, is to proclaim it on the basis of objective truth and untruth.

Schleiermacher also postulated a natural basis for these two communities. i.e., a naturally-given common type, by means of which the members forming

---

[93] For Schelling's virtually equivalent viewpoint, see pp. 61f. above.

the association form a unity (thereby a process of reason) even before the association becomes effective, just as the state has such in nationality. He now appropriates this nationality as the natural basis for the scientific association; school and academy are based on national knowledge (in truth, however, only because they are cultivated by the state); yet he still does not know of any such for the church, and hopes for its future discovery, as difficult as that may be.

So for Schleiermacher, the relationship between the state on the one hand and these two communities, scientific association and the church, on the other, is the complete lack of any connection as a matter of consistency, since they are based on different anthropological sides (or objective rational functions) that have nothing in common. "The latter are destined to be released from the dominion of the state into the sphere of the individual as such. Whether they then get organized or not is of no concern to the state; whether, if they do manage this, the state should take any notice, depends on circumstances." He merely establishes the inevitable negative connection, that the state must make room for the other connections, must ensure their external subsistence, and conversely that these must not embody anything dangerous to the state in the extreme sense of the word. Except for this, he demands complete freedom of belief in the sense that the state should not only be non-confessional but not "generally Christian" either.

The State Constitution

If the state is a process of developing nature, of subjugating external objects under the common control of the people, then the determinative grounds of the state must also be based on natural conditionings and laws. To wit, the manner in which a group of persons arranges itself, unifies, allocates positions, allocates the functions it must establish in order to achieve such common control of the outside world, is determined by natural laws. The scientific treatment of the state is therefore a "*physiology of the state.*" But especially since the state is supposed to be a manifestation of the peculiarity of the people, which pertains to the side of nature (since all difference comes from nature, while reason is universally the same), every metaphysics of the state ("metaphysical politics" – "state ideal") such as given by Plato and Fichte, is inadmissible.

Schleiermacher wishes his doctrine of state to be treated from this point of view. He presents the process of state formation in which the hordes are a precursor as a necessity of nature, in which higher formations emerge from lower precisely in this process, but in which purpose in the strict sense is not in question. For him, democracy is the lowest stage of the (simple) state, monarchy the highest. He also considers the estates-oriented or constitutional monarchy to be the final formation of completed monarchy, but without using those names. He also teaches the construction of this as well as other forms from the concept and the relation of the legislative and executive powers, albeit in a peculiar way. That is to say, the essence of the state is for the collective mass of people to receive rules and put them into practice – the legislative and the executive power. He transfers both of these originally into the mass; its experiences and perceptions of life are the source of the law, and by executive power Schleiermacher understands compliance firstly as it emanates from the mass. But the diversity of life experiences (actually the valuation of life), which comes with the division of labor and diversity of interest, prove insufficient, which makes necessary a "permanent magistracy as an intermediate member." So Schleiermacher does not reckon the magistracy to the concept of legislative and executive power. It becomes necessary only when the actual legislative power, popular valuation of life, and the actual executive power, compliance on the part of the people, factually prove insufficient. Such authorities as intermediate members are the representative bodies, but especially the king. The king, in the developed constitution, is therefore the end of legislative power and the beginning of executive power. Public opinion evolves the law up to its sanction [by the king], and compliance begins with him until it is finally implemented by the mass.

In the state organism thus developed, however, Schleiermacher rejects *popular sovereignty*, in which the executive power (that is, according to him, the compliant, obedient mass) stands above the legislative (permanent magistracy, king, parliament), just as much as he rejects ministerial accountability; the legislative power (the parliament) stands over the executive (this is again the king as the beginning of the executive), but the ministers must be accountable to the king, and in this regard the estates merely have the right of petition by which they refer their complaint in the matter to the prince. The desire for a different relation rests on the misconception of the necessary safeguard, i.e., mistrust. But this comes from another side and must be eliminated there; namely, mistrust arises only because the state engages at all in a sphere that does not pertain to it, but instead to individual life, especially religious and scientific. Ultimately, this is the most important practical tendency in Schleiermacher's political doctrine: these two spheres should remain free from any state interference; the state should be completely separated from religion and church as well as from science, as touched on above.

Verdict

The greater abundance and depth of thought, and in particular the recognition of the ethical world as an entirety, as something which coheres in itself and does not consist solely of relations between individuals, such as has distinguished science from the older conceptions since Schelling, is also in evidence with Schleiermacher. From this arises in particular his doctrine of ethical goods, through which he conceives the basic institutions of common existence, family, state, church, school, as the center of ethics, with the duties of the individual derived therefrom. But he also shares the entire fallacy of the pantheistic-speculative standpoint which was demonstrated above in the systems of Schelling and Hegel. Such nebulous "reason," which receives its content only through nature and is still supposed to be the yardstick of nature, which is not realized except in and through personalities and yet is to have first created those personalities, is not able to explain the world, neither the natural creation nor the ethical world. Admittedly, all earthly existence falls under the four categories: conceptualizing and constructing activity, universality and particularity (peculiarity); but for these categories to hit upon any natural existence, especially that of man, or any ethical relation in its specific meaning, is the same delusion that we encountered at every stage of rationalistic development.

For Schleiermacher, too, there is therefore only a clever balancing and symmetrizing with those opposites in which his presentation moves; there is no real explanation or indication of the origin or the necessity of ethical configurations. This is not to deny that with his development of and proper appreciation for ethical relations, he greatly encouraged ethics, especially in terms of subjective morality; but like Hegel, he did this not by virtue of his philosophical categories, but despite them. But there is even more to it than that. By this philosophical point of view, the innermost essence of ethics is lost to Schleiermacher, just as it is to Hegel and their predecessors, because in absolute terms it too is not the quality of a will, located in the will itself, but merely a triumph of thinking, thought-activity, consciousness ("reason") over non-thinking, unconscious nature. In this he takes up the position of the creator, i.e., demiurgic reason, and this has only the purpose (or rather the necessity) of subjugating matter, its other inherent potency, to the power of thought; what appears to be a quality of will, virtue, is only a means for this process of subjugation, not what is supposed to be original and ultimate. In the absolute world conjuncture, the entirety of ethics has no actual ethical, but only an intellectual or artistic meaning.

Above all, however, Schleiermacher, in accordance with his point of view, completely excludes the true basic relationship of ethics, a relation between *twofold* living personal wills, divine and human,[94] according to which good and evil are absolute and positive opposites either agreeing with or disobedient to ethical power, and according to which the various relations grounded on the person of God, namely unification with Him, and on the divine nature and the perfection of human existence in terms of this unification, establish the distinction of spheres, religion and morality, church and state. He must therefore conceive ethics according to arbitrary and subordinate relations, which are to be attained precisely by using that contradiction of nature and reason. Evil is merely nature not yet become reason, with regard to which, indeed, ethical disgust remains entirely unexplained; religion is only a similar, coordinated moment in the all-encompassing sphere of ethical goods, its innermost essence being merely the variety in anthropological organ, or, if you like, the variety in reason-function (peculiarity-aspect, feeling), not the great object and goal, God and man's personal union with God. Its content, the eternal acts of God which it reveals, steps back as irrelevant, and only the way in which it stirs people up is the decisive factor.

But the peculiar implementation that Schleiermacher gives to the pantheistic-speculative standpoint is that, regardless of the objectivity of the scientific conception which it necessarily includes, the results predominantly stand on the side of subjectivity, bare individual human freedom. Certainly, the ethic for him is not the task and fulfillment of the individual, but of objective, world-forming reason, and therefore of the human community in which it is realized. But the way in which he arrives at the content of the ethic does not consist in higher orderings, but only in the development of personality. The process of reason strives for nothing else than this. For him, the innermost essence of the

---

[94] See Vol. II, Book I [*Philosophical Presuppositions*], §. 28.

state is not an order over the people, whether it is a government placed by God to maintain justice and peace, as in the Christian view, or as an architecture of rational determinations, as with Hegel; instead, it is only the revelation of the individuality of the people in the manner in which the people makes nature useful to itself.

Likewise, the innermost nature of the church, which according to the Christian view is a divine institution to proclaim God-given doctrine and to convey the miracle of the sacrament that God Himself gives, and which consequently has no place in Hegel, is only the expression and the realization of the (subjective) religious feeling of people in community. Divine punishment becomes the mere natural effect of sin, civil punishment is the defense of the community against the offender, a necessary consequence of which is the struggle against the death penalty, to which Schleiermacher dedicated a sermon. The public (state and church) and the private are not opposed to each other as objectivity and subjectivity, but only as the subjectivity of a mass (a popular unity or great association of feeling) and the subjectivity of an individual. Schleiermacher's practical position in relation to the state is therefore the direct opposite of Hegel's; Schelling's standpoint divides these extremes. With Hegel, everything should be determined from above by government; resistance of the estates and above all of individuals against the objective-rational must be given no power, nor even a hearing; with Schleiermacher, on the other hand, everything should come from the individuality of the individuals, and no power should compel this individuality. This can also be seen very clearly in his pseudonymous writing on liturgical law. According to this, no change in the liturgy may be made as long as any individual conscience finds itself burdened by it. It is not the contrast between monarchy and democracy, but the contrast between state or church power and individual will. This is also the basis of his absolute separation of state, church, and school.

Consequently, Schleiermacher could not have arrived at an actual, independent theology. Since he allocated religion to the mere manner of characterizing (conceptualizing) activity, much like Hegel allocated it to the imagination, he, like Hegel, of necessity had to deny the objective truth of religion, only attaching value to it as a subjective mode of conception and impulse of feeling. It is a fundamental violation of all correct thinking that despite this, Schleiermacher concedes independent truth to the results of religious feeling and thus establishes a dualism of human knowledge in terms of its objective content: what the thought teaches us – a pantheistic world conjuncture in which impersonal reason (which is nothing in it itself, but only comes to content and existence in nature) formed the world and determined the morals – and what feeling teaches us, a God, the characteristics of Whom are love and mercy, and hope for everlasting continuity. Schleiermacher postulates an agreement of these directly opposed postulates as something transcendent, the manner of which is unknown to us,[95] since within our thinking it is already quite clear that such an agreement is absolutely impossible, and on the other hand is not at all necessary, because the religious feeling that Schleiermacher shows to be a necessary product of the (impersonal) process of reason, cannot possibly be something that is independent of this process, something higher than it, but must necessarily be explained from it and can very well be explained as the refraction of the pure objective truth through the subjectivity of sensation. If world-forming, impersonal reason also creates a longing for a loving God and a Redeemer, should such a God be created objectively, contrary to that reason, thus retroactively cancelling the originally producing impersonal God? It is only the deep personal grasp of certain basic facts of Christianity, the need for redemption, and redemption by the Savior, which Schleiermacher raises above all these contradictions and directs to a Christian doctrine. Fairness dictates that this must be counted less as a weakness of a philosophical conception than as a strength and intensity of the religious disposition; for it is no less scientifically superior to recognize a large, powerful object inconsistently, than to deny it for the sake of the consistency of philosophical thought. But it must be obvious from the outset that a Christian doctrine of faith which is thus inserted within a general philosophical conception that contradicts it, cannot possibly be the genuine doctrine of faith. As great and lasting as Schleiermacher's achievements for the scientific construction of theology may be, the Christian faith content in his dogmatics is fundamentally tarnished and weakened.[96]

Schleiermacher accomplished less for the doctrine of law and state than for other disciplines. His view of the state is infinitely more objective, richer, more

---

[95] *Der christliche Glaube* [Christian Faith], I, 174.

[96] For details see my *Fundamente einer christlichen Philosophie* [Foundations of a Christian Philosophy], p. 185.

lifelike than that of the earlier Kantian-Fichtean era. For him it is based on original community and has positive objectives. But Schleiermacher strips the state of its innermost ethical significance. For the subjection of external nature and external human facilities is not what is ethical in the highest sense; on the contrary, justice and punishment, the ethical center of administration, and the majesty of an ethical authority as an end in itself, the ethical center of the constitution, have no place in his doctrine. The administration of justice does not manifest itself as the realization of the idea of justice, but only as the distribution of the goods wrought from nature; it is thus only a means to that goal of the subjugation of nature. The abolition of the actual ethical point of view for subjective morality extends only to the scientific conception; here, however, it also extends to the results. The whole purpose of the state is then predominantly a mere technical one, which is why the state has no inner bond with the church and the scientific community, but only an external one by which it vouchsafes them space and the ability to protect themselves against it. These are purely distinct spheres without real unity; only an ideal abstract unity exists, simply in the philosophical conception. Reality contradicts Schleiermacher's notions. Throughout history, states have as little restricted themselves to the purpose of subjugating nature as to the Kantian purpose of the protection of individual rights; everywhere they have likewise striven to realize ethical ideas as necessary and sacred in themselves.

Accordingly, it is also entirely logical that with Schleiermacher the highest scientific doctrine of state is not ethics but physiology. The question is not what the ethical meaning *per se* is of kingship, the courts, popular representation, the administration of justice and police, but only the ways in which, according to natural laws, the technical task of the state (the process of developing nature) is achieved through those institutions and their functions. Indeed, the highest and most essential aspect of the doctrine of state is hereby abandoned; for such is ethics and not physiology, and has as its task the ethical significance of the institutions, and therefore does not at all coincide with an abstract state ideal that ignores popular, national particularity, as Schleiermacher postulates as an alternative at the beginning of his politics. In the same way, the development of states in world history is not recognized in its deepest meaning. For this is an advance of ethical ideas and not a mere physiological process of natural and mechanical impulses, as Schleiermacher treats it. But the aspect of the doctrine of state which is thereby actually practiced is not represented entirely purely. For the physiology of the state can in terms of its nature only be a purely historical science. As such, it has entirely historical material as its object, and as its lodestar merely whatever history has to offer in the way of constitutional artifacts, administrative goals, leading ethical ideas. The state physiology of Schleiermacher, by contrast, has a standard and purpose for the investigation which has already been given prior to and outside it: the process of developing nature. It assumes from the outset that the aim of the state can only be this, and only examines how the natural conditions of the state relate to it. These are historical investigations according to an *a priori* point of view. Added to this is Schleiermacher's other way of thinking, abstraction from specific reality and transposition to the sphere of the most universal thought relations. This often leads him to overlook the simple, immediate, and true meaning of the political elements, and to look at them in terms of relations that come as more of a surprise than as getting to the heart of the matter.

So for example, he declares civil jurisdiction to be an integral or complementary part of the legislative function, because of "the way it specifies dubious law," the way, then, that "the negotiations and results of the administration of justice everywhere provide the basis for the clarifications and improvements of the legal code," ignoring all the distinctive characteristics that differentiate it from legislation: application to specific cases, effect on a specific entitled person, the restriction to an existing legal norm. Thus he ranges the administration of criminal justice and the military together under the concept of "state defense" or "warfare against the internal and the external enemy," overlooking that the former has as its essence the realization of the idea of justice, according to which it unites with the administration of civil justice, while the latter pursues physical force through technical means. Thus, he reckons *observance of the law* to the executive power, overlooking the fact that the essence of political functions is not the realization of a norm but the realization thereof by virtue of political authority, even where it does not exercise actual coercion. In the same way, he considers the main aspect of legislative power to be the inducements from which the content of the law comes, the life experiences of the crowd, rather than the sanction. Thus he declares it to be a departure from pure democracy, even actual aristocracy, when some become "spokesmen" by "knowledge and power of speech," and even when these "popular leaders" have "successors like them" among their students, overlooking the fact that the essence of the form of government is whose will it is that actually decides, not who influences that will at any particular time; otherwise a monarchical state would also be changing its constitution depending on whether the prince is influenced by popularity, court environment, clergy, etc. Because it is not a mere conception and implementation of the physiological point of view, there is no lack of valuable contributions in Schleiermacher's politics, and in itself its promulgation is meritorious. As the work of a highly gifted and educated mind, it will always retain its value and interest; but it can hardly be ascribed a profound influence on the scientific doctrine of state or practical political views.

Schleiermacher's most peculiar and important achievement in the area of philosophy is his ethics. The basic system, as shown above, is untenable; how could a system of ethics count as the true one which knows of no evil in the actual sense, no punishment, no reconciliation! But it was not just that Schleiermacher significantly promoted the appreciation of ethical relations in the implementation, but that he brought to life a whole side of ethics which until then had not been recognized, at least not to such a degree, and he did so in a scientific manner. This is the side of particularity (individuality), this innermost center of the person. The freedom from external constraint of the higher spiritual spheres, religion and science; personal human tolerance vis-à-vis other beliefs; the worth of every individual in free social interaction; all of this derives from the fact that the human being has an aspect of particularity in his innermost being that does not coincide with anything else, and perhaps no one has emphasized this aspect as a primordial product of "reason" (God) and, as one might say, the primordial right of man, with clarity and energy as Schleiermacher has. From this also follows the indestructibility and the necessary unfolding of people-individualities, and the equally new and to a certain extent true and fruitful idea of Schleiermacher's that even the diversity of confessions is based not only on truth and error, but also on different individualities. It is because of his excellent representation of this aspect of ethics that Schleiermacher occupies his high position not only in science, but also in the nation. This lays the foundation for a beautiful, noble humanity, which must be regarded precisely as a fruit of the Protestant church and Protestant education. Freedom is thus understood in its deepest and most ethical root, in a way that corresponds with the German spirit. When freedom is erected not so much on the naked valuation of the individual will, as in Rousseau, or on the inviolability of individual property, as in Locke, but instead on ethical individuality, then it not only has a higher dignity, but also cannot break away from mores as in those cases.

It is also Schleiermacher's lack, as can be seen from the above examination of his point of view, that he makes this one essential aspect, which he represents in its noblest manner, the exclusive principle, such that he also denies the most essential truths in the religious sphere as a mere diversity of individual views, and thus abolishes the immutable, objective doctrine of the gospel; that in the political sphere he destroys the internal connection of the state with the church and with science, and not only demands freedom of worship, but also combats any proclamation of a public national confession, and such like. There are two poles of the ethical world, objective truth and necessity, and the freedom of human individuality. They are in contradiction in our imperfect state and must restrict each other. The principle of state religion must not be fully realized with its consequences because it will then destroy the religious freedom of the individual, and the religious freedom of the individual must not be fully realized with all its consequences because it will destroy state religion. It is necessary to find the proper measure depending on the feeling and the need of the times. Schleiermacher positions himself absolutely and fundamentally only on one side, on the latter side. It is an imperfect condition, a lack of free individual feeling, when along the lines of the Augustinian theory regarding the state, the One Church realizes its full consistency. It is a condition of destruction (the loss of all common national faith) when, in accordance with Schleiermacher's theory, the relinquishment of religion entirely to individuals and their voluntary connections is a need or possibility. Yet whoever represents even that one side, the one of free individuality, with the lively warmth and innermost penetration, and ever only in its ethical root as Schleiermacher does, nevertheless deserves full recognition even from those who may have it as their nearest and dearest vocation to represent the other side, in opposition to the prevailing movement.

BOOK VI: HISTORICAL LEGAL PHILOSOPHY

PART I: THE WRITERS OF THE COUNTER-REVOLUTION

Until the French Revolution, the doctrines of liberalism and the constitutional system were considered to be infallible, the ideal for state institutions; nothing less was expected from their realization than the fulfillment of human existence, the rule of absolute reason. With the Revolution, both were realized in turn; but rather than meet expectations, they led to a chain of evils and atrocities which could not be accidental, but only the result of their principles. The sight of collapse or impending destruction awakened resentment against them as well as an understanding and enthusiasm for the former order, from which emerged scientific views precisely opposed to those of the previous two centuries. This issued forth in the writers of the *Counter-Revolution*. Their common tenets and motives are: *Legitimacy*, i.e., power based on inherent regard or majesty (more deeply, on divine sanction) as opposed to popular sovereignty; the *original unity of the state*, as opposed to the establishment thereof through the assembly of individuals and contract; the *organic constitution* of natural elements and members, in opposition to abstract democracy and constitutional mechanism; *corporative unification* as opposed to the absolute isolation of citizens; the *customary order* as opposed to upheaval and reconstruction out of one's own reason. These are indeed indestructible truths; they are the foundations of state-building. Although the applications that Counter-Revolutionary writers make of these basic doctrines cannot everywhere be endorsed, they themselves are fully justified. Just as the Revolution represents true postulates, so does the Counter-Revolution represent true principles. The former struggles for what the present should gain as a new benefit, the latter for what must be preserved at all times.

In the implementation, they are mostly filled with an image of the past, the spirit of patriotic institutions which the Revolution did not comprehensively destroy, and of course each draws this image from the history of his own nation. This makes them so different from one another. But the ones who have had the most impact are those who imbibe this spirit of national history without the admixture of their own personal ingredient. As such, there are three Counter-Revolutionary writers who stand out above all others, corresponding to the three most important nations in Europe: Maistre, Burke, and Haller.

Maistre

Maistre's political writings[97] have no systematic form, and hardly any internal order; he treats the most diverse things like someone leading a brilliant conversation in company. But the focus of his political convictions is: man makes no states, no constitutions, no kings; God makes them, and if man undertakes to tear himself away from God to present them as his own work, then with such an iniquity he necessarily embraces what is bad, and destroys rather than builds. Among the various constitutions, hereditary monarchy is the most perfect, the one commanded by God, and deep divine wisdom proves itself in the excellence and sustainability of this constitution; on the other hand, it necessarily follows from the rationally human approach that electoral monarchy, which has not proven itself, is considered to be better. A necessary member of the perfected constitution is the nobility. The separation of this class as higher in right and honor, as well as the selection of lineages for these things, is God's work, and the infringement of this order is therefore sacrilege. But finally, above the whole structure of the secular state stands the higher regard for the Roman Catholic church and its head, the Pope, appointed by Christ as His successor. What the Revolution is after – protection against arbitrariness and injustice, the guarantee of lawful and gladdening government – has its element of truth; but it could not come from below, as the Revolution undertakes it, by the exaltation of the people over kings, but only from above, from an even higher authority than the monarchical. The submission of princes and peoples to the leadership of the Pope will fulfill all that the Revolution seeks in vain. This nimbus of royalty, this divinely established dividing wall between the nobility and the citizenry, and finally the overarching of the entire state structure by the higher glory of the church – this is the spirit of the old French monarchy, and the supporters of the *ancien régime* probably have no better author to rally around than Maistre.

Among the writers of the Counter-Revolution, Maistre is the most deeply moved by religion; he has a sacred view of the world. He everywhere sees the direct rule of God, His institutions and means, His goals and intentions. The energy of devout sensation and imagination which is characteristic of the

---

[97] *Essai sur le principe générateur des constitutions politiques* [Essay on the Generative Principle of Political Constitutions]; *Soirées de St. Petersbourg* [The Saint Petersburg Dialogues].

French and Italians animates his writings. But his political viewpoints are in glaring contradiction with the real conditions of life and the real demands of the present. This is likewise due to the one-sidedness of his ethical and religious viewpoint. He considers earthly history and the earthly order of men to be an immediate and visible kingdom of God. He therefore recognizes divine guidance and divine will only in external authorities, not also in the further development of the conditions which God also directs, not also in the inner consciousness of the community, which is also an organ of divine influence. Rather, monarchs [die Einen] rule in the name of God with visible juridical authority, while others merely have to obey them passively. What emanates from these agents is divine, and what emanates from the others is human rebellion. History should not proceed from inner development, but from external guidance. This is how the floors of the building ascend. The nobility is God's guardian over the commons, the princes over the nobility, the clergy over the princes. In his reaction to the more recent, certainly profane conception, he pushes the theocratic conception further than even the Middle Ages, in that he bases not only the supreme authority but also the inner social condition, the separation of the two estates, on God's inviolable institution and sanction.

But it is the infallibility of the church that completes this system and makes it possible to be thought. For the multiple instances of depravity, injustice, and delusion of God-ordained rulers are not objectionable insofar as they only relate to individual actions and injustices against individuals, which God will one day judge, but only insofar as they could spoil the moral condition of mankind as a whole. But this is prevented by the hierarchy, into whose protection and authority the complete preservation and development of the ethical (and therefore the complete higher spiritual) element of humanity is given, and which never errs. The doctrine of the church is therefore also the most important position in Maistre's entire view, and for the formation and the progress of this doctrine he denotes an important moment. While up until the French Revolution, the papal system and the episcopal system contradicted each other in the sharpest manner, Maistre – and as far as I can discover, Maistre *first of all* – provided for a higher union of the same, which has currently found the most widespread acceptance among Catholics who are faithful to their church.[98] He

---

[98] *Du Pape* [The Papacy].

teaches with the papal system the true supreme power of the Pope, rejects the assertion of a higher authority of the ecumenical council over his doctrine and person, and indeed denies the ecumenical council itself any meaning where it is without its ordained head, the Pope. But he also recognizes with the episcopal system the independence of the episcopate. He does not want the Pope to decide on matters of faith without the consent of the council (the Pope not without the bishops, the bishops not without the Pope), just as the King of England passes laws with his Parliament; accordingly, the bishops appear as the necessary mediating organs of the Pope, not as the papal system teaches, not as mere assistants for whatever use or disuse (the doctrine of the *episcopus universalis*). Maistre's view is followed, perhaps with even more detailed development, by the most famous Catholic canon law teacher in Germany, Walter; it dominates Catholic education in Germany. The same is shared by the present French clergy, which is much different in this regard than that of the old France. The un-Catholic, indeed in its deepest ground un-Christian, spirit of the new France has pushed the clergy toward the Pope. According to this view, the church is a restricted monarchy; the Pope is sovereign but with necessarily complementary elements, and if the Catholic prerequisite is conceded that the church is such an external, state-like kingdom, it is the only correct one, the organic view. This brings peace and harmony to the church and enables it to face hostile powers in readiness. Maistre's doctrine of the church is so much the keystone of his whole conception and has had – whether through him, or through similar motives from elsewhere – such an influence on the public condition in France and Germany, that it could not remain entirely unnoticed in a history of legal philosophy.

Burke

Burke is without comparison the most powerful and dignified of the writers of the Counter-Revolution, and indeed one of the most outstanding political writers of all time. He derived his views from his own experience as a well-tried statesman in the country with the richest public life and the most richly developed institutions. His political doctrine is based on a religious mindset; he is enthusiastic about certain features of the Middle Ages, especially the chivalrous sense of honor and devotion to higher things. But he everywhere stands on the ground of real and present relations, and acknowledges their stipulations with a sober eye. Burke's understanding is quite practical. Philosophical grounding is not his business. As far as he concerns himself with this, he has no other means and conceptions than the familiar ones from constituting state charters and the like; but he does not deal with it very much either; on the contrary, it is precisely one of his primary principles that those philosophical doctrines, both those of the rights of man and nations and those of unconditional obedience to authority, be kept far from the state, and that only experience-based and immediate needs of concrete conditions are to be determinative. This is not a rebuke; the living knowledge of basic political truths and their deeper ethical justification are two different tasks, to the solution of which the same person is rarely called. But Burke's teaching is such pure vision, it is so interconnected and penetrates so deeply into the innermost core of political relations, that it is an ethics or philosophy of state in action, the deeper expression of which someone else has to find the words.

He fights the French Revolution on the soil of the true English educated mind. The original regard of public authority, in the monarchy of the king, but within constitutional limits – the historically well-structured constitution of manifold estates, corporate entities, authorities, especially the importance of large landholding therein – the permanence of civic institutions in which freedom is an entail of forebears, not an achievement of today – the legality and prosperity of the most varied forms of state depending on the needs and the special history of a state – the "manly liberty" which consists in certain well-defined rights, and above all the sanctity of acquired rights – these notions, which factually dominate English history and English institutions, brought to scientific clarity in a masterly manner, form the content of his immortal book about the French Revolution.[99] There is nothing of de Maistre.'s overwroughtness and medieval fantasy. He does not consider the monarchical form to be a commandment of God, but recognizes each form in its own way; he does not see the nobility as a race chosen by God, but only a political class that is significant because of its large landholdings. He knows nothing of merely passive devotion to authority; but freedom and the right of the subject, the independent activity of the nation on behalf of its conditions, are as natural and necessary to him as the regard of the kingdom. Indeed, he even justifies rebellion and

[99] *Reflections on the Revolution in France,* 1790.

dethronement in cases of extraordinary need, and rejects them only where they manifest themselves as a matter of principle and course, as the result of the higher authority of the people over the government.

As truthful and sound as the principles that Burke contrasts with the doctrines taught in France at the time, his judgments about the actual state of contemporary France are often inaccurate. In his bias against the movement, the innermost motif of which he recognizes as wrong, he also takes all the evils against which it is directed under his wing. But his political theory is not without flaws either. He fights the errors of the Revolution and illuminates the immovable foundations of the state against which they are directed. But he does not go into the real ideas that underlie the Revolution, the necessary expansion of the political doctrine that they require. He protects the goods that the existing state offers; but he fends off the goods that are to be added to them. He rejects the historical significance of the Revolution, the transformation of the civil condition on its old foundations, which he considers to be pure error and iniquity. Burke is thus the purest representative of conservatism. Maintaining, which is the task, he fulfills perfectly; but he does not sufficiently engage in building on what exists, which is also the task. And yet, if this could somehow be propounded in a fair way without inclusion of the erroneous principles, there would be nothing in Burke's doctrine to reject it. As far as theory is concerned, then, one can accuse him of lack, but not of error.

Burke has been widely accused of having previously enthusiastically defended the same principles of liberalism and democracy that he subsequently fought with such outrage. One might believe that he observes this from Burke's opposition during the first reign of George III, in particular his pamphlet at the time, *Thoughts on the Cause of the Present Discontents* (1770). In fact, however, there are few statesmen who remained as faithful to their innermost political views from beginning to end as Burke, though he exchanged parties at the time of the unprecedented world-historical catastrophe; and the accusation of apostasy is based on a misrepresentation of the question at issue at different times, and in particular the sense in which Burke took it. The opposition with which he began his political career and which is expressed in that writing is directed against the king's intentions as he understood them, which under Lord Bute appeared to be headed toward establishing a court government and a power of royal arbitrariness in England through the destruction of what had been established as constitutional custom and mores. It is this constitutional custom that Burke represents. He opposes the separation of court and administration wherein the unaccountable entourage of the king really governs, and accountable ministers are made its unwilling instruments. He opposes the corruption of elections through which the king, instead of the people, allocates parliamentary posts, which are therefore filled by the court party. On the other hand, he praises the traditional way in which the king takes his ministers from the leaders of the two parties, which builds the connections of the most powerful families in the country, so that the government is supported by the confidence of the nation, indeed by its pyramidal structure of landed estates. All this is nothing other than a defense of the existing, historical, well-structured constitution of England, the "*real* rights" of the English people, and therefore "masculine liberty," that is, precisely what he professed in the later period. There is no question of a new freedom to be introduced, no debasement of the royal regard among the people, no dissolution of the English nation into an egalitarian democracy.

Just as loyal, i.e., just as in accordance with the English constitutional custom, are the means Burke proposes for the protection of what exists against the undertaken innovation: rejection of positions [so offered] by all honorable men, refusal to vote in Parliament as long as the ministers do not vindicate their independence from the court, expression of popular sentiment in the meetings. On the other hand, he vehemently rejects any attempt to change the constitution in order to gain greater power over the king, in this manner to overthrow the court government: motions for more frequent parliamentary elections, for the exclusion of civil servants from Parliament, and the like. The constitution is so artful, so intricate that one should not change anything in any way; one should not proceed according to speculation and abstract principles at all, but only according to what experience provides. Thus, in this supposedly liberal period, Burke already appears to be the same conservative statesman and the same enemy of all abstract principles, as in the later one. He could have published these thoughts about the present causes of discontent and his reflections on the Revolution at the same time, if the court party had existed at that time, and would not have been in any fundamental contradiction with himself. No less did he make known this conservative attitude when he was elected as a member of Parliament by the city of Bristol (1774). Here, too, he explained that the machine of a free constitution was not a simple set of wheels, but was just as intertwined and delicate as it was beneficient and precious, and that in particular the true lawful rights of the sovereign form the keystone of its noble and solid vault. His speeches in favor of the Americans are likewise in the same spirit.[100] Against the taxation of the colonies on the part of the mother state, he appeals to the particular law and custom, that it was never a manner, and that it was against English constitutional law to impose taxes while refusing all rights of approval, and above all he refers to the impact, that it would be unbearable for the Americans to be subjected to trade restrictions and taxes at the same time, and to the need for conciliatory measures.

On the other hand, he rejects all theoretical questions of principle ("metaphisical distinctions") with respect to unrestricted supreme power as well as to freedom, as things which can only be discussed without disadvantage in schools. It is a presumption regarding political limitation that those who do not accept the principles of liberalism cannot have a sense of freedom and justice, of a well-founded constitution, of order in the state budget; this presumption constrains the advocates of liberalism to see only contradiction in any deeper harmonious political character which, as circumstances dictate, here confronts the revolutionary movement, democracy, leveling, there the oppression of well-founded people's rights and people's interests by force. True, a change undeniably occurred in Burke's political position, but it lies in a very different field than that of the supreme principles. Rather, his partisanship for the aristocratic element of the English constitution against the monarchical, for the power of the Whigs, is what he then abandoned. The Whiggism of then was not in itself liberalism, least of all in Burke's view. It consisted merely in the outstanding families who had conducted the revolution under Charles I and James II being the masters of the government, which was precisely the given condition of the customs of state and power relations. Burke came back on this because of the Revolution, while he recognized the need for independent royal power, and while revolutionary sympathy emerged among his previous aristocratic friends. He thus corrected an error in which he was previously involved; but this error was not in any connection with the principles of the Revolution or with liberalism. His change of party position was not a change of system and political outlook, and was not a contradiction.

---

[100] *Speech on American Taxation.*

Haller

The main content of Haller's doctrine[101] is, in the spirit of the ancient German territorial constitution, the *private-legal character of princely power*, which he attempts to justify scientifically. He recognizes the theory as developed by Grotius to be the cause of the Revolution, and undertakes to counter it with an equally fundamentally and systematically developed theory. He is therefore the rationalist among the Counter-Revolutionary writers. He does not pursue lively and varied views like the others, but, as with natural law, implements a supreme principle with logical consistency in all relations.

This principle is divided into two theses. Above all, he opposes the prevailing doctrine that states have arisen through reflection, i.e., through reason vis-à-vis the state of nature; rather, they arise through nature itself. It is the law of nature that the stronger rule, the weaker obey. Superiority on the one hand and necessity on the other establish all human relations, such as the relation between man and woman, between father and child, between teacher and student, between doctor and patient – so also the relationship between ruler and subject. On this natural ground is based all state power, not on the artificial one of a state contract. This is the first thesis in Haller's legal-philosophical foundation of the state. But it does not get one very far. Because if the regard of the ruler rests only on his strength and superiority, it would cease as soon as he is no longer the stronger. The father's power ends when the child is of age, the regard for the teacher with the maturity of the pupil, and the guidance of the doctor with the recovery of the patient. So also with the strength of the people and the power of the king. This would justify any usurpation, even that of the French people; for if it had not been the stronger, it would not have dethroned its king. But Haller immediately adds a second thesis, the very core of his doctrine: the dominion that a man has thus obtained through his strength or other superiority, he now possesses as *his* right, for *his* purpose, and henceforth it may not be snatched away from him and his heirs by anyone. *It is a private right*, like any other private right, and for this reason inviolable, just like property acquired by occupation through a natural advantage, a fortuitous superiority, but which, thus acquired, from that point may not be taken by any other person, even if

---

[101] Haller, *Restauration der Staats-wissenschaften* [Restoration of the Sciences of the State].

that other person has the advantage of physical superiority. Dethroning the king is then just as illicit and criminal as robbery, and for the same reason. Haller thus declares all public authority in the state to be the private law of the ruler, which was created by himself, his natural strength, not by divine institution, which exists for himself, for his purpose, not to serve a higher order. In this way he believes he has restored the inviolability and sacredness of the magistrate, and he imagines that natural law and the Revolution were wide of the mark simply by considering the state and all regiments within it as something public.

His entire system is nothing else than the application of this one thesis of the private-legal nature of rule, and it is easy to grasp any claim of his, because it is basically one and the same.

The states are dominions like other dominions, e.g., patrimonial power or the power of masters over servants, only that they are independent (sovereign) dominions, and do not have a higher dominion over them, as the patrimonial power does. This, and not the totally different vocation of state power and domestic power, is the distinguishing characteristic between them. The prince obtains dominion through titles of private acquisition, originally as implemented by natural superiority (similar to occupation), afterwards by ordinary titles: inheritance, purchase, exchange, gift, marriage. Yet he possesses them for his personal purposes and for his arbitrary use, like any other right. All so-called affairs of state are therefore only private matters of the prince; the territory is his land, which he may distribute, give away, sell, dispose of by testament. Civil servants are his servants, of no other sort than court or princely private servants, only obliged to him and his instructions of service like any servant vis-à-vis his master, not to the laws of the country; taxes are his income, war is his vendetta, the government of the country is his right, and not his duty. He does not need to use his power for public purposes, indeed he does not need to use it at all if he does not wish to. He may, for example, fail to administer justice to his subjects. He is only morally obligated to do this, not legally.

But Haller is far from teaching an unbridled power of the prince. He recognizes subjects' rights no less than the prince's right; on the contrary, he even rejects any encumbrance of the natural rights of subjects, such as their personal freedom and wealth, through princely power, precisely because he does not accord it a public purpose. According to him, subjects are not obliged to pay (direct) taxes that they do not voluntarily assume; they are not obliged to serve in the wars (vendettas) of the prince – military conscription is absolutely proscribed. And these subjects' rights are of the same kind and rank with the prince's right, since this too is only private law. Therefore, if the prince violates their right, the subjects are empowered not only to emigrate, but also to armed resistance, as any private law can be protected against private attack through self-defense. Indeed, this uniformity of princely law and the rights of subjects leads Haller to the conclusion that the subjects must all be entitled to the actions which constitute the function of the state administration, only to a lesser extent. He therefore grants them the right of war or vendetta as much as the prince, and considers it a crying injustice (a result of the godless new orientation) that private vendettas and duels are forbidden. All of this, however, is ever only an external limitation of princely power, not an internal moderating and ordering of its use. It is a boundary to the sphere of state power, not a boundary for the princely will within this sphere. The prince is limited here by the rights of the subjects, just as an owner is limited by the rights of the leaseholder or pledge-holder. But with regard to the exercise of princely power itself, i.e., the provision of what Haller recognizes to be a matter of common rule, such as civil and criminal legislation, use of royal revenues, welfare administration and the like, no limitation thereof by subjects and estates, no constitutional norm that binds and determines them is admissible. Everyone, prince and subject, manages his affairs purely for himself. The former cannot be restricted for his power, bound to a norm or to consent and participation, while the latter cannot be encumbered in his rights. This is the extreme and all-pervading opposition of Haller's doctrine to the present evaluation of the state and the actual arrangement of states at the present time.

Already Haller's first thesis, that state power is based solely on the natural law of the strong, is one-sided and therefore incorrect. In its origin as well as in its continuation, it rests just as much on ethical consciousness, on duty and obedience, as on external natural superiority. The latter can lead to power over slaves, but not over subjects. The consciousness of the moral necessity of the civil bond and its purposes, the consciousness of being subject to a particular magistracy by virtue of certain events, be it descent from the firstborn, election by the majority, or by actual defeat, hence the moment of reason, i.e., of mores, is likewise an essential moment in the emergence of states. But Haller's second thesis claiming that state power is a mere private right, is completely wrong. In the same way as the natural law he combats, he overlooks the higher order and the inherent regulation of life relations and institutions. As a result, all dominions and all legal ties appear to be completely the same; the entire social condition dissolves into a mass of individual rights standing side by side without an organic, uniform bond and inner permeation. Above all, however, this profanes the power of the state and princely standing; for the sanctity of the magistrate is based only on higher ethical vocation, and it must therefore cease where the magistrate uses power not for this vocation but only for his own satisfaction and benefit. Haller's doctrine renders impossible the divine consecration and empowerment of thrones which he wishes to protect against the Revolution.

The impetus for all of this was given him by the natural law doctrine of transferred power. He viewed the factual reclamation thereof by the French people, the judgment of the king and the entire series of atrocities, as flowing from it. This doctrine seems to him to be an irrefutable consequence when one takes state power to be public, for in that case it only exists for the people, through the people, and depends upon the will of the people. Therefore, he sees no other way scientifically to oppose the Revolution than to deny this public character of state power, which in his sense is to consider this not to be right of the people and for the people, but a right of the ruler and for the ruler himself. But with the Revolution he presupposes a completely erroneous concept of the public. The truth of the matter is, what is public is not what exists for the people, above all what exists through the people and according to their will; rather, it is what exists for the purpose of a higher order, and what by virtue of its own inner necessity is no less superior to the people than to the prince. His inability to think of an independent and inviolable right of the ruler except as a private one manifesting itself for his satisfaction, is no less a limitation of the concept. So there is a middle term between the Revolution fallacy and Haller's fallacy, and that is precisely the public character of state power in its true understanding. It does not preclude the original competence and inalienability of the right of monarchy, but only its arbitrary use.

Haller took the model of his doctrine from the condition of the Middle Ages, especially the German territories. There existed precisely the traits that he praises as healthy and accomplished: the arbitrary division and alienation of land, patrimonial government, mere princely servants, princely vendettas, princely revenues, and on the other hand, no military conscription, no power of taxation, finally the right of private individuals to armed resistance against the sovereign. However, the German territories were not states in the full sense; they were only provinces, and originally, to a certain extent, only the manorial estates of the German state, and even in them the private-legal character was not as glaring and exclusive as it is in Haller's doctrine, according to which even the administration of justice is a princely private right to be exercised at will, for there were always public necessities facing the territorial lord. Moreover, the drive behind historical development in the German territories and in all European countries from earliest times has been to overcome this private-legal character; in particular, the church as representative of a higher dominion already attempted everywhere to ease the expressions thereof and indeed completely to banish them. But it is precisely this dark side of the Middle Ages, which it itself recognized as such, that Haller develops into a severe exclusive theory. As such, his view is nothing more than a caricature of the Middle Ages.

Haller is wrongly accused of wishing for or teaching princely absolutism. His doctrine in itself is so little absolutist that the princes, if they were to carry it out completely, could only perceive it as a weakening of their princely power. But the result shows that his doctrine leads to absolutism, in that the freedom of the subjects and the guarantee of their rights, which he grants indeed to an exaggerated degree, such as freedom from taxes and conscription, are no longer possible; while on the other hand, that which is possible and necessary in the newer state formation, participation in the care of the public condition, he rules out.

If Haller's teaching is therefore completely untenable in terms of its ethical-political side, it has the great merit of having brought to clear awareness the natural side of law and the state and to have successfully attended to it.[102] Haller provides abundant and accurate observations about natural causes, impacts, and conditions both for the supreme state authority and the internal social structure of the community (manorial estates, corporations), which in themselves as well as by contrast with the abstract conception from which we suffer at the present time, can be made fruitful if one frees them from the false viewpoint of private-legal power of rulership to which they are consistently related in Haller's

---

[102] Vgl. Leo, *Skizzen zu einer Naturlehre des Staats* [Delineations of a Natural Doctrine of State].

system. But even more than this: The idea that natural power relations, even in view of a higher ethical order, form a basis for political relations, that is, ethical relations of obedience, has been brought to awareness by Haller, albeit with the exaggeration whereby he passes them off as the legal basis and exclusive significance and guideline thereof.

Adam Müller

Adam Müller deserves special mention among the German writers of the Counter-Revolution. Müller is the product of a German philosophical education to a greater degree than the others, and therefore tries to refute the Revolution from a philosophical point of view. He finds the ground thereof in the abstraction of the state, whereby individuals position themselves outside of it. He excellently explains the unsustainability of this starting point, which he compares to the spot outside of the earth (δός μοί που ατῶ) once demanded by the Greek mathematician. In this way he also combats the static nature of the logical concepts on which natural law is built, to which he opposes life, movement, which never stands still.

As far as his own philosophical treatment is concerned, it is of no value; he uses some concepts from the first stage of Schelling's system, and treats everything in accordance with them. This is not his real achievement either. Rather, it fulfills two basic notions: the divine conferment in all human rights and conditions, and the organic reciprocal conditioning of both the various spheres of life (e.g., law and welfare) and people (rulers and subjects) in them. To this, among other things, one can attribute his particular affection for feudalism.

These living features are deeply penetrating; they distinguish him advantageously from Haller. But from these true and commendable basic notions, Müller cannot build a world. He sees them only in the past of the Middle Ages, which he does not have a mind to bring back. He has no idea as to how they might be reborn in another form appropriate to the new age. His *Elemente der Staatskunst* [Elements of Statecraft] are therefore a profound polemic against the newer doctrine; they are one of the noblest apologies of the Middle Ages; but they are not a book for establishing and governing a state here and now. Müller's positive achievement lies less in politics than in economics. In this field, he has not only opposed the prevailing doctrine, but offered true and productive principles in its place, which, however, still look forward to their elaboration.

The mistake common to the Counter-Revolutionary writers is that they do not recognize any true motive in the revolutionary direction themselves. For this reason, they necessarily have to accept the previous condition as completely sufficient, which in reality cannot be sufficient, because in that case no Revolution would have taken place. This mistake is most evident in Haller, because he is fighting the truest motive of the Revolution, which is to elevate state power from a patrimonial character to a public, state-oriented one.

PART II: THE HISTORICAL SCHOOL OF JURISPRUDENCE

Historical Knowledge in General as the Defining Characteristic of Our Age

One of the things which distinguishes our age's entire way of thinking is *historical knowledge*. Our age views bygone times as particular in themselves, and sharply distinguishes them from the present. The different ages, and indeed the different peoples during these different ages, each had a peculiar appreciation of their living conditions, a peculiar archetype and goal of their life activity. This is the ethical intellectual specificity thereof, call it manner of thinking, spirit, individuality, or, with the artificial expression of Hegel and Schleiermacher, the "consciousness"[103] of an age and people. Language, science, art, mores, law, each in their particular character proceed from it with inner necessity and in reciprocal conditioning, as one great indivisible revelation of its inner life. This rules out the otherwise customary manner of transposing current conditions and ethical conceptions in order to shed light on earlier epochs; it rules out the explanation of great national achievements as stemming from deliberation and intention, that is, in short, the pragmatic view as described above (pp. 1 ff.). Our age, however, has no less of an idea of the coherence of all ages. A tradition and a further development of conditions and concepts runs from the beginning of the human race through its entire history. The present is only a moment in this uninterrupted current; it is therefore everywhere determined by the past, it cannot separate itself and start again, neither in its institutions nor in its thought, and it is not truly understood apart from its genesis in the past. This is the historical knowledge and viewpoint of which we can boast as the greatest asset of our way of thinking over that of all previous generations. The expression hereof in the field of jurisprudence is the *Historical School of Jurisprudence*, established by Savigny and Niebuhr on the basis of Hugo's exploratory work, and extended by Eichhorn into Germanic law.[104]

---

[103] In this sense, Hegel in particular speaks of a Greek, a Roman, a Germanic consciousness.

[104] In addition to Savigny's work *Vom Beruf unsrer Zeit für Gesetzgebung und Rechts-*

Basic Concept of the Historical School of Jurisprudence

The essence of the Historical School of Jurisprudence is a *view of the emergence of law:* law is an aspect of the entire life of a people, inseparable from its other aspects and activities, such as language, mores, art. Like these, it therefore originates not from choice and deliberation, but through an inherent sense and drive, through a consciousness of the necessity that manifests itself in observation; and usually it is fixed through symbolic acts. Later, when legal activity became more complex, the jurists who scientifically processed those principles of law that arose directly from national consciousness for detailed application, came to be singled out as the legal profession. A "technical element" was thus formed upon the foundation of the "national element." Legislation was finally added as a means of ordering individual legal relations where necessary, but not to re-form the entire legal condition. Yet the legal profession and the legislator are themselves only organs of popular consciousness; they only develop the latter's creations, or give specific (precise) form to its general impetus to development. Since the law is the outgrowth of popular consciousness, be it directly, be it by means of the legal profession and legislator, it is, like the external conditions and way of life of the people, undergoing continuous development; it cannot break off from the past, not close itself off to the future. This is the course of events among all peoples, it is the natural origin of law, and (this is undoubtedly the underlying message of *Über die Beruf)* one ought not distance himself from it even in times of free reflection, when the temptation to do so becomes manifest. Accordingly, the basic tenets of the Historical School are: the coherence of law with the people and popular consciousness; its original unreflective origin; the requirement of continuity in its further development.

It thereby opposes the entirety of the previous ways of thinking, first the pragmatic view by which all legal norms and institutions have arisen from deliberation and intention for one purpose or another, but no less natural law, because natural law constructs law upon a general (abstract) principle which has not the slightest connection with the entire further existence of a particular

---

wissenschaft [On the Vocation of Our Time for Legislation and Legal Science], which provides a concentrated presentation of the historical view of law, we refer generally to the works of the above-mentioned writers.

people, and demands a law that, being rationally necessary, is a finished product for all times, and therefore allows for no further development.

Relation to the Scientific Treatment of Positive Law

This contrast initially has an effect on the scientific treatment of positive law, and here it is Thibaut in particular who represents the earlier way. This outstanding civil jurist forms the culmination of the earlier way of thinking; but he was unable to enter into the new one. He got bogged down in the manner of thinking of the earlier natural law, which among other things is manifested in the abstract form of his system; but he was even more suffused with the pragmatic view. Feuerbach must also be mentioned as a luminary of the earlier school.

The orientations diverge already in the doctrine of the *sources of law*. The earlier school considers legislation to be the only true source of law, it being the sole conscious, deliberate introduction of law, for which reason custom and tradition are held to be a source of law not in and of themselves but only by the allowance of the legislator; by contrast, the Historical School holds custom to be the original and main source of law, since it expresses the unintentionally instinctive work of the national legal consciousness; and even regard for the legislator is only the result of customary law, namely the constitutional position of ruler and subject, which among all peoples is originally formed through custom and not through statute. If this were all, it would always only be divergence in one single, albeit very important doctrine. But in fact, with the Historical School *the whole way of treating law* has become something else. Previously, the law was treated merely *dogmatically;* since all its norms were regarded as absolutely free and deliberate acts of the legislator, one had no other task than to make them understood at the moment in which they were enacted. Scientific activity then consisted only in determining the will of the legislator, partly based on rules of language and presumptive legislative reasons, partly to bring the entire body of the law into an external order by means of certain logical categories having nothing to do with the particular content, such as subject, object, acquisition, loss, exercise of rights; for which reason they were applied equally to all legal matters.

The Historical School of Jurisprudence brought about a salutary reform in two respects. For one thing, it established a more *inward view of law*. Instead of making the will of the legislator (which, moreover, only has meaning for written law) into the first and consistent guiding principle, it made the fixed legal concepts and characters of the legal institutions of the relevant legal system (Roman or Germanic) that principle. This makes the presumed will of the legislator only a secondary principle, in that it only applies to individual provisions and oftentimes even can only be understood in terms of that deeper consideration. Consistent with this, it also provided those general, uniform, logical pigeonholes by which to master the legal material, and sought in every legal matter the inner order that results from the particular content and meaning of the legal institution in question, which demands a unique particular point of view for each. All of this was actually done by Savigny and the gifted among his successors, without their being aware of it, it being the result of the liberation from the external logical view, the awakening of a more living outlook. For example, compare Savigny's system of institutions and legal history (made known by Pernice) with Thibaut's system. At stake here is not just a matter of the conformity to nature and the beauty of scientific arrangement, but of the correctness of practical results. When for example Thibaut deals with the specific institution of property relations, possession, under the general category of exercise of rights, or the specific institution of the law of obligation, cession, under the general category of assignment of rights, the order is not merely confusing, but it also leads to erroneous conclusions, e.g., to transfer what is prescribed by the assignment of an inheritance to the category of the cession of obligations.

For another, the Historical School founded the *historical treatment of legal science*, which is the reform that it intended and fundamentally avowed; it is the necessary consequence of its insight into the uninterrupted course of development to which law, like all human conditions, is subject. It cannot be denied, of course, that legal history had previously been carried out and held in high esteem. But it was always regarded only as an external aid, which one used for a purpose, namely to recognize from the conditions under which the legislator enacted the law his motives and intentions, which one can then also leave off as soon as this purpose has been achieved, much like the knowledge of the Latin language is an *external aid* for the understanding of the Roman legal corpus, which can be dispensed of should there come an adequate translation, since it itself is not what one needs to know, but is only what leads to that. The Historical School, on the other hand, recognizes, in terms of this insight, the history of law as an *essential integrating side* of law itself. The men of the earlier way of thinking always think of history and the past merely as a *transitory* cause of the present. This is a mere product that, once created, has nothing to do with its cause; in legal practice it is indeed only a question of what is current and what is standing. In this way of thinking Feuerbach says: "History explains how something has gradually *become;* but history does not teach how and what this something *is*. What belongs to history has already died in life."[105] But the past is not merely transitory, it is an *immanent* cause of the present; the past is still contained in the present as past, as what it was. In terms of its major content, the current legal condition is, without prejudice to the newly added elements, the epitome of earlier legal terms and legal institutions, the true meaning and current application of which can only be sought in the meaning they had when they were created.

The very highest concept of our practice itself – that of *common law* [106]– offers a convincing example. All the effects of this concept which are current are nevertheless the effects of a past concept; for its cause no longer belongs to our lives, for which reason we can do nothing to change it, it is rigid and fixed like everything that has died, and yet it has a lively effect on the present and there is no legal relation that it has not touched. Viewed in this way, the history of *standing* law can be an aspect of legal science, because it is immanent in its existence. In the same way, one can only conclude that a history of Indian law, Persian law, or such-like, should be required, or considered to be more beneficial than Roman law – as Thibaut and Feuerbach have said – if one regards legal history not as an essential part of the legal condition but rather as a means of general cultivation. For this reason, Savigny rightly limits our historical studies to Roman and Germanic law.

As a result of these scientific characteristics, the Historical School has provided an insight into our existing law, Roman and Germanic, of which one till

---

[105] Feuerbach, "Vorrede" [Preface] in Borst, *Ueber die Beweislast* [Concerning the Burden of Proof].

[106] [This refers to the modified Roman law – the *Usus Modernus* – which was applied as a form of general equity in German legal doctrine and practice. For more on this, see, e.g., Franz Wieacker, *A History of Private Law in Germany,* trans. Tony Weir (Oxford: Clarendon Press, 1995).]

then had no idea. In particular, Savigny has recovered the real understanding of Roman law which, since the older French school, had been lost in ignorance or the transplanting of more recent conceptions, and Eichhorn with herculean power penetrated the monstrous body of Germanic law in such a way that not much progress has been made since. No impartial person can fail to recognize that not only since but also through the Historical School of Jurisprudence, a complete and fruitful transformation of jurisprudence has been brought about, the likes of which may not ever have been seen before. There is no longer a civil jurist, whether he confesses himself to be a follower of the Historical School or an opponent, who treats Roman law in the manner of Thibaut or who does not follow the pattern for which Savigny's law of possession everywhere set the precedent.

This is not to disregard the aberrations that are tendered from the viewpoint of the Historical School and which have not been refrained from. The insight that the entire development of law is of a piece, that is, that no period of Roman and Germanic law is not without influence on our current legal condition, entails the temptation to regard all periods equally highly and to pursue them with the same zeal. This has often given rise to micrology, the antiquarian treatment of jurisprudence, and the overestimation of legal historical discoveries, particularly vis-à-vis the dogmatic practical penetration of standing law. All of this is quite harmful, but it does not lie in the purpose and orientation set by the Historical School of Jurisprudence, but rather in the misuse of those who have practiced it. Law always remains a practical science, its ultimate goal being the application to life and the present, the maintenance of law and justice. Contemplative gratification in legal history must always remain deeply subordinated to this. No limit should be placed on legal-historical investigation *per se*, the less so because the connection which may be found between it and the present condition cannot everywhere be foreseen. A limit is desirable only for general study and educational presentations; it is found in the awareness that one wishes to know not the history of law, but the law in a historical manner. Above all, however, it must be demanded that the interest which the practitioner of jurisprudence fulfills is predominantly to be practical, the correct application of standing law. In particular, it has been noted of Savigny's achievements that he closed his account of Roman law, especially as contained in his book on possession, with the Justinian legal corpus, and that his history of Roman law was a history of literature rather than a history of dogma. Savigny certainly never defended himself against this even when others attempted to do so, and the accusation, the material correctness of which is of no interest here, says nothing in itself beyond this, that a certain man was unable to exhaust the fulness of the task of legal science. Just as little can the preference for Roman law and reduced receptivity to Germanic law, which is characteristic of the personality of another luminary of the Historical School,[107] decide anything about the general direction given here to legal science.

The main objection to the Historical School from the part of the earlier school is that it is *impractical.* There is a certain truth in this. The real understanding of Roman law – and it has first of all to do with the application of Roman law – comes into conflict with practice because practice has often been established as a result of a faulty understanding of Roman law. This conflict is necessary because a more thorough insight, which should improve practice, must first appear to conflict with practice until it itself has become practice. Now there are certainly several institutions that have grown out of a misunderstanding of Roman law, which are nevertheless not just misunderstandings but at the same time serve a real need in current conditions, and therefore must not be sacrificed to the written sources. It may then happen that in many cases the genuine knowledge of Roman law is used to inflict violence on such institutions, and that, on the other hand, a legal scholar such as Thibaut, who has immersed himself in later doctrine and practice which conflicts with the sources, defends their role in the real needs of life and legal practice. But in fact, the historical view does not teach that norms of an earlier time should be applied where the lively constructive power of law has already established a different appreciation and a different structure of relations; rather, it teaches the opposite;[108] and this conflict appears only in the first stage of the historical and source-related treatment of law. When such treatment completes its course through Germanic law and the more recent doctrine, precisely it is what separates what is really new in the existing practice from what is only scientific impotence. For example, Savigny indisputably replaced previous practice

[107] [A reference to Georg Friedrich Puchta.]

[108] Savigny, *System des heutigen Römischen Rechts* [System of Modern Roman Law], vol. I, p. 93.

regarding the institution of possession as a whole, and Thibaut, standing on its ground, was unable to prevent it. But it was precisely the continuation of Savigny's work in the spirit of the historical viewpoint, particularly in the areas of canon law and procedural law, which showed which provisions of practice, even when divergent from the Roman sources, were to be preserved.

This is the great change that the Historical School has brought about in the scientific treatment of positive law. If it were to exist as a school forever in the way it first appeared, that would of course be detrimental, for it would then manifest all the one-sidedness to which it is tempted, in the nature of the case, to combat the earlier way of thinking.[109] In reality, however, we are not talking about a school with peculiar catchphrases, manners, axioms, but rather about a far-reaching expansion and liberation of legal study. It is not that there are two parties of legal scholars facing each other; instead, current legal science is being confronted with a heightened knowledge of the past.

In Relation to Legislation

The Historical School opposed the previous way of thinking with regard to the development of law and legislation no less than it did regarding positive law. According to the earlier view, the legislator appears as the creator and master of the legal condition; he can give a new law every day that has no connection with the previous one, but can only be explained by himself, and which he should explain either in order to establish the absolutely rational legal condition – the wish of some – or to eliminate the difficulties and complications of our legal condition brought on by foreign sources and the variety of the particular statutes entail – the wish of others. The latter, in particular, is called for by Thibaut in his treatise *Über die Nothwendigkeit eines allgemeinen Bürgerlichen Gesetzbuches in Deutschland* [On the Need for a General Civil Code in Germany]. But according to the Historical School, the legislator is only an organ of the national legal consciousness; he is to allow the further development of the law by other organs, custom and legal science, and only where such wavers, or where a contradiction arises with the immediate need of life, does he come to the rescue. Legislation should therefore only apply to individual provisions or matters, not to the refashioning of the legal condition as a whole, neither in terms of its

[109] Savigny, *System des heutigen Römischen Rechts*, vol. I, p. XVI.

content, by which it changes the received norms wholesale, and thus without any particular reason, nor in the manner in which it validates them, by reducing the entirety of received law to a single code whereby only inclusion in the code decides the validity and meaning of the legal provisions – *codification.*

In this sense, Savigny opposed Thibaut's proposal. He would like to have achieved the national unity of the German legal condition not through a common codification, but predominantly through a common scientific manner of thinking and practice, and the aspect with which he in the main opposes codification, with regard to which he denies the vocation of the times to legislate, is the "*technical element,*" or as I prefer to call it, the *structure of the law*. His reasoning, in particular from the latest attempts at codification, everywhere goes to the issue, not that unjust, unsuitable provisions have been given, but that neither the legal concepts of the existing condition have been understood nor have others been chosen with clarity to take their place, which means that fluctuating, indefinite concepts have been included in the code which, when applied, must lead to confusion. With Bacon, he calls a method of this kind "ex vinculis sermocinari" [making a purely verbal (unsubstantiated) connection]. A clear recognition of existing legal concepts is therefore an indispensable condition of new codes; if such exists, however, a new code is hardly needed.

It is this [supposed] position on legislation on the part of the Historical School, which goes by the name of "natural growth," that its opponents chiefly combat. According to it, law is a mere natural fact, it grows like a plant, human intelligence plays no part, and it is only by leaving it to itself that good comes of it. But that is not really the Historical School's doctrine. It does not wish to exclude conscious deliberate further development, but what motivates it is a duality: for one thing, that the beginning, the original emergence of law in every people arises not from reflection, but is really natural; for another, that afterward, the free intentional formation of law always has its roots in this, which was originally unintentionally formed, or was handed down by a previous generation, so that free formation is not absolutely beginning, is not intangible. In terms of the idea, it is not legislation that should be contrasted with natural growth, but absolute legislation breaking with existing law that should be contrasted with law based on custom. In asserting this idea against the prevailing orientation, the Historical School may have expressed too much aversion to deliberate state power regulating with prudence and energy of will. But its polemic against the very widespread view and manner of codification is entirely well-founded, and the fact that Thibaut's proposal was rightly combatted and the vocation of *that* age to legislate was denied, is confirmed most decisively by the fact that a codification for Germany, if it would have taken place at that time, would, per Bluntschli's credible observation, have taken place entirely in terms of the formation of Roman law, which means that the revival of Germanic law which has since taken place, if it were not stopped in its tracks, at least would have had less influence on the legal condition. At present, the following questions no longer may be answered *in abstracto* by any reasonable person: legislation or scientific development, general German or particular state legislation, Roman or German national content of the laws? Always and everywhere it will be about the particular object, the particular need, the particular level of maturity and certainty of legislative knowledge. The Historical School has freed us from the schematic and mechanical conception of the legal condition, and has everywhere opened the way to the impartial appreciation of real life with its wealth and its individual need; this liberating doctrine must not itself be made into a schema to which life and need have to conform.[110]

In Relation to Legal Philosophy and Politics

Legal philosophy was never made the object of treatment by the Historical School, and especially by its luminaries. Legal philosophy was not part of its task as a school of positive jurisprudence. There may have been an inner reluctance regarding legal philosophy, because the entire operation initially manifested itself as a struggle against an erroneous version thereof and the false confidence that was put therein. It also proceeded from men whose peculiar talent consisted in grasping life and history in all its wealth through immediate observation, of maintaining the ethical standard with sure discretion, yet not of breaking it down into concepts and grounding it in metaphysical deduction. The school therefore did not indulge in this aspect of legal science. Hugo's *Lehrbuch des Naturrechts als einer Philosophie des positiven Rechts* [Textbook of Natural Law as a Philosophy of Positive Law] can by no means be regarded as a product of the Historical School, even less as a document of its philosophical confession.

---

[110] Regarding all of this, see Vol. II, Book I [*Philosophical Presuppositions*], §. 16, and pp. 401ff [Vol. II, Book III (*Private Law*), §. 49].

This book is priceless in its polemic and rich in reasonable remarks drawn from real life, but it is utterly unclear in its standpoint. For the most part, it pragmatically sets aside all ethical standards and judges only according to expediency, from which arise those shameful defenses of slavery and torture that it contains; on the other hand, it turns and sets the standard for reasonableness without any awareness, either express or even discernible in the application, of what that reasonableness might be. To this end, it contains no trace of what is peculiar to the Historical School, the ethical individuality and life task of peoples, and the continuous and traditional nature of legal development. Although the spirit of the earlier way of thinking still prevails in him, here he skeptically dismantles his previous works.

This lack of philosophical confession often led to confusion within and misunderstanding without the school. In fact, it was submitted as its confession that there is no absolute ethical standard of law, but only the relative standard of appropriateness in terms of conditions and level of culture, or that any scientific study of such a standard (legal philosophy) was vain and to be dismissed. But this runs against its spirit. There is no relinquishment of ethical judgment about laws and institutions, but awareness that this judgment is based not on pure concepts of reason and abstract principles – wherein philosophy had hitherto sought it – but rather on the fullness of human knowledge, and especially that it likewise must be drawn from historical development itself, that, presuming the general criteria of justice and ethical life, the entire received individuality of laws and institutions that has been established over the course of time is something which is ethically binding, which should not be given up without necessity, and which needs to be further developed in the direction in which it points. The Historical School does not remove the absolute ethical standard, but only combats what was considered to be its content at the time, and it asserts the relative or rather the individual standard that was overlooked up to that point.[111] Precisely a deeper philosophical truth is that on which it stands in its ultimate foundation, unspoken and perhaps for most unconscious, and this is the recognition of living divine workings in history. From this comes the reverence for the previously existing, from this comes human reticence regarding the modification thereof, the looking to a higher power from which the most

---

[111] See Vol. II, Book II [*Principles of Law*], §. 64.

essential and the best is to be expected. Piety, according to its innermost motive, is that cautious nurture of history, the preservation of every peculiar institution, the awe regarding everything that has come about apart from our doing. Even the high and independent value given to the detail of positive-legal provisions in past and present presupposes a world conjuncture according to which it is not logical law but personality and freedom that is the primary cause of all that exists.[112] It is therefore not without reason that Thibaut, in his final pamphlet against the Historical School, written not without irritation, describes it as a pietistic orientation (as he understands piety).

The Historical School then, far from eliminating philosophy, i.e., ethics from law, itself contains a new and deeper philosophical principle. But this always refers only to the way in which the law arises, how it is to be introduced and developed, and not to the content, which is precisely ethical institutions and laws. It does not rule out a philosophical doctrine dealing with this, but neither does it provide one. As such, it only provides a characteristic, an element of legal philosophy. But this characteristic is indeed a ray from the entire spectrum of true legal philosophy; a test for every legal-philosophical system is whether such a system can absorb it harmoniously. But precisely this entirety of legal philosophy cannot be constructed from the principles of the Historical School alone; it must be drawn from other sources. The Historical School cannot be blamed for the fact that it has no pronounced philosophical creed, and that the philosophical doctrine which it actually represents relates only to the origin, not to the content of the law. But this does constitute a real lack in its viewpoint. Because of this, it only emphasizes one side of the law, its being the product of popular consciousness, and not to the same extent the other side, its being a higher power, the ethic over the people and the popular consciousness, which lays a requirement on the people, which measures and judges the people; and that therefore in the legal profession and in the legislator it sees only organs and representatives of the popular consciousness, and not organs and representatives of the law as such, as an independent higher power.[113] This may also give rise to the, if not fundamental, at least factual gravitation toward the custom-oriented growth of law as opposed to energetic calculated arrangement.

---

[112] See Vol. II, Book I, §. 12 of the 2nd edition of this work.

[113] See Vol. II, Book II [*Principles of Law*], §§. 20 and 22.

Just as the Historical School has no material legal-philosophical principle, so it has no political system. But it has a political character regardless. Above all, its basic doctrine regarding the emergence of law is of the greatest political importance: this respect for what already exists, this reticence in terms of which every generation is to do its part for a development that runs through all ages, and not engage anew in the construction of the human community as a whole. It thus enters into the most decisive opposition to the Revolution, no less than the actual writers of the Counter-Revolution. But it is saved from Maistre's one-sidedness of seeking the guidance of God only in the actions of public, in particular ecclesiastical, authorities, since on the contrary it considers the internal transformation of national consciousness and the gradual, unintentional transformation of conditions to be the essence of history. It is no less preserved from Haller's aberration, to replace the natural law theses with another thesis and the same logical departure therefrom. In general, it differs significantly from all Counter-Revolutionary writers in that it does not in any way undertake to complete the shape of the world through certain (past) institutions. This cannot be emphasized enough: what is truly historical is for history not to be relegated to the past, but to see to it that uninterrupted becoming be recognized in it; and it is truly religious if divine guidance is not arbitrarily restricted to earlier formations, as if they were its unsurpassable works, but that the new future formations that it furnishes are received with implicit devotion.

In addition to this political character trait, which is given with the basic doctrine of the Historical School, the meaning and the way of thinking in which the school's legal view is rooted do not lead to a certain political doctrine. Nevertheless, they do lead to a certain political disposition, namely to an ample and impartial appreciation, open to the innermost motives, of all political structures and aspirations. In the most distinctive manner, and developed in a political doctrine, at least in the basic characteristics, this disposition comes to expression in Niebuhr, the man who, along with Savigny, is the founder and representative of the historical view. His Roman history, his letters, his posthumous lectures on the French Revolution, together yield an entire political viewpoint. It is a genuine German political viewpoint, characterized by justice, abundance, and sincerity, by firmness of principles together with free affiliation to historical conditions, by a conservative basic tone together with love for every germinating new development. The closest thing to it is Burke among the English, and the Doctrinaires [see p. 22 above] among the French; but it is less biased and blunt than the former, and has more ethical depth than the latter.

WORKS CITED

Borst, Nepomuk; Feuerback, Anselm Ritter von. *Ueber die Beweislast im Civilproceß.* Leipzig: F. A. Brockhaus, 1824.

Burke, Edmund. *Reflections on the Revolution in France.* Indianapolis & New York: Liberal Arts Press, Inc., 1955 [1790].

—. *Speech of Edmund Burke, Esq. on American Taxation, April 19, 1774.* London: J. Dodsley, 1775.

—. *Thoughts on the Cause of the Present Discontents.* London: J. Dodsley, 1770.

Goethe, Johann Wolfgang von. *Faust: A Dramatic Poem.* Trans. Esq. A. Hayward. 2nd ed. London: Edward Moxon, 1834.

Haller, Carl Ludwig von. *Restauration der Staats-Wissenschaft.* VI vols. Winterthur: in der Steinerischen Buchhandlung, 1816–1834.

Hegel, Georg Wilhelm Friedrich. *Encyclopädie der philosophischen Wissenschaften im Grundrisse.* 2nd ed. Heidelberg: August Oswald, 1827.

—. *Encyclopädie der philosophischen Wissenschaften im Grundrisse: Tl. 1: Die Logik.* Ed. Leopold von Henning. 3rd ed. Vol. VI. Berlin: Duncker und Humblot, 1840.

—. *Grundlinien der Philosophie des Rechts (Naturrecht und Staatswissenschaft im Grundrisse).* Ed. Eduard Gans. Berlin: Nicolaischen Buchhandlung, 1821.

—. "Über die englische Reformbill." *Allgemeine preußische Staatszeitung* 115, 116, 118 (1831).

—. "Verhandlungen in der Versammlung der Landstände des Königreichs Würtemberg, im Jahr 1815 und 1816." *Heidelbergische Jahrbücher der Litteratur* (1817): 1041–1088, 1153–1232.

—. *Vorlesungen über die Geschichte der Philosophie.* Berlin: Duncker und Humblot, 1836.

—. *Wissenschaft der Logik.* III vols. Nürnberg: Johann Leonhard Schrag, 1812.

Hugo, Gustav. *Lehrbuch des Naturrechts als einer Philosophie des positiven*

Rechts, besonders des Privatrechts. Berlin: Mylius, 1798.

Jouvenel, Bertrand de. *On Power: Its Nature and the History of Its Growth*. Boston: Beacon Press, 1962.

Leo, Heinrich. *Studien und Skizzen zu einer Naturlehre des Staates*. Halle: Eduard Anton, 1833.

Locke, John. *Two Treatises of Government*. Ed. Peter Laslett. New York: New American Library, 1965 [1960]. First edition 1689.

Machiavelli, Niccolò. *Il Principe*. Rome: Antonio Blado d'Asola, 1532.

Maistre, Joseph de. *Du Pape*. Anvers: Janssens et van Merlen, 1820.

—. *Essai sur le principe générateur des constitutions politiques*. St. Petersburg: Pluchart et Comp., 1814.

—. *Les Soirées de Saint-Pétersbourg*. Anvers: Janssens et van Merlen, 1821.

Montesquieu, Charles de Secondat, Baron de. *L'Ésprit de Loix*. Geneva: Barrillot & Fils, 1748.

Savigny, Friedrich Carl von. *System des heutigen Römischen Rechts*. Vol. I. Berlin: Bei Veit und Comp., 1840.

—. *Vom Beruf unsrer Zeit für Gesetzgebung und Rechtswissenschaft*. Heidelberg: bey Mohr und Zimmer, 1814.

Schelling, Friedrich Wilhelm Joseph. *Briefe an Eschenmayer*. n.d.

—. *Darlegung des wahren Verhältnisses der Naturphilosophie zu der verbesserten Fichte'schen Lehre: eine Erläuterungsschrift der ersten*. Tübingen: J.G. Cotta'schen Buchhandlung, 1806.

—. *Ideen zu einer Philosophie der Natur*. Leipzig: Breitkoph und Härtel, 1797.

—. *Philosophische Untersuchungen ueber das Wesen der menschlichen Freiheit und die damit zusammenhaengende Gegenstaende*. Reutlingen: Ensslinsche Buchhandlung, 1834.

—. *Vom Ich als Princip der Philosophie*. Tübingen: Heerbrandt, 1795.

—. *Von der Weltseele... nebst ein Abhandlung ueber das Verhältniß des Realen und Idealen in der Natur, oder Entwickelung des ersten Grundsätze der Naturphilosophie an den Principien der Schwere and des Lichts*. Hamburg: Perthes, 1798.

—. *Vorlesungen über die Methode des akademischen Studiums*. Tübingen: J.G. Cotta'schen Buchhandlung, 1803.

Schleiermacher, Friedrich. *Der christliche Glaube nach den Grundsäzen der evangelischen Kirche im Zusammenhange dargestellt.* Berlin: G. Reimer, 1821.
—. *Die Lehre vom Staat.* Ed. Chr. A. Brandis. Berlin: G. Reimer, 1845.
—. *Grundlinien einer Kritik der bisherigen Sittenlehre.* Berlin: Im Verlage der Realschulbuchhandlung, 1803.
—. *Grundriß der philosophischen Ethik.* Ed. August Twesten. Berlin: G. Reimer, 1841.
—. "Über die Begriffe der verschiedenen Staatsformen." *Abhandlungen der Königlichen Akademie der Wissenschaften in Berlin* (1814–1815).
Stahl, Friedrich Julius. *Fundamente einer christlichen Philosophie.* Heidelberg: J. C. B. Mohr, 1846.
—. *Philosophical Presuppositions.* Aalten: WordBridge Publishing, forthcoming.
—. *Principles of Law.* Aalten: WordBridge, 2007.
—. *Private Law.* Aalten: WordBridge, 2007.
—. *The Doctrine of State and the Principles of State Law.* Aalten: WordBridge, 2009.
—. *The Rise and Fall of Natural Law: Volume 1A of the Philosophy of Law: The History of Legal Philosophy.* Aalten: WordBridge Publishing, 2020.

INDEX

aristocracy, 9, 14, 15, 164
Aristotle, x, 4, 14, 32, 74, 105
Bodin, Jean, x, 14
Borgia, Caesar, 5
Burke, Edmund, 24, 172–76, 197
Christ, Jesus, 30, 88, 110, 170
Christianity, 15, 16, 88, 105, 107, 108, 109, 162
church
  expression of subjective religious feeling (Schleiermacher), 161
  surrogate of the democratic state (Schelling), 57, 65
Clermont-Tonnerre, Stanislas-Marie de, 19
Constant, Benjamin, 19–22, 23, 25
  sovereignty, 21
constitutionalism, 17, 25, 173, 175, 187
  Doctrinaires, 22–25, 198
  English constitution, 8, 26, 113, 176
  mechanism replaces ethics, 13
  organic, 169
  organic versus mechanical, 25–27
Counter-Revolution, 22, 116, 169, 170, 172, 182, 197
Delaunay, Claude-Jean Veau, 11
democracy, 14, 15, 158, 161, 164, 169, 174, 176
dialectic, 45, 70–83, 86, 87, 88, 91–102, 127, 134, 138–47
Doctrinaires, 22–25
  sovereignty of law, 23
Eichhorn, Karl Friedrich, 185, 190
ethic, the
  conflict between private law and morality (Hegel), 86
  Hegelian, 87, 101, 104, 118, 119
  Historical School of Jurisprudence, xiv, 196
  national, 31
  natural law and pragmatic politics disagree on, 29
  objective (Schelling), 53
  personal versus impersonal (Schelling), 55
  problematic character of reason as source, 3
  Schelling's, approaches the Greek, 64
  Schleiermacher, xiii, 160
  source sought beyond human will, 38
  speculative philosophy, 133
ethical world, 64, 84, 85, 86, 98, 101, 119, 149, 159
  Schleiermacher's construction, 150–54
ethics, 3, 11, 32, 64, 85, 111, 115, 117, 137, 138, 149, 150, 151, 152, 159, 160, 163, 165, 173, 196
family
  and ethics (Hegel), 87, 91
  improvement over earlier concepts (Hegel), 112
  insufficient concept of (Hegel), 96, 98, 101
  right of, 37
  Schleiermacher, 150, 151, 153, 159
Feuerbach, Paul Johann Anselm, Ritter von, xiii, 112, 123, 124, 187, 189
Fichte, Johann Gottlieb, 41, 42, 43,

47, 51, 52, 54, 57, 61, 64, 66, 68, 69, 70, 71, 79, 101, 127, 138, 149, 157

God
- impersonal, 54, 55, 59, 65, 69, 73, 75, 78, 84, 106, 107, 123, 134, 145, 149, 162
- personal, 58, 65, 79, 99, 110, 129, 130, 131, 134, 138, 146

Goethe, Johann Wolfgang von, 49, 53

Göschel, Carl Friedrich, 16

government, xii, 8, 9, 12, 13, 14, 15, 18, 19, 20, 22, 23, 26, 30, 89, 113, 114, 115, 123, 161, 165, 170, 174, 175, 176, 178, 180
- Hegel's predilection for government action, 111–15
- the substance of the state, xii, 114

Grotius, Hugo, 83, 177

Guizot, François, 22, 23, 24

Haller, Carl Ludwig von, 112, 169, 177–82
- private-legal concept of sovereignty, 178
- right of resistance, 181

Hegel, G. W. F., x–xiii, 38, 45, 49, 52, 56, 58, 65, 69–126, 127, 130, 134, 140, 141, 142, 143, 144, 145, 146, 149, 150, 151, 159, 161, 185
- dependence on Schelling, 77–78
- family and ethics, 87
- fulfillment of rationalism, 79
- hostility to acquired rights, 113–15
- improved concept of the family, 112
- insufficient concept of the family, 96, 98, 101
- lack of all historical principles, 112
- law contradicts morality, 86
- legal system fundamentally different from abstract natural law, 83
- pantheistic character of his system, 78, 107–8, 121
- predilection for government action, 111–15
- relapse into subjectivity by his followers, 124
- reverence for historical constitution, 122
- system derived from Schelling, 59
- the family and ethics, 91
- the state as the
  - unity of family and civil society, 87
- the state as the conceptual integration of individual wills, 106
- the state as the highest realization of God, 75
- the state stands over the people, 123, 125

Historical School of Jurisprudence, xiii–xiv, 116, 185–99
- aversion to state power, 193
- charge of utilitarianism, 195
- customary law the original source of law, 187
- exhibits deeper historical recognition, 16
- opposition to natural law, 33

historical, the, *passim*
- germ of, contained in speculative philosophy, 39
- knowledge of, characteristic of Stahl's age, 185
- not bound to the past, xiv, 197

Hoffmann, Ernst Theodor Amadeus, 144

Homer, 135

Jakobi, Friedrich Heinrich, 50, 57, 58

Joseph, 10

Jouvenel, Bertrand de, xii

Kant, Immanuel, xii, 42, 46, 51, 52,

61, 69, 71, 73, 79, 83, 97, 112, 130, 133, 140
law
contradicts morality (Hegel), 86
customary, 176
customary order, 169
original source of law (Historical School), 187
decree of the sovereign
criticized by the Historical School, 192
historical. *See* Book VI, *passim*
beginning of the historical view of law, 38
origin of, 38–39
Savigny the founder of the historical view, 53
natural, xv, 3, 6, 7, 10, 11, 17, 29, 33, 63, 64, 65, 96, 97, 108, 155, 177, 178, 179, 180, 182, 186, 187, 197
Hegelian, 38
legitimacy
defined, 169
Doctrinaires' understanding of, 23
historical duration as divine sanction, 25
prescriptive understanding of, 23–24
liberalism, 6, 17, 19, 22, 124, 169, 174, 176
expression of natural law, 3, 17
Locke, John, 6, 8, 27, 166
Louis Philippe, 24
Louis XI, 5
Luther, Martin, 30
Lycurgus, 30
Machiavelli, Niccolò, 4, 5, 6, 29
the result of politics without God, ix, 12
Maistre, Joseph de, 170–72, 173, 197
Marheineke, Philipp Konrad, 123
monarchy, 5, 8, 14, 15, 17, 19, 30, 62, 158, 161, 170, 172, 173, 180
constitutional, 112, 116, 158
Hegel, 88
Montesquieu, Charles de Secondat, Baron de, ix, 4, 6, 8, 9, 14, 15, 16, 17, 19, 21, 22, 27
as unethical as Machiavelli, 13
national character, 30–32
morality, xiii, 63, 64, 65, 83, 85, 86, 91, 100, 101, 108, 112, 151, 159, 160, 163
contradicts law (Hegel), 86
divorced from politics, 13
Moses, 29
Müller, Adam, 116, 182–85
Napoleon Buonaparte, 18
Neander, Augustus, 101
Niebuhr, Barthold Georg, 116, 185, 197
Niethammer, Friedrich Immanuel, 61
Paul, apostle, 67
philosophy
historical
originated in speculative philosophy, 39
legal, *passim*
speculative, x, 16, 119, 127, 138, 175, Book V, *passim*
considers the world to be the free act of the personal God, 138
contains the germ of Christian philosophy, 39
contains the germ of the historical, 39
Plato, 11, 13, 127, 130, 133, 135, 139, 140, 142, 145, 146, 157
Puchta, Georg Friedrich, 191
reflection, 83, 122, 177, 186, 193
definition, 44
versus speculation, 44–45
Revolution, July, 123, 124

Revolution, the, 17, 21, 22, 24, 38, 45, 95, 113, 123, 169–85, 197
right of resistance (Haller), 181
rights, 187
  entitlement, 38
  general principle of, 25
  historical, 23
  hostility to historical (Hegel), 113–15
  human, 182
  individual, 21, 52, 133, 163
  natural versus historical, 173–82
  origin of, 87
Rousseau, Jean-Jacques, xiii, 6, 9, 17, 21, 83, 112, 115, 123, 166
Royer-Collard, Pierre Paul, 22, 24
Savigny, Friedrich Karl von, 101, 116, 185, 188–94, 197
  founder of historical view of law, 53
Schelling, Friedrich Wilhelm Joseph, x, 41–68, 69, 70, 76, 77, 78, 79, 92, 115, 117, 121, 127, 137, 142, 149, 150, 152, 159, 161, 182
  church and state, 62, 65
  copula, 47, 48, 58, 135, 139
  Hegel's dependence on, 77–78
  recovery of objective will, 38
  restored objectivity to legal doctrine, 63
  shift toward personal God, 57–59
Schlegel, Karl Wilhelm Friedrich, 5
Schleiermacher, Friedrich, xiii, 116, 149–66, 185
  church and state, 156–57
  church as expression of subjective religious feeling, 161
  elevation of personality, 165
  historical understanding of the state, 164
  physiological doctrine of the state, 163
  revelation of national individuality, 161
  the state divorced from church and science, 166
separation of powers, 8, 9, 17
Sieyès, Emmanuel Joseph, 17–19
Socrates, 67, 128
Sophocles, 135
sovereignty
  Benjamin Constant, 21
  of law (Doctrinaires), 23
  of reason, 24
  popular, 6, 20, 21, 116, 123, 158, 169
    Rousseau, xiii, 112
  private-legal concept of (Haller), 178
  royal, 9, 21, 25
    Burke, 176
    connection with religion, 20
    English based on custom, 22
speculation, 138, 142, 146, 175
  essence of, 44
  versus reflection, 44–45
Spinoza, Baruch, 51, 61, 70, 76, 77, 83, 92, 108, 118, 134, 149
Spinozism, 12
  worldview regrounded by Hegel, 77
state, the, *passim*
  and ethics (Hegel), 87
  as unity (speculative philosophy), 133
  aversion to state power (Historical School), 193
  conceptual integration of individual wills (Hegel), 106
  divorced from church and science (Schleiermacher), 166
  highest realization of God (Hegel), 75
  mechanical view of, 3–27, 33, 112,

194
original unity of, 169
physiological doctrine of (Schleiermacher), 163
revelation of national individuality (Schleiermacher), 161
right of the, 37
Schleiermacher's doctrine an improvement on Kant and Fichte, 163
shortcoming of Hegel's concept of, 97
stands over the people (Hegel), 123, 125
unity of family and civil society (Hegel), 87
Thibaut, Anton Friedrich Justus, 187–94, 196
Tholuk, August, 110
will
general, 86
objective, 38, 61, 83
subjective, 86, 87

www.ingramcontent.com/pod-product-compliance
Ingram Content Group UK Ltd.
Pitfield, Milton Keynes, MK11 3LW, UK
UKHW020444061026
15625UKWH00032B/732/J

9 789076 660813